THE GOOD, THE BAD, AND THE VERY UGLY

THE GOOD, THE BAD, AND THE VERY UGLY

A Hollywood Journey

SONDRA LOCKE

WILLIAM MORROW AND COMPANY, INC.
NEW YORK

It is the policy of William Morrow and Company, Inc., and its imprints and affiliates, recognizing the importance of preserving what has been written, to print the books we publish on acid-free paper, and we exert our best efforts to that end.

Library of Congress Cataloging-in-Publication Data

Locke, Sondra.
    The good, the bad, and the very ugly : a Hollywood journey / Sondra Locke.
        p.   cm.
    ISBN 0-688-15462-X
    1. Locke, Sondra.   2. Eastwood, Clint, 1930–   .   3. Motion picture actors and actresses — United States — Biography.   4. Motion picture producers and directors — United States — Biography. I. Title.
PN2287.L55A3   1997
791.43'028'092 — dc21
[B]   97-33262
                                                                      CIP

Printed in the United States of America

First Edition

1   2   3   4   5   6   7   8   9   10

BOOK DESIGN BY OKSANA KUSHNIR

www.williammorrow.com

TO
GORDON

And his magical dog
"Christmas"

Prelude ~

Since I was a child, I have always loved and collected fairy tales. They were old and familiar friends to me, yet here was one I had never found . . .

> . . . the Prince was a prince but he proved not to be Charming at all. He was dark; he was like Bluebeard and he carefully guarded the heavy iron door that held his secrets and hid all the shadowed bodies inside. The maiden, whom he called his only love, his Princess, glimpsed behind that door and saw too much. Then he brought all his power and darkness down upon her. They all said she had been foolish and naïve ever to have believed in him. She was neither, for he had worn a clever mask to hide his secrets well . . . and she had a trusting heart. But still, she was not alone. There was her beloved lifelong companion who was clearly "Other" yet only called himself the Fool. It was he who would emerge as the wise one, a prophet to whom the hidden powers would reveal themselves. As a tale it was intriguing, full of so much Dark, yet so much Light . . .

There were times I wished I had only read it . . . and never lived it.

THE GOOD, THE BAD, AND THE VERY UGLY

Chapter 1 ~

The press was having a field day. Movie stars in court with a David vs. Goliath slant.

"Once they starred together in films, then they became lovers, now more than a decade later they are bitter enemies in Locke vs. Eastwood.*" —* Michael Tuck, CBS-TV

"The Eastwood case is making big headlines. Eastwood's former lover is suing him for fraud." — Ann Martin, CBS-TV

"Sondra Locke said it was the ultimate betrayal and Eastwood says he was only trying to help." — Channel 7, ABC-TV

"Sondra Locke says Dirty Harry played dirty pool with her career, and she's fighting back." — Hard Copy

"Big names, lots of bitterness in a Los Angeles courtroom today. There were opening statements in a lawsuit against Clint Eastwood." — Geraldo Rivera, *Rivera Live,* CNBC

"Did Clint Eastwood try to sabotage the career of longtime lover Sondra Locke? Opening statements began today in that star-studded trial." — Christine Lund, ABC-TV

It was September 9, 1996, and the crowd was all over me — mikes on poles, cameras, and, of course, the reporters scrambling for position, all at the same time thrusting their microphones in my face. "Did you . . . ?" "Have you . . . ?" "Is it true . . . ?" Tell us . . . ." "Did you know that Clint just said . . . ?"

When I was a little girl with wispy hair and knobby knees playing "movie stars" — as we called it in the South — the scenes I made up were always fun and exciting. They were always golden moments, fantasies about magical and glamorous occasions when people loved you, flashbulbs popped, and reporters jotted down your every wondrous word. They were never like this, never about an ugly situation; never were reporters asking about something as sad and painful as this legal nightmare in which I found myself. But this was real life and it had happened; I had made the journey and now I was standing on the edge of a precipice. And the truth was—the view was frightening.

ABC-TV Channel 7, John North: "Sondra Locke and Clint Eastwood fell in love and began living together on the film The Outlaw Josey Wales. Thirteen years later they were involved in a 'palimony' lawsuit which they settled. . . . Sondra Locke says that settlement was a phoney. She wants Eastwood to pay."

During part of Mr. North's report, ABC aired a film clip of Clint from *Unforgiven.* It showed him facedown in the mud wallowing with pigs. I enjoyed it, but I knew Clint wouldn't. His carefully crafted public image—so cool and laid-back—would never allow him to appear worried, or upset, or even aware of "such an insignificant" news report. Of course, I knew otherwise. I knew that somewhere, wherever he was, he was tuned in, and he was jumping up and down, having a fit like Rumpelstiltskin's.

CBS also ran a movie clip. It was from *The Gauntlet,* and was a scene in which a violent Clint punches me in the face, slamming me against a wall and down onto a bed. The clips, which had been chosen by the news reporters, all portrayed *me* as the sympathetic or injured party. I was amazed. It hadn't been that way when we split up. Then Clint, the American icon, was always the hero. Now it was different.

NBC-TV, Manny Medrano: "Their thirteen-year relationship ended in a very bitter fashion. Today the parties are back, behind me in the Burbank Courthouse, and this time Sondra Locke is suing her ex-lover Clint Eastwood for fraud. In 1989 Locke filed a palimony suit against Eastwood after the end of their thirteen-year relationship, accusing Eastwood of cruelty including forcing her to have two abortions, tapping her telephones, and changing the locks on their home. They settled that lawsuit out of court with a deal at Warner Bros. for her to direct films. But Locke charges that that deal was bogus and destroyed her career at a time when all she wanted to do was just work again and become financially independent."

CBS-TV Channel 2, Mary Grady: "Studio executives all say that Sondra Locke is a very good director based on her work in the critically acclaimed film Impulse. But she never got the opportunity to prove her skills in the three years that she was at Warner Bros.

"It's really interesting watching these two. Eastwood goes in through the back door. Locke goes in through the front. They don't talk to each other. They don't look at each other. Clint Eastwood says he was only trying to help, but Locke says his 'help' has nearly ruined her career. Thirteen years ago theirs was the classic Hollywood love story. They were inseparable, making half a dozen movies together. But the fireworks finally fizzled. And now the onetime soul mates are bitter enemies.

"In court today Eastwood admitted to jurors, 'Yes.' He paid Warner Bros. more than one million dollars to get his ex-lover a film development deal. Locke says that because it was Eastwood's money that paid for the deal the studio never took her seriously, never made one picture with her . . . she says Eastwood faked a film deal to trick her into settling her 1989 palimony suit."

"What does this say to women out there who *work* for a living," Clint said to a gaggle of television reporters. "That they should just go out and knock somebody over?"

I could only laugh at this comment. Clint often had a peculiar, almost alien way of speaking, but here he seemed to be comparing himself to a 7-Eleven store that I was trying to "knock over." His statement was also ridiculous because this lawsuit was all about work, work that I had been *denied*. When I had settled with Clint after our splitup in 1989, I had agreed to his proposal only because he had promised me a real Warner Bros. contract to produce and direct films. I had been working and supporting myself since I was sixteen, and certainly in 1990 when my life seemed to be falling apart, I desperately wanted and needed to work more than anything else. But the years had passed by and I hadn't *worked* under the deal Clint delivered. And why not? Why hadn't Warner Bros. given me a picture to direct for them? The powerful Clint Eastwood had set up the deal for me, had promised that I would work. I'd already directed two films for Warner Bros., and the most recent one, *Impulse*, had gotten the coveted two-thumbs-up from Siskel and Ebert, who also said it was "the best-directed film" they'd seen in a long time. I had gone to my office on the Warner Bros. lot daily for three long years, and had collected $1.5 million from them. I had been available and taken endless meetings. I had pitched more than thirty projects to them, including *Oh Baby* (which later became *Junior*) with Arnold Schwarzenegger. I had even asked to be assigned to a project they already owned, *Addicted to Love*, but instead they hired a first-time director, someone who wasn't even under contract to them. I hadn't been allowed to *work* on anything. Not only had I not been given the opportunity to direct or produce a single film, I hadn't even been given the opportunity to "develop" a story or an idea, the first stage of the process. Why not? In my mind the answer to that question was clear. What Clint wanted, Clint got, and Clint did not want me to work, especially under the deal he had delivered. And I believe that was because in 1989 I had fought him when he had expected me to just go away with nothing. He had wanted me to simply evaporate but I had dared to challenge him. I had done the unthinkable, I had publicly exposed him. He told me then that he would "never settle with me," yet he had, and it was clear to me and to many others that he was paying me back for that. He would show me who was boss, have the last laugh. He would arrange a work contract for me in which I would never work. I would live in false hope of that work promise for three long years of my Warner Bros. deal, collecting my Warner Bros. paychecks. Then, to add insult to injury, I would eventually learn of the secret deal between Clint and Warner Bros., a deal that had been carefully hidden from me. The money Warner Bros. pretended *they* were paying me was, in fact, all coming from Clint Eastwood's pocket. They were laundering his money. It was a shell game, a sham. I was stunned and outraged at the way I had been tricked and cheated a second time, but I realized my options were few. I could walk away defeated, or I could risk more and fight. There was very little in between. No matter the odds, I knew I had to try and swallow my fear, stand up, and fight.

These very real fears — of losing, of embarrassment, fear of further retaliation from Clint and Warner Bros. — relaxed somewhat when, at the very outset of my trial, I sensed that the media was suspicious about the deal Clint had secured for me at Warner Bros. They were presenting this fraud trial seriously, not in some tabloid fashion, and they were ultimately favoring me in their reports — just a few examples of the many seeming miracles that unfolded during my lawsuit against Clint. And it was certainly unexpected, for in this litigation the legal experts had been the first to predict that Clint Eastwood and Warner Bros. would crush me. I was taking on two of the most powerful and wealthy players in the entire entertainment industry.

CLINT STOOD ON the courthouse steps addressing a bank of cameras: "The . . . uh . . . breakup . . . was not a pleasant one. *She* said a lot of untruths in the . . . in the press . . . and . . . uh . . . but I had to keep my mouth shut."

Clint was slamming me to the press, just as he had in 1989. Yet he also seized every opportunity to perpetuate the image that *he* had *never* spoken out about our relationship, and that it was *I* who had always berated *him* to the press. It was a lie. I had even been offered an enormous sum of money to talk to the press. Clint's old friend Jane Brolin (supposedly mine as well) admitted under oath, during one of our 1989 preliminary hearings, that it was *she* who had spoon-fed the stories and lies about me to the tabloids—and been well paid for it. And at whose behest? I had no doubts; after all, she later admitted she had been brought in to be his henchwoman to help "get rid" of me. Still I was shocked when, during that same hearing—over Clint's and his attorneys' strenuous objections—the judge demanded that Clint's wills be submitted into evidence. From his most recent will, made after the "lockout," I was, of course, excluded; however, Jane Brolin, for the first time, was curiously made the beneficiary of $1 million.

Clint's verbal assaults against me in 1989 had been carefully worded press releases designed to sound harmless but, in fact, attempted to discredit me and misrepresent the whole situation. He told Mary Murphy in *TV Guide*: "I don't blame Sondra. I blame myself. How could I have been so blind about her character!"

My character? It was he who, while I was at work, had changed the locks on the home I had virtually built. It was he who had thrown my clothes in boxes and sent them to Bekins for storage. It was he who had secretly and illegally tapped my telephones. It was he who had manipulated and tormented me for months before our breakup.

Then on the *Today* show, or *Good Morning America*, I can't recall which, he accused me of attacking his "children's inheritance." His children's inheritance? When the bulk of my initial settlement request to him had been my home and its contents? A home in which his children would never live, a home he had bought for me and told me was mine? A home I had spent years renovating and filling with very personal collections. His accusations were all lies, but even more scurrilous was the way he made them while pretending *not* to make them. "I haven't talked about her . . . I've tried to take the high road."

And now it was years later . . . 8:00 A.M. on the morning of September 9, 1996, the first day of the trial for fraud, and Clint was still at it. "You have to wonder about the case," Clint said to the reporters who surrounded him as he paused on his way toward the back entrance of the Burbank Courthouse, "because . . . uh . . . all I did was try and help the woman."

After thirteen years with "the man with no name" I had now become "the woman with no name." After our breakup Clint had seemed unable to utter my name. Just like that, I was no longer Sondra. I was reduced to the pronouns "she" or "her." In W magazine, he once referred to me as "the person." On another occasion I had become "the nonperson." Maybe my stock is rising, I thought. At least now I was "the woman."

As the reporters followed him, Clint continued. "I gave her many acting roles. I started her as a director . . . and . . . uh . . . now she's suing me for it," he said with a theatrical world-weary sigh. Then with the downcast eyes of the perennial victim, he geared up to conclude his calculated performance, "No good deed goes unpu-uh-uhhh . . . unpu . . . nished."

He had flubbed his exit line. And there were no retakes here, Clint, not today. This is real-life television news. I'd come to know him so well. I knew how carefully he had worked on and planned that statement.

I knew he expected that "no good deed goes unpunished" would be repeated and repeated in the press like his "Go ahead—make my day" line from *Dirty Harry*. It would become the catchphrase of the whole affair. Clint Eastwood—as sage and victim. Everyone would rally to his side. That phrase would assure his again being perceived as the "good guy" who had done nothing except munificently bestow good deeds and bounty upon an ungrateful "woman" who was only out to get some more of his money. In "Clint's world" he was always the victim.

Well, it didn't happen that way. Clint was the only one to utter the phrase. I had a feeling we hadn't heard the last of it, and I was right. A few days later he dug it up again, being very careful not to flub it that time: "No good deed goes . . . un-*pun*ished!" he enunciated victoriously.

IGNORING CLINT'S STATEMENT, John North of ABC quickly asked him, "Is it true that you paid money for Ms. Locke's Warner Bros. deal?"

Even before North could complete that question, Clint had spun on his heels and was beating a hasty retreat. "I'm not gonna talk on that," he mumbled through a stunned expression, then quickly bolted for the courthouse.

Clint must be reeling, I thought. Someone had dared to ask him a direct question. That was not allowed. In Clint's world questions weren't permitted. He issued statements—proclamations. And they were expected to be written down and taken as gospel. Shouldn't they all be grateful? After all, Clint Eastwood had deigned to speak to them. They were only there to write down his every word and then scurry breathlessly back to their TV stations to share them with a waiting world.

As Clint entered the courthouse from the back, I came in through the front and my only words were "I'm glad finally to be here, finally to get the chance to tell my story." And I was.

Certainly, Clint's and Warner Bros.'s attorneys had worked diligently to prevent me from ever doing that. After I had filed my suit against Warner

Bros. in March 1994, and subsequently a separate case against Clint in June 1995, the attorneys of both had filed motion after motion, all claiming that I did not have a case. They said I didn't deserve to have my day in court, or to be heard by any jury. It seemed to me that they would say black is white or white is black on any separate day of the week, whatever suited their purposes. When all other strategy had failed, Clint's attorney tried to get a continuance by claiming, "Mr. Eastwood is not available until 1997."

Judge D. M. Schacter of the Burbank court seemed unimpressed. "We're *all* very busy," he responded during a preliminary hearing. "And Mr. Eastwood doesn't have to be here every day if he has pressing matters elsewhere." The ruling was made, the train was rolling, and I was on it.

Inside the courtroom Clint (who suddenly *was* available every day) and I sat like bookends at opposite ends of the two seven-foot tables that had been shoved together lengthwise. To my left was my attorney Peggy Garrity, a sole practitioner with offices in Santa Monica, California. To her left was Melanie, a young South African attorney who had recently come in to assist.

"Could you please keep to your own table?" Ray Fisher, Clint's attorney, said to Melanie. It was very crowded at the tables and Melanie's chair had crossed the territorial line of demarcation where the two tables met.

"I'm sorry," replied Melanie.

Ray Fisher, who worked at the powerful firm of Heller, Ehrman, White & McAuliffe (and was a president of the Los Angeles Police Commission and would later be appointed as deputy in the U.S. Attorney General's office), peered down his nose at her with an air of condescension.

To his left was Clint, and on the other side of Clint was Fisher's younger associate, Ms. Nancy Cohen. Various other of Fisher's "spear carriers" — as Judge Schacter referred to them — sat in the public section of the courtroom immediately behind him. They were there, it appeared, to do Fisher's bidding at all hours of the night and day. And backing them all up was Kevin Marks from Clint's business law firm of Gang, Tyre, Ramer & Brown. Marks always sat behind Clint's "team" in the front row that was meant for observers. He rubbed his beard and scrutinized every detail, and at every available break, he consulted with Fisher and Clint. In fact, he seemed to be the real one running the show.

I turned and watched as the potential jurors were brought in. All twenty-four of them had shown up that morning not knowing to which trial they might be assigned. There had been no earlier publicity on my case, and I wondered what they thought as they walked in and saw Clint Eastwood and me sitting at the litigants' tables. It was impossible to tell; their faces remained expressionless as they took their seats in the jury box.

The jury selection process began with questions by the judge. He asked the jurors where they lived, what they did for a living, did they have a husband, wife, and children, did anyone in their families have cancer, did they watch movies or read tabloid magazines, did they know who Clint Eastwood was, how many of his movies had they seen. He asked them if they knew who I was, how many of my movies had they seen. Once the judge had completed questioning the first twenty-four potential jurors, each of the attorneys began with his own questions.

Watching the jury being chosen was an extraordinary experience for me, not at all as I had expected. They were intelligent, open, real people, which was refreshing after all the years I had dealt with "Hollywood types." I listened to their answers and watched their reactions. And I found myself being moved by them. I pictured their lives as they spoke one by one: the female television news producer, the three male engineers, the master chess player, the mechanic who liked to sew and cook for his children, the grandmother, the young bank teller who aspired to produce music and always read *Rolling Stone* magazine, the single mother who worked for Pacific Bell and passionately spoke of Toni Morrison's books and how they had affected her. I loved listening to their opinions, and to the details of their lives. Somehow the anxiety that these men and women would hold my fate in their hands fell away and I looked at them as individuals apart from me. The experience became poignant, even profound. I realized that whatever these jurors determined in this court would be acceptable to me. I knew they would try to do the right thing.

Whatever the final outcome, I would be content with it. Clint could tell his story and I would tell mine. I already felt vindicated by the simple act of being there, in front of those potential jurors, of having gotten to that point against so much power and against so many odds. I was finally about to be heard.

Questions to the potential jurors went on all day—that first, long, tense day at trial. Still, I couldn't stop; my day wasn't over. From the court in Burbank, I hurriedly drove to Hollywood, where I was in postproduction on a small independent film I had directed. My old friend George Dzunda had recommended me for it, and the entire budget was $1.3 million. The film, *Do Me a Favor*, which starred Rosanna Arquette, Devon Gummersall (of TV's *My So-Called Life* and *Relativity*), Peter Green, a brilliant actor, and Cuba Gooding, Jr., was on a tight schedule, so even after being in court all day I had no choice but to work at night with my editor, Julie Rogers. I was earning very little—but it didn't matter. It was the only job I had been able to get since I had entered into the bogus deal with Warner Bros., and I was grateful to be working again, to be doing the only thing I had ever wanted to do—to make films. And I was glad for the distraction.

When I finally got home around midnight, I was beyond exhaustion. Once I had dragged myself inside, the dogs—my three wild babies, Ginger, Spot, and little Hannah—jumped up and down, squealing and licking me until each was satisfied—three miniature poodles with little tails that couldn't stop wagging. I stood there for a moment, feeling a sudden surge of renewal because of them. Animals are so pure and innocent, I thought, so trusting. I started toward the stairs but stopped. Maybe a cup of chamomile tea would help me relax, and I could fall into a much-needed deep sleep.

I pressed the black playback button on my answering machine as I stood waiting for the water to boil. A voice I didn't recognize reverberated through my small kitchen. "Two of the most despicable, disgusting people in America are both are on trial this week, the same week. I wanted to touch base with you and let you know there is a whole slew of people, people that you don't even know, who are so supportive of you and what you are doing. And I wanted to let you know that . . . you're doing it for a lot of us. God bless you."

Recently my life had been moving so quickly that I could barely remember what day of the week it was, much less keep up with current events. I had forgotten that O. J. Simpson's civil trial was beginning virtually at the same time as my suit against Clint.

It was eerie that other people who had been in the Eastwood inner circle were making that same comparison between Clint and O. J. Simpson. After five years of silence, Fritz Manes (who had been Clint's oldest and closest friend since junior high school and the producer of a good number of Eastwood films) had telephoned me earlier during the Simpson criminal trial. Despite his having been close to Clint for nearly forty years, Fritz had been summarily fired one day with no warning. Clint hadn't even told Fritz himself; he had quickly left town, allowing his business manager to do the job for him. It was the kind of heartless betrayal that left Fritz wounded for years. "Fritz'll *never* produce another film," I had heard Clint say afterward. And since then, he hadn't.

"Sondra," Fritz had said to me when he phoned, "I couldn't help but think of you during this awful O.J. trial. It's so bad. You know, maybe you don't realize it, but I think you were lucky because the real difference between O.J. and Clint is that Clint didn't take his vengeance out on you physically."

In no way were the comparisons meant to equate what had happened to me with the horror that was committed against those two innocent people in Brentwood that night. The abuse I had felt from Clint was not physical. Rather, the comparisons existed between two men who were considered to be beloved American icons—"good guys"—and who in reality were nothing of the kind. It was the public face vs. the private truth.

I had watched the Simpson criminal trial on television, and as a portrait of the real O.J. emerged, its resemblance to Clint was chilling. The whole ordeal made me sick. I found myself watching the exact same legal games of power and manipulation, which only a superstar's money could buy, paralleled my own ghastly experience with the courts.

Even Frances Fisher (Clint's girlfriend following me—and the mother of his third child of record at that time, and certainly no relation to Ray Fisher) issued a press statement that appeared in Marilyn Beck's column immediately upon O. J. Simpson's acquittal in the criminal trial: "Once again the illusion of stardom has overshadowed a man's infidelity and cruelty. When corruption and denial take precedence over morality and conscience, all I can pray for is that eventually the court of our Higher Power will see that justice is done."

When asked if she were drawing a comparison between O. J. Simpson and Clint Eastwood, Frances answered, "If the shoe fits." I laughed.

The teapot began to whistle, so I poured the steaming water over my chamomile tea bag, then made my way upstairs.

How had I arrived at this place in my life? I wondered. It had been an unusual journey, full of intense highs and lows with what seemed like very little middle ground in between. From nowhere to everywhere and back again. But perhaps everywhere *was* nowhere, and nowhere was everywhere; things are not always what they seem. Understanding the meaning of things had always been important to me. For years after the breakup with Clint, I had struggled for understanding of who he really was behind the mask he had presented to me. Was he ever the person I thought him to be? I struggled with understanding myself and why I had not been able to better anticipate his ultimate, evil betrayal of me and circumvent some of the pain and loss it brought. Why did I now find myself at forty-something fighting Goliath when I had spent my whole life avoiding conflict? Maybe it was *because* I had always avoided conflict. And what of Gordon? And that extraordinary aspect of it all? Who could say exactly, why and how so many amazing events had brought me to this moment. I had learned that life is deep and wide and I'd come to believe there are very few accidents.

Chapter 2

I was the Cinderella girl, they all said . . .
a fairy tale come true . . .
discovered by Hollywood out of nowhere

Among my earliest memories are those funny little butterfly-shaped bar-
rettes, all fuzzy and flocked like the cards you get on Valentine's Day. My
mother bought them at the five-and-dime, the one on the corner, downtown
on the square in Shelbyville, Tennessee, where I was born.

The center of the square held the stately old courthouse, sitting grandly
on its own little island of grass, with a cupola and clock on top, surrounded
by streets with parking meters and stores: Castner Knotts, Ben Franklin, the
Fair Store, the bank, the hardware store, and Turner's Drug Store, where I
got my cherry cokes from the fountain. On one corner there was a funny
little metal booth, sort of like an outhouse but with its own air conditioner.
Inside a man made the fresh popcorn that I'd get as a treat whenever we
went downtown. Then there was the Family Shoe Store owned by the
family that would one day become so important to me, and just three stores
down from it, across the street, was the most wonderful place of all, the
only movie house in town, the Princess Theater. There was also the Bedford
Theater, but people whispered that inside "the pictures" weren't the only
things moving; everyone said that big rats would run across your feet in the
dark. So no one went, and it closed forever.

Shelbyville was a quiet town. It seemed that nothing ever happened;
nothing ever changed—that is, until August each year when the annual
Tennessee Walking Horse National Celebration was held. Mysterious people descended on the little town of nine thousand until it was popping at
the seams. Each time I walked the two miles from my house on Horse
Mountain Road to the small grocery store near the celebration grounds, I
saw them there, cantering their horses to the organ music. My own bare

feet hopping up and down on the scorching August asphalt, I would watch the high-stepping horses with their ribbon-braided manes flying. I imagined that the owners who paraded them so proudly were all interesting and rich and lived fine lives. Sometimes famous politicians and celebrities were guests of honor there.

The tiny grocery store was one of my special places. It sat on a residential street, among the houses with their green lawns, and probably had once been only a garage with floors of dirt, but to me it was a world unto itself. The worn and wavy wooden floor felt like smooth soap underneath my bare feet as I entered, and no matter how hot the day, it was always mysteriously cool in there. The long narrow room had wooden shelves that ran along one side, across the back and up again to meet the sales counter on the next, and were mostly filled with canned vegetables and loaves of bread which I loved to look at all lined up and stacked so neatly.

Throughout the long walk there, I would try to decide what treat I would buy that day. Sometimes I would get a Popsicle, the kind with two sticks so you could break it in half and share it with someone. There was grape or orange or banana-flavored; the banana was the best, and I would suck on it until the color would disappear from the top, leaving only the frozen ice behind. I always wished they would make them with two different flavors, one side one flavor and the other side another, like the ice cream bars that were vanilla on the inside and orange on the outside that we called Dreamsicles.

Sometimes I would only get a soft drink. I especially liked buying them because I loved the big red metal ice-water chest they were all kept in. When I lifted its lid to choose, I would see the bottles lined up, each flavor in its own long metal slot: Dr Pepper, Orange Crush, RC Cola, Grape Nehi. It was the major decision of those lazy summer days. I would grab my choice between my fingers by its crinkly bottle cap and slide it along the long slot, through the cold water and chunks of ice, and out into my hands. Popping off the top in the built-in bottle opener on the side of the old chest, I'd listen for the lovely sound it made as it fell into the already collected pile in the hidden pocket underneath.

"Will that be all for you today, Sondra?" the owner, who knew everybody by name, asked me.

"Yes, thank you," I said, and put my coins on top of the counter.

"Your mama doesn't need any bread today?" he'd ask, because my grandmother, whom I called "Momma," would often send me for light bread.

"No, not today."

Then he would ring up my purchase on his old cash register, making the big red sale flag pop up in its little window.

As I would turn to leave, he would smile and call out goodbye and the little bell on the door would jangle as I closed it after me, marking the end of the adventure.

Summers went on that way. I played hopscotch with Carol and Helen up the street, savoring the sounds of my favorite little piece of glass as I tossed it onto the pavement and the skips of my shoes dancing their way along the eight chalked-in squares and back again. Most of my time I spent alone, lying on the old quilt under the big shade tree in my front yard, reading, dreaming, or drawing houses I wanted to live in—always with a lovely staircase. My dog, Queenie, my constant companion, would always be looking over my shoulder. Queenie was beautiful. She didn't have a pedigree but looked a lot like Lassie. We'd lie there together smelling the grass and I'd braid clover chains or read books and listen to the buzz of the big yellow bumble bees in the hollyhocks, which I stayed very far away from after I stepped on one with my bare foot. They weren't at all like the gentle giant June bugs that my brother, Donnie, caught and tied strings on, then ran with as if they were tiny kites. I hated that. Poor little June bugs.

Twilight was my favorite time of day because the crickets would begin their serenade and then, as soon as the sun had set, the fireflies would come out. Everybody else called them lightning bugs, but in all my books they were called fireflies. That was so much prettier I thought. The way they could light up never ceased to fill me with awe.

"Momma," my mother's mother, lived with us, and I loved to help her with the chores. We had an old washing machine with a wringer attachment on top: two rubber rollers that rotated against each other and squeezed out the excess water from the clothes. My job was to take the soggy clothes from the water after they finished washing and put them into the wringer. I loved doing that until one day, as I poked the clothes there my fingers got a little too close and the wringer caught them. I screamed and screamed, and Momma came running to rescue me. Momma was my favorite person then, with her wonderfully big tummy and long gray hair which she wore pushed into waves on top and twisted into a knot at the nape of her neck. I wanted my hair to wave like hers but it was always perfectly straight and fine, and when Momma would braid it for me, the braids were thin, not thick and fat like the ones I coveted on little girls in the movies.

"My hair is too skinny for braids and they show off my big ears and make them stick out," I'd say to her.

"No, they don't, honey. They look real pretty."

We would often sit in the big swing on the screened-in front porch while I watched her shell peas for dinner. Momma would have all the peas in her lap and one by one she would shell them into the pan I held for her. The swing would creak rhythmically as we sailed to and fro, back and forth together.

Sometimes a sudden summer shower would arrive.

"It's sprinklin'," Momma would say.

I'd sit on the porch smelling the dampened dusty yard as the sweet rain beat down upon it, until the distant rolling thunder would turn into loud cracks as the lightning came closer and closer. Then I'd run inside and jump on the big feather bed in Momma's room, and making sure that my feet and hands were safely in the very center of the bed, I'd hide there under the covers until the storm rolled away.

In Shelbyville, even though the seasons were very mild, we had every one of them. The summer wasn't too hot; the winter wasn't too cold. The highlight of winter was when it snowed. It was magical. The town was transformed into one of the villages from the books of fairy tales I loved to read. And best of all, it was dramatic because, no matter how light the snow, the schools shut down and everyone stood, with red cheeks flushed and happy, watching all the big yellow buses line up to take us home. But autumn was my favorite; then the leaves would change and suddenly almost overnight they'd come alive with incredible colors—oranges, golds, and deepest reds.

Autumn also meant Halloween. I loved Halloween because the teacher would bring out the big box of colored chalks for me to draw pumpkins on the blackboard, and everyone would decorate the bulletin board with black cats and witches made from orange and black construction paper. We would get out our funny little blunt scissors, and our paste and glue. I could never decide which to use. I loved the small jar of white sweet-smelling paste with its own brush in the lid, but then there was the glue in that little glass bottle shaped like two bubbles, one bigger than the other. On top of the smaller bubble was a red, rubber nipple that let the honey-colored glue ooze out when pressed against the paper. The way the bottle fit perfectly in my hand was so satisfying. Halloween was exciting because it was mysterious and slightly scary with the big carved jack-o'-lanterns that glowed on dark porches, and everyone transformed themselves into fairies and witches and demons and monsters.

But there were the darker memories, too. When I was about five years old, some strange man and my mother took me and ran away from home to a motel, where I remember eating Post Toasties out of tiny cardboard

boxes. I marveled at the little box that you cut open, and like magic, it
became its own bowl to pour the milk into. The cornflakes tasted so much
better that way. I don't remember why we ran away that day. My mother
occasionally ran away. Many times I would sit outside our house with my
hands over my ears, trying not to hear the arguments between her and
Daddy as she threatened to leave him. What I do remember is that I was
wearing my little white nylon socks with the tiny ruffles on the edge and
my shiny black patent leather shoes with the single strap around the ankle
when Daddy found us on that particular day and took us home.

My father was a carpenter and my mother worked in the pencil factory.
I remember she was always washing her hands to get rid of the black that
was left behind from the lead she graded; she sometimes brought home big
boxes of Valomilk candies that she had bought at the pencil plant. They
were circular in shape and the chocolate coating was pleated around the
edges. Inside was a creamy marshmallow center that was all stringy when
I would break the candy apart.

"Now you can't have one before dinner," she would remind me.

I always helped Momma cook the dinner: chicken, mashed potatoes,
sliced tomatoes with kernels of corn on top and big long scallions, which I
pulled from the garden Daddy always grew. There would also be blackberry
cobbler that Momma and I made from fresh blackberries we picked on our
special walks in a nearby woods. And of course, we'd have big glasses of
iced tea with slices of lemon. All of us sat around the supper table: Pauline,
whom I called Pah-yee because she didn't want to be called Mother; Alfred,
whom I called Daddy; Donald, two years younger than I, whom I called
Donnie; and of course Momma. My parents were simple, uneducated people, and when it came to the realms of fancy and to the yearnings of my
heart, there was no understanding. And, where there was no understanding,
there often seemed to be anger. Anything that was out of the norm, or not
exactly like them, frightened or threatened them. Sadly, I was not like them
in any way—not in the way I looked at the world and not in the thoughts
or questions I had. My questions seemed only to annoy them, probably
because they never had answers for me. An invisible wall seemed to separate
us, as if we spoke a different language.

When I made straight A's in school, my parents seemed genuinely proud
of me, but when my teachers called for permission to skip me ahead a
grade, my parents wouldn't allow it. I didn't understand, and like everything
else, they wouldn't explain it. Maybe they couldn't; maybe they didn't understand it themselves.

My childhood felt as if I had been dropped off at an extended summer camp from which I was waiting to be picked up. There had to be something more. In books there was more, but my reading seemed only to annoy my mother. I could never read when she was at home. "If it's gonna make you cry, just give it to me," she would say, snatching the book away. "All you do is read anyway. You read too much. It's not good for you."

"But, Pah-yee, the little lame prince is in trouble," I pleaded. "Please let me find out what happens."

"No. Go on outside and play."

"Can I play my Victrola, instead?" I would ask.

She would usually pause, then say yes, so I would turn on the little red Victrola with the yellow pictures painted on its side and pull out my favorite record about old Paint the horse. It too was yellow, and I loved watching it spin as it sang to me.

I thought and I dreamed and I waited for something to happen; I knew it had to happen. My life seemed a mystery waiting to be unraveled. It was like the photograph of me I kept finding, an afterthought thrown in a drawer and stuck to this or that. In it, I was sitting alone, as a sad but expectant infant staring into the camera. Someone had used the back of the picture to scribble long-forgotten phone numbers and to blot bright red lipstick. Underneath the blot was the name, written in pencil, Sondra Smith. The Smith had been repeatedly crossed out and replaced with Locke. Sondra Locke. For a long time I wondered about that.

I was always excited with the approach of weekends, for then I'd get to go to the Princess Theater downtown. I spent my happiest times there, sitting scrunched down in the dark with an RC Cola and a box of popcorn, staring at the screen, that *magic window* that could take me where everything meant something, where women were beautiful and led bold lives. And so, it was perfect that it would be at the Princess Theater where I would first see someone who would later change my life forever.

One particular Saturday afternoon at twilight, when I was eleven years old, I was waiting for Pah-yee to pick me up after the matinee. It had begun snowing and the wind had already formed beautiful white drifts against the buildings, but it was nice and warm inside the Princess's lobby, where I stood staring through the big front window, pretending to be an artist and painting frosty patterns with my warm breath against the cold glass. I no longer remember what the movie was, because the only Technicolor image my heart carried away with me that afternoon was the one I saw, not upon the screen, but through the window in the lobby. It was truly the *magic window* that day, for on the sidewalk across the street from the Princess was the most amazing sight that I had ever seen in real life. It was right out of

the pages of Ouida's A *Dog of Flanders*, the book I was reading during
Christmas vacation.

He looked about my age, was wearing a long stocking cap with a tassel on the end and real Dutch shoes, big blocky wooden ones with pointy toes, and he was pulling a red wagon with a white, curly cocker spaniel inside, all decorated for Christmas with ribbons and red balls around its neck. He crossed the street and seemed to be heading straight for me. But suddenly, with the snow swirling round him, he vanished down the side of the theater. He was gone. My heart was pounding. I looked around; no one else seemed to have noticed him. How was that possible? I knew he was real but how could he be in a town that was full of nothing but farmers and walking horses and pencil factories? I wanted to get in that red wagon with his dog and go away with him; somehow I knew he would have answers to my questions. I held on to that glimpse of whoever he was. The promise of magic, if for only a few seconds, had at last materialized in my everyday life.

My junior high years at the Shelbyville Mills School seemed like separate little lifetimes, each with its own beginning and end. I was a cheerleader, and I adored my white cheerleading sweater with the big gold and blue letters SMS, and the little blue felt skirt. It was all gored and sassy and I loved to watch it as I twirled around.

At the end of the eighth grade my grade point average was the highest, so I was valedictorian, which meant I would make the valedictory address. I would be standing all by myself, on the stage of that huge auditorium. I marched up proudly to the microphone, in my white linen sheath dress, my new white pumps with their Queen Anne heels, and my new sophisticated poodle cut. I felt quite grown-up. That day was memorialized in photographs taken of us afterward. There we were, sitting on the sofa, none of us smiling, in the knotty pine living room my stepfather had recently added onto the old house where we lived on Horse Mountain Road.

SHELBYVILLE CENTRAL HIGH SCHOOL was a large, sprawling redbrick building that swallowed up approximately one thousand sleepy kids from all over Bedford County. Like many students who came in from the countryside, I arrived every morning and departed every afternoon on the big yellow school bus. The classroom was the one place where I had a chance to prove myself and I continued to excel. I felt safe there and I liked it.

My most vivid memory of freshman year was Latin class. It was not because of the song that Mrs. Mummert drummed into our heads: "In Latin class each morning, if you'd happen by our way . . . You'd hear us conjugating and this is what we'd say. . . . *amo, amas, amat* . . ." It was because of the boy with the large green eyes who would turn from his seat at the front of the classroom and steal glances at me in the very back where I sat. Almost from the start I was completely intrigued by him. I knew he was smart because often when the teacher would ask difficult questions only four or five hands would shoot up, and his would always be one of them. Then he would turn and, looking back conspiratorially over his shoulder at me, make sure that my hand was also in the air. It seemed that we were sharing something, something that was completely mysterious to me. His name was Gordon and often during class I was aware that he was drawing or sketching. "He's a real artist . . . one of his pictures won a ribbon at the State Fair in Nashville," said a girl who had gone to Madison Street Junior High School with him. He wasn't like everyone else; he seemed self-contained, a world all his own. I'd seen some of the other boys make fun of him, but he never seemed to be afraid of them, or be fazed by it at all.

One afternoon after the final bell had rung and Latin class was over and I was making my way to the school bus, Gordon charged up and thrust a piece of paper in my hand; he had drawn my portrait. It was wonderfully done, and I was stunned. He just looked at me and whispered, "You know, you're different. You're different from all the others." I thought about it all the way home on the school bus that afternoon, and finally decided that he'd meant it as a compliment, but in time I would discover that it was he who was *truly* different.

It started with small glimpses, little things that would occur from time to time. Once, around Halloween, our freshman English teacher, Mrs. Morton, instructed us to write a scary composition. Gordon created his story around the horrifying French death instrument, the guillotine, and shocked us all by informing us that it was still in use and that the executioners were called *bourreaux*, men who were born into their professions and were shunned. In France there was no "bogeyman"; the children there were told that the *bourreau* would come and take them away if they were bad. I was fascinated; I had never even heard about the guillotine. And too, he seemed to be able to predict things. He had written away to Zibart's Bookstore in Nashville for a book called *A History of the Guillotine*. No such book existed, they said, but a month or so later, a letter came informing him that one had been published under that exact title. An eerie coincidence, I thought. Then, one Monday, I was very nervous about a science project that was due at the end of the week. Gordon said, "Don't worry, you won't have to have it on Friday. I'm doing mine over the weekend." In spite of my insisting that the teacher expected them on Friday, he seemed completely unconcerned. Sure enough, I awoke Friday morning to the kitchen radio announcing the news that an unpredicted heavy snowstorm had covered middle Tennessee and there would be no school that day. I can still summon up my feeling of awe that was tinged with an eerie spookiness—spookiness because I thought about a local man, a Mr. Warner, who had once lived in that grand, butter-colored mansion on North Main Street. It was said that he had "the gift," that he could tell futures. People had come to him from miles around, I'd heard . . . And one of them had murdered him.

I wasn't sure what to think about Gordon's "predictions." On Monday morning I waited for him. "Tell me how you knew that," I implored excitedly. "Shhhh. Be quiet," he whispered. "I only told *you*. Besides, I don't know how. Just sometimes I seem to know things."

At first, it seemed that Gordon was standing away somehow, quietly, in some place entirely all his own—watching and missing nothing. Then there were times in class when he would suddenly join in, making a hysterically funny comment. Other times, he was extremely serious and seemed far older than any of us. Just when I was getting a sense of who I thought he was, he would do something totally unexpected, and I would wonder, "Oh my God, who was that?"

Sometimes I was shocked. Once in algebra class, Freddie, one of the big football stars, had been teasing Gordon about his "artistic hands . . . full of genius" as one of the teachers had described them earlier that day. Gordon tried to ignore him but Fred wouldn't leave him alone. "Let me see those hands," he said as he grabbed one. "Why, there's not a scratch on 'em, they're so soft. Mind if I hold it a little while—honey," he said, winking at the rest of us.

Gordon seemed completely unperturbed and answered, "So, you've grabbed hold of my hand like it's some girl's, h-m-m, well, that gives me the prerogative to do what a girl might do in such a situation." And with that he hauled off and gave Fred a furious slap, leaving his handprint red and burning on a suddenly sheepish Fred's cheek. That story circulated through the school for days.

I wondered what Gordon's parents were like. His father owned two stores in Shelbyville, the Family Shoe Store and the Shoe Box. One Saturday, I went shopping there, just to meet them. His father seemed charming and warm, and his mother was beautiful with a vibrant but sweet personality. I told her how talented I thought Gordon was, and she began excitedly to describe the painting he was currently working on. I couldn't help but contrast the pride she took in him with the way nothing I ever did or said mattered to my own family.

I came to accept that it would never be any different for me at home. They didn't physically abuse me, nor were they deliberately cruel, but there seemed to be no connection. I knew if I tried to broach some thought or subject, something outside my mother's direct experiences, she would reply, "What in the world are you talkin' about, girl?" My pain came from a total *absence* of any warmth, nurturing, and guidance as a very young child. There was no word of encouragement for me, no interest in anything I said or did or wondered about. The painful truth was I just didn't feel loved.

Mysteriously, even though I barely knew Gordon then, I felt an immediate *connectedness* to him. He didn't seem to trust easily, and neither did I, but slowly an extraordinary bond formed between us. And, as I entered his world, I found solace and also began to find myself. I was fascinated by how he found meaning in what he called "omens and signs." He seemed to read the layers of life the same way I would read a book. But most wondrous of all, he himself seemed like a character from a movie or a book.

One Saturday afternoon after working on the sophomore class float for the football homecoming parade, Gordon said, "Come home with me; I only live a half block from here. We'll make a snack."

We approached the charming two-story stone house on Belmont and I just knew that inside there would be a staircase like the ones in my summer drawings. As we approached it, Gordon pointed at the roof. "Look, it has seven gables. Count 'em. Mama's a romantic; she's never gotten over Nathaniel Hawthorne." As we opened the front door, I marveled at the little built-in music box that tinkled "Bless This House." The living room walls were a soft pink ("It's called apple-blossom, but it's more a shell pink," Gordon informed me). The large windows were framed with ruffled and crisscrossed white organdy swag curtains, just like the curtains I'd seen on all the television shows where families lived ideal and happy lives. The furnishings were in an antique French style and in the corner was a large television console that was gold! "This is the most beautiful home I've ever been in," I exclaimed. "I've never seen a gold television before."

"Neither has anybody else, but you can have one too," Gordon said. "All you have to do is go down to Edward's paint store and get yourself a can of Florentine gold spray paint just like Mama did." He bounded through the dining room and into the kitchen. "Margaret," he called, "would you please make us a snack?" As I followed him through the dining room, I noticed the beautiful dining set, all-white wicker with rose-colored velvet cushions. "Come on into the kitchen, Sondra; Margaret's gonna fix us a snack. What would you like?"

"Uh, oh anything at all," I said.

He stood staring at me, waiting, as if determined that I should make a choice. "It's hard for you to ask for anything, huh? We'll have to do something about that. Margaret, we'll have cheeseburgers and French fries, please, if that's all right."

"Sure it is, baby, if that's what you want."

It was clear that Gordon and Margaret adored each other. She was black, about thirty years old, with sparkling eyes and high cheekbones. "Margaret's been fussing at me because her skin's irritated," he said, pointing to her temples. "I told her that her hairline here is wrong; it's not wide enough and we could fix that by removing a half inch or so of the hair on each side—you know Rita Hayworth and Lana Turner both had to have their hairlines changed—anyway, she shouldn't complain because she looks one hundred percent better since I put Nair on it a coupla days ago."

"Honey, that stuff 'bout burned me alive," she said, laughing.

"Yeah," he responded, "but it made your cheekbones look even more beautiful."

"Well, that's the last time we're doin' that, I can tell you," she said as she began to cut up fresh potatoes.

"Margaret and I are seriously thinking about running off to Hollywood together." Margaret laughed as Gordon jumped up and scurried out onto the enclosed back porch. He returned with what I would later come to think of as one of his best friends, his big gray Voice of Music tape recorder. "Have you ever seen *Marie Antoinette* on the Million Dollar Movie?" he asked excitedly as he rewound the reels on his tape machine. "Norma Shearer stars in it, and Robert Morley. This scene is between Madame du Barry and her arch-rival the Duc d'Orléans" . . . (I was impressed with the way Gordon pronounced the name; he sounded so French. *"Or-lay-ohn"* — "Joseph Schildkraut plays him," Gordon went on, "he was wonderful as Anne Frank's father in *The Diary of Anne Frank*."

"I've been teaching Margaret to act," he went on as he pushed the big fat piano-key play button and the reels began to turn. "She's playing Madame du Barry here. She speaks first." He needn't have told me.

"Ah—Hiz Grace of Orleeens. Ah bin waitin'. Hiz Grace's late. Ahha-hum."

"The loss is mine, Madame." Gordon spoke the line, but the voice wasn't his. It sounded nothing like him.

"Ah ha hum. Flatt-uh-er. Ah believe you wonts somethin'."

"U-m-m. Let's see, why of course I do, Madame, I want to be Grand Admiral of France," responded Gordon in a very regal, very baritone, and very un-Southern Duc d'Orléans.

"Ah ha hum. An' kin we resis 'im? He haf all the charm of a sailah," Margaret's Madame du Barry continued. "And ah've known many sailahs."

I couldn't hold back any longer; I burst out laughing—partly at Margaret and her acting, but mostly at how much fun it all was. "What is that 'ah-huh-HUM' Margaret said at the end?" I had to ask.

"She's Elvis, of course," Gordon teased. "You know, when he sings 'I'm All Shook Up.'" He sang in a perfect Elvis. We were all laughing uncontrollably. "No. 'Ah ha hum' was *supposed* to be a little satisfied laugh." He then demonstrated it perfectly.

"I'm not studying you two," Margaret said, and laughed, handing us our plates heaped with French fries and plump cheeseburgers. "He can try to make an ackress outta me until Glory comes, but it ain't gonna work. You two are messes and I've gotta go do ma ironin'."

Margaret was wonderful and I marveled at the close and easy relationship they had. The whole afternoon was all about the kind of fun and closeness that I had never really had, but it became that because, as I was leaving, I discovered something truly amazing. I paused in the living room to take one last look around, and that was when I noticed them, on the hearth in front of the fireplace . . . a pair of wooden shoes. I asked haltingly. "Did you ever actually wear these?"

"Uh-huh, sure. I used to wear 'em, but in the seventh grade I outgrew 'em. That's when Mama snitched them and painted them pink—apple-blossom pink, of course. Aren't they awful?"

"No," I said earnestly as I reached to pick them up. "They're wonderful." I turned them over, looked at their bottoms, and, sure enough, I saw the scrapes and pitmarks of wear. It hit me.

"Do you have a curly white dog?" I asked.

"Yeah, that's Wiggles. And then there's Honey; she's mine. They're in the backyard."

"You're the one . . . the one I saw when I was in the sixth grade . . . downtown when it was snowing . . . pulling your white dog decorated for Christmas . . . in a red wagon . . . aren't you?"

"You saw me?" he answered slowly.

When I told Gordon about that day, and how it had affected me, it was his turn to be amazed. "It's an amazing omen." He grinned. "It's a sign."

Finding that piece of the puzzle gave me an overwhelming sense of elation, like stumbling upon something important you'd thought was lost forever. Somehow it was right and completely perfect that the magical image I'd carried with me had turned out to be Gordon.

And though I vowed that as soon as I got back home, I'd ask if I could paint my room apple-blossom pink (just like Mrs. Anderson's living room), I knew not to discuss my afternoon at Gordon's. It would be just for me; I would keep it my secret.

Not long after that day I wrote a poem, which, perhaps for the first time, succinctly expressed what I felt living there in the house with my mother, my stepfather, and my brother: I felt *invisible*. After I had studied my poem for only a few minutes, my hands suddenly flew into a frenzy and tore it into tiny bits and flushed it down the toilet. It was too scary. I *was* invisible. I knew there was so much inside I wanted to share, but I had no place to put it. In time Gordon explained what he'd meant when he told me I was "different." "I think that you're a lot more animal than human. I can't explain it. You're not silly like the other girls at school. There's a depth about you, a poetry in your soul." Gordon made me proud of myself and made me want to be all those things he described. But Gordon looked at everything in a way that never ceased to fascinate me. He seemed always to be after something that was *underneath*. And there was nothing nebulous or spacy about the way he could see and rely on what he called his omens and signs. When I asked him how he was able to come up with answers or explanations from the same observations and data that anyone else had, he told me that Number Two did that. Number Two, he explained, was the part of himself that had come forth to help and guard Number One. Gordon smiled. "Number Two made survival possible — he has an animal's instincts; he knows things and can see things and hear things that other people miss. Without him I might have killed myself a long time ago." That struck deep into my heart. He then told me he had first become aware of Number Two when he was seven or eight. It was completely fascinating; I had never before heard of anything like it.

"It's probably the most important experience in my life so far," he explained, "but I learned early on not to talk about such things, so normally I don't . . . but I will for you . . . Okay, it was in the summertime," he began, "and I can remember the hot sun and that I was very hurt and had been crying because of something my brother and his gang in 'Post 80' had done to me and I was running across my backyard to get inside when suddenly I saw a tiny white kitten. I stopped and studied it for a moment, then ran under the house and got myself a piece of rope. I made a little noose and tied one end to a tree branch. Then I picked up the kitten and slipped the noose over its neck, and just as I was about to release my hands, I suddenly heard this voice, inside my head I guess, but it didn't sound like my voice. It really scared me. 'Stop! You are not going to hurt the kitten, as you've been hurt. You are not your brother—you're not like them . . . *you* are the *kitten.*' " Gordon sat quietly for a moment. "When I looked at that kitten— and I was just a baby then, Sondra—I understood, *really* understood, that the kitten *was* me." He stared at me for a few moments, then added quietly, "Number Two comes from God." I sensed what he was conveying to me was very important, and though I didn't really understand it at the time, eventually I would.

The second time he invited me to his house was another Saturday afternoon. I was on my way to the public library when I saw him come running down Depot Street toward me. He told me his grandmother, Ma Belle, and her sister, Great-Aunt Beaudine, were visiting. "You have to meet Ma Belle, Sondra," he said. "And Great-Aunt Beaudine used to be in vaudeville. And, she still thinks she is," he said, delicately tapping his forefinger against his temple.

Two hours later, I stood listening to the tinkling of "Bless This House," and this time Ma Belle herself opened the door. I had heard all about her, of course. She was Gordon's mother's mother, and usually lived at Gordon's six or seven months out of each year. Her name was Isabelle, but she was always called Ma Belle. "That means 'My beautiful one' in French," she was always careful, casually, to inform. Gordon had told me that she was always dressed to the nines and in full makeup, and often in a big Southern belle picture hat, even to sit around the house. And anytime a camera was near, she would pose glamorously, usually with a *McCall's* magazine opened, all the while pretending to be completely unaware of the camera. I had never known any colorful characters like her and I was entranced by Gordon's stories. Especially how during the Depression, she had opened her large home for boarders. No one knew what she did with the money. One night her daughters decided to have an impromptu party and when they rolled back the rug for dancing they discovered a field of fresh spring green bills, hundreds of dollars, precisely spaced there. Ma Belle, ever the true Southern belle, was not going to entrust her *till* to the bank. After all, those Yankees "might be comin' again."

"Come on in, darhlin'," she trilled. "Gordie had to run down to the market for me." She wore a lilac-colored taffeta dress that rustled when she took dainty steps in her tiny ("size five quad, dear") high-heeled shoes. Heavy amethyst and pearl bracelets covered each of her wrists, and around her neck was a matching necklace, and of course a large picture hat (gray

with violets) was positioned perfectly atop her dark brown hair. Then, as if
to explain why she was wearing the hat indoors, she said, "Oh, you caught
me just as I was about to go on downtown, honey."

It was then that I heard a feeble croak come from behind me. "Now
that's not true, Belle dear," it said. "You weren't going anywhere. You only
put that hat on because you knew we were expecting company and you
wanted to show it off. Isn't that so, dear?"

Ma Belle laughed coquettishly. "Well, it *is* lovely," she mused, examining the violets on the hat, touching them fondly. "It's a John-Frederics."

I turned to look behind me and found "the croaker" peering at me
intently, her head bobbing gently to and fro. "Weren't you on the circuit
in vaudeville? You and your sister did a toe-tap routine; we worked together
around 1915, I think. You come right on over here, honey. Sit down with
Miss Beaudine and let's you and me get reacquainted," she said to me. I
couldn't imagine what on earth she was talking about, but I didn't say a
word. She looked ancient and a little scary lying on the sofa, propped up
against a mound of pillows, all covered with an afghan . . . I studied her
carefully as she chattered on about vaudeville and her years on the Or-
pheum circuit. She had heavy dark-red lipstick that had run into all the
deep lines around her mouth, and her saggy eyes were heavily lined and
made up just like Elizabeth Taylor's in *Cat on a Hot Tin Roof*, I thought.
Her jowls and the sagging skin of her neck rested gently on the ruffled
collar of her dressing gown. Her hair was gorgeous and long and blond and
flew out wildly around her face. Suddenly she looked at me and whispered,
"Help me, dear, they wanna lock me up again, you know." I'm sure my
eyes must have grown to twice their size and I began to stammer some
reply, when suddenly, in one fell swoop, the blond hair went flying from
her head and the whispery croak was replaced with *Gordon's* hoots of laughter. "You didn't know it was me, did you?" he gloated. "Tell the truth. I
fooled you. Didn't I . . . didn't I"?

"Oh my God," I cried out in total shock. I'd never in my life experienced
anything like that moment. It was surreal. "I don't understand how you
could make your face change like that. It's impossible. How did you do it?"

"You wanna see? Come on up to my room," he said. "You can watch
me take it off."

"That's right, Gordie honey," Ma Belle prompted. "Go get all that off
before your daddy gets home. He'll have a fit if he sees you."

Just for a second Gordon looked sad. "I'll bet Lon Chaney and Perc
Westmore didn't have to run and hide when their daddies came home."

But then he was off again, "I wish you had been here last week; I made myself up as Quasimodo in *The Hunchback of Notre Dame*. It was great; I looked just like Charles Laughton."

"But even your voice," I said. "You can really act!"

He looked up as he began to apply cold cream to his face. "Oh yeah, I'm a wonderful actor. Wanta see me cry?" he asked casually.

I nodded, and in perhaps six or seven seconds large tears began to trickle down the corners of his eyes. I was completely mesmerized, but before I could comment, he said, "Incredible aren't they? I taught myself to do that when I was six, and I must say it's come in handy on occasion. Maybe I'll teach you sometime."

I was amazed how he had created all the wrinkles and sagging skin with only cotton, toilet paper, spirit gum, and nose putty. "Who taught you to do this?" I stammered in complete fascination.

"Nobody. I read all about it in a book."

What he seemed the most interested in talking about was the extraordinary wig that appeared to be growing right out of his skin. "When I was a tiny thing," he said. "I saw *A Star Is Born* with Judy Garland, and there's this scene where she walks past James Mason, and he doesn't recognize her. See, she's got a rubber nose on and they've changed her eyebrows, but the main thing is she's suddenly blond and you could see the hairline with all the hair growing out. Then . . . he snatches off her hair! I couldn't get it out of my mind; it was like magic. So I had Mama write to New York about it." Showing me the delicate hairline, he continued. "See. Each hair on the hairline is tied one at a time into this fine net that's almost invisible. I made this one."

"You made it?" I couldn't believe it.

"Yeah, I did a lot of research, I ordered my wig needles and some hair from New York. The hair only cost about twenty dollars. It took almost a hundred hours for me to make it. It's the Rolls-Royce of wigs. Look," he said, placing the wig on my head and turning me toward the mirror; "It's like magic, isn't it?

Transfixed, I stared at my reflection. That afternoon began my apprenticeship in appreciating the unreal as real and vice versa, for Gordon was fascinated by illusions of all kinds. His room itself was a place of wonder to me. It was the only room on the second floor, like some safe little tower, all to itself, and it was filled with books — a whole section devoted to beautifully illustrated fairy tales, records, and no end of fascinating artifacts. A bald mannequin's head, old toys, papier mâché masks, movie stills, sketches, and finished drawings were scattered all around. There was an amazing variety of what he called "little people"—little figures, his best friends from grammar school days, he said. The most unique one lay perfectly positioned below a glittering silver blade that could fall rapidly between the two posts of a little guillotine. In a flash its tiny head would fall into a waiting basket. "See, you can reattach the head this way. I made it with one of mother's big hairpins," he told me.

"Why do you like the guillotine so much?" I asked.

"It's forbidden. That always fascinates me." He laughed. "It's really strange, you know, I never got over the very first time I ever saw one in the movie *House of Wax* with Vincent Price. It was weird; from the minute I looked at it there seemed something oddly familiar to me. Then, too, it's terrifying and yet there's a sense of romance. You know, like the French Revolution—life one second and death the next—it's so dramatic. And fairy tales are full of beheadings, Jack the Giant Killer, the Goose Girl. Victor Hugo and Charles Dickens wrote about it, Toulouse-Lautrec painted it. There's even an oil portrait of it in the Louvre. You know in France, no photographs of the guillotine are even permitted; it hasn't been photographed in fifty years! One day if I ever have the money, I'm gonna go to France and investigate," he said determinedly.

"Oh this is beautiful," I said, noticing another of his little people. It was a female circus aerialist, dressed in a detailed blue costume complete with tiny feathers and sparkles and seated gracefully on a miniature trapeze that hung from the edge of one of his bookshelves.

"I made her; I sculpted her in clay then cast her in plaster. It's Betty Hutton, Holly in *The Greatest Show on Earth*. C'mon," he said suddenly. The next thing I knew we were in his attic and I was watching him swinging in large arcs on *his own trapeze*, rhapsodically describing the Cecil B. DeMille film and why it was so special to him—the magic of the circus, the marches and the waltzes and the incredible costumes. He said he could actually go back in time to the day he first saw it and smell the Strand Theatre's popcorn and hot dogs, and feel the blast of summer heat as he and his mother walked out of the air-conditioned movie theater into the blinding sun of that August afternoon.

Suddenly at the very end of one of his arcs on the trapeze, he let go and flew backward. I gasped; then he quickly caught it by his ankles. "That's an ankle drop. It's the first trick Betty Hutton does in the movie," he told me as he sailed by.

I thought he was magnificent. What fascinated me most about that afternoon was how everything that was *unreal* seemed so much more true and vivid than my own *real life*. Knowing Gordon was turning my once gray, colorless world into brilliant Technicolor. He brought a *bigness* to ordinary life because he was bigger than ordinary life; in fact, he was more alive than anyone I had ever met. Compared to how I felt when I was with him, everything else seemed flat and lifeless. Whatever we were doing, Gordon could find the magic. And I believed that somehow he'd been sent to show me how to find it too.

I can remember once we sat in a frozen porch swing as twilight turned to darkness, and watched a thick snow falling silently, visible only in the golden shafts of light from streetlamps. "There's no magic in putting on our overcoats," Gordon had said, so we sat swaddled up in the bundles of blankets he had promised would be much more special, toasting marshmallows over a single candle's flame. As we sat in the frozen silver silence, he reached out toward a naked bush shining with ice that grew beside the porch and snapped off two branches. "Gently bite the ice off, Sondra, it's sweet," he spoke softly. And as we watched the candle burn down and gutter, he told me secrets. "If you really listen you can hear the falling snow," he told me. "Shut your eyes and listen," and suddenly it seemed that I could: a whisper that shimmered in some secret place far behind the quiet.

Gordon hesitantly spoke about God. He told me how he disliked churches and didn't think they had very much to do with God at all. "God's not cooped up in some building with a steeple on top for one hour each week. Look at this, now this is God," he said, pointing at the incredible snow whirling around us and gradually turning Belmont Avenue into an image right out of Currier and Ives. "My dogs, Honey and Wiggles, have more God in them than all the churches in Shelbyville put together." I had never heard anyone talk about God the way Gordon did. I was completely intrigued and I too began to perceive God in a new light.

"I had an experience when we still lived on Franklin Street," he told me. "It really goes beyond my being able to describe it verbally—God is beyond words. It was Sunday and I had played sick so I wouldn't have to go to church. I was home alone and it was pouring rain. I was lying on the cold linoleum kitchen floor, watching as the rain came down in torrents while my cheek rested on Wiggles's back. I could feel him breathing up and down as the cool air breezed through the kitchen, and the rain pounded down on the porch with such force that where it struck, it made bursts that splattered in on me and looked just like sparklers on the Fourth of July." He told me that suddenly he had felt a peace, a euphoria that was unexplainable and amazing, come over him—it was almost as if he'd *become* Wiggles, and the rain, and the linoleum as well. At that very same moment he experienced something mysterious that centered on his cherished little cherry tree that was bending under the force of the rain, there in his backyard. "That gray, rainy Sunday morning I could *feel* God," he said quietly. "I could feel him all around me."

"Have you ever since then?" I asked.

"No. Not like that. Not since then."

For a time there was only the icy swing creaking back and forth, then he again spoke. "God is love they say, right? Well, how about this for love." He began to tell me a story that happened when he first moved to Shelbyville. "You know that old, white, tiny wood-framed house right by the railroad tracks, where all the kudzu grows so crazily? Just a block and a half from the back of the Princess Theater?" I nodded. "Well I used to walk right by that house every time I'd go to the shoe store, and a nice black woman was always sitting on the porch with her dog. Once I said hello and told her how pretty I thought her dog was. She said his name was King, and as time went on, sometimes I would sit on the porch stoop and talk to her. I called her Miss Lady. Well, my visits with her soon became a cause for great concern to an old biddy who lived on my street. She called my parents and told them that 'Christian duty' decreed she inform them that their son was keeping company with 'undesirables.' "

"I can't believe that! What happened?"

"Well, my father had just opened a business and was eager to be accepted, so he forbade me to speak to Miss Lady ever again. And when I asked why, all I got was a whipping and a 'because I say so, that's why.' Of course, I knew the reason was that she was a black lady and I knew the reason was *wrong*. Everybody's got to find somebody else to pick on, or to be better than. God, it makes me sick. And I'll bet it makes God sick, too. I decided then that I didn't want to go to church with those kinds of people. The truth was that Miss Lady always seemed much kinder and had a lot more God in her than that old white-haired witch who had told on me."

Of all the things I envied and admired about Gordon, I think what I admired most was that. Not only could he see the truth, he was never afraid to tell it. He reminded me of the child in the fairy tale "The Emperor's New Clothes" who was the only one with courage enough to say the emperor wasn't wearing any clothes.

In my sophomore year Gordon asked me to go with him and some other classmates to see a play at Middle Tennessee State College in Murfreesboro, and, surprisingly, my mother consented. Gordon had never been to my house and I felt a certain trepidation, wondering what he'd think. After all, we didn't have a golden television set. But when he came to pick me up, I felt a great sense of relief. The introductions were made comfortably, and miraculously, my mother even seemed almost charmed by him.

When we got outside, Gordon paused on our screened-in porch, and whispered, "You are absolutely nothing like your family. It's amazing. That man is not your father, is he?" He didn't wait for an answer. "There must be something very interesting going on here. I can see your resemblance to your mother's bone structure; so obviously, you just took the name Locke when she married *him*, right?" I nodded, not knowing what else to do. "And your brother, he's obviously got a different father too."

I don't know how he knew that, but somehow he did.

It had been sometime during grammar school when I learned that Alfred Locke, the thin, dark-haired carpenter whom I called Daddy, was not my real father. I had immediately thought of the photograph of me I'd found in the drawer, the one with the name Smith crossed out on the back. Was my real father's name Smith? I searched for my birth certificate and there it was, Raymond Smith, a native of New York City. I knew it would do no good to ask my mother; she never answered questions, so I begged Momma to tell me the truth. "Honey, don't worry your pretty little head about that," Momma said. But finally she told me how Mr. Smith had been in the military, stationed nearby. It just hadn't worked out and he went away before I was born. Although Momma would not admit it, I knew Mr. Smith never married my mother.

After a pause, Gordon smiled brightly. "Oh, I know what, you're illegitimate, Sondra." A look of shock must have passed over my face because he quickly comforted me. "Oh no, you should feel special. That makes you a mystery. It's wonderful to be a mystery," he said tenderly. "Your father, whoever he was, was clearly very special, because so are you."

"Really? Do you think I should try and find him?" I asked.

"No, why would you want to?" he asked.

"Well, you know who your father is."

"That means nothing. I wish *he* were a mystery. He certainly doesn't care anything about me," Gordon replied matter-of-factly. It was not the first time Gordon had said something like that about his father.

I was to learn firsthand what a sad relationship Gordon had with his father. One afternoon Gordon had just finished a beautiful drawing of a medieval cottage that he'd spent days on, and I was admiring it. Mr. Anderson didn't even pause to look at it as he walked by, casually unwrapping a piece of his favorite Juicy Fruit gum, and tossing the wrapping on top of the drawing. "I think he only copied it out of a history book, didn't he?" he said coldly.

"Oh why don't you go kill a baby rabbit and throw it down the sewer," Gordon said, getting up angrily from the dining room table. "C'mon let's get out of here, Sondra."

His father yelled back at him, "Don't you talk to me like that; I'll stomp you . . ."

"I've been hearing I'm gonna be stomped since I was three," Gordon retorted, grabbing my arm and pulling me out the back door and down the stairs into the backyard. "Follow me," he whispered. We made our way around the side of the house and settled into large bushes that grew near the side porch at the front of his house. Once we were safely hidden, I asked what he meant about the rabbit and the sewer, and he began to tell me a story that I will never forget.

"Well, when we lived in Jonesboro, Arkansas, I think I was six. There was an open field across the street behind a large apartment building. My brother and his Post 80 gang were all playing there and I had tagged along, trying to be part of the group, I guess, when all of a sudden we all caught sight of a little brown wild rabbit. Everyone started chasing it and one of the boy's dogs went after it, managing to bite its back, but still it had gotten away. Now I could always run faster than all the rest of the boys — probably because I had to in order to get away from them — so I was the one who caught the rabbit. And I ran back home with him, put iodine on his little back, then wrapped him up in a towel, named him Baby Jesus, and began to try to nurse him back to health. He was so small and helpless that on the first day I had him, I wandered around the house with him crying, which, I guess, drove Daddy crazy. But in a week or so Baby Jesus had begun to recover and I could take him out of the wire cage Mama had gotten for me to keep him in, and he'd even let me pet him without running away.

"Then one Saturday my brother got invited by a friend to go to the matinee, at the Strand movie theater, and, as usual, Mama said he could go 'If you'll take Gordie with you.' Daddy was outside working in the yard and I put Baby Jesus and his cage in the shade where it was cool and asked Daddy if he would move him when the sun came around to that side. He said he would, but when I got back from the movie theater, I went running to the cage and my little rabbit was just lying there on his side. He didn't move. I reached in to pet him and he felt so hot, and he was as hard as a rock. I knew he was dead and I began sobbing. And I began screaming at my daddy, 'You killed him, and you did it on purpose.' I remember I was crying so hard I couldn't get my breath. He squatted down, grabbed me, started shaking me and ordered me to stop crying and 'act like a man' and to get the rabbit out of the cage. Then he marched me to the corner of our house, at Flint Street and Cherry, and made me drop my little rabbit down the sewer."

I sat there in stunned silence. It was so horrible; the story was so awful that I didn't know what to say. All I could do was hate Mr. Anderson. I would never be able to look at him without thinking of that story.

"I've always known who he is. That's how he gets his kicks," Gordon went on. He told me that, for as long as he could remember, the slightest thing he did that was deemed wrong resulted in a strapping. And always Mr. Anderson had strapped him until he peed. Until one day when Gordon retaliated by peeing on Mr. Anderson. Despite the circumstances, Gordon was never a victim. Gordon's relationship with his brother, Bill, had never been a good one either. Bill even organized his Post 80 club specifically so he could exclude Gordon from it, something that later on, as an adult, Bill even admitted. "As far back as I can remember all my brother ever did was call me names and make fun of me. He liked nothing better than tearing up every picture that I'd draw. And he taught all the other boys in the neighborhood to treat me the same way and call me the same names that he did."

Being different has its penalties, I thought. As I looked at Gordon that day, I swore to myself that I somehow would never, ever let anybody else hurt him again.

"Daddy's in there now figuring out what to do," Gordon said, chewing on a blade of grass. He was staring far off at nothing, but it was as if he could *see* his father. "He doesn't want me outside talking to you, not after what just happened. He's going to come up with some way to try to get me back inside the house. You'll see."

Within five seconds I heard the sound of a door opening and his father's voice call out, "Gordon! There's a phone call for you." Gordon turned and looked at me, smiling. "I told you," he whispered. "There is no phone call; we would have heard the phone ringing." He looked up toward the window above us. "That's Ma Belle's bedroom and her window is wide open and the phone's right by her door." He smiled.

It staggered me the way he was able to see into the hidden truth of who and what his father really was. In time I could tell that Mr. Anderson also *knew* Gordon could "see" him, and was threatened by this. Of course, early on in our relationship, I had figured out that Gordon seemed to "know things," but over time it became obvious that he had a completely preternatural clarity and insight. He had an uncanny understanding of people and why they acted the way they did. And often, just like with Mr. Anderson, he could even predict how they would act in the future.

Off and on I would say to him, "You must be psychic"—for it was the only explanation I could comprehend—and Gordon, grinning enigmatically, would assure me that he wasn't. That aspect of Gordon, though I found it fascinating, was at the same time unnerving.

Almost as unnerving was the fact that Gordon simply seemed to have become a completely different person at the start of our junior year. In a matter of weeks he had become the most popular, most outgoing person in the entire high school. At his house on Belmont Avenue he was given his own private phone because the family phone had begun to ring unceasingly for him. The other kids were coming to him for constant advice on their girlfriends, their boyfriends, their grades, their parents. It seemed as if everyone wanted to know Gordon and everything he had to say. Even the football star Fred, whom he'd slapped in algebra, was going over to Gordon's and driving him home from school—he was teaching Fred to draw! He held court in the corridors, and in the classrooms, even some of our teachers deferred to him. If our high school were the audience, Gordon had become Oprah.

What had caused his extraordinary metamorphosis? He told me how a couple of weeks before school started he and his father had had a horrible fight. Mr. Anderson had called him names, said he was "antisocial," and accused him of not having any friends—"I'm ashamed of you! You're no son of mine. I'll send you to the Dale Carnegie Institute or some goddamn military school," he had threatened. It had all mushroomed into what sounded like a truly ugly scene, with Gordon telling him to "go on and try," as Mrs. Anderson stood crying.

"Then Number Two decided," Gordon told me. "I would make him eat his words."

And just by deciding to do it, he did it. Soon everyone except me had forgotten about the old Gordon. He was friends with the freshmen, sophomores, juniors, and even with the seniors. He alone was allowed to go to all four class parties. He even had his own radio report on the local DJ show, giving hysterical renditions on all the goings-on and gossip at Central High. In the school newspaper he even wrote a gossip column that everyone either feared or wanted to be in.

After a brief stay in the hospital during his senior year, he "took to his bed" for two weeks and had approximately three hundred seventy visitors at Belmont Avenue. Oh yes, and they all signed in. It was like the end of *Pollyanna* where Hayley Mills lay in bed as the entire town came to cheer her up. Gordon was surely a magician, I thought.

One day he decreed, "You might become an actress!" I thought he was teasing me about the dramatic readings I gave in our English and speech classes. "You could read the phone book and sound like Medea," he once said. I turned red and then he added, "Still, you're better than the college actress we saw in the play Middle Tennessee State. I can teach you if you'd like." So we began to work together in his attic using his big gray Voice of Music tape recorder. We'd tape movies on television and listen to them over and over, studying inflections, timing, and phrasing. After he made me imitate the performances, he'd then help me understand the psychological reasons the actresses had made their choices. Next, I'd have to play the scene with my own interpretation and completely *different* line readings. Before the end of the spring term I would win first place for best dramatic reading at Middle Tennessee, performing a monologue from one of August Strindberg's lesser-known plays.

Still, my confidence was limited. "I might be able to play Laura in *The Glass Menagerie*, but I'd never be able to play someone as flamboyant as Blanche in *A Streetcar Named Desire*," I said.

"Oh no?" Gordon said, slapping a red wig on me which he then made me wear to school. "Be brazen!" He laughed. Everyone turned as I walked into French class. "Sondra, your hair looks so sophisticated!" The rest of the day I felt quite glamorous, and maybe just a tad flamboyant, and I was certain no one knew it was a wig.

I loved looking at all the pretty models in *Seventeen* magazine and dreamed of their glamorous lives. "Make me look like them, Gordon," I said, "you can do it." And he would happily re-create their glamorous makeups on me. Well, at least he'd do *half* my face. "Finish the other side, Gordon! I look stupid." "Oh I will," he'd say. Then he'd be bored with the thought of repetition, his creative moment would pass, and instead he would move on to a record or a book or want to go outside to his big backyard with the huge maple tree and roll around in the grass. "You don't believe it but you can do anything you make up your mind to do," he'd tell me, "that's one of the things I love about you. Why don't *you* do the other side of your makeup—if you try, you'll learn to do it as well as I can." And I did. Then he'd call Ma Belle and his mother in to admire my artistry, and they would bring big silver trays of snacks for us to eat. Ham, egg salad, pimento cheese sandwiches, Cokes, and barbecue potato chips. Mr. Anderson no longer picked on him the way he once had; now in fact, he seemed a little afraid of the most popular person in school. Certainly he had had to eat his words—Dale Carnegie's help had not been needed.

The summer before my senior year my family moved from Shelbyville to nearby Wartrace, only a twenty-minute drive away. I liked the new white house with its pink trim on the big corner lot in Wartrace. It was much better than Horse Mountain Road; it felt lighter, brighter somehow. And I loved all the trees in front, and lying under them. The yard was big enough so that Daddy could have a really big garden in the back, and Mother could have lots of chairs on the front porch, and I could sit and watch the train, which ran through the center of Wartrace and right past our house, and imagine where it was going.

Since no Central High School bus went as far as Wartrace, my parents had to buy a second car so I could drive to school. I loved the little Renault Dauphine and the freedom she brought with her. That little car was the only obvious difference about me as I began my senior year at Central High, yet I was suddenly the center of attention. When some of the other girls, the ones with well-to-do fathers, first saw it, they gushed, "Oooh, oh, Sondra! You have a brand-new car; it's adorable! Did your daddy buy it for you?" They didn't know that my new status symbol was really just a practical way to get to school and accomplish a host of chores and errands to help out at home. Perhaps at one time I'd have found their interest flattering, but that was long past.

In truth, in spite of not knowing what I would do when school was over, I was ready for the senior year to come and go. To make the time pass more quickly I worked part-time as an office assistant for the principal and even took extra classes because I hated study hall and its silence. It reminded me of home, where I spent most of my time in my newly painted pink and white bedroom with the pink princess phone I was allowed. Then when the living room television set was replaced, I inherited the old one for my room and— just like Gordon had told me I could—I sprayed it white to match.

My drama lessons continued that year in Gordon's dusty attic in front of one of the large spare mirrors from the Family Shoe Store, with Gordon's trapeze above, gently swaying to and fro. He'd lay Honey on the floor in front of me and tell me a heartbreaking story of how she had died, and I would sob. Then, through equal parts ranting, raving, beseeching, and al-chemy there came the time that Honey was happily gnawing on a bone somewhere else, but I, still pretending she was there . . . and remembering . . . could feel the tears again coursing down my cheeks. I was becoming an actress, he said.

Chapter 3 ~

Along with becoming so popular, Gordon had also become the star of high school theatrics, and Mr. Patterson, the English and speech teacher, fancied himself something of Gordon's mentor. His unusual inscription in Gordon's junior annual had read "How exquisitely excruciating has our relationship been this year. I now wonder who or which was the potter and which the clay. I've learned much from you and hope you have from me."

And so, he decided that Gordon should direct one of the three one-act plays the high school was planning. Gordon accepted and chose a thriller entitled *The Monkey's Paw* based on W. W. Jacob's short story. In the play, two bereaved parents are given an enchanted monkey's paw from the Far East. Once in their possession, this terrifying relic has the power to grant them their dearest wish. They quickly wish for the return of their beloved son, who had been tragically killed in an industrial accident. Too quickly perhaps, for instead of wishing that the accident had never happened and that their son had never died, they wish only for his return, which means his return will be from the grave. The play ends with the sound of leaden footsteps approaching the cottage. We all realize with horror exactly what is waiting for them on the other side of the door and as the father reaches out and slowly begins to open it . . . the lights dim and the curtain falls.

This play would mark a turning point for me, because Gordon decided that I would play the mother and he would play the father, as well as direct. He designed lighting that was dark and moody. At two key points in the dialogue, candles that were lit on stage mysteriously extinguished themselves (thanks to an aquarium tube that led backstage). At another key moment in the play, he directed me to give the audience a big shock by having me, with by back turned, suddenly drop an entire tea tray service onto the floor. He even used music cues from the spooky television series *One Step Beyond*. All this was unheard of for a little school play.

As dress rehearsal approached I was nervous because we knew that some rowdy boys had been hiding in the auditorium balcony during the other two plays' rehearsals and had pelted the cast members with tomatoes and eggs. Sure enough, in the middle of our rehearsal, we began to hear whispers coming from the darkened balcony. Gordon, like some maestro, threw up his arms and stopped the play, screamed out into the darkened theater, berating the hidden offenders, then dramatically rang down the curtain, and stormed off. "I fixed that. They're gonna pay," Gordon huffed. From the balcony you could hear a pin drop. And no tomatoes or eggs were forthcoming.

On performance night we were such a big sensation that Mr. Patterson entered us into statewide competition, beginning with the regional at Middle Tennessee State University. We won first place there, and so were invited to the state competition at Johnson City, Tennessee. Unfortunately, it cost money and the school refused to sponsor us. Undaunted, Gordon said, "They can't stop us. We'll do it on our own. Mama will drive us to Johnson City!" I'd never known anyone with as much determination as Gordon when he wanted something, especially if someone was unfairly trying to stop him.

What a wonderful time we had on that trip. All morning I spent leaning my head out the back car window to catch the wind in my face, daydreaming, mesmerized by Gordon's hair. He had just shampooed it and I watched as the wind was drying it, whipping it about like so many golden threads. Mrs. Anderson had even packed us a picnic lunch for the five-hour drive and along the way we stopped at a big open stretch of countryside and ate in a meadow. It was my first adventure anywhere without my parents. I could just as easily have been off to Paris; I was that excited.

That night at the Howard Johnson's motel was chaos. It seemed everything was going wrong: The tape recorder for our music had begun to stick; there were rumors that we might not even be allowed to use music at all, or the tube for blowing out the candle, or even the all-important door for the finale. Finally in frustration we all gave up and went to bed, hoping for better news in the morning.

I shared a room with Mrs. Anderson and grew even closer to her; that night it felt as if she were my mother. Together we each set our hair and told stories. I watched her winding that beautiful long hair around her finger and into curls, then securing them with those big strong hairpins, the ones Gordon loved to make things with. As I coasted into sleep I could hear the echo of her voice telling me all about how she had "finally found Gordie that pair of real wooden shoes he'd wanted for so long . . . at a costume shop in Memphis, ones he could really wear . . . he wanted to be a real Dutch boy . . . or an elf. In his fairy tale picture books, elves and dwarfs often wore wooden shoes too . . ."

The next day, like magic, everything fell together. The door was pinned on, the aquarium tube carefully placed at the candles, the tape recorder was set, the lights came on, the stage manager whispered, "You're on," and the curtain opened. It was incredible. I could hear a pin drop in the audience as Gordon said his first line. And we were off.

When our performance was over, we sneaked into seats in the very back of the auditorium to watch the rest of the plays, our competitors. There were twelve of us finalists who had been chosen from over two hundred plays across the state, and all were good. I never dreamed of really winning anything, it was my very first play, but Gordon turned to me and said, "There's only one actress that's any real competition for you." Still, when the big moment of award-giving finally arrived, my pulse quickened. "Best actress . . . goes to . . . Sondra Locke." I could hardly believe it. Gordon and Mrs. Anderson both flew out of their seats and grabbed me. Dazed, I managed to stumble down the long aisle and up onto the stage to receive my plaque. Then, "The winner in the one-act play competition given by the National Thespian Society for the state of Tennessee is . . . 'best play' goes to . . . Shelbyville Central High School, Gordon Anderson, director." I screamed, again jumped straight out of my seat, and watched with joy as Gordon ran up that same long aisle to get his large trophy. Finally it hit me: I was the best actress in the entire state and Gordon was the best director, despite the fact that all the other directors were teachers. It couldn't have been more thrilling if it had been Broadway and the Tony Awards.

Two months later, my four years in the sprawling redbrick building came to an end. Gordon and I were chosen to be among the so-called class Superlatives. I was most studious and Gordon was the funniest (Baron of Humor and Duchess of Studiousness! Very regal). For those honors we were dressed in formal attire and had our pictures taken for the annual. I ranked highest in the class, was again valedictorian, and that May I wrote and delivered my valedictory address. Its theme was "We are a part of all that we have met." The more I had been around Gordon, the more I had understood that was true. But mostly I understood I had become a part of Gordon. At times I felt inexplicably that we shared one soul, and for the very first time I had an inkling of what that word — soul — really meant. In some mysterious and wonderful way . . . it felt as if we *were* each other.

ONCE HIGH SCHOOL was over, the sense of security I had had in the classroom went with it. I suddenly felt lost; I didn't know what to do and I had

no money. So I went to work. Of all things, I got a job doing light book-
keeping in the office of a chicken plant in Shelbyville. There is nothing
I've always hated more than business and accounting. But then, I laugh
when I recall the summer Gordon's father had insisted that he take a job
in one of the pencil plants. Gordon said he didn't need a summer job; he
earned money painting portraits of people around town, but Mr. Anderson
wouldn't hear it. Gordon said, "He wants me to do manual labor. He wants
to get me good and dirty." So Gordon went to work at the pencil factory,
where he operated the machinery that pressed and glued the two sides of
the wooden pencils around the lead. His boss was almost always unpleasant,
and on those occasions when he was particularly mean, Gordon would
"accidentally" jam his machinery. Pencil parts flew everywhere. But they
didn't fire him until one day at the end of the official ten-minute morning
coffee break, Gordon began demonstrating his self-taught tap-dancing skills
that he'd learned from religiously watching the *Mickey Mouse Club* on TV.
All the other workers stood happily applauding while Gordie tap-danced his
heart out. And with that, Gordon was sent packing. No one could have
been happier about it than Gordon.

Gordon's job was bad, but mine seemed worse. Chickens were being
slaughtered, plucked, and packaged just on the other side of the wall from
where I sat, logging my stacks of statements. I hated it. I stayed in the office,
refusing even to look inside the plant. At least I was earning some money
and I was saving it—just like Ma Belle. When I arrived home, I would
make dinner for everyone. And life went on that way throughout the summer. Except for the times when I was with Gordon, the world again seemed
drained of color. Before the summer was over, I was "let go" and I was
glad, because that meant I had more time to spend with Gordon before his
father shipped him off to Middle Tennessee State College in Murfreesboro
in September.

I didn't know what I was going to do. When I look back, it's inconceivable that I hadn't developed some plan, but then my parents hadn't prepared
me for making plans. I always did well at everything, but so far everything
had been mapped out for me. My only dream was of being an actress in
movies, but I knew that was impossible. I felt like a train that was ready to
travel but the tracks had run out and so there it was, left sitting alone in
the middle of some pasture. Going on to college was, of course, something
that made sense to me. School was the only place I'd belonged, but then
I knew it cost money that my parents neither had nor would have viewed
as a necessary expense. Gordon's mother was disgusted that the teachers at
Central High hadn't seen fit to ensure I had been given a scholarship.

"Sondra honey, with your school record, I'm sure you could have had a scholarship to Vassar or Radcliffe — or, in fact, anywhere you wanted to go," she said to me.

"Well, none of the teachers said anything about it," I replied. I didn't tell her that I had never asked to meet with the guidance counselor, because, I guess, I was too proud to admit I had no money.

"Well, I wish I'd known in time. Gordon, why didn't you tell me?" Mrs. Anderson said.

"Because she doesn't need to go to Vassar with a herd of other girls. Something special is gonna happen to her."

What? Mrs. Anderson and I both wondered out loud.

"Well, I don't know, but something will. I can feel it." We were all perched on her bed with the Andersons' dogs, Wiggles and Honey, when suddenly Gordon got up in a huff. "I can't tell you how depressing this talk about college is. God did not intend for me to go to college. The prospect of going to college is the single most horrendous thing that has ever happened to me in my entire life. It's clear that nobody in this house has any understanding of who I am. I am an artist," he moaned dramatically, "and, since I never intend to teach, the whole concept is idiotic. I feel besmirched." He turned to me and continued, "And you don't need to go to college anyway. Everything wonderful about you will just be contaminated. How many more years do you have to go on making straight A's before you finally realize you're smart?" He exited his mother's bedroom in high dudgeon. "I'm going outside," he harumphed. "You'll find me on my trapeze."

When Gordon's favorite movie, *The Greatest Show on Earth*, was released, it finally played for two evenings at Shelbyville's 41 Drive-in. Gordon and I went, and I, too, fell under the spell of the tinsel, and the excitement. And when we left the drive-in that evening, we had more than just our memories, because Gordon had lugged his big gray tape recorder out to the projection booth and had talked the projectionist into plugging it directly into the projector's audio output. So now we could listen to the whole movie and at Gordon's insistence we did so — *ceaselessly*. Since he had the entire soundtrack of the film, he would take his tape recorder into his backyard, settling it in the deep grass, where it would play the aerial music cues while we swung ten feet off the ground on his trapeze, pretending to be Betty Hutton and Cornel Wilde.

Gordon had recently gotten a super-8 camera with a zoom lens and a tripod and he decided that we would do a remake of *The Greatest Show on Earth*, lip-synching the dialogue. Word spread and Gordon began collecting twenty-five dollars from all of the eager boys and girls who couldn't wait to make their "screen debuts." Eventually Gordon coerced me into making costumes on Momma's sewing machine and I was amazed at how easily plumes, sequins, glitter, three yards of satin, and an old aqua bathing suit could be transformed into really beautiful circus costumes. I was to play Holly and Gordon would be Sebastian. Another friend, who was a whiz at all things mechanical, was rather miffed when he was assigned a role *behind* the camera as our director of photography. The first shot of our production would take place at Shelbyville's old train depot, and was from the scene where the aerialists Holly and Sebastian meet each other for the first time as the circus train prepares to roll out of winter quarters. "But, Gordon," I said, "that scene only requires street clothes. What about our beautiful circus costumes?"

"I know, it's disgusting, isn't it?" he replied. "But I don't know how we can film any of the circus scenes when we don't have a big top." Then his face brightened. "I know what! We can still wear them when we swing on the trapeze in the backyard."

At 9:00 on a Saturday morning, approximately thirty of us converged down at the railroad tracks. Large red paper backings with "Ringling Brothers Barnum and Bailey" that Gordon had painted in gold scroll letters were put up and Scotch-taped in place onto several abandoned boxcars. Gordon got everyone in position, hollered, "Action!" and filming began. Extras carrying suitcases and sparkly old costumes—from dance recitals and proms—hurried past the camera. A Jeep with Buttons the Clown rolled by. And our home movie camera on its tripod rolled in on a furniture dolly for a medium shot of Holly and Sebastian. Gordon was so nervous that I might get out of synch with Betty Hutton's voice that he was doing her lines right along with me. Finally, after five or six takes, everything went perfectly and Gordon announced that it was a "wrap." Our production at last was under way! Sadly, it was short-lived. At the end of the day, as we rushed to get the cartridge of film to the local lab, we discovered that our trusted cameraman had *forgotten* to put film in the camera.

"Oh my God," I said. "I don't see how he could have forgotten to load the camera."

Gordon's eyes narrowed. "He didn't forget anything! If he couldn't be in front of the camera himself, he was going to make certain that the rest of us wouldn't be, either. Welcome to show business, Sondra."

It was a wonderful summer and it was also poignant, because it was a turning point. Childhood was drawing to a close and I worried what would happen to us. Gordon and I had become so close that I couldn't bear the thought of life pulling us apart. Perhaps it was that fear that crystallized my true feelings for him. I realized our bond was more than best friends; I knew I had fallen in love. Our friendship took a deeper, richer turn when Gordon confided to me that he'd been in love with me since junior year. Suddenly there were no more distractions. And even now, as I look back and reflect upon the sweetness of that time, I see only Gordon and me. It's late afternoon and the hot sun is losing its power as the sky transforms to rose and amber. A soft breeze blows and we're the only two people in the world—the two of us atop a hilly landscape of summer green.

Now I truly belonged to someone and the power of that first love experience elevated my spirit to a new level of excitement about life and the future. Even my mother's behavior was unable to tarnish it. She had sensed something new between Gordon and me and she didn't like it. She didn't want me to have a steady boyfriend—especially not Gordon. "All he does is fill your head with silly dreams and notions" was her complaint. But the truth, I'm sure, was that both my parents were uncomfortable with Gordon's scrutiny of them and could tell that he saw and understood too much. And even though Gordon was always friendly and polite to both of them, they eventually came to resent him. But I was in love. I had found something extraordinary, something that at last made sense to me. I wasn't about to let it go.

At least my grandmother, Momma, understood and liked Gordon. A country woman all her life, she loved the stories Gordon told her about his grandmother, Ma Belle. She had never known such a creature and was fascinated with the tales of furs and jewels and breakfasts in bed. "Why, you know, she sounds like somethin' outta the 'Rabian Nights," Momma would marvel. About Gordon she'd say, "Now's he's a sweet 'un, honey." Then chewing on her little twig—a habit of hers—she'd look far away at something only she could see, rock back and forth in her old rocker, then say, "I'm jus' thinkin'. You know what's interestin' about 'im? That little boy can see what's what. And sometimes, honey, that can be a curse." I'm sure she had no idea how deep a truth she had spoken.

As Gordon's relationship with me became more pronounced, his father began to make his life miserable regarding me. Mr. Anderson perceived himself as one of the finest "upstanding citizens" in Shelbyville, and he made it clear to Gordon that I was not suitable. "How in the hell do you think it makes me feel when I have to tell Calvin Daughtry [the druggist across the street from his shoe store] that my son is 'going' with Alfred Locke's daughter?"

When Gordon told me this he declared, "I couldn't believe it. He's so pretentious. I told him, too. I said, 'Just *who* do you think you are, anyway? I'm afraid you only *dreamt* you "dwelt in marble halls" when in fact you had twelve brothers and sisters, walked barefoot behind the mules to school, and never went to college, yet it was fine for you to set your sights on Mother—the college valedictorian from the big white house, whose grand-father was one of the finest doctors in town. You're such a hypocrite. Where in the hell do you get off judging Sondra anyway?' "

Though I knew I was an outsider, and not from a rich family, it had not really occurred to me that I was looked down upon, especially by someone like Mr. Anderson. Though I was hurt and embarrassed, I managed to consider the source.

As fall approached Gordon became depressed because his father was virtually forcing him to go to college at Middle Tennessee State University, which his brother, Bill, was also attending. Hearing that, I decided that if Gordon were going there, I would go too. I counted my money and applied for (and got) a last-minute scholarship for my tuition and board. Together it was just enough. I could hardly wait. My parents, as usual, seemed threat-ened; they had been happy when I was working at the plant and came home every night. It was something they could relate to. But I was bound and determined to go. It was my own life, and I had to begin to make my own plan, and, even if it was only a forty-minute drive away, it was a be-ginning. So, together Gordon and I went to MTSU.

The theater at MTSU was the same theater in which we had won best play in the region for *The Monkey's Paw* and our reputations seemed to have preceded us; the heads of speech and drama were both aware that I had been named Best Actress and Gordon Best Director in the state. There, we continued our interest in dramatics, and, although most of the larger roles usually went to upperclassmen, we were both cast in major roles in the fall play, *Life with Father*. Gordon was cast as Whitney, one of Father's four sons, and I had the ingenue's role, Mary. In the next production, *The Crucible*, I played Mary Warren and Gordon was in charge of all makeup. I was disappointed he wouldn't audition for a role. "Who wants to play a Puritan?" He laughed. "Nothing but all those drab black and white cos-tumes."

Amazingly enough, my mother and father decided to come see *The Cru-cible*. I couldn't imagine what had prompted them to do this, and their presence gave me a certain unexplainable anxiety. Then, in the middle of one of my highly charged dramatic moments as Mary is making her hys-terical accusations and is being challenged by the court authorites, suddenly I heard my mother's voice ringing out through the hushed theater, "Hey you. Leave that girl alone, you hear me?" I was horrified. I wanted to disappear. I was so stunned I thought I was going to lose control of my performance, and once I had moved away to my next mark and looked back to where I'd been standing, I realized that, in another way, I had lost control. It was mortifying.

I could sense that Gordon was never happy at the school. He appeared in the midwinter operetta, and was again in charge of the makeup but was feeling more and more stifled. He felt he had exhausted the school's creative reservoir—and, as usual, he had no interest in completing "the other side of the face." He told me he had had it and would "run away" if he could. So instead of going to class, he spent his days deep in the library stacks reading old issues of *Theatre Arts* magazine and *Life* and *Look*. On the day they took the freshman class pictures, he refused to have his own taken and convinced me to do the same. "We aren't going to be part of MTSU's history. We weren't here. It never happened." As ever, I was thrilled by Gordon's sense of special destiny, which always seemed to materialize when we needed it. As the year was ending, he wrangled an invitation to the summer session of Pasadena Playhouse and was off to California for three months. Of course, I couldn't afford to follow him and remained in War-trace with nothing but my longing. That summer seemed interminable and lonely without him. Every morning I would walk across the railroad tracks to the little post office, and hope for a letter or a postcard from him and . . . mythical California. The afternoons I spent sitting on the front porch watching the train clatter through town, speeding away, and imagining where it could take me too—maybe even Pasadena—if only I had a way.

Finally Gordon returned, armed with new amazing stories and photos of himself onstage in several different plays that had been produced at the playhouse. He was especially excited because at the end of his stay, during the showcase productions, he had been approached by two agents who wanted to represent him. Of course, that wasn't possible because Gordon was only there for the summer, but it was still encouraging. It all sounded so exciting and impossible and I was mesmerized with all his stories.

It was during the same summer, just after Gordon returned, that everything suddenly blew up between my mother and me. The event itself was un-important and could have been spurred by any number of things. It was inevitable. It followed on the heels of a series of little abuses—this time it was over a telephone conversation I had had with Gordon the night before when everyone else was already in bed. "I don't want you on that telephone at night," she said.

"It's my phone," I defended myself. "You told me it was mine; I even picked the color."

"Oh yeah?" she countered. "Well, that was then and this is now." Then she hurled the final words: "If you don't want to do exactly as I tell you, you can pack your bags, girl, and get outta here. This is my house, not yours."

I was nineteen years old. These were words that had been said in so many different ways, but never out loud. And they were words that gave me the anger, the courage, and the initiative to go.

Boldly, I packed a bag and left. I had no idea where I was going and was walking down the road when miraculously I saw Gordon's station wagon driving toward me. I had forgotten that we had planned to do something that afternoon. When I explained what had happened, he was livid. He wanted to go back to the house and confront my mother, but I convinced him not to. I asked him to take me to my cousin Dwight's house, hoping that my mother's sister would take me in. But smiling in that I'm-hatching-a-plot Gordon way, he said, "Maybe in a coupla days, but for now you're coming home with me, and I'm not gonna let anyone know you're there. Now I know Mother would be happy to have you, but if she knows you're there and your parents call and ask for you, I know she'll feel she has to tell them the truth. Instead, I want them to stew in their juices, wondering where you are. Let them call everybody, maybe even my house, and find that none of us have seen you. Then maybe your mother'll learn you can't go around treating people the way she's been treating you."

And so I hid upstairs in Gordon's room, and he smuggled food up for me. I felt safe and happy and a few days later, after my aunt and cousin Dwight had taken me in, I learned that no one had called them or the Andersons to ask of my whereabouts. That really hurt. The next day, when no one was home in Wartrace, Dwight took me back there so I could retrieve a few more of my things, especially my television; it seemed important to me, maybe because I'd spray-painted it white.

The next afternoon I was alone at my aunt's house when my mother and Donald arrived. I thought and hoped that she had come to tell me she was sorry, but all she said was, "I want that television back."

"Don't do that. It's not fair. You gave it to me; it's mine," I cried as I ran to the back bedroom.

They followed me. "Donald, hold her down," Mother said as she bent down to unplug the television. Donald, who always did what he was told, pushed me back onto the bed and, using both his hands and knees, pinned me helplessly down.

"Get off of me," I screamed. I couldn't believe the hideous scene and began to sob. "Don't," I begged. "Please stop."

I can still remember vividly the way Mother victoriously looked at me as she marched out of the bedroom with that sad spray-painted little seventeen-inch television set, and the way she said, "Come on, Donnie, let's go *home*." I numbly walked to the large window in the living room and stared as they backed out and drove away. To me, she hadn't just come for the TV. She had come to hurt and humiliate me. I vowed then that the television was the last thing — literally and symbolically — she would ever again take from me.

I would never again live in that house and for nearly thirty years I would have only a handful of conversations and short visits with my mother. It made no sense for any of us to spend our lives pretending to have relationships that did not really exist. And even though it is my nature to feel responsible and guilty, even when I am not, remarkably I never felt that way about my decision to walk away from my parents' home.

After a few weeks, I decided, for my aunt's sake, to move. Carolyn Dickens, my best girl friend and high school basketball teammate, asked me to stay with her and her father. Together we shared the household chores and cooking, and I got a job answering telephones at a tiny real estate office in Shelbyville. Once again I was carefully saving up my money. During this time Mrs. Anderson became even more like a second mother to me, and I spent all my extra time at their house. Gordon, it seemed, had developed a new plan for himself; because his father insisted that he had to stay in school, he had agreed to enroll in George Peabody College in Nashville at the beginning of the new semester right after Christmas. That would certainly be more interesting than Murfreesboro. "You can't stay here in this town," he said. "Move to Nashville with me." I couldn't imagine how I could do something as daring as that. Where would I stay? How would I get a job? But, somehow I knew that if I was with Gordon, all the questions would be answered.

On Christmas Eve I left the real estate office early so I could go to the Andersons for the holiday celebration. I was looking forward to it, even though that old feeling of not having my own family throbbed inside. But Christmas morning at the Andersons turned out to be the most unforgettable I'd ever had. There were two packages for me from Gordon; each one was beautifully wrapped and looked like a shoe box — from the Family Shoe Store, I was sure. When I opened them, I was speechless. He had managed to compress in those boxes two complete outfits I had seen in a fancy new shop that had just opened in town. The owner was from New York, everyone whispered, and all the clothes he carried were exclusive! And the prices reflected it. The two outfits together cost over three hundred dollars — a lot for Shelbyville in the sixties. I will never forget them, and I kept them long after I stopped wearing them because they were far more than dresses to me. One was a wine silk velvet with long gathered sleeves and a small Peter Pan collar, with delicate smocking and tucks across the yoke. The other was a muted, light blue–gray A-line mohair jumper with a large patch pocket on each side. The blouse that went with it was cream silk crepe with long full sleeves, a round collar, and a self-tie that could be knotted into a large, soft bow. They were the most wonderful gifts I had ever been given. I began to sob. "Oh, Shana," Gordon said, using one of his nicknames for me. "You deserve much more than this. And some day you'll have it. I promise."

"But how could you buy these?" I stammered.

"Well, I'd saved up around two hundred and seventy-five dollars, you know from my artwork and from painting the Episcopal bishop's portrait last summer. The rest of it," he said with a mischievous look at his mother, "I snitched from that little green coin purse Ma Belle keeps all those thousands of dollars rolled up in, all color-coded with rubber bands."

"Gordon, you didn't!" I said.

Mrs. Anderson shook her head and, reaching up in that familiar gesture of hers to push one of her large hairpins back into her French twist, said, "Sondra honey, what're we gonna do with him? If he doesn't end up an artist or an actor, I'm afraid he may end up in the electric chair."

After the holidays, we moved to Nashville. Gordon settled in at the Peabody dorm and I found a single room, upstairs in a big white two-story house with a red door, and then I began to look for a job. I applied at one of the largest employers in the city, the National Life and Accident Insurance Company and, thank God, they took one look at my application and routed me over to one of their smaller operations, WSM, a broadcasting station. What great luck, I thought. I had no idea what I'd be doing, but the atmosphere sounded right. I jumped at the job. I was assigned to the "traffic department," which meant that we figured out what program or commercial appeared at each point in the day. Eventually I went through several jobs there, including the sales department, which I didn't like, and the public relations department, which was my favorite because we planned all sorts of promotional activities. We were the NBC affiliate in Nashville and each fall season would be kicked off with a big party. This was especially exciting because generally the stars from the upcoming TV series would do publicity tours and would show up for the party. The cast from *The Monkees* came to town, and I remember Robert Loggia, in particular, who was starring in the new series *T.H.E. Cat* about a cat burglar. He arrived in Nashville to promote his new show and flirted outrageously with me. Somehow having occasional brushes with real-life successful actors kept me inspired.

During this time, I made a few attempts to repair the breach with my family, but never successfully. I don't know why I expected otherwise. One such attempt would be so humiliating that it would be the last. Getting around Nashville without a car was difficult. I traveled back and forth to work on the bus, but was saving money to buy a car. I shopped around and finally found a used English racing green TR-3, which *spoke* to me the moment I saw her. I immediately named her "Leapin' Leaner." Fortunately I had just enough for the down payment. But the bank said I needed an "adult" to co-sign the loan papers. After I'd exhausted all options, I screwed up my courage and picked up the phone to call my mother. It took her only seconds to reply, "No, Sondra. I'm sorry. We can't do that; we just signed for Donald to get one."

"But you don't have to pay anything, Mother. I'll pay; I have it all figured out. It's just that the bank needs a grown-up to vouch for me. Please. I've no one else to ask."

But she only replied no.

I said a quiet goodbye and hung up, wondering why I continued to have any expectations of her. Later, I swallowed my pride and asked Mrs. Anderson if she would co-sign for me. She answered without hesitation, "Why, of course, honey. That's exciting. What kind of car do you think you're going to get?"

Gordon had been at Peabody only a week or two when fate provided him with a new friend—a perfect person to look after him, run his errands, and make sure he went to classes. His name was Arthur, but everyone called him Artie. He was from a small rural community about forty miles from Nashville, and he became Gordon's close friend, confidant, and as he himself put it, "his indentured servant." I always suspected he was in love with Gordon, but he seemed content to accept, as he put it, his fate. In fact he would become a dear friend to us both, and would, years later, figure into some extraordinary occurrences. In addition to being extremely smart, he was a gifted musician who played both piano and organ and was possessed of a quick and lively wit—a wit very much in evidence in an inscription he wrote in Joan Fontaine's autobiography, which he gave to Gordon years later in 1978. His words on the flyleaf echoed their first meeting in the Peabody dormitory halls, which was, at least for Gordon, fortuitous. Artie, who loved Gordon's sense of theatricality and mischief— though he enjoyed pretending he didn't—said that Miss Fontaine's book title, *No Bed of Roses,* was the perfect phrase to describe life with Gordon as he knew it. He wrote:

A tarnished moon shone brightly o'er the yard
And calm and peaceful times embraced betimes
The past was dim, the future all forgot
When at this time: Behold! Diana's Kin appeared—
The shining flame, the watchman of the art.
With burning azure-verdant eyes he spied
And with the flaming tongue he spoke
The Fatal words to doom or praise.
The thread of life was spun more length
When "Hello, Wally" sealed the fate.
My fate: "Have a steak from the Campus Grill in my room when I
get back from the Circle Theatre."
"Register for my classes; I've got to go to Knoxville for a
Weekend party."
"My key is under the trash can at the end of the hall."
"Call Sondra and tell her I've been hurt."
"Take all my calls when I'm paged on the intercom."
"Tell them I have the body of DAVID . . . well,
work it into the conversation!"
"Rewrite this act. My part should be bigger anyway."
"Let me put ketchup on you in the shower—just like Psycho!"
"Write London and tell them why I haven't sent the
Money for the blonde wig."

Gordon and I continued to pursue the theater. The first play we did together there was *Life with Mother* at Theater Nashville, an amateur theater that hired its own professional resident director, a woman from the East named Anita Grannis. It was exciting for me that a professional director had chosen me for her production.

No sooner had that play finished than Gordon was trying out for the scarecrow role in the Nashville Children's Theatre's next production of *The Wizard of Oz.* Nashville Children's Theater was one of the finest in the United States and Chuck Doughty and his wife, Carol, professionals with many years' experience, were respectively its director and choreographer. Their productions were always eagerly anticipated and children from all over middle Tennessee were bused in.

"Come on and try out with me, Shana," Gordon insisted. "You'd be a wonderful Dorothy. It's a grand theater, huge and really professional. They fly all the scenery."

"You know I can't sing!"

"Yes, you can. I'll fix you all up and teach you a song."

This time I didn't believe he could pull off that particular magic, but try he did, making me rehearse endlessly with Artie, whom he dragged along as our accompanist. The audition was overflowing with children and adults who were eager to become part of the wonderful *Wizard of Oz*. I wore the soft mohair jumper Gordon gave me for Christmas, and put my hair into two short pigtails. After I read two scenes for the director, he said, "Excellent. We'd like to hear you sing a little later." When that terrifying moment came, Artie accompanied me on the piano while I sang "Whistle While You Work" (a song chosen not only because it was easy to sing, but because we all adored Disney animation, especially *Snow White*). Artie gave me a nod on the downbeat and I managed the song rather well, but then Mr. Doughty said, "Very nice. Now we'd like you to do 'Over the Rainbow' for us." I thought, Please, dear God, let the floor open and swallow me. Let's just say the song was beyond my capabilities.

When they called Gordon's name, he read the lines brilliantly, sounding exactly like Ray Bolger. And his pantomime gestures made it seem like he didn't have a bone in his body. I could tell he Doughtys were very excited and Carol eagerly asked, "Did you bring something to sing?" "Can you by any chance dance?" as if that were too much to hope for.

"Sure," Gordon replied. He quickly went into a chorus of "If I Only Had a Brain," then turning toward the piano said, "Hit it, Artie" and went into an eccentric tap. My mouth fell open. Even if Gordon had never done something before, he could make it up on the spot, and somehow, it would look and seem totally professional—with no lessons, and no rehearsal. I could never understand where it came from.

Two days later Gordon got the part of the scarecrow, but, alas, Dorothy went to a girl with a trained voice. It was some consolation that later Mr. Doughty told Gordon he had loved my audition and thought my look was perfect and, except for my singing—or lack of it—he would have chosen me.

After that Gordon and I had a dream come true. We had wanted for a long time to do *The Innocents*, William Archibald's dramatization of Henry James's chilling novella *The Turn of the Screw*, about a governess and her two preternatural charges. Gordon's enthusiasm for the play must have been contagious, because Chuck Doughty loved the idea and said he would direct it with me and Gordon as the two children, and two other well-known local actresses as the grown-ups. He also asked Gordon to design the costumes and the poster. Chuck took his ideas to the Circle Theater and agreed to mount the play and direct it providing there were no auditions and he could have the cast he wanted. Even though it was unprecedented to precast a play, the Circle Theater quickly agreed. Unfortunately, this generated ill feeling in some quarters, not toward the director but toward Gordon. This was the first time I realized that it would be Gordon who would always get the blame for anything anyone close to him did. If I were to throw a brickbat at someone, somehow that person would ultimately blame Gordon. At that time I wasn't able to understand exactly why. I thought it was just a mysterious consequence of his personal power.

After *The Innocents* I was cast in other choice roles at the Circle Theater and Theater Nashville,* including Rosalie in *Oh Dad Poor Dad Mama's Hung You in the Closet and I'm Feeling So Sad* (*The Nashville Tennessean* reviewer called my character a "candy-coated vulture"—I loved that—and went on to say, "Sondra Locke, a talented actress, is apparently stuck with wicked-child portrayals." I guess they *were* always the most fun for me: When I played the social worker in *A Thousand Clowns*, I found it boring). Then there was Laura in Tennessee Williams's *The Glass Menagerie*. "Miss Locke [gives] a fragile, brief, and totally heartbreaking delineation of this sad, lost child woman . . . We are sorry that the director did not advise fewer placings of her hand over her mouth and suggest that opening the mouth wide and leaving it open can be annoying and distracting." I laughed. An exquisite phrase from that play by Tennessee Williams reminded me of my own early years and struck a chord in me that would forever resonate: "the long awaited but always expected something that we live for."

Word of my work in the local theaters began to spread and soon caught the attention of the on-air producers and directors at WSM, who started asking me to appear on camera. Gradually, I also began doing voice-overs for radio commercials and soon was modeling for newspaper and magazine advertisements and finally television commercials as well. It seemed I had achieved a certain level of local fame for myself.

For almost a year Gordon had been struggling with a deeply personal issue. It was something he had first confided to me the summer he returned from California and the Pasadena Playhouse. He had told me that numerous men there had pursued him and made sexual overtures, and that he had actually found himself attracted to one of them, although he had done nothing about it. I was relieved by that fact. But then, five months later, my heart sank when he told me, matter-of-factly, that he had had his first sexual experience with a man. He had decided it was time to find out. "I don't know. Maybe I'm gay," he had said hesitantly.

I was stunned. I didn't want it to be true because I didn't want to lose him, so I minimized it. "How can you say that? The very least you can say is that you're bisexual." But his look did not give me the confidence I sought. Despite how I had hoped the issue would go away, it hadn't. And even though I was crushed, I was still able to recognize how extraordinary it was that he had told me so readily. I guess a small part of me was not surprised that he needed the love of a man. After all, he had never had it from his own father or his brother. His father had only humiliated Gordon because he couldn't bend him to be exactly who he wanted him to be. He was a cold, insensitive, and unevolved man who never appreciated Gordon's uniqueness and his special gifts. And his brother, Bill, was the cliché of the tormenting older brother. It used to break my heart when Gordon would tell me about his early childhood, and how he had loved it, in the first grade, when the school crossing guard, an older boy, helped him to safely cross the street. He had felt so happy, he said, when he took his hand, that he would often pretend to forget something so he could go back and make several trips across the street. Homosexuality was not openly discussed then as it is today and I was as confused and uncertain as anyone else, but I was certain about one thing, if Gordon was gay, there could be absolutely nothing wrong with it.

One evening, as he was eating a hamburger alone at the Campus Grill, he noticed a darkly handsome man in his mid-thirties staring at him. His name was Anton and he taught at Vanderbilt University. He was the sort of professor that young girl students twitter about, always freshening up their lipstick for before entering his classroom. He began to chat with Gordon from his stool at the counter, and in his deep French accent, apologized for staring. He went on to explain that it was because Gordon looked exactly like the illustrations of the hero called Prince Eric in a children's book that had been one of his few childhood treasures growing up an orphan in France. He invited Gordon home for coffee and offered to show him the book. Within the week Gordon moved in with him. Initially I felt left out and jealous. But gradually, in spite of my hurt and jealousy, I grew to see that Anton was a special man and we became friends. He was totally enamored of Gordon and called him his Little Prince Eric or "mon petit Apollon." I had to admit it was somehow perfect. Gordon had a dark and dashing Frenchman—just like the Great Sebastian in The Greatest Show *on Earth.* At the end of Anton's teaching contract at Vanderbilt, he decided to return to Tulane and his home in New Orleans. Gordon chose not to go with him; he told me that although he'd miss him, and that he was a wonderful man, and though he did love him, he hadn't actually been *in* love with him, and wondered if there were something wrong with him because he hadn't.

This began Gordon's conscious exploration to find that answer. After Anton there was, almost humorously, a series of Toms in Gordon's life. Tom number one—whom Gordon met at a party and who instantly dubbed Gordon the "love of his life"—was tall, blond, very handsome, and from Huntsville, Alabama. Then there was Tom number two from Knoxville, who was tall, blond, even more handsome, and a fraternity brother of number one Tom. Tom number three was tall, *dark*, and handsome and had always been heterosexual until Gordon crossed his path. It seemed that Gordon had plenty of admirers but none of them gave him the answer he searched for. Further complicating it all, Gordon was frustrated by the deep feelings he said he still had for me.

And he longed to go to New York to see if he could become a professional actor but his father had told him that was out of the question, until an influential doctor in Shelbyville, who knew Gordon's entire history, had spoken frankly with Mr. Anderson, confronting him with the accusation that Mr. Anderson had done little for Gordon except to hold him back and punish him for who he was. He accused Mr. Anderson of being threatened by the fact that Gordon was a gifted child when, in fact, he should have embraced it; he should have taken Gordon's hand and grown. It was a remarkable gesture and one that changed Mr. Anderson's decision. Gordon was allowed to enroll in New York's American Academy of Dramatic Arts. This time I didn't go with him.

A month later, when I was putting him on that Greyhound bus for New York, it didn't seem possible that we were going to part, but I understood and I was happy for Gordon. Earlier, Gordon's mother had given him a shoe box filled with fried chicken and pimento cheese sandwiches and tearfully told him goodbye. I alone stayed until the bus pulled out.

"It looks like it's going to rain," he said.

"I know—I hope it does," I replied, beginning to crumble.

He smiled at me and held me, studying me at arm's length, "You and your black patent leather raincoat." He laughed, although his eyes were filling with tears.

"I know it was too expensive but I had to have it. And," I added, justifying my splurge, "it's really an all-purpose coat, after all." I had seen it in *Mad-*

emoiselle and had ordered it all the way from New York almost a year earlier and then had come the new fashionable miniskirts, so I had had to take up the excess length and shorten the hemline by folding it up inside and holding it with electrical tape on the lining.

Gordon shook his head, then reached down and gently touched the electrical tape as if it were made of cobwebs. "I love this," he said, eyeing my handiwork—his lips quivering. Then, I began to sob and he hugged me tightly. By then we were both crying; we kissed and held each other until the bus's door was ready to close. I remember looking at him and thinking *he's only a baby* and New York's so *huge*. I said a silent little prayer for him as he mounted the steps. Then he turned in the doorway and said, "I love you, Shana," and as the doors began to close between us, he murmered wistfully, "You know I never could bring myself to tell Mama, but I never much liked pimento cheese."

And with that the door closed, the bus pulled out, and he was gone.

Gordon's stay in New York proved to be a big success. No student at the Academy of Dramatic Arts was allowed to perform on the professional stage, but special dispensation was made for Gordon, who had convinced the entire school that he was a once-famous child star from Hollywood. I smiled when I heard that; it was so perfectly Gordon. He had won one of the leading roles in an avant-garde off-Broadway play by Venable Herndon, who later wrote the screenplay for Arthur Penn's *Alice's Restaurant*. The play, *Until the Monkey Comes*, was a biting social indictment concerning a group of young, rich, and vain people. Gordon's performance received raves from the New York critics. (He had had to change his last name because there was another Gordon Anderson in Actors' Equity.) Jerry Tallmer of the *New York Post* wrote, ". . . exquisitely and poignantly turned out by actor Gordon Addison, and in fact perhaps the most sympathetic character in the play." Another said, "Gordon Addison is brilliant as a narcissus who manages to keep his feet dry, and observing him performing this feat is on a level with observing the best performance of the season." And, in that year's look-back at the season, *Variety* picked Gordon's performance as one of the "most outstanding performances of the year," alongside the likes of Dustin Hoffman, Faye Dunaway, Gene Hackman, Shirley Knight, and Frank Langella. It was amazing. He had gone to New York, been cast in a play, become a member of Actors' Equity, received wonderful reviews, and was soon represented by one of show business's most powerful agencies, GAC—and all so quickly.

While in New York he also met someone special and moved in with him. Gordon told me that his name was Brad and that he was a talented artist. I was happy for him, but sadly it seemed that life was taking us further and further apart in so many ways. I was adjusting and I was dating, but it still seemed strange and impossible not to be with Gordon.

But when he came home that next Christmas of 1967, and stayed for six weeks, it seemed as if he had never been gone at all. He brought me a little porcelain figure of the Lady Mouse from Beatrix Potter's "Tailor of Gloucester," which I adored. I had gotten the lead as Helen of Troy in Jean Giraudoux's *Tiger at the Gates* for Theater Nashville, and Gordon designed my look (I warned him that this time he'd have to finish my entire face) and my wonderfully elaborate hairstyle. His makeup gave me a perfect Hellenic nose and brow. Then by adding fake hair to mine, he created a coronet of braids that gave the impression of a small crown with a long switch that hung well past my waistline pouring from its center like a golden waterfall.

"I'll never be able to duplicate this hairdo when you go back to New York, Gordon," I complained. "Can't you just make it simpler?"

"No!" he insisted. "This is the *right* way; you can do it if you try."

And, as usual, he was right. Even the newspapers agreed: "Sondra Locke's entrancing golden hairdo entwined with strands of pearls brought forth many complimentary remarks during intermission of *Tiger at the Gates* in which she played Helen of Troy." While home, he perfected my performance as well. Though I complained vehemently of his uncompromising taskmaster's approach with me, I was very proud when my reviews proved him right: "Sondra Locke's Helen is coolly impudent, as prettily sparkling as blown glass, equally indifferent to flattery or passion, a tantalizing, slender-throated witch with a fall of golden hair and long demure eyelashes. Miss Locke's professionalism points up the shortcomings of most of her fellow performers by its very excellence."

Gordon's uncompromising nature had won out yet again. Yet we live in an imperfect world, I thought, and to get along one *has* to compromise or be painfully overwhelmed. That was one of the dynamics between us: I was always *too willing* to compromise and Gordon would *never* compromise. So far he had never been able to "find the happy medium," the ambition he'd selected to go under his senior class picture in our yearbook.

After the holidays he returned to New York, but somehow in his heart he never returned. He had said to me, "I don't know what I'm going to do when I go back. In some ways I don't even want to go back. I became an actor and was judged a good one. There must be something more for me to do." I was concerned, but, also, I had to laugh; again it was like making up only one side of my face. He had been to New York; now he was ready to do something else. Still, I had thought that being a professional actor was what he had always wanted and things seemed to be going so well for him, but he explained it this way: "That's the point. I am, always have been, and always will be . . . an actor. If Margaret Mitchell had left *Gone With the Wind* moldering in her drawer instead of showing it to the man who eventually published it, she *still* would have been a writer. Artists who paint brilliant works for their own pleasure or as gifts to family and friends *are still* artists. They don't need gallery showings." I understood, and was reminded once again of Gordon's unique insight and view of life.

My Nashville life was on automatic pilot. I was selected for a big commercial for Southerland mattresses. "You might go to the Bahamas/wearing a gown or your pajama/On a Southerland dreamliner you just might/sail away to dreamland every night" went the commercial. It was a full-scale production, shot in color. I was balanced atop the mattress as if I were surfing while it sailed across an ocean, islands with palm trees blowing in the wind behind me. And, of course, there were the "beauty shots" of me at the end blissfully dreaming on my mattress. Images from this TV commercial were used for print advertising as well. And shortly thereafter, I began to do quite a bit of modeling for Rich-Schwartz, one of Nashville's premiere department stores.

I continued to date and off and on was involved with a few different interesting men: an advertising executive, a sculptor, a television announcer, one of the actors I had been in plays with. I had not fallen in love, but I was enjoying my freedom and my independence and that had been enough to keep me happy. Still, a part of me was missing without Gordon. When he called me in March, I sensed that something was up. He begged me to come to New York. He said he had not been happy since he had left me. If he sent me the money, couldn't I come for a long four-day weekend? I was very excited, not only to get to see Gordon, but to see New York. I'd never been outside Tennessee. He told me that his lover, Brad, would pick me up at the airport because he had to work until 2:00 P.M. at his "fill-in" job at the Waldorf-Astoria. When I asked him how Brad was, there was a pause and then he answered, perhaps a little too brightly, "Oh, he's just fine." Uh-oh, I thought, bye-bye Brad.

When I landed in New York, Brad was there to greet me and I could see that Gordon hadn't exaggerated. He was good-looking, rugged, and muscular, more like a construction worker than the artist I'd heard he was. He was polite and affable but eyed me suspiciously. As we waited for my suitcases, I asked how Gordon was. "This morning he seemed fine. At this very

moment I can't say how he is, but, whatever he *is*, I can tell you *it's* on
wheels." Brad didn't stand on ceremony. On the ride in from the airport
he made the rather startling pronouncement, "Gordon's mine. We're married." What could I possibly say? Gordon came home to their walk-up on
Madison Avenue (close to Altman's) around 3:00 P.M.. We hugged and
exchanged greetings, then he turned and leveled his gaze on Brad. Smiling
sweetly, he began, "Tell me, Sondra, I'll bet the first thing Brad said to you
after you met him was 'Gordon belongs to me,' or maybe, 'we're married'—
right?" I was speechless. I tried to make light of it and, stumbling, answered,
"Well . . . not the first." Brad's face flushed a deep red and he left the room.
Instantly I felt sorry for him. Gordon could definitely be a handful.

Even with the ongoing tension over Brad, I had a wonderful time. We
saw Ethel Merman in *Annie Get Your Gun* and Shirley Knight, who was
brilliant in *We Have Always Lived in the Castle*. For the most part Brad
stayed out of the way, but I knew that something was brewing and finally
I had to know. "What's going on? Is everything okay?" I asked. Gordon only
sighed, as if the weight of the world were bearing down on him, and left
the room. Soon he returned with a letter from which he proceeded to read
to me. In it Brad extolled Gordon's "great inner and outer beauty, his
goodness, his purity, and his innocence," telling his mother that he now
finally had found what she had had throughout her life, "the great love,
one that will forever keep me monogamous."

"Now tell me, Gordon, *who* was *that* he was just describing?" Gordon
shot me a pious look, but I continued. "Boy, that's some accolade."

"Yes, isn't it? And all so true," he mused, smiling mischievously.

"Okay, what's the story?" I asked, knowing that with Gordon there would
always be a good story to go along with it. "This is to his mother. How do
you happen to have it?"

"Well, he writes her nearly every two weeks," Gordon explained. "I can
always hear him typing a letter to her for fifteen minutes or so, but this
time he was typing for three hours. He would type, then wad up the paper
and begin all over again. I couldn't imagine what he was typing that required such perfection. The next morning when I went to the wastebasket
to find out, there was nothing there. He had 'the nerve' to have carefully
emptied it!"

I laughed when Gordon punctuated his story with a comical little moue
of self-righteous indignation. "It was as if he didn't trust me! But he did
leave the letter for me to mail. So I steamed it open, and when I saw the
truth and the beauty—the brilliance with which he'd captured *moi*—I knew

that God intended that I should make a copy." I sat there laughing as he told me how he then carefully resealed the letter and sent the original on to Brad's mother.

Suddenly he slapped the page with his other hand. "This is how he supposedly feels about me—right? Now, I'll tell you the nitty-gritty. One evening, about a week after I'd returned to New York, the phone rang. It was a very convivial-sounding woman who asked for 'Gordon,' and then launched into this detailed, complex story about how she'd been meaning to call me, she'd so enjoyed talking to me at some bar or another, and she'd just love to get together again. I told her she had the wrong Gordon, that I remembered nothing about this, and that I didn't go to bars. When she persisted, I cut her off and said goodbye. Then she called back and I was more emphatic. I told her she'd made a mistake and hung up.

"Then, about ten minutes later, the phone rings again. This time, it's a very attractive male voice on the phone, who finally gets around to explaining that he'd had the woman, a close friend of his, call me because he was shy, but what he really wanted was to meet me, because ever since he had seen my photograph he was 'smitten.' I asked where he'd seen it, figuring he'd seen it in a magazine from one of the modeling jobs I'd taken. But he said no, that he had seen the photo in *my very own apartment.*"

"Wait, wait, wait, I'm confused," I said.

"Well, it seems while I was home for Christmas and Brad was writing me every other day pledging his undying love and faithfulness, he had invited at least this one man home to play around with. And while he was there, Brad had shown him the photographs of me. And so now, the man was calling to meet *me.* He said he was a photographer, and he made it clear he didn't just want to *take my picture.*"

"So, did you meet him?" I asked.

Gordon looked at me as if shocked. "Sondra. Of course, I didn't. I told him I wasn't interested and hung up."

"Well," I hesitated, "what did you say to Brad?"

His eyes narrowed and he smiled. "Nothing . . . yet." Poor Brad, I thought, with a shudder. I was glad I wouldn't be around for it.

As soon as I went back to Nashville, Gordon moved into the guest room and locked the door every night. Two weeks later, Brad came home and Gordon was gone.

"Don't worry about me, Shana," he comforted long-distance." But I did worry, until he called the next day to tell me he had been taken in by a friend he'd met at the Academy of Dramatic Arts, and was living in a *penthouse!*

• • •

Despite his having landed in luxury, reports from Gordon confirmed that he was continuing to withdraw from his life in New York. He had been "called back" for the third time on a play he thought "stunk." And so, instead of going to his callback, he went to the Guggenheim Museum. When he told his agent he didn't see why he should be expected to go to audition for parts in plays he wasn't interested in, his agent became completely exasperated, telling him that was no way to build a career. Shortly thereafter, Gordon sat down and wrote me one of his long letters, telling me that he wasn't happy without me. He said he was fed up with the people he'd been meeting and that sexually he wasn't certain about anything any longer. He said he loved me, that he knew somehow we were meant to be together. Out of the blue he proposed we should get married and go to California together. In mid-May, he returned to Tennessee.

I was thrilled he was coming home. I agreed to his proposal, and however conventional or unconventional our marriage might turn out to be honestly did not concern me that much. I was very young, but I had come to feel that, for me, sex was the least important element in a relationship and the one thing that time had proven to me was that my love for Gordon came from such a deeply connected place that it transcended everything else. In spite of our separation, there remained an indefinable feeling akin to destiny between us. Gordon and I were like one person; we would go to California and find our dream together, and somehow all the rest would work itself out.

Chapter 4 ~

Once we made the decision to "run away" to California, we weren't exactly sure how we were going to follow through on it. While we allowed it to stew, Gordon went back and forth between my apartment in Nashville and his parents' house in Shelbyville. Mr. Anderson had sold both shoe stores, gone into the school supply business, and was on the road most of the time, which delighted Gordon. He could live there in peace. Some weekends I'd drive to Shelbyville, and we'd stay together with his mother and Ma Belle. We'd sit on Ma Belle's bed while she had her evening sherry, creamed her face, and told us stories about her girlhood. And Mrs. Anderson listened to Gordon and me take turns reading passages from Tolkien's book *The Hobbit*, which I had just discovered. We both loved all Tolkien's books and gradually began calling each other by the nickname Hobbit. I even called Mrs. Anderson "Mama Took" after one of my favorite characters in the series.

Life drifted pleasantly while we considered and waited. But the uncertainty of our new plan began to bear down on Gordon. Because we'd decided to marry, he seemed suddenly to feel that he needed to become some stereotype of a "husband," and he didn't know how to cast himself in that role. I was hardly conventional myself and I certainly did not expect that of him. Still, he expected it of himself and it created a depression he couldn't seem to shake. It got worse, until it peaked around 2:00 one morning when I awoke to discover that he wasn't in bed. I went into the living room and found him sitting on the floor between the chair and the wall. I could tell he had been crying.

"What's the matter, Hobbit," I said, sitting down next to him on the floor.

"It's me. It's just me. You're so wonderful and I love you so much and you deserve someone who can take care of you, not some funny thing like me."

Tears welled up in my eyes as I hugged him and said, "You've taken better care of me than anyone in my whole life."

As he continued to talk, I was less conscious of what he was saying than I was of an unexplainable feeling of urgency or pressure filling the room — or filling me. It was somehow pleasantly disorienting, impossible to convey. I would never forget the quiet intense strangeness of the way Gordon then said, "I was in here behind this chair praying that God would help me be able to make everything work out. If I could have anything, I'd wish that it would be you who'd be the success. I wish you'd be famous!" I comforted him and soon everything seemed to return to normal, then he turned to me and briskly stated, "Oh by the way, Barbara and Turner are coming for dinner day after tomorrow." "Oh and Rick and I are playing racquetball after the office tomorrow. Did my new suit from Brooks Brothers arrive yet?" I finally caught on to his joke and began laughing.

"Come on, Hobbit," I said. "I'll go to the store."

"Oh, Shana," he sighed forlornly. "Do you think anybody makes wing tip wooden shoes?"

"Everything's gonna be fine. Let's go to the store. I'll make us a banquet."

"Now? At three A.M.? It's starting to thunder and lightning."

"When did that ever matter to you? Come on. You ride along with me," I said. "We can run through the rain just the way we used to, remember?"

He rode along in "Leaner" but wouldn't come inside the store. "I'll have steak and French fries, just like Mama used to make on Saturday nights, and a salad with radishes, and French dressing, the orange kind," he added just as I closed the car door and made a dash through the pouring rain.

The thunder and lightning raged as I whipped up the dinner that, somehow, came out just before the storm blew out all the electrical power in the area. I got some candles and set the table. "Let's eat in here, Shana. It's better," Gordon said, referring to the low coffee table in the living room. And we sat there on the floor and ate, and watched the rain pound against the big tall A-frame glass window of my living room. There was something magical and haunting about that early morning, and though the crisis passed, my sense that something different was going on inside Gordon did not. Then a series of unexpected things occurred.

David Howland, an acquaintance of mine, asked if I would act in a little low-budget thriller he planned to make. Howland worked for a local company that produced half-hour religious/educational dramas for schools, churches, etc. I had played the lead in one that he directed and found it an exciting experience, so I convinced Gordon that he and I should star in this personal project of Howland's. Since Howland imagined that this film of his would launch him into the "big time," and since *Nashville* magazine had just done an article on Gordon and his New York success, Howland was ecstatic at the idea of getting him for his movie. I thought it would improve Gordon's spirits, but from the outset it proved to be a bad idea, which only got worse as the low-budget film disintegrated into a home movie. Parts of the story just didn't make sense and Howland's ideas were embarrassing. I was managing to cope, but for Gordon the pathetic nature of the situation became intolerable.

"His poor wife is going to have a miscarriage trying to push that big camera around on that homemade dolly. For God's sake, you've got to get us out of this, Sondra," he said early one Saturday morning as we waited for Howland to knock on my apartment door and transport us to another day of horror.

"How? I don't know what to say."

About that time the knocking began. On this morning it was to the rhythm of "shave—and a haircut—two bits" followed immediately by Howland's voice singing, "You outta be in movies." I looked at Gordon and he pulled the covers over his head.

"Gordon, don't do this. It'll all be over soon," I reasoned.

"I can't take another day. It'll turn into a disaster soon; I'll say something that will hurt his feelings and I don't want to! Look at it this way: You're saving him from wasting his money; he's never going to be able to do a thing with this mess."

I was so furious at Gordon and the predicament that I picked up the little ceramic Beatrix Potter Lady Mouse he'd brought me from New York and dramatically drew it back, threatening to throw it at him.

"Go ahead, murder poor Lady Mouse!" he taunted. "I always knew this day would come."

This only made me laugh. I knew he was right. I quietly walked to the front door, and told Mr. Howland that we just couldn't continue. We quit.

Then, miraculously, a group of Nashville businessmen I had met through working at WSM approached me with the proposal that they wanted to finance a small film that would feature Gordon and me if we could come up with a script. This appealed to Gordon and he asked Venable Herndon, the playwright whose play he'd been in in New York, to do a treatment for us. We loved his treatment, but the local businessmen weren't ready for Venable's avant-garde Cocteau sensibilities. They suggested Gordon write the script instead and paid him five hundred dollars. *Gilly, Gilly, Ride a White Horse* was a charming reverse Pygmalion story in which an ambitious girl discovers and makes over a plain, shy, young man she stumbles across into a teen singing sensation à la Pat Boone, fooling everyone in the process. In the script his transformation and subsequent success become their ticket to escape from the South and head for the bright lights of Hollywood. Gordon's wishful thinking, I decided.

Finally, he completed it, and I drove down to Shelbyville to see him and to pick it up. It was a Sunday afternoon and Mrs. Anderson made us one of her wonderful Southern lunches with homemade biscuits and gravy. Afterward I helped her wash the dishes, and then Gordon and I wandered out into the big backyard and settled in the grass with Muffin, the beautiful blond cocker spaniel puppy that we had bought for his mother. When her dog had died, Mr. Anderson had decreed that she could have no more animals. It had made us both so furious, because she deeply loved animals, that we ignored him and got it for her anyway.

I sat there in the grass, petting Muffin, and watched Gordon performing on his trapeze that still hung on the big shade tree there in the backyard. He was still wonderful on it. Later, we found Mrs. Anderson in her bedroom reading her Sunday paper, *The Nashville Tennessean*, with Skeet, her parakeet, perched on her shoulder. Gordon, Muffin, and I were sprawled across the bed when something caught her eye.

"Listen to this. Movie auditions were held in Nashville," she said, scanning down the article. "Brownstone Productions out of New York is conducting a nationwide talent search for an unknown ingenue to play Mick Kelly, a starring role in *The Heart Is a Lonely Hunter*, Carson McCullers's coming-of-age novel. The film will be directed by Joseph Strick, who last directed the film version of James Joyce's *Ulysses*."

Gordon grabbed the paper from her and quickly began scanning the article. "Why didn't you try out for that, Sondra?" Mrs. Anderson asked.

"I didn't know anything about it. What else does it say?" I asked.

"WHO COULD CHOOSE? is the caption under the picture," Gordon began reading. "Four girls have been chosen to represent Tennessee at auditions in Birmingham this Friday, August fourth." He glanced at their photographs. "They look wrong to me. They don't have the right look for McCullers. They're too cutesy. Think about Julie Harris in *Member of the Wedding*," he said as he showed me the newspaper photo. "These girls look like cheerleaders—they'd make much better Gidgets."

"They're gonna get screen tests, it says!" I cried. "Nobody told me about it. I didn't even get to audition."

I wondered why no one in the theater community in Nashville had told me about this. I had starred in many of the productions at the Circle Theater and Theater Nashville. Had they intentionally tried to exclude me? Obviously so, since it's pretty hard to keep big news like that off the gossip loop in a small theater community.

"So no one told you about it, huh?" Gordon said. "Well, it's just petty jealousy. I hate that kind of crap. We'll just see about that, won't we? And screen tests are very expensive. It doesn't mean a thing that these four girls were picked by a tookie puny Nashville theater board. These girls haven't even seen this talent scout the paper is talking about."

I could tell that it had all made him angry. Suddenly he was up; he had a new purpose. "Screw Nashville. We'll just get into the auditions in Birmingham. Somehow, we're gonna have to get a copy of that book," he said. "Let me think, it won't do any good to go to the library here; it's closed on Sunday. We're driving to Nashville," Gordon said with an instant determination that surprised even me. "If the public library there isn't open, the college ones will be." He had turned into a whirlwind. "Just let me get some things," he said, running up the stairs to his room.

"My stars and garters, what is he up to now?" Mrs. Anderson looked at me and asked. I just shrugged. "Well, I hate to see you all go so soon, it seems like you just got here; but, if he's got his head set on it, I guess there'll be no stoppin' him." She sighed. "Honey, why don't you let me make you some pimento cheese sandwiches and you can take some of that cold fried chicken from lunch and—"

Gordon had reappeared. "Don't have time, Mama," he said, cutting her off.

"Well, at least take some biscuits with you. You're gonna get hungry later," she said.

We just gave her a kiss on the cheek and ran outside to my little green TR-3. After a breakneck ride to Nashville, we found a copy of the McCullers novel in the Vanderbilt University library. Since we were not students there and couldn't check it out, Gordon, undaunted, simply stuffed it down his pants, and pulling his shirttail over it, we made a casual exit. Then we tore up the street to Chambers restaurant, where Gordon began poring over it. I ordered a ham sandwich and potato salad, but Gordon wasn't interested in food.

"How can you eat at a time like this?"

"Well, we did come to a restaurant, didn't we?" I replied.

He ignored me and continued leafing through the book, rapidly finding all the descriptions of Mick Kelly. "She is," he read, " 'a gangling, tow-headed youngster . . . that at first glance was like a very young boy.' Just like I thought. She's a lot like Frankie in *Member of the Wedding*—a tomboy, sensitive, and yearning."

Gordon looked up at me from the book. I was wearing false eyelashes and a miniskirt and my hair was longish and straight, like Julie Christie's in *Darling*. "Well," he said, looking at me apprehensively. "This is gonna take some work."

After dragging me all over town to collect an assortment of odd supplies that he wouldn't explain, we finally arrived at my apartment. The next thing I knew, he was dunking my head in the kitchen sink, pouring an ash rinse over my golden blond hair, and while it was still wet, he pulled it back so tightly into a single braid that it hurt.

"Ouch! That's too tight; you're pulling the roots out!" I screamed.

"You have to look fourteen. You have a small and delicate head, like a child's, and this will show it off much better. Plus, the smaller your face, the larger your eyes will look."

That was just the beginning of my torture. Next, he mixed up bleach and covered my eyebrows with it. "That'll make your eyes look even bigger," he said. "Pale blond eyebrows, like children's, is what we want. Now, I think you need a 'skinned' knee," he said. "Where's the food coloring?" He dabbed a dampened Kleenex against the bottle of red, then rubbed it gently onto my kneecap. When he added the Band-Aid, it looked perfect. My breasts, not very big to begin with, he bound with Ace bandages. Using six different shades of indelible brown pens, he created freckles on my face. Then using red food coloring and acrylic matte medium, which when dry and torn looked exactly like peeling skin, he created a perfect peeling sunburned nose. Tearing through my closet, tossing things right and left, he decided I should wear a little white cotton print dress which he thrust over my head. Finally, he stepped back to study his handiwork.

"I *am* a genius. It's true; it's true," he sang. "You look perfect," he said, taking me by the shoulders and walking me to the mirror.

I was astounded. Staring back at me was an entirely different person.

"Call that photographer you know," he said. "We need photographs."

I DIDN'T THINK my small car was up for the trip to Birmingham, so I had borrowed an obliging old boyfriend's station wagon. We had picked it up and were finally on our way when the sound of a siren and flashing lights made my heart sink. A cop. It seemed I hadn't exactly made a complete stop at that last stop sign.

I quietly accepted my punishment, but when the officer walked away, I went into a fit. "I'm not going," I pouted. "This is just an omen of how things are gonna go on this pointless trip. Bandages on my breasts! Ink on my face! The whole thing is just a waste of time anyway. It's never going to work out."

Gordon just stared at me, then coolly picked up the envelope with the Mick Kelly photos. Pulling them out, he said, "Oh well, since we're not going, I guess we won't be needing these, will we?" With a calculated expression, he held one up and slowly began to tear it.

"Stop! Don't," I yelled before he could tear past the half-inch white margin.

He smiled. "All right . . . then enough theatrics. Let's go. We'll stop in Shelbyville on the way."

What could be taking him so long, I wondered as I waited in Mrs. Anderson's living room for Gordon to reappear. "Gordon, what are you doing? Don't you think we'd better go now?" I called up the stairs, eager for him to come down so we could leave.

He didn't answer, so I climbed the stairs, opened the door, and saw him there, scrunched down between his twin beds.

"What are you doing?" I asked.

"Oh, nothing really. I'm ready. I'll go write Mama a note."

When he left the room, I walked over to see what he had been doing there. I bent down and saw some tiny scribbling on the baseboard. Leaning closer to it, I made out the small letters—P.D.G. I knew immediately that they stood for Please Dear God, a special prayer and a code that Gordon had invented as a child. At important times he would often write P.D.G. or other secret codes in hidden places.

Finally, we were in the car. I had just started the engine when Gordon suddenly said, "Wait." He opened the passenger door, leaned out, and picked up a pebble from the driveway.

"Look, at this; it's just a pebble. It's ordinary right now, but it's going on a trip and things could happen that would make it different forever," he said as he dropped it in my purse. I understood that this little pebble would be our talisman.

Hours later we arrived at the outskirts of Birmingham, where I registered at an inexpensive motel just off the interstate while Gordon hid in the parking lot. I got the key, went to the room, and waited for him to sneak in.

The next morning Gordon went into action and brought Mick Kelly to life again. Then we jumped in the car and headed for the Town and Gown Theater.

"How do we know when the auditions are starting, Gordon?" I asked.

I followed him as he walked toward the pay phone booth next to a Piggly Wiggly market. "And how are we gonna get into them?" I went on. "What if they won't let us in? After all, no one is expecting us. My name's not on any list." I jabbered nervously while he dialed.

"Oh god, you're driving me nuts. Sh-h-h," he whispered. And then— "Hello, Town and Gown Theater?" I heard him ask in a charming Southern lady's voice. "Way-ull, Ah tell ya Ah I'm jus' so mad at my ah daughtah! She has gone and lost that little bitty piece of paper she was given with the time of the auditions for tuh-day. Whut ay-am Ah evah gonna do with her?" Someone had obviously given him the information because then Gordon merrily trilled, "Why thank you so much, darlin'. We'll be right they-ah." He hung up. "Three o'clock at the Town and Gown Theater."

As we walked back to the car, he gave me my final instructions. "Now remember, you're only seventeen years old."

"I know, I know."

"And don't forget, if they ask, give them my address and phone number in Shelbyville. They're gonna be looking for the real Mick Kelly and they'd love to find her in a tiny Southern town like Shelbyville not Nashville. And don't forget the Southern accent."

It had been extremely difficult, but Gordon and I had both taught ourselves to drop our natural Southern accents. Now, for my first professional audition, I needed to find it again.

We walked into the theater. It looked huge to me. Sprinkled throughout the audience were at least three hundred Mick Kelly wanna-bes from all over the South. Way down front, the proscenium stage was empty except for a table and a couple of chairs. Gordon noticed a stack of papers on the table near the entrance. A girl with carrot-colored hair was standing there mouthing lines from the pages, and Gordon reached around her, grabbing a set for us. I looked over his shoulder as he scanned the pages. They were scenes for the movie. Oh God, I was suddenly so nervous.

"Come on, let's go outside," he said.

I followed him back to the station wagon. "You have to study these lines. You *have* to be the best," he said as we closed the car door.

Over and over he made me repeat the lines. "Slower there . . . throw that phrase away . . . make sure you have a transition in your voice here." And on and on. The final scene took place at the grave site of the character of Mr. Singer. As Mick lays flowers on his grave, she says, "I loved you, Mr. Singer. I loved you."

"Now, when you say the last 'I loved you,' I want you to put a little break in your voice like you're choking back tears; you're just about to cry."

I tried it.

"No, no, the last one has to be softer." He directed me like a conductor. Finally, after several tries, I had it.

Inside the theater Gordon was still instructing me as we sat down next to a girl who had obviously just cut her hair to look like Julie Harris in *Member of the Wedding*. Her mother introduced herself as a journalist from *The Birmingham News*. She seemed hopeful that her daughter would be chosen by the casting director and was there, ready to write all about it.

The girl looked me over carefully. "Oh, your nose is all burned. It's peeling!" she said, reaching toward me. Quickly my hand went up in a defensive gesture. I could tell she was about to pull the "peeling skin" off, but Gordon stopped her short, "Don't touch that nose!" The girl pulled back, as if she had been struck. "I mean, it's real sore . . . it's hurtin' her somethin' bad."

I whispered, "You didn't have to snap at her, Gordon. She was probably just trying to help."

"Hah! Grow up. How many strangers in your life have been eager to help you peel your sunburn. I know sabotage when I see it," he snorted.

All three hundred of us sat there, waiting for the important casting director from Hollywood or New York to arrive—each of us with our dreams, each of us wanting that part, each of us with heart pounding. Suddenly I spied them, the girls in the WHO COULD CHOOSE? picture in *The Nashville Tennessean*. And, almost as if they could feel my eyes on them, they turned. One of them, wearing what was her idea of a tomboy's getup—a man's sweatshirt that was all frayed and torn, blue jeans tucked into men's big black rubber fishing boots, and a chain with what appeared to be a shark's tooth around her neck—stood up, glared at me, and then stomped up the aisle toward the lobby. She had recognized me and I just knew she was going to turn me in.

Soon she was back with a man in tow. He was wearing a bow tie and a proprietary air. The girls all began animatedly whispering to him, at which point, his head swiveled toward me; he nodded, then began to walk toward us. Uh-oh, here it comes, I thought. We're going to get kicked out. I wasn't one of the "chosen."

"Hello, I'm James Hatcher, director of the Town and Gown. And what group might y'all be with?"

"We've come from Shelbyville," Gordon responded in a thick good ol' boy Southern accent. "I've brought my cousin here. I think she'd be perfect for the part."

Where did that accent come from? Cousin? What was he doing? I was certain we were going to get kicked out. Strangely, though, there was an odd familiar feeling about it all. Suddenly I knew what it was. That's it — we're in an episode of *I Love Lucy*. Gordon is Lucy and I'm Ethel and we're both disguised and trying to get into show biz. I almost looked around for Fred and Ricky.

Before Mr. Hatcher could respond to Gordon, he was upstaged by the entrance of a very tall lady in a big hurry. It had to be the casting director, because she acted as if she knew exactly what she was doing and headed straight for the empty stage. As soon as old Hatcher saw her, he dropped us like hot potatoes and scurried across the theater to greet her.

He followed her onto the stage, and they both soon began glancing in our direction. After a conference that seemed endless, Mr. Hatcher returned to us, "It's okay for you to stay and read for Miss Dougherty. Better study your pages, now," he said, shaking his finger at me.

Gordon and I waited and watched as Miss Dougherty called one girl after another to the stage. Finally it was my turn. As I stood up, he whispered, "Don't forget your sunburned nose. Pick at it like I showed you. Like you're a tomboy, but only do it once; and when you do it, you mustn't be looking at her. Don't worry, she'll see it . . . she'll be watching every move you make. Now don't forget."

I took a deep breath to steady my nerves. "I won't forget." I walked toward the stage, and as I climbed the stairs, my head was spinning. What kind of chance did I have to win a starring role in a Hollywood movie? Please Dear God. I sat down before her. She looked at me curiously, as if I were an interesting little bug, then asked my name, age, home town. "Shelbyville — seventeen years old."

"Okay, Sondra, would you like to begin? I'll read the other characters in the script."

And so I began. I don't know how long I was there, on the stage with her, because I felt as if I were inside some incredible vortex with no beginning and no end. Instead of only one scene like everyone else, she asked me to read all four. And though I seemed to be in a trance, I did remember to pick at my peeling nose, only once. When I finished, she said, "That's very nice," she said. And then — "Could you please wait in the theater?"

I walked carefully back to Gordon and sat down on the edge of my seat. While I recounted every word she'd said, he absorbed it all, at the same time studying the room, taking everything in like a radar dish. Then suddenly his neck stiffened and around the theater whispering began like buzzing bees.

"What is it?" I asked.

"Oh my God—that looks like—yes it is—she's quite a bit older, but it's Mary Badham," Gordon said, adding with emphasis, "a star sweeps in!"

And, sure enough, in she swept. "Scout" from *To Kill a Mockingbird* herself. Mary Badham still lived in Birmingham, where she had been discovered in a talent search for that film about six years earlier. She blew past us with her own entourage and headed straight for Miss Dougherty. My hopes were dashed like a rag doll in a tornado. "Well, I guess that's that. She'll probably get it," I said, turning to Gordon, who was following her every step, sizing her up. We watched as Miss Dougherty greeted Mary warmly and ushered her and her people offstage and out of sight. How could I possibly compete with someone who had been nominated for an Oscar? "Oh no," I muttered. "After all we've done."

But Gordon's brain was clicking. "She's had an agent for years. They would have submitted her long before any of this. I don't think she's going to get it," he said, playing out the entire scenario in his head. "Her brother is a producer in Hollywood at Universal Studios, I think—they are the ones who made *To Kill a Mockingbird*. Maybe this is just some sort of a courtesy thing."

That sounded good to me, but it didn't convince me, because Mary stayed on and on in some private place with Miss Dougherty. Finally they were back and Mary Badham left the theater. I was recalled to the stage and again read the now-familiar pages.

"Thank you, Sondra. That was wonderful," she said. Miss Dougherty sat silently looking at me for a moment, then said, "I'd like to have you meet the film's director."

Meet the director! I must have grinned from ear to ear.

"Now I can't promise you anything because it will ultimately be the director's decision, but I liked your reading very much and I think he should meet you. His name is Joseph Strick, and he's in New Orleans right now," she said.

The director was in New Orleans? Maybe that meant he was there for other auditions. Never mind, I couldn't think about it. I had made it to second base. "Yeah, I sure would like that. I'd like to meet the director," I drawled in my Mick Kelly voice.

"We'll be at the Roosevelt Hotel in the French Quarter," she said, scribbling down the address and phone number. "Do you think you could be there by ten o'clock tomorrow morning?"

How many miles was New Orleans from Birmingham? I hadn't a clue. Who cared? Say yes to everything—"Yeah, that's good"—Smile—"I'll be there"—Not too overanxious—"Thank you"—Now pick at your sunburned nose like Gordon told you, just once more, for good luck and walk away.

Gordon knew things had gone well the moment I began to hurry toward him with the slip of paper in my hand. Success! We were off to meet the man who had directed *Ulysses*. But not before Mr. Hatcher, who now all too eager to court me, suddenly became my guardian.

"I absolutely insist that you come into my office and call home. I feel responsible for your welfare now, and I need to know that your parents know where you're going."

"She'll appreciate that, sir. I'll get her on the phone right away," Gordon said, then shot me a look. I had no idea what he was going to do.

"Hi, Aunt Marge, it's Gordon," he said. "They seem real interested in Sondra for the movie! They want her to go to another audition in New Orleans. It's okay? Sure, we have the gas card. Thanks! Bye."

What a performance, I thought, because I knew there was no one on the other end of the line. Just then, Mr. Hatcher reached for the phone but Gordon was too quick for him; he was already hanging up. "Oh, I'm sorry, she was just on her way out."

Looking a little disappointed, Mr. Hatcher said, "Well anyway, you called and let them know, so I feel better."

As we turned to get out of there, we bumped into yet another obstacle — an elderly Southern matriarch in a blue dress with hair to match, a "dear old thing" as they say in the South. "Jimmy, I doooo believe," she tinkled to Mr. Hatcher, "that it might be wise to pick up a loooovley little frock for her. Somethin' real sweet. And I can call Westelle. I just know she could do something woooondorous with that poor little pigtail."

For an instant Gordon's eyes glazed over in horror. "Oh, what a good idea, ma'am," he said, smiling, in his most grateful good ol' boy accent. "I don't rightly know how to thank you for thinkin' of that, but we wouldn't want to impose. Jus' so happens mah daddy's sister lives only forty miles due south from here, and she's a beautician with three girls, so she'll be able to get us all fixed up." Then before anybody could say another word, we made a run for it.

Gordon carefully wrapped the piece of paper Miss Dougherty had given me with the New Orleans address around the pebble from his mother's driveway and off we drove . . . New Orleans bound! One quick look at the map told us that it was not just around the corner, but if we drove nonstop, we could just about make it on time. We zoomed through the night with Gordon behind the wheel, and me in the backseat trying to sleep so I could once again pass for fourteen. The last thing I remember as I drifted off was Gordon singing Rudolf Friml's "Only a Rose," one of the songs used in *The Greatest Show on Earth*.

We reached the outskirts of New Orleans at about 4:00 A.M. and began checking motels, hoping to find a room where we could get at least a couple hours of sleep. But every motel was booked because of some big sports event that weekend. Gordon then suddenly remembered that his cousin Missy lived in New Orleans, and, even though it was 4:00 in the morning, we were desperate enough to call her. Gordon dialed only to find out that Missy was, of all things, in Scotland. It was like a bad dream. I *had* to get some rest, I was supposed to look fourteen years old in five hours!

Gordon hung up the phone. "The house sitter's calling Scotland."

Finally the phone rang with the news that Missy had okayed it, and laughingly added that it all sounded "exactly like Cousin Gordie." At least we had a place to lie down for the next few hours.

We arrived right on time at the Roosevelt Hotel in the French Quarter and Miss Dougherty greeted us. Gordon waited in the lobby while I followed her up to Mr. Strick's suite. My heart was pounding. So much depended on the next hour.

I entered his suite with its tall windows, and Mr. Strick, a quiet man with a gentle manner, greeted me. He had olive skin, dark hair, and bright eyes behind his dark-framed glasses. "It's nice to meet you, Sondra," he said, smiling warmly at me. "Marion has said some very nice things about you. Thank you for coming all this way. Did you fly in this morning?"

"No, sir, my cousin and I drove all night to get here."

He and Miss Dougherty both looked stunned. "Oh, Sondra, I feel terrible," she said to me. "I just assumed you'd fly in; it never occurred to me that you'd be driving. I'm so glad you got here safely."

"Thank you, we're fine. I'm so excited to be here," I said, shuffling the audition pages from the Town and Gown. Then Mr. Strick handed me a thick, soft-bound manuscript with a pretty yellow cover that said *The Heart Is a Lonely Hunter* by Thomas C. Ryan in gold letters. I actually had my hands on the whole script for the movie.

"So, this is what a real movie script looks like," I said in character. "It sure is pretty."

They smiled and Mr. Strick gestured for me to sit on the sofa.

"Can I get you a Coca-Cola or anything?" he asked.

"Oh, no, sir," I said. "I'd be too nervous to even drink it."

He laughed gently and said, "We'll leave you alone to look it over before we begin."

"Okay," I said.

Soon they returned. Miss Dougherty sat down on the sofa next to me, and Mr. Strick pulled up a chair. "Would you like to read something for me now?"

"Yes, sir. Which scene would you like me to read?"

"Let's just start at the beginning."

I closed the script.

"Don't you need that?" Mr. Strick asked.

"No, I think I know it now."

They looked at each other in surprise.

"You must be very quick, Sondra. You must have a good memory."

"Yes, sir."

Miss Dougherty gave me my cues and I began playing the scenes. At the end of each one I would look up at Mr. Strick for instructions, and each time he would smile and say, "Go on, to the next one." I reached the very last line in the very last scene. "I loved you, Mr. Singer," and, remembering just how Gordon had told me to quiver my voice, I finished with . . . "I loved you."

Had he liked it? I glanced at him nervously.

"Very lovely, Sondra," he said, standing up. "I'm so glad Miss Dougherty suggested I see you."

That meant the audition was over. I didn't want it to be. I felt lost. My feet didn't want to carry me out of there, but I forced them to move me toward the door. Looking down, I realized I was still holding the yellow script. "Oh, I guess you'll want this back," I said, offering him the script.

He paused and smiled, then said, "Why don't you take it with you."

I hugged the script against me. Was it a good sign that he had given it to me, or was he just being nice? As I passed the big window on my way to the door, I glanced out. My eyes fell on a large white truck parked on the street, and on its side was painted in big red letters: GORDON'S GIN. It was definitely a good sign. I couldn't wait to tell Gordon.

It was a two-day trip back to Shelbyville and Gordon made me recite every last detail and gesture from the audition until I thought I would go mad. And all along the way, we kept our eyes open for another "sign." When we arrived home and parked the car on Depot Street in front of the Family Shoe Store, there it was! Up the street on the movie marquee: "Harper Lee's *To Kill a Mockingbird*."

We were speechless. "Look at that," Gordon said. "This movie was only released five years ago! It's too soon for it to be rereleased. This isn't Nashville; this isn't a revival theater. I can't believe it. What's this movie doing here in Shelbyville now, two days after we were just with Mary Badham." He stared at the marquee. "It's a powerful sign," he said.

"And you know what else is eerie?" I said, amazed. "That script you wrote, *Gilly, Gilly*? It was about being discovered and a 'make-over,' just like you've done to me. It's like what's happening to us, right now."

~

I WENT BACK to work at WSM in Nashville, and Gordon was in Shelbyville. We waited for any news from Miss Dougherty. None came until about a week later. The phone rang at Gordon's house. His mother knew exactly what to do if they called. "Sondra honey, it's for you; it's Miss Dougherty; she's calling from New York," she said excitedly, handing over the phone.

"I've been so nervous," the Mick Kelly voice began excitedly. "I was hopin' I'd hear from you. I read the whole script. It sure is a wonderful story," said *Gordon*, pretending to be me, pretending to be Mick Kelly.

"I'm glad you liked it," Miss Dougherty said. "Mr. Strick would like to work with you a little, and we want the writer to meet you. Can you come to New York?"

"Oh yes," Gordon exclaimed. When Miss Dougherty asked to speak with my mother, Gordon said, "Oh yeah, sure, she's right here. Mama, Miss Dougherty wants to speak to you."

Gordon's mother took the phone and said, "Well, of course, Miss Dougherty, it would be marvelous for Sondra to get to go to New York and meet the movie people." Mrs. Anderson was quite an actress herself. She wrote down the flight information, and then said, "Oh, Miss Dougherty, Sondra has something she wants to ask you."

"Miss Dougherty? Is it okay if I bring my cousin Gordon to New York with me?" Gordon asked her. "I wouldn't be as scared if he comes 'cause he's been there before."

"That would be fine, Sondra," she said to Gordon.

Instead of phoning, Gordon drove to Nashville and told me he had come because a new film was opening. I naturally assumed he would have called the minute he had any news, so I couldn't bear to ask, but after a while he said, "I wonder if we're ever gonna hear anything from New York about the movie?"

"I don't know; it's all I've thought about. I'm sick of thinking about it. What do you think? I hope you've been doing a lot of praying about it!"

"No. I don't think I'd call it praying. It's more like I've been jitterbugging with Him. He's so worn out from listening to me that He's never gonna want to hear the sound of my voice again." Then he asked me, "Would you rather be flown to New York and put through more auditions and maybe a screen test and then, after all that, still not get it, or would you rather never hear from them and have it be over now?"

I thought about it, then said, "I'd rather go—I'd rather go and at least try."

He picked up a magazine from the coffee table as if he were going to start reading it, then nonchalantly said, "Well, you're going! They called; they're flying you to New York! And I'm going with you."

I screamed, jumped into the air, and fell on the sofa. Gordon grabbed me, and we hopped up and down, up and down, dancing around the room. "We're going to New York—we're really going! I can't believe it—we're going to New York!"

~

"HELLO, MISS DOUGHERTY. I'm here. I'm in New York City; I jus' can't believe it. I'm calling from the big public library with the lions out front. It was the first thing I wanted to see, you know, in 'real life,' because I saw it in the movie You're a Big Boy Now. I loved that movie." Gordon and I were actually calling from an inexpensive restaurant off Times Square. But Gordon insisted I tell her we were at the library. That would be just like Mick Kelly to go to the very spot of an actual movie location she had only glimpsed on-screen. Miss Dougherty seemed to love that image of me—just as Gordon said she would. "Well, get checked in and come on over to the production office," she said. I had imagined I'd be staying at some place glamorous like the Plaza, but somehow it didn't matter when I learned Warner Bros. had booked me at the YWCA.

That afternoon at Brownstone Productions—which was producing Heart along with Warner Bros.—I began my two and a half weeks of unbelievable stress and tension, waiting to see if I were really going to be chosen for the leading role in this major motion picture. I became even more anxious when I learned that Miss Dougherty had auditioned over two thousand unknowns across the country. And there was still the possibility that the whole thing was just a way to garner publicity and stir up public interest for the film, and the role might go to some famous actress. After all, a similar nationwide talent search had been conducted for the coveted role of Maria in West Side Story; yet it had gone to Natalie Wood, an already famous star.

It was wonderful to see Mr. Strick again. I was drawn to him; from the moment I had met him in New Orleans, I had found him very special. He introduced me to the two producers: Marc Merson, who seemed easygoing and likable, and Thomas C. Ryan (who also wrote the screenplay), whom I found a little unsettling. There was an edginess and an intensity about him as he moved around the room, studying me like some exotic specimen in a zoology class. Of course, I was there to be studied, but his whole manner made me very uncomfortable.

They asked me to read scenes for them, Miss Dougherty taking the other parts. Afterward, they smiled and said, "Very nice." Miss Dougherty then asked me to wait in the outer office. I sat amidst a beehive of activity, excitedly taking it all in, until I was again summoned to read more scenes. Occasionally Mr. Strick would direct me: "Give me a harder edge, Sondra," or "Make it softer—give me a wistful, yearning quality." Each time I would do as he asked. "That was lovely, Sondra" was all he'd say. And again, I would be banished into the outer office.

Another unforgettable aspect to my whole New York experience was the saga of our "accommodations." I was tired of the Y, and of course Gordon couldn't stay there, so he made contact with Anita, his best friend from his American Academy days, and she found a place with a friend of hers where all three of us could stay. But when we reached the address, we were all shocked. It was in the meatpacking district, which was incredibly smelly and awful. In shock, I stared at Gordon as we climbed the long stairs but was pleasantly surprised when we suddenly found ourselves in a charming refurbished loft.

There we met Luna. It was apparent from the start that Luna didn't make a move without her tarot cards. She promptly informed us that she was a witch and that her cat, who was named Familiar, was, in fact, her "familiar."

Cautiously we settled in, but only for a few days, until Luna found out that I might be getting a role in a Warner Bros. film. "She said we have to get out immediately," Anita told us. "And I'm supposed to tell Sondra that she's 'put a hex on' you, and you may as well go back to the boondocks. You're not getting the part." Anita only shrugged, "What are ya gonna do? She wants to be a Movie Star too—just like everybody else."

So just like that, we were orphans of the storm, at least for several hours, until dear Anita once again found us shelter. This time it was with someone she knew only casually, a friend of a friend, a quiet girl named Dinette, an artist. We all agreed that this time Anita would say that we were just tourist friends from out of town. Hollywood could not be mentioned.

Dinette was on the droll side. Attempting to be friendly, Gordon said to her, "Anita tells us you're an artist. That's great, what are you painting now?"

"Trees" came back the flat reply.

"Oh, I love trees; what kind?"

"Pine."

"Vines?" Gordon had misheard.

"No, pine, They're all pines. That's all I paint. You wanna see?"

"Of course, I'd love to." We marched behind her into the master bedroom, where, all lined up, were numerous landscapes. They all looked precisely the same and each was waiting for a sky. We stared at them. "Well, how interesting." Gordon stammered, "You do the skies last, I see."

"I don't paint skies; someone else paints the skies. I only paint trees, pine trees."

The three of us exchanged glances. I was beginning to feel New York was altogether insane. "Oh, I get it," Gordon continued, "it's sort of an assembly line. You paint the pine trees. Someone else paints the babbling brook, and another person paints that little cottage."

"No, the girl who paints the brook paints the cottage."

"Well, I'll say." He was obviously at a loss. "It's very . . . I mean they're . . . How interesting," he finally managed. Then as we turned to leave the makeshift gallery, he clutched both Anita's and my arms and whispered sotto voce, "God help us."

Each day I lived nervously on the edge, wondering when the screen test would come. Eventually, they began to audition actors for the other roles and Mr. Strick wanted me to read opposite them.

Once during my reading sessions, they asked me to minimize my Southern accent. That was a snap, I thought. I took it down to maybe three fourths, but they didn't seem to hear the change. "Try again, dear," they asked. I gave them half, but they just stared at me. Suddenly, Tom Ryan declared, "She needs a vocal coach!" All heads turned. "How would you feel about that, dear?" Mr. Strick inquired. Mick answered, "Gosh, tha'd be great—a real voice teacher. I think it'd be excitin'." So the next day I was at the studio of Dorothy Dixon, one of New York's best vocal coaches.

Coming out of Mrs. Dixon's studio that morning was a pretty blond woman. She was wearing sunglasses, vibrant red lipstick, and a silk scarf tied discreetly over the back of her hair. As she passed by us, she tossed us a dazzling smile and said hello.

Gordon, who never missed a thing, immediately grabbed my arm. "Sondra, that was Betty Grable. She's on Broadway now starring in *Hello Dolly!*" I watched in wonder as she walked away unnoticed down the street.

"God, just think . . . the voice student immediately before me was Betty

Grable," I said. Gordon looked at me meaningfully. "Well, Shana, I guess this is it—this is what they call 'the big time.' " As Gordon settled down on the front stoop to wait, I climbed the stairs that led to Mrs. Dixon.

Mrs. Dixon listened to me read from the script, then began instructions. I, of course, was constantly trying to figure out exactly how much of the accent to drop at each read-through; I couldn't let anyone know my Mick Kelly accent wasn't real. Mr. Strick might send me home. Mrs. Dixon thought I was an amazingly quick study and sent me away with congratulations, but then she'd be told by the production office that I needed just a little more work. It all became incredibly frustrating, even for her. She thought I sounded perfect. Finally, swearing her to secrecy, I blurted out a complete confession about my accent. She laughed warmly and said, "Oh, I see what it is. This is for *Hollywood*. Accomplishing the task at hand must be difficult and lengthy, and, by all means, it must cost a great deal of money." As I left that afternoon she said, "Don't worry. I know just what to say when I speak with them tomorrow. And, Sondra dear, I want you to give them just the slightest *blush* of Southern on a word here and there. I'll tell them that at last you have *graduated* and then they'll be satisfied." She was right. Suddenly everyone was ecstatic with me, even though I sounded exactly as I had one week before.

Gordon and I had become friendly with Shari Leibowitz, the production secretary, a savvy New Yorker with a good sense of humor. One day at lunch she confided the most amazing thing to us, "Some of your pals back in Nashville have been extremely interested in what's going on with you." She reached in her purse for a letter. "The Circle Theater wants to make sure all of us up here knows that you *broke audition rules* and that you shouldn't be considered for our film at all. And a Mr. David Howland wrote to Actors' Equity to inform them that you should *not* be allowed to appear in any of their union films because you had walked out on one of *his*." She arched her brow and gave me a look. "That Nashville must be something else. And I thought Hollywood and New York were bad enough."

She was laughing but I was incredulous. I could not imagine they had all gone so far. "You don't think Mr. Strick will pay attention to this, do you?"

"Oh, Sondra, of course not. It's ridiculous and also kind of sad. The guy from Equity called our office, actually laughing. He said that he informed Mr. Howland that they couldn't help him with his problem. Actors' Equity is only for *stage* performers! Motion pictures have a different union."

"That's show biz," said Gordon, laughing.

• • •

By day, the Mick march went on. I learned that in addition to all the nationwide auditions, advertisements had been placed in major newspapers all across the country, inviting young girls to send in their photographs and bios for consideration. Some were wonderful and touching—from girls who, just like me, dreamed of becoming actresses. Others were hysterically funny, or downright absurd, like the one from a *Playboy* playmate, Sue—who enclosed her centerfold with those vital statistics which she just knew made her absolutely perfect for the role.

By this time cousin Gordon had become quite cozy with all the girls in the production office. Often, when one of them would have to leave her desk for the ladies' room or a cup of coffee, she would ask him to watch the phone. If a call came in concerning the casting of Mick Kelly, he responded in the voice of "Marge," with a distinct New York accent and "she" would tell them confidentially that the role had already been cast. "Gordon, they're gonna catch you!" I would warn him. "They're gonna be mad at us!" But Gordon paid no attention. One day as he was rifling through the drawers, hoping for some memo concerning me, the door unexpectedly flew open and in came an agent, pulling a young girl. "This is Lorna Luft, Judy Garland's daughter. [Garland was at the time performing her one-woman show at the Palace Theatre.] She'd be perfect for the young girl in your film."

Gordon, caught in a compromising situation, began stuffing envelopes, pretending to be an office assistant. "So sorry . . . already cast," he replied, smiling.

Like punching the clock, I kept reporting back to Mr. Strick, and finally one day I was surprised to see Marion Dougherty, Marc Merson, and Thomas Ryan, looking rather solemn, all collected together in Mr. Strick's office. They stared at me for what seemed an eternity. I felt queasy.

"Sondra," Mr. Strick gently began, "we all think you're wonderful . . ." then he paused long enough for me to think here comes the *but* . . . it's not fair; they hadn't even given me a chance to make a screen test. I felt my hands getting cold.

". . . and *we want you to be our Mick!*" I screamed. I jumped up and hugged them all, laughing with exultation, tears streaming down my face. I don't even remember leaving the office, or getting in the elevator. My life was changed. I remember nothing until the elevator doors parted and I saw Gordon waiting in the tiny entrance lobby.

"I got it! I got it!" I cried. "They want me to be their Mick!" We began hugging each other, jumping up and down. Except this time, we were dancing, arm and arm, down East Fifty-seventh Street in New York City.

The first thing we did was telephone Gordon's mother in Shelbyville— she too was beside herself with excitement. Next, I heard Gordon's voice saying, "The number in Nashville Tennessee, for *The Nashville Tennessean*, please." He turned to me slyly. "Don't you think we should share our good news with dear Mr. Howland and all those supportive people at the Circle Theater?" The next day's front-page headlines ran TENNESSEAN GETS STARRING ROLE IN MOVIE! I wished I could have seen their faces.

Then came the next best part. I was sent to the costume designer Albert Wolsky (a sensitive, gentle, and extremely talented man who years later won an Academy Award for *Bugsy*). I stood in one of the dressing rooms at the famous costume house Brooks Van Horn as he measured me and searched for the right "look" for Mick.

Bob Willoughby clicked a photograph as I stood in my little Mick camisole. He was a very famous still photographer who had been hired by Warner Bros. to take some photos of me which would be used as publicity for the film. I was to spend the rest of the day with him being photographed all around New York. He was the most wonderful photographer, and to this day, the photos he took of me are my favorites, especially the ones of me on the Staten Island Ferry (wearing Shari Leibowitz's sweater); they're more than photographs, they're truly poems. Years later they would hang in galleries in Mr. Willoughby's many private showings.

We were almost on our way home to Shelbyville—and not a moment too soon for we were about to lose our most recent "accommodations."

"You won't believe what's happened, Dinie," Anita said excitedly. "Sondra just won this big talent search to star in a Warner Bros. movie. Can you believe it!"

Pause. "Gee, that's great," Dinette replied with no emotion, and then after a moment, "Excuse me." She abruptly disappeared into the other room, and just as we were debating where we should go to celebrate, there came a primal scream from her direction. We barely had time to react before Dinette came speeding into the room, lurching to a stop, grabbing onto the doorjam, screaming obscenities at us. My God, I thought, what now? Every time one of us tried to placate her, she only screamed louder, then ran to her bedroom, slamming the door.

"She really needs psychiatric help; she's flipped her lid," Gordon said.

She had done more than flip her lid; she'd obviously been dialing as well, for in short order Dinette's mother showed up with one of "New York's finest" in tow. "Whad'n de name a hell's goin' on in heah?" she shrieked in a thick Brooklyn accent, eyes bulging, her towering, teased, bleached-blond coiffure wobbling dangerously. Then turning to the cop, she jerked her thumb and bellowed, "Officah, get 'em de fuck outtah heah."

Gordon spoke up in his most patrician tone, "I'll get our things." He disappeared into the bedroom returning with our bag. I had wondered why, on our way out past the still-screeching duo, Gordon had turned and smiled at both of them so very sweetly. I later learned that on his way to fetch our things, he had made two quick stops: one at his shaving kit and the other at Dinette's closet! Her shoes would never be the same.

Back in Shelbyville more waiting began—this time, for the cameras to roll. That wait was interrupted by one heart-stopping phone call. Joseph Strick had left the production. Mr. Strick and others in power did not see eye-to-eye. I later learned that Mr. Strick had wanted to go much darker with the entire film and had wanted to emphasize the inference of homosexuality between Mr. Singer and Mr. Antonapoulos when, apparently, no one else did. Robert Ellis Miller, who had recently directed *Any Wednesday* starring Jane Fonda, was being brought in and I was told that he was "reviewing" the cast. Oh great. That's it, I thought. The new director would certainly want to recast everyone—especially me. Soon, I was summoned back to New York to read for him. And although certain other actors were re-placed—most conspicuously Jackie Vernon, who was to portray Mr. Singer's mentally handicapped friend, Antonapoulos, was replaced by Chuck McCann—nevertheless I remained. Hallelujah. I went to FAO Schwarz, the toy store, and bought giant Raggedy Ann and Andy dolls—as large as myself—for Gordon and me, and again returned home triumphant. But I will always wonder what Mr. Strick's vision of the film would have been like. How my Mick Kelly would have differed.

I had quit my job at WSM and was hiding out at Gordon's house waiting for the film to start when the pink phone in Mrs. Anderson's kitchen rang. My whole body could sense something bad as Mrs. Anderson said, "Just a moment," and handed me the receiver. "It's your mother, Sondra." Oh my God. My stomach fell as if I had hit the downslide of a mile-high roller coaster. I glanced at Gordon, whose expression gave me courage.

"Hello," I said.

"Hey, girl," she replied. Her tongue sounded thick from too much al-cohol. I hadn't spoken with her in three years but I had heard she had bought the One Spot, a local café/bar. I was embarrassed, wondering what Mrs. Anderson had thought of her slurred speech.

"So. I hear you're gonna be a big Hollywood movie star, huh, girl?" she launched in.

"Well, I don't know about that," I responded. Avoiding. She had never before wanted to hear about anything I'd ever dreamed of or tried for; why should I have to discuss this with her now?

"You gonna buy me a m-e-e-enk coat?" she asked. "That's what they all say around here! Pauline's gonna be wearing furs and jewels." Her tongue seemed to be getting thicker.

"I doubt I'll be able to do that, Mother," I said, my voice slightly shaky. I hated this whole situation. I just wanted to be able to disappear, wake up, not have to deal with it.

"Well, why not?" her voice began to sound more belligerent. I thought of all the ways she had tried to hold me back, make me feel I was wrong and invisible. The night she had told Donald to hold me down while she took my television away. The coldness in her voice as she refused to co-sign the loan so I could buy a car. Her voice began again, rambling. I don't know what she was saying when I suddenly I blurted out, "You didn't even say 'I'm proud of you' or congratulate me." I was angry. "I'm hanging up now. Mr. Anderson is trying to sleep. Please don't call back here disturbing people. Goodbye." I hung up and then began to cry. Gordon and Mrs. Anderson put their arms around me. The phone began to ring—and ring—and ring. "Don't answer it," Gordon said. And no one did. We just stood there staring at it until it stopped.

Finally it was the day before I was to report to location for the filming in Selma. Gordon and I had planned to be married on September 25, and we had wanted to do it our way with a justice of the peace, a stranger who might have gone somewhere in the woods with us and performed the ceremony. But Mr. Anderson was determined we should be married at a certain church by a certain minister in Nashville, in a very traditional way. Mrs. Anderson, a romantic, wanted the flowers and rice. So Gordon and I went through the formal ceremony, mostly for her. At least it was simple and informal. Gordon wore a cream suit and I wore the palest green spring dress, and the only people present were Gordon's family. Mr. and Mrs. Anderson, Gordon's brother, Bill, and Gordon and I gathered at the chosen Presbyterian church in Nashville, in front of a minister we had never met. None of it mattered because Gordon and I were officially united now. After a quick dinner we jumped into our carriage, "Leapin' Leaner," and were off to Selma to meet a whole new world.

We arrived at the film location in Selma around 3:00 A.M. the following morning. "Sondra Locke's room key," I proudly said to the all-night desk clerk at the Holiday Inn where Warner Bros. had booked the entire company. The desk clerk smiled and stared shyly as she handed it to me. She must be one of those Hollywood people, I imagined she was thinking.

Gordon and I made our way up the outside staircase of the two-story U-shaped building. The next day *it* would all begin. I would be a real actress, on a real movie set. And though it was late and I was exhausted, I was certain I couldn't get a wink of sleep . . . and I was right, but it would be for quite a different reason. I was summoned into the producer's room.

"YOU CAN'T HAVE a TR-3! You're Mick Kelly! What do you think all the reporters will say about that? Huh? Huh? And what do you mean Gordon is really your husband and not your cousin? I won't have it! I'll replace you. I swear. In a flat second. I'll pick up that phone right now," Tom Ryan, the screenwriter and co-producer of the film, screamed at me.

"Come on, Tom. Leave her alone. We'll work this thing out." The voice of reason was that of Marc Merson, the film's other producer.

Ryan, who was holding a glass of scotch, suddenly whirled on Merson and threw the entire drink in his face. As the scotch dripped from Merson's chin, Ryan slammed down his glass and yanked out his false teeth with a flourish, hissing, "That's show biz."

Merson sat there for a long moment, not moving, then raising his arm he calmly wiped his face dry with the edge of his shirt cuff. He looked worse than I did. And I was in shock.

To merit this outburst I had clearly done something wrong. Hadn't I? But what? It had to be something more than arriving in my TR-3, something more than marrying Gordon—or was there something in my contract I had missed? Or had Mrs. Dixon "told" on me, that I didn't really have that accent? I had conned them! That's it, I thought, and now they were embarrassed and angry, thinking how each day I had fooled them. Gordon was right. They had never wanted an *actress* . . . they wanted the *real* Mick Kelly and now they had finally discovered that I was just Sondra Locke.

I wanted to keep this role more than anything. It was the kind of break that happens only in movies.

Ryan whirled on me, "The whole world is expecting Mick Kelly and she's fourteen! We've set up an interview for you with Edwin Miller at *Seventeen* magazine! What are you going to say to him? We've told him you're seventeen—you'll have to take the fall there, explain to him that you lied to us. You'd better straighten it out, or else."

I really couldn't imagine that the "whole world," or even Edwin Miller, would care how old I was as long as I looked right and could play the part. Ryan's hysteria reminded me of Kim Stanley in the latter part of *The Goddess* when she was having her nervous breakdown. Whatever he says, I should just agree, I thought. "All right, I will. I'll call him. Whatever you say." I could feel my tears forming.

"And you'll have to hide that sports car and *never* be seen driving it again!"

"All right, I will. I'll put it in storage in the morning."

"And Gordon will have to leave this location. My God, we begin filming on a public street Monday, with you pulling a red wagon! You can't have a husband! The idea! He has to go!"

I paused. He was about to rip out my heart. The tears burst forth drowning my eyes. "All right, he will."

I had surrendered. I had given him everything he wanted. My precious Gordon, who had made it all possible, was about to be sent away. I had betrayed Gordon — without choice, I told myself — and I had also betrayed more than Gordon, I had betrayed myself. And it would not be the last time.

Our honeymoon night was destroyed. I slept restlessly and I could tell from his swollen eyes that Gordon had spent much of it crying. As he left for his departing plane, he put on a good front for me. But I knew that when he returned to Shelbyville, he returned deeply wounded. He had been locked out of Post 80 all over again. As strong of heart and will as Gordon was — stronger than anyone I would ever know — at his center he was, and would always be, that tender soul whose rabbit Baby Jesus was thrown down the sewer. This time I felt responsible for his hurt. If only I could have been braver, stronger — as brave and strong for him as he had been for me. It no longer mattered that I had a big starring role in a Warner Bros. movie. That only made me feel guilty. After all, it had always been Gordon who had more talent, Gordon who deserved it more than I did. Without question I felt that was true. I called Gordon at least once a week and wrote him almost every day during the shoot, and to me he was always right there beside me, but that didn't change what had happened.

My Dear Hobbit, I felt a little better today, knowing that you are okay. I've never been so miserable in my life. I love you so much, Cumba. I'm so happy we got married. I still have my bouquet and your little boutonniere. As soon as I get some money I'm going to buy a big thick notebook and take notes while I'm on the set and I'll send you those. It has started to rain outside and that makes things worse. I suppose I'll turn on the TV so there will be noise in the room. I feel like going out in the rain. It's so sad. Anyway, it will be wonderful for us. And we can go see the movie hundreds of times. I love you. I'll write you again tomorrow.

During the time that Gordon waited in Shelbyville, he created the most beautiful portrait doll of me as Mick Kelly. Her face was so much like my own, her arms and legs fully articulated, and he even made a tiny wooden wig block to fashion one of his handmade hair-by-hair wigs for her. And just as he'd done for me, he braided her hair into a pigtail. I thought of it and of Gordon's extraordinary talent and cried.

Still, I stiffened my upper lip and did my best to try to experience and enjoy my own great luck. It's funny, when I look back on that time—the "discovery," our marriage, running away to conquer the world—except for that awful night it seems in many ways the most wonderful time in my life. Everything was like the first morning of spring and so much was new and fresh and full of expectations. I barely smelled the peculiar stench of the nearby Selma paper mill which everyone else complained of endlessly; nor did I even notice the greasy Selma food they all hated. It *was* the best of times . . . but without Gordon to share it, it was also the worst of times.

Seventeen magazine was calling; *Look* magazine was calling; *The New York Times* was calling—all wanting photo sessions and interviews with me. The most wonderful moment of all, though, was when I stood in front of the big two-story rambling white wooden house and watched as the crew rolled in the big lights, the camera, and all the other equipment. Before that moment, I had never even seen a real thirty-five-millimeter movie camera, except in the glossy photos that Little Gordie had written to Paramount for when he'd first seen *The Greatest Show on Earth* production—and on which he'd inscribed to himself in his best version of a grown-up's penmanship, "To Gordie, the best little actor I've ever worked with, Love, Betty Hutton!"

In the McCullers's novel Mick's family is very poor and must bring in a boarder. That man is the central and leading character of *The Heart Is a Lonely Hunter*, Mr. Singer, a deaf mute played by Alan Arkin, the star of our film. Alan, in many ways, *became* Singer to me. He was gentle of manner and assumed a protective though somewhat reserved role with me; and it's only after years of exposure that I now can reflect on a certain sense of tranquillity I felt around him. Apart from his great abilities as an actor and his generosity of spirit both on and off the set, I mostly recall his interest in jazz, his brand new 280SE convertible, and his ten-year-old son, Adam, who visited from New York and developed a crush on me. Finally, Alan made one statement to me that I would never forget, "As an actor you always think you'll never work again." Surely not you! To me he was impervious to such a feeling. After all, he was a *movie star*. I had seen him in *The Russians Are Coming! The Russians Are Coming!* and I had heard how brilliant he was in numerous Broadway plays and he'd just done the film *Wait Until Dark*. He was sitting on top of the world. How could he possibly feel that he would never work again? I decided he was only saying that to make me feel better when I'd get scared, but unfortunately I learned that what he said was all too true. After each job, we actors feel that we are just another member of the unemployed, and are certain that we'll *never, ever* work again.

Chuck McCann played Antonapoulos, the mentally handicapped and childlike friend, who brings much pain to Mr. Singer, and whose own death ultimately triggers Mr. Singer's suicide. Stacy Keach, in his first movie role, was cast as a roustabout who briefly befriends Mr. Singer. Laurinda Barrett played my mother and I will always remember with great fondness the Sunday afternoon when, to "get into her character," she sewed a little cotton flowered dress for me on a machine she bought at a local store. As I stood watching, and trying it on as she pinned and sewed, I began to feel younger and younger, and more and more like Mick, and more and more like she was my mother. Laurinda was tall and handsome, and had a pleasant manner and a very wide, warm smile. Her mother was Kay Brown, the well-known talent agent for David O. Selznick's New York office, the person responsible for pushing him to buy *Gone With the Wind* for the screen and was at the center of the great search for Scarlett O'Hara. I couldn't imagine anything as glamorous as having been a part of Hollywood during that era.

One of the secondary plots of the film focused on a black family in the Southern town. Cicely Tyson, an extraordinary actress, was playing Portia, the daughter of the local black doctor. Cicely, who was a sophisticated New Yorker, and apparently unaccustomed to the ways of the South, told me that the film company had had to make special arrangements for her to stay in the same hotel with the rest of us. Even though in September 1967 Selma, Alabama, was a surprisingly quiet town, no one could forget the racial riots that had recently taken place there. I looked at Cicely with fascinated eyes. She was mysterious to me. She had acted on Broadway, was self-possessed, gave off the air of someone who had seen the world, and lived what I imagined was a rich and exciting life in New York City with the famous jazz musician Miles Davis.

On the set, I felt completely at home. Though I had never heard of any of the technical concepts that a film actor must learn—like hitting the marks, or the eye-lines, or clearing for camera—it seemed almost as natural as breathing to me. James Wong Howe, the very famous cameraman whose credits included *Hombre*, *Hud* (for which, as well as for *The Rose Tattoo*, he won an Academy Award), *This Property Is Condemned*, and *Picnic*, and who had worked since the days of the silent movies, seemed impressed that I instinctually knew what to do and wondered if I had studied dance because of the "elegant" way I moved. I was incredibly flattered. It was a great privilege to work with Mr. Howe. I could listen for hours to his stories of Hollywood during the silent era when he had started as a slate boy; I especially loved hearing how he had finally become famous by successfully determining how to photograph Mary Miles Minter's extremely pale blue eyes, which were threatening her career because on-screen they appeared entirely white. Though *The Heart Is a Lonely Hunter* was publicized as "a million-dollar movie!" it was still a small film and could not afford someone like James Wong Howe. He told me he wanted to make the film so much that he cut his price and even agreed to two free weeks' filming.

My director, Robert Ellis Miller, was an easygoing, well-spoken, intelligent, and personable man. He always treated me in the most deferential and appreciative way. I don't recall him being very hands-on as a director, though sometimes he gave me "line readings" as a way of getting me to change how I intended to play a moment. I always wondered if the reason he didn't push me harder was because he *liked* what I was doing or if he thought I was by nature similar to the character of Mick and he didn't want to "throw" me. But I liked him and always felt safe and comfortable working with him. It was exciting when, before the start of filming, he rented the local theater and ran his latest film, *Any Wednesday*, for all of our cast and crew. Afterward champagne was served! Even I was allowed.

The people of Selma's reactions to having Hollywood descend on them were unforgettable. Once when Laurinda Barrett and I had the day off, we went downtown to see the Selma square. Everyone stared openly, and all the sales ladies ran up to me saying, "You are Mick, aren't you? Can I have your autograph?" I signed, thrilled. It was my first. Sometimes the conversations we overheard were very funny, like the two ladies in the school supply store:

"Have you seen any of them yet?"

"I saw one yesterday."

"What kind of people are they?"

"I don't know."

"Who's feeding them?"

"I don't know. We sure aren't. We were asked to, but we didn't want to bargain with them."

"I think the Pancake House is feeding them."

I had to laugh when they spoke about us as if we were some strange new species or breed of animal.

I continued to write Gordon almost every day.

My dear darling, Well, today was my first day. It was very exciting, but long, long waits. It was about 3 P.M. before I finally got to act. It took all morning to shoot Alan Arkin getting off the bus. They used the local fire truck and put the camera on the big tall chair that reaches high in the air, and just as the bus pulls in and Alan gets off it, the camera is dropping down. We got to the Kelly house about 1:30 after lunch. Then I got my makeup put on. We all do our own arms and legs. I got you some sponges from Mr. Greenway—like all the makeup men use. It's so exciting that he did the makeup for Audrey Hepburn and now he's doing me! Except he keeps wanting to accentuate my eyebrows, and make them bigger and darker. I'm afraid to say anything to him, so I just go to my dressing room and wipe the eyebrows off. He doesn't seem to notice.

Dear Hobbit, Another night of all-night filming. We thought we weren't going to be able to film outside because it was raining earlier. But we filmed the scene where Mick is sitting outside the theater listening to a Mozart concert inside. Of course, there was no music and I had to imagine the sounds. I kept reminding myself of the part in the story where Mick begs her mother for piano lessons but they can't afford them and her heartbreaking line "I just wanna be somebody, Mama." That helped me capture the emotions she must have been feeling. Mr. Howe told me the light looked beautiful on my profile. I love you, Hobbit. I made them agree that you could come the last few days of filming. I can't wait. Don't worry. Everything's gonna be okay.

My dear darling Gordie, I miss you so much. Tom Ryan has been awfully nice lately. It's getting cold and I thought I was going to have to ask you to send my coat, especially since we're working nights now. But the very next day after the first night shoot, a package arrived. You wouldn't believe it; it was all wrapped with a bow on it and was delivered to my room with a note that said, "To a great actress from a very grateful writer." It was from Tom. Ha! I was really shocked because he had never spoken to me after that night. [That ocher-colored wide-wale corduroy coat that Tom Ryan bought for me in Selma on the square would live on for years in Gordon's attic in Shelbyville, alongside the old turquoise bathing suit I had sewn so many shiny sequins on for our home movie production of *The Greatest Show on Earth*.]

Dear Gordon, Today we filmed the hardest scene for me in the whole movie. I have to describe the music to Mr. Singer who, of course, can't hear it and can only get images of it from reading my lips as I talk about it. Of course, I couldn't hear the music either because they can't play the music which I'm supposed to be listening to while I'm acting the scene for the camera — because the soundtrack has to be only my voice, or they could never cut it together later. Then after they cut it together they add on the music. But you know all this. Anyway, it was hard but fun because I was the only one in the scene with any dialogue. And it was a challenge interacting with Singer without dialogue. I hope I don't look ridiculous.

Finally, when the filming was almost completed, Gordon was allowed to visit me. Coincidentally, we were also filming the very ending of the McCullers story. The scene takes place on the anniversary of Mr. Singer's suicide when Mick is carrying flowers to his grave site. It is a sadder and more grown-up Mick Kelly who says, "I loved you, Mr. Singer . . . I lo-ved you." It was perfect that Gordon should be there for that scene. It was, in so many ways, the first Mick moment of our whole journey, when we had sat in that station wagon in Birmingham while he directed me for my first audition. And recalling that direction, I concluded the moment, with the big Panavision camera rolling, and the Warner Bros. crew watching, with a catch in my throat and a tear in my eye, as I softly whispered "I loved you, Mr. Singer . . . I lo-ved you."

But Robert Ellis Miller interrupted; he wanted me to play the scene with the same energy I had used earlier in the film. I knew it was wrong; Mick had changed. So I kept playing it the same way, glancing at Gordon, who seemed to agree with me. Miller also began to look at Gordon, and said to me, "Now, Sondra, I don't want Gordon's presence to change your performance." I continued playing the scene the way I thought it should be, and ironically, years later Mr. Miller said to me, "You were wonderful to work with, but obstinate, Sondra." I was shocked because I had never thought of myself that way. "Yes," he said, "I remember that any time I attempted to direct you in any way with which you disagreed, you would do as I asked, but in some way that proved me wrong. Then you would turn around in the very next take and do it your own way. Maddeningly, your way would always be best in the dailies!"

Finally having Gordon there made everything complete. I showed him all the sets and gave him the grand tour of Selma. After all the melodramatic attempts to keep my *husband*, Gordon, out of things, it was decided that he could, after all, be seen and discussed. In fact, when *Look* magazine arrived on the set to interview me, the journalist loved the *real* story of how I had gotten the part and made it and Gordon an important part of the article.

My favorite interview was one in which the journalist read between the lines of what had happened. "Miss Locke merely enters a room . . . doesn't sweep in à la Loretta Young. Nor does she do the grande entrance of a Katharine Hepburn. It is in this 'mere entering' that gives a glimpse of the little girl still inside the fragile frame. I've just spent four fascinating hours with this elfin being of indeterminate age. She can be fourteen or almost forty. Sondra has the chameleon-like quality of being what her surroundings are. Particularly the median age of her 'surrounders.' . . . as to 'the nation-wide search' bit . . . I think she found 'them.' "

Chapter 5 ～

The beautiful line from Tennessee Williams's *The Glass Menagerie*, "The long awaited but always expected something that we live for," again reverberated in my mind, but with none of its poetry as I began to realize that my life as an actress was going to be all about waiting. And now another wait began, this time for the film to be released. I had earned Screen Actors Guild minimum wage of $350 a week for a total of $4,200, which was all I had in the world, so Gordon and I decided to stay with Mrs. Anderson in Shelbyville until *Heart* was edited and available for other producers and directors to see.

I heard very little from Michael Selzman, my agent in Hollywood. Gordon had somehow learned that George Schaefer was planning on making the film version of *We Have Always Lived in the Castle*. I was dying to play Merricat, the young girl murderess who was the younger sister of the character Shirley Knight had so beautifully portrayed onstage. Gordon took another photograph of me, this time looking like the perfect Merricat. I sent it to my agent and hounded him to get it to Mr. Schaefer. A letter came from him saying that he "very much liked the look of Miss Locke" and expressed interest in meeting me closer to production time. We were excited but unfortunately the film project never came together.

My agent also sent me the script for the screen adaptation of the novel *True Grit*, which was being made starring John Wayne. Apparently the producer Hal Wallis was interested in me based on rumors he had heard about my performance in *Heart*. Gordon and I both read the script and were disappointed. I was convinced that my next film role should be a character entirely different from Mick Kelly so that I wouldn't become typecast by Hollywood. Unfortunately the girl in *True Grit* was too much like the role I had just played. Also, I couldn't imagine that the film would remain true to the book and not be pasteurized, and glamorized somehow, particularly since John Wayne's character, Rooster Cogburn, was over the hill and had only one eye. "You know John Wayne always wears a toupee,"

Gordon said. "I doubt he'll suddenly remove it for this character, and be photographed bald, wearing an eye patch like this character."

"Let's wait for the right thing," I said to my agent. "Nobody has even seen my movie yet." He hung up frustrated. Of course, the joke would be on me as far as striving for versatility. I learned, no matter how hard you try, in Hollywood there is no avoiding typecasting, and if you do, it only becomes a problem; then they don't know how to cast you at all. John Wayne *didn't* remove his toupee and won an Oscar anyway.

The editing of *Heart Is a Lonely Hunter* was finally completed and the director needed me to "loop" a few lines of my dialogue, because there were sound problems on the original track. It seemed the time was right for us to go to California.

Sadly, I sold "Leapin' Leaner"—at least it fittingly went to Gordon's best friend, Billy Palmer (our son from *The Monkey's Paw* and Buttons the Clown from our home movie of *The Greatest Show on Earth*)—and bought another more appropriate car for our trip across country—a yellow Mercury Montego. Its backseat was stuffed to popping, and so was the trunk, as we pulled out of the Anderson's driveway. I turned back for one more glimpse, remembering; it seemed only yesterday that Gordon had first taken me there, to that stone house on Belmont Avenue with the musical door and the golden television, and only moments ago that he'd picked up that little stone, our talisman, from its driveway on our way to Birmingham. Now it was safely packed among our things and we were again off to the unknown. Before leaving it all behind, we made one last pilgrimage—to East Side School, where Mrs. Anderson was now teaching fourth grade. Driving slowly past, we honked our horn several times, waiting for her to appear in the big paned window, smiling and waving goodbye.

Days later we finally reached Tucson, Arizona, where we planned to stop and visit an early childhood friend of Gordon's named Brenda. There was one twist to our visit that would later seem ironic. The three of us decided to go to a drive-in movie because Brenda wanted to see *The Good, the Bad, and the Ugly*. "A Western?" I groaned. "Isn't there something else? I hate Westerns." She assured me it was different from most Westerns. "Remember Rowdy Yates from *Rawhide*? He's starring in this, and he's really cute!"

I'd never seen *Rawhide*, but Gordon knew about it because *Rawhide* was always one of Ma Belle's favorites, and Rowdy was her favorite character. She was completely infatuated with him. I finally acquiesced and went along. Gordon talked through most of it, and I happily fell asleep in the backseat of the car, mumbling an apology, "I don't get why you think he's so great. I don't think he can act at all; it's more like a nonperformance;

all he does is whisper. I guess this whole movie just isn't my cup of tea."

Before leaving Brenda's I phoned my agent, who was finding us a temporary place to stay in L.A. while we looked for an apartment. He told me that he had arranged a small suite at the Sunset Marquis, a moderate-price resident hotel where many visitors in the film business stayed.

When I hung up the phone I suddenly burst into tears.

"What on earth is wrong, Hobbit?" Gordon asked.

"Nothing," I said. "It's just that our hotel is so expensive. How can we survive?"

Gordon managed to cheer me up, but not permanently; I would always suffer inordinate insecurities over the insane and unreliable profession I had stepped into.

The trip on to Los Angeles continued uneventfully, until one night around 10:00 P.M., on a winding stretch of deserted highway in New Mexico. It would be many years before I would be able to put what happened there into some kind of perspective. The road was like an undulating snake with one curve after another. There were not many cars and we were probably going sixty miles an hour, when the beam of our headlights cast their glow on an enormous steer, standing no more than thirty feet away, right in the middle of our path. At that speed there was no time to do anything — not to pray, or even to scream — but just as our car bore down on it, the steer seemed unexplainably, without its legs moving, to be simply pulled out of our way. It was impossible to describe. It was as if it were standing on a board and unseen hands had instantly spun it away like the hands on a clock. We pulled over and sat there, shaken, comparing notes and recovering from the knowledge that we would have both been killed instantly if the impossible hadn't occurred. We both understood that what had happened had no rational explanation. We felt somehow we'd been protected and both felt blessed.

It was evening as we at last approached Los Angeles. At least according to the map and the signs, we were there, but the freeway and the lights seemed to go on and on and on. Finally, we found ourselves on the southern end of La Cienega Boulevard, a long winding street that travels from somewhere near the Los Angeles airport for miles and miles north until it dead-ends at the base of the Hollywood Hills, colliding with Sunset Boulevard. I couldn't help but think of Gloria Swanson moping gloriously around her huge mansion. And there Gordon and I sat in our yellow Mercury Montego, a little dusty from the trail, waiting for the traffic light to turn green so that we could go left onto the Sunset Strip. I was so excited that my heart pounded, but I was also scared as we checked into and made our way up to the little suite. We soon discovered that Van Heflin was staying there, and so was Ricky Nelson, people we had only seen in movies or on television. In our rush to get settled, we soon found an apartment nearby. It was owned by Sonia Mitchelson — the mother of Marvin Mitchelson, the attorney who would later pioneer the law commonly referred to as "palimony" in the case of Michelle Triola vs. Lee Marvin — and was an old two-story ersatz Regency modern complex built in and around a garden, which sounds a lot more enchanting than it actually was.

Just when I breathed a sigh of relief about that, I became apopleptic about the cost of even shopping for groceries. Just going to Gelson's or Carl's or Sher Mart could set off my deepest anxieties. I was certain we wouldn't survive. But Gordon, who kept assuring me everything would be fine, was having a wonderful time.

"Hobbit, look over there. Can you believe it?" he said to me one day when we were browsing the aisles at Carl's.

He had spotted Norma Shearer. I, of course, wouldn't have recognized her wearing her turban. There she was, Marie Antoinette herself. I instantly thought of the scene from her film that gordon and his maid, Margaret, had enacted, the one Gordon had played for me on his big gray tape recorder that first day I'd gone to his house. I felt a tug at my heart and a sense of the impossibility of where fate had brought us.

I wished I'd been part of that golden era, for then I would have been under contract and wouldn't have to be hawked every day by my agent, whom I found it hard to deal with. I hated calling him. He seemed to enjoy telling me unconstructive things that only upset me: " 'He' [the producer or director] didn't like your hair, he didn't like your teeth, you're too young, you're too pretty, you're too plain, 'he' likes so-and-so better than you," or finally, "sweetheart, not much is going to happen until your pic opens, ya know?" Half the time I'd hang up and fling myself on the bed for a good cry. Agents and businesspeople would always be the Catch-22 of my life. It was becoming clearer and clearer that I, in fact, had a real aversion to thinking about or talking about business. In fact, anything to do with money made me nervous and depressed; I loved everything artistic and creative but business was the natural enemy. I had no understanding of it, no affinity for it, and I didn't want to learn. And that unwillingness would eventually come back to haunt me.

The day finally arrived when I went to Warner Bros. to "loop" lines for *Heart*. I could hardly wait, because I'd been told that for the first time I would be shown a scene projected on the big screen. It was thrilling walking around the Warners lot while Gordon pointed out all the street façades that had been used in so many old movies. We arrived on the soundstage and were greeted by Robert Ellis Miller, who, after hellos, explained to me what "looping" entailed, even though it was something Gordon had already told me about in high school. When Mr. Miller showed me the scene I was to loop, I just stood there. I didn't know what to say. I had incredibly mixed feelings. It was exciting to see myself on the big screen in an actual movie but I didn't like my performance in that scene. I remembered clearly the day we'd filmed that particular scene, and I hadn't been happy with it even then—looking at it now only confirmed those feelings. I tried to improve it by changing my performance in the looping. Unfortunately, Mr. Miller didn't agree; he had liked the way it was. "Don't change your performance, Sondra. I just need to get rid of the traffic sounds in the background that are overwhelming the dialogue." Maybe he was right; I didn't know anymore.

Funds were getting low and I stressed to my agent my need for a job as soon as possible, but the only roles he came up with were on television, which everyone felt I should not do, or smaller roles in feature films. Most of those were the leading man's "daughter," or parts that were poor rehashes of a Mick Kelly–like character. It was already clear that my dreaded typecasting was going to be a problem; in meetings everyone seemed surprised and even disappointed that I wasn't a gawky tomboy like Mick Kelly. I was baffled.

Compounding this was the fact that that there were so few great parts for someone my age. It was 1968 and there was no "youth market." The leading ladies of that time were Elizabeth Taylor, Joanne Woodward, Audrey Hepburn, Faye Dunaway, Anne Bancroft, and Vanessa Redgrave. And most films then were almost totally male-driven, even more so than now, if that is possible, and I was definitely too young to play opposite stars like Steve McQueen. I looked seventeen, and had just played a fourteen-year-old. After looking around, I was beginning to understand how unique a script like *Heart* was.

During those first months there was only one character I really wanted to portray. It was the female lead in *The Sterile Cuckoo*; her name was Pookie and she was colorful and neurotic, needy and impossible, vulnerable and endearing. The film was being directed by Alan Pakula, who had also produced *To Kill a Mockingbird*. Recalling the connections between that film and my auditions for *Heart*—like seeing Mary Badham and then the *Mockingbird* title on that theater marquee after Gordon and I returned from New Orleans—I wondered if this too were a sign.

My agent said that Mr. Pakula had heard about me and wanted to meet me. I was thrilled, even though I had heard that Liza Minnelli was already attached to the project. I brushed it aside, thinking you never know. Gordon and I poured over the script. Just like for the audition for Mick Kelly, Gordon directed me, word for word, even inflection for inflection this time. Pookie was a much more difficult character for me to capture, but finally I got it.

During my audition Mr. Pakula was mild-mannered and gentlemanly, and when I opened the script to read my heart began to beat faster. I could again feel that sense of euphoria of creating something special. Gordon would have been very proud of my performance that day; it was both frantic and vulnerable, just as he had shown me, and Mr. Pakula was very responsive. Afterward, as he walked me to the door, he said, "That was the best audition I've heard; I only wish I had met you six months ago." That did not bode well. Even though Pakula continued to rave to my agent, they *had* committed to Liza Minnelli six months earlier. I was excited to have met him but annoyed with him as well. I couldn't understand why he had asked to meet with me for a role he had already cast. Maybe it was as a reference for the future, or perhaps he thought Liza Minnelli might possibly drop out. Who knew what was really going on? In any case, I was terribly disappointed. Liza's Pookie was a very different Pookie than mine would have been but was wonderful, and losing out to someone with so much talent reduced my disappointment.

Finally the Los Angeles cast, crew, and press screening of *Heart* came. Not surprisingly, Tom Ryan called me to give me advice on how I should look for the occasion: "Sondra, I thought you'd want to hear this. I spoke with Eva Marie Saint and she's seen some photographs of you and thinks you look best with a straight hairstyle and a simple dress. She said, 'Sondra is just not the wavy type.' I thought you'd want to keep that in mind for the big screening next week."

I guess he thought that if a famous Oscar-winning actress like Eva Marie Saint said I should look a certain way, then I would immediately go for it. I had enjoyed many of Ms. Saint's performances but I didn't believe a word Tom Ryan said to me, and even if I had, I still intended to do what I wanted to do. Or certainly what Gordon advised to do — and that was "look as beautiful as you can. This is Hollywood. It may be the only thing they care about."

I was astounded that in the next day's *Daily Variety*, Army Archerd wrote about us in his column. "There wasn't a dry eye in the house at the finale of *The Heart Is a Lonely Hunter* for newcomer Sondra Locke's farewell to Alan Arkin. Miss Locke, who plays a plain 14-year-old in the pic, surprised crew members who'd never seen her outta character. She's a sexy-looking twenty-one-year-old wed to thesp Gordon Anderson."

The Hollywood premiere was followed on July 31, 1968, by a big "world premiere" at the Penthouse Theatre in New York City. Warner Bros. flew Gordon and me there and put us up in a suite at the old Dorset, a wonderful old hotel with a European feel about it. Mr. and Mrs. Anderson, and Gordon's brother, Bill, and his new wife also came and we booked rooms for them at the same hotel. Mrs. Anderson had never been to New York, and I loved watching her excitement almost as much as feeling my own. The most endearing moment occurred one evening around 6:30 P.M. when Mrs. Anderson, wearing her robe and slippers — just as if she were at home — and holding a large glass pitcher, knocked on our door. "Honey, can I borrow some ice from you. I know you all have a kitchen and we don't," she asked. I smiled, filled her pitcher with ice, then said, "You know, Mother, you can call room service whenever you need anything." "Oh, I don't want to bother them. They've got enough to do!" she replied. Then, completely oblivious to the stares of the New Yorkers dressed smartly for the theater and their nights on the town, she shuffled back into the elevator among them. That was Mrs. Anderson.

The premiere was glorious. The black limousine collected all of us and swept us across town to the Penthouse. As we pulled up in front of the theater, our car was virtually beseiged with photographers. I couldn't believe what an event it was. I had so many times imagined it in my mind, but never expected that it would be that grand. I peeked through the limousine windows at all the cameras crowding in on us, then turned and looked at Gordon, who smiled, squeezed my hand, and whispered, "Here we go." Chills ran up my arms, and I was on a cloud as the Warner Bros. executive Joe Hyams opened the limousine door and pulled us through the wall of photographers into the evening ahead.

First there was champagne then the screening followed by dinner. Finally seeing the film was an experience beyond words. It seemed not at all real in some ways and once it was over it was as if I hadn't seen it at all. My focus was so divided, my feelings so mixed. I thought the film never completely captured the rich world and characters McCullers had created in her novel, and even my own performance disappointed me in places. But then, I would always and forever be disappointed with every performance I gave. Still, after all the hard work and struggles, Gordon and I were ecstatic. And through the rest of the evening the cameras never stopped flashing. The real beauty of that evening was marred only by Mr. Anderson. The same Mr. Anderson who had never felt that I was good enough for his son roughly pushed Gordon aside and grabbed my arm. All so he could be the one escorting "the star" in the press photos. As the silverware he had swiped from our dinner table clanked loudly in his pockets, I pulled my arm away and stepped over to take Gordon's hand.

Around midnight when we returned to our hotel, the phone rang. "Why haven't you called Bob and me?" The voice was loud, aggressive, and drunk. It was Tom Ryan.

"What do you mean?" I asked, not having a clue what it was all about this time.

"Why haven't you called and thanked us for your reviews? How dare you!"

Now it was my turn.

"Mr. Ryan, you're *drunk*," I said disgustedly. "Never call me again like this. I've taken your crap because I felt I had no choice, but that's over. The truth is I have no reason to thank you for my reviews. They are my reviews—good or bad. It is you who should be thanking me!" As he screamed more expletives, I quietly replaced the receiver on the hook. We never spoke again. Some years later I heard that he had become very disturbed and was in a mental hospital. And after that I heard he had died there. It was sad.

However, in my heart I was certainly thanking God—and the critics—for my reviews: "Newcomer Sondra Locke reveals a rare talent that bears watching." . . . "Sondra Locke, an extraordinary actress who has both the scrawny look of Julie Harris and the wispy quality of Geraldine Page" . . . "Sondra Locke, the newcomer who has every chance to speak, complain, express all the emotions and succeeds beyond all expectations in one so young and inexperienced." . . . "Sondra Locke is stunning." . . . "Sondra Locke is impressive, blessed by her haunting eyes and the depth which she can bring the maturity of her later scenes." . . . "Sondra Locke is the find of this film." . . . "Miss Locke manages to touch the right nerves of compassion every time." . . . "Sondra Locke . . . whose physical and emotional portrait of adolescence sets the screen aglow."

I could hardly believe my good fortune. But the review that meant the most to me did not come from a film critic. It came from a music critic in *New York* magazine, who in writing an article about music in films referenced the use of Mozart in *Heart,* and in particular my scene in which I try to describe it to Mr. Singer. *"It is a wonderful thing, the scene in which Mick tries to share this love of hers for music with the deaf mute Singer as*

they both listen to recordings of Mozart symphonies. Her language, her im-
agery is childlike, but somehow infinitely more meaningful as verbalization
than hundreds of musicological-analytical tomes. By some miracle of perfor-
mance by a remarkable young actress named Sondra Locke a sense of the
wonder of music's power is re-created."

The review was further gratifying because that particular scene was such
an important and difficult one, partly because I was describing music that
couldn't be played for me during the scene. And also, the scene was crucial.
I understood that it was meant to reflect the very heart of Mick's yearning
and the silence of Singer's.

However, let it not go unsaid that wherever there are raves, embarrassing
"punches below the belt" follow not too far behind: "Miss Locke is deriving
hers [performance] from cheap fiction, bad direction or other movies."

I believe one thing has served me well through the years, that I never
completely believed any of the raves I ever received, and never completely
believed the pans either. A certain distance from them has kept me
grounded.

While we were in New York, my agent, Phyllis Wender, invited Gordon
and me to drop by her apartment, and for some reason, I would always
remember that visit. We arrived at her house at the exact hour she'd suggested, only to discover that she was eating her dinner. She invited us to
sit down, not to join her, but to watch her. It was highly peculiar, I thought.
Then I became mesmerized at the meticulous way she ate her steak and
broccoli—knife and fork held European style—and, most important, she
used an individual crystal saltcellar with its own tiny spoon. Compulsively
she salted, separately and adoringly, each piece of meat just before it entered
her mouth. "Uh-m-m-m," she said to Gordon right in the middle of savoring
a bite of salted steak, "I *wa-a-anted* her to have that part." She indicated
me by jabbing the air with her bone-handled steak knife. Gordon and I
glanced at each other. The "she" she referred to was me, and the "part"
was Mick Kelly. Somehow Phyllis had rewritten history, assuming that she
had gotten me the part, even though she had never even *met* me—much
less wielded power for me—until after I was already cast in the film. Alan
Arkin was her client and he had asked her to help with the Warner Bros.
paperwork once I was already hired.

Warner Bros. was beseiged with offers from magazines to interview and
photograph me: *Mademoiselle* said that Gordon and I "might very well have
been the brainchildren of Truman Capote, Eudora Welty—or Carson
McCullers." They photographed both of us together in a two-page fashion
layout, and years later I looked at this and understood why some

people had commented, "Her husband is more beautiful than she is," because Gordon looked amazing! *Vogue* also photographed me, as did *Harper's Bazaar*. The most unusual and fun layout was for a magazine that no longer exists called *Eye Magazine*. The article was entitled "The Many Faces of Sondra Locke — because her childhood sweetheart played Svengali, she learned how to become a bright new star." In it I was costumed and photographed as many different characters: Rima (the Audrey Hepburn character from *Green Mansions*), Charlie Chaplin, Verushka (a famous ultra-high-fashion model of the time additionally well known for her posing session in the Antonioni film *Blow-Up*), Gigi, and Scarlett O'Hara. For the Scarlett shots, the original "Prissy," the wonderful Butterfly McQueen, was lacing me up in the photo. Gordon and I could hardly believe that we were actually meeting the real Prissy from a movie we had both loved so very much. At the time she was performing off Broadway in the musical *Curly McDimple*, to which she gave us tickets.

In between my photo sessions and interviews Gordon was busily turning New York upside down looking for "treasures." And he found a few too many, but that was no problem, for by that time Gordon had discovered Red Arrow. "Shall we Red Arrow this to your hotel, Mr. Anderson?" That meant the cost would go on our hotel bill, which Warner Bros. was picking up. "Oh yes indeed!" exclaimed Mr. Anderson to every clerk!

"Gordon! What have you done?" I screeched when I saw the pile growing in our hotel suite.

"Well the men from Warner Bros. said that anything you want you should just ask for!"

"Yes, but I don't think this is what they had in mind!"

"I didn't get that much. Look at this beautiful little umbrella I got you from Bendel's. You need it; I heard it might rain."

And, I suppose I *needed* the little glass cube that held a sculpture of the bust of Oberon (from *A Midsummer Night's Dream*) dressed with the most amazing miniature dried flowers and real butterfly wings.

The full amount totaled around three thousand dollars, as I recall. No one said a word as we checked out, but a few months later I got a bill from the Warner Bros. publicity department. Naturally I burst into tears. "What'll I do? I can't pay this," I sobbed.

"Just call up the people at Warner Bros. and tell them," Gordon advised, nonchalantly munching on an Oreo.

"Easy for you to say. Who'll I call? *They're* the ones who sent me the bill!"

"Well," he said, savoring another bite, "I think you should go to the top and call the head guy." His sense of entitlement was never wanting.

So I called Kenneth Hyman, then president of Warner Bros.–Seven Arts. I don't know exactly what I said, but by the end of the conversation he said, "Don't worry about it, Sondra. Consider it paid." And it was. No one ever mentioned it again.

Back in L.A., I came down from the clouds and returned to the anxiety of hoping for a new movie. The exciting trip to New York had also left me with some depressing news. While in New York I had met Lucy Saroyan, daughter of the wonderful writer William Saroyan, and she had told me that the director Frank Perry had wanted me for Sandy in his film *Last Summer* and was very disappointed that I had "passed." I was devastated; I would have loved to have worked with Mr. Perry, but my agent had "accidentally on purpose" forgotten to report his interest to me. Mr. Perry's film would have been another job for SAG-scale wages and most likely that was not attractive to my agents. They'd rather I do nothing but wait until the release of *Heart*. It was a great disappointment, especially since I needed a quality job at that time; our funds were quickly dwindling. In fact, things got so tight that I'd decided I would have to take a job on television. One came through from the series *The F.B.I.* but Gordon wouldn't let me do it. "I don't want you to do that, Hobbit. I know all the movie people are going to love you when they see you in *Heart*. I'll get a job instead."

I couldn't imagine what job Gordon could possibly get. He was an artist, an actor, and I was the perfect example of how elusive employment in those fields can be. But he was determined, and soon had a job selling books at the Broadway department store. I would be forever touched by that gesture.

Over the past year my relationship with Gordon had grown even more special, even though the physical aspect of our life together had not continued in the way we both had expected. Then one afternoon he told me that, for the first time since he'd lived in New York, he'd been with a man, that he now felt he understood himself, and *knew* he was exclusively gay. My first feelings were torn and confused but gradually I knew that it truly didn't matter, our relationship was about so much more than that. But then that wasn't exactly true either. It did matter, but only in the sense that I loved him so much I was jealous of anyone else who might get too close. I thought about the day I discovered some old photos of Brad (his lover in New York) and how I'd torn them into tiny pieces and thrown them away. When Gordon asked about them, I lied. I said I didn't know what had happened to them. But, of course, he "knew" and later forgave me.

I was happy for Gordon that he now felt settled and clear about his homosexuality, and in fact, he felt a great relief about it. He told me how he was tired of hearing so-called experts talk about it as situational or behavioral, or all their other reasons why gays were gay. "I'm not interested in hearing a lecture on a dog given by a cat," Gordon said. As far as he was concerned, you were born that way. It even occurs in the animal world. After all, who would *choose* to deal with those problems. He held me as he talked for hours, explaining that no matter who he met or who he might ever love, he would never stop loving me.

I felt the same way. Just like Gordon himself, our relationship was something "other." Gordon was my only family, my closest confidant, my hero, and even in the sweetest, purest sense my child—just as I had, in many ways, been his. I felt I would always love and protect that vulnerable pure child in him, and the powerful Gordon who "knew" things would always take care of me.

From the first screenings within the industry to major reviews of the film, there were many predictions that I would be nominated for an Academy Award. Truthfully, I did not count on it. I remember Gordon and I attended a dinner party one evening at a home where Casey Robinson and his wife were guests. Robinson was the author of many of the screenplays for films that had become classics of Hollywood's Golden Age (*Dark Victory*, *The Corn Is Green*, *King's Row*). He told me how much he admired my performance, and he also gently said I shouldn't be too disappointed if I weren't nominated because my film was not the most high profile. Gordon, of course, disagreed with him and was certain that I would be. Just one of his "feelings," he said.

Warner Bros. too seemed very high on the idea and had taken out full-page ads in the trade magazines touting Alan, Chuck McCann, and me as Oscar candidates. Warners had decided that even though I played the leading female role, they would suggest that voters consider me for Best Supporting Actress instead of Best Actress, hoping I'd have a better chance since there were so many great leading performances that year. In fact the five actresses ultimately nominated in the Best Actress category were quite daunting: Katharine Hepburn, Dame Edith Evans, Audrey Hepburn, Faye Dunaway, and Anne Bancroft.

As word spread that I might be a serious contender, I was suddenly approached by several large publicity firms and I finally agreed to sign with Rogers Cowan and Brenner. They set to work getting me "out there," something I hated even more than I expected, for that meant going to parties with a bunch of strangers who were also there because their press agents had sent them. It was a system hard to fathom, yet it had worked for others. On one occasion we were bused to the Hollywood Bowl for a Trini Lopez concert, where we sat next to Eva Gabor. We were schlepped to Chasen's to have lunch with Marilyn Beck, who would write only about the mascara and lipstick I used. But the real highlight was going to a party at Charlton Heston's house! Gordon was beside himself. Destiny was at work and little Gordie would finally meet Brad, the circus manager of *The Greatest Show on Earth*. We must have been dressed at least an hour before time to leave our apartment and the hands on the clock would not move fast enough.

Finally we pulled up to the large modern structure in the hills of Coldwater Canyon. We wandered about looking for Mr. Heston, but with no luck. Soon we found ourselves in a small library where we noticed a whole row of all his leather-bound scripts, among them *The Greatest Show on Earth*. Gordon delicately pulled it from the shelf, as if it were the Gutenberg Bible, and opened it. There on the pages were the lines that he'd memorized from listening to the film so many times. It was truly an extraordinary moment for him. "I'd love just to swipe this," he said. "After all, I love it more than anyone. It probably means more to me than it does to Charlton Heston, but that would be sacrilegious." He sighed as he carefully replaced it.

After watching the film *If It's Tuesday, This Must Be Belgium* and a few more hours of wandering past others like Elke Sommers, we grew impatient. We just wanted one glimpse of Mr. Heston before we left, but eventually learned that Mr. Heston wasn't home. He was merely lending the credibility of his home, his screening room, and his name to the affair (something called the Bel Air circuit). Welcome to Hollywood. Gordon went home extremely disappointed.

Gordon's childhood friend Brenda had decided to move to L.A. She and her mother were in town and looking for an apartment for Brenda. One afternoon as we were driving them around we randomly turned left on a street named Havenhurst Drive, located not too far east of La Cienega and west of the famous Schwab's drugstore, supposedly where Lana Turner's legendary "discovery" had taken place. Suddenly Gordon yelled, "Stop! Pull over." I didn't know what had happened; he sounded so adamant and excited. I thought perhaps I was about to hit something, so I slammed on the brakes. He pointed across the street at an Old World Spanish-style building; hand-painted above its archway entrance, in a beautiful aqua scrolled lettering was its name, the Andalusia.

"But there's no VACANCY sign posted there, Gordon," we all said.

"I know, I just want to look at it; it's so beautiful," he replied.

We wandered around, taking in the beauty of the extraordinary building, when the manager and owner, Mrs. Uhl, with her crimson hair, approached us in the garden. "May I help you, dears?" her voice and bracelets tinkled. When we praised her building, she warmed up. Soon we were getting a tour of the most beautiful apartment, which in fact was available. There had been no FOR RENT sign displayed because of a very long waiting list. Anyway, it was too expensive for Brenda. We thanked her and went on our way, but the mystical-like connection Gordon and I both felt toward the Andalusia and Mrs. Uhl did not go away, and months later we would find ourselves returning in a most unexpected way.

In early 1969 the 1968 nominations for the Golden Globes were announced by the Hollywood Foreign Press Association and I was nominated for two of them: Most Promising Newcomer (along with Ewa Aulin, Jacqueline Bisset, Barbara Hancock, Olivia Hussey, and Leigh Taylor-Young) and Best Performance by an Actress in a Supporting Role (along with Ruth Gordon, Barbara Hancock, Abbey Lincoln, and Jane Merrow). The Golden Globes are usually considered to be a sneak preview of the Oscars.

Warner Bros. offered to buy my dress and naturally I took them up on it. I chose a dress (no famous designer) that was very simple and could have stepped right off the pages of a Jane Austen novel. It was directoire made of a dull, heavy silk with a silk organza overdress, cream and bone in color. I wore no glitter or sparkles, no jewelry except for a beautiful two-inch-wide choker which Gordon made out of antique ribbon and tiny seed pearls. The only real color was on the cape that I found in the costume department at Warner Bros. It was cut velvet, in soft muted hues of rose and green and sienna, and had probably been made for one of the old Warner Bros. films I had watched on The Late Show or the Million Dollar Movie back in Shelbyville. It could have been in *Don Juan* with Errol Flynn, or maybe *A Midsummer Night's Dream* with Mickey Rooney, Anita Louise, Olivia de Havilland, and James Cagney. I'll always remember that when we walked into the Coconut Grove at the Ambassador Hotel that night, Susannah York stopped me and commented, "What a beautiful cape, Sondra." I was very flattered and continually surprised that people I had only seen on the screen now knew me. I was one of them.

Gordon had done my hair, also very simply, pulled tightly up onto the crown of my head and twisted into a standing figure eight, with tiny curly tendrils falling delicately around my face. The whole effect reminded me of something from *Can-Can* or of La Galou from *Moulin Rouge*.

Just after we arrived at the awards I was faced with a dilemma that made me very uncomfortable. Three of the Most Promising Newcomers of the evening were nominated from Warner Bros. movies—Leigh Taylor-Young (*I Love You, Alice B Toklas*), Barbara Hancock (*Finian's Rainbow*), and me. Leigh Taylor-Young couldn't attend the awards and the Warners representative of the evening asked Barbara Hancock and me if we would go up together and accept for Leigh if she won. I was embarrassed. I thought it was a tacky idea, but I didn't know what to say. I didn't have to wonder long because Gordon came to the rescue.

"You mean like sorority sisters? Sondra's never even met her," he said. He and I looked at each other.

But suddenly we were saved; a member of the foreign press came over and said, "Miss Barbara Stanwyck would like to meet you." I was so flattered that Barbara Stanwyck wanted to meet me that I virtually floated over to her. She was totally down to earth and warm. "Congratulations, Sondra. I wanted to meet the little girl who discovered Warner Bros.! I do hope you will be nominated for Oscar as well," she told me. I was stunned. Barbara Stanwyck!

No one had to pick up the award that evening for Warner Bros. because Olivia Hussey from *Romeo and Juliet* won as Newcomer, so that dilemma was solved, and Ruth Gordon won as Best Supporting Actress for *Rosemary's Baby*.

It was an exciting period of time, all the parties and the bustle. I was ecstatic to be there. One of the pre–Golden Globe parties was especially fun because it was at the home of a Greek, and dancing was had by all. I looked around at one point and there was Gordon holding hands and doing kicks between the ever-youthful Bob Cummings (of the old *Bob Cummings Show*) and Peter Graves (of *Mission Impossible*). As I watched them dance, I could practically see Bob Cummings surrounded by Shultzy and Margaret and Chuck, and hear his famous weekly line as he posed with a camera, "Ho-o-ld it. I think you're gonna like this picture."

In spite of all the celebrating, I was really beginning to understand Alan Arkin's fear about never working again. I received one interesting script called "Color of Evening," adapted from Robert Nathan's novel, but then the whole project fell apart for lack of funds. Finally came *Run Shadow Run*, which was to be produced by Twentieth Century–Fox with Noel Black as director. He had just directed an excellent and quirky film called *Pretty Poison* (which had gotten a rave review from Pauline Kael). *Run Shadow Run* was a twisted tale about a talented but dark young documentary film-maker. When he finds real life no longer exciting enough, he begins manipulating people and circumstances so he can photograph them. The director was interested in me for the female lead, the girlfriend, who was described as sexy yet fragile and beautiful. After Mick Kelly's plainness, I needed exactly this kind of chance to expand my career.

Then the torture began. My agent would inform me, "The director really loves you, but they have to wait and see who the male star is going to be, to see if you fit together." Then, "You're one of several girls they're really interested in." Then, "You're at the top of the list." I waited and prayed that I'd finally get a call that I was the one they wanted and negotiations would begin. But I had one more mountain to climb in order to snare *Run Shadow Run* — Richard Zanuck, the head of Twentieth Century–Fox. "He's seen your performance in *Heart* and thinks you're a great actress but he's just not *sure* you're sexy enough for Melisse." I was summoned to meet him.

It was all planned. I dressed carefully, tucking my long blond hair underneath a cinnamon-colored cloche hat. Gordon told me, "At just the right moment, you should suddenly sweep your hat off your head, oh so casually, and let your long hair cascade down your back." I practiced. The meeting date arrived; as I let Mr. Zanuck study me, I sat soft and silent and then like Rapunzel, I let down my hair. Years later, Dick told me he had never forgotten that little touch.

I'll always remember the Saturday when I was called and told I had the part. There would be life after *Heart*. I had gotten my second picture and this time I had competed against Hollywood's younger leading ladies.

The cast began to fill out and Robert Forster (who had just made a splash in *Medium Cool*) would play opposite me. Several other actors such as Sam Waterston and Ken Kercheval, who would go on to much subsequent success, completed the supporting cast. Then just before filming began the Oscar nominations were announced.

The night of Monday, February 24, Gordon and I went to bed knowing that if we were awakened by a ringing telephone, it most likely meant that my agent was calling to say I'd been nominated. When shortly after 8:00 A.M. the phone did ring, I felt as if I'd never been asleep at all. I was excited beyond words or description. The very first person we called was Gordon's mother in Shelbyville; she was called out of her classroom so we could share our incredible news.

Immediately, the barrage of interviews for television and radio began. I was photographed in every possible kind of situation. In one I stood like some high-fashion model, posed in front of the Century City fountain while the owner of one of L.A.'s most exclusive jewelry stores seemed to be offering me a velvet tray laden with the most exclusive pieces from his store. I wore the directoire gown that Warners had bought me for the Golden Globes. Rona Barrett loved the story of how I'd gotten the role in *Heart*, and interviewed me, even filming Gordon for her report. I'll always recall the way she ended her interview with the words: "And now an Academy Award nominee in her very first picture, and starring in *Run Shadow Run* for Twentieth Century–Fox . . . Sondra's not Lonely, she's Lovely."

Hollywood became a veritable beehive of activity, leading up to the Oscars, and I was asked to be a presenter at the Third Annual Costume Designers' Guild Award.

Gordon and I were seated around a large round table. On Gordon's left sat Candice Bergen, who was beautiful, delicate, and much smaller than she appeared on-screen. To us she was "Lakey Eastlake" from *The Group*. She seemed rather bored with Hollywood's self-congratulatory glitz, *and* the bad taste. When the female singer began thrusting her microphone in and out of her mouth in a highly suggestive manner, Miss Bergen disdainfully started torpedoing her water glass with after-dinner petits fours. I watched with fascination.

I will never forget a gesture she later made on my behalf. When the emcee introduced Eva Gabor, he said, "Nominated for an Academy Award for her very first film etc. etc. . . . . Miss Eva Gabor." Miss Gabor said nothing about the mistake but when Miss Bergen presented next she whispered to the emcee that he had made a mistake and had read my introduction for Eva Gabor's. I overheard her as she quietly told him to reread my introduction before he called me to the stage. It was a lovely, generous thing for her to have done and I was touched. She never even knew that I had overheard her.

When we had first arrived at our table that evening, Gordon was struck by a beautiful blond woman sitting next to Martin Landau and Barbara Bain, who were across from us. She emanated an aura of glamour and drama, and her escort was tall, dark, and handsome. As Gordon peered at her, he whispered to me, "Good Lord, is that Claire Trevor?" Then after a few more peeks, he said, "No. Oh my God. It's Lana Turner!" And it was. The quintessential movie goddess was sitting right across the table from us, ablaze with diamonds and shimmering in her beaded gown! While we studied her, I began to notice that her dashing escort, a handsome designer, couldn't take his eyes off Gordon. In fact, his interest in Gordon did not wane, as the evening did. He tried all sorts of ways to make contact, "I'd love to send you an invitation to my next showing. How can I reach you?" Gordon, withholding the phone number and address he was so clearly hint-ing for, coolly but charmingly replied that he should send it to my agent, giving him the name. The man's face fell ever so slightly. But he did not give up.

Toward the end of the evening, I remember Barbra Streisand grandly sweeping onstage in a long emerald green gown that evoked the Renaissance. She humbly told the costume designers' guild that had she not become a performer she just knew she would have found her niche in their union, she would have become a costumer. At that moment I distinctly heard Lana Turner quip, "Yeah, I'll bet."

The high point of the entire evening for both Gordon and me was hearing Lana Turner *actually* say (so it wasn't just some mythic Lana Turner story), "If they don't hurry up and serve dinner, I'm going to go catch a plane somewhere."

A week or so later, the biggest event of them all occurred—the pre-Oscar party the Academy gives each year to honor the nominees. It was an incredible affair, and what an experience it was to enter the large elegant room and find Atticus Finch (Gregory Peck in *To Kill a Mockingbird*), Eve Harrington/Nefretiri (Anne Baxter in *All About Eve* and *The Ten Commandments*), Anastasia/Clio Dulaine (Ingrid Bergman in *Anastasia* and *Saratoga Trunk*), Auntie Mame (Rosalind Russell), Elmer Gantry (Burt Lancaster), and Gypsy Rose Lee (Natalie Wood) all milling about. Soon the publicist from Warner Bros. who'd been assigned to look after us was introducing Gordon and me to all of them.

"Miss Bergman, I'd like you to meet Sondra Locke and her husband, Gordon Anderson. Miss Locke is a nominee this year for Best Supporting Actress." Ingrid Bergman smiled at me and warmly shook my hand, exchanging hellos and wishing me the best of luck. What a magnificent-looking woman she was. She towered over me by what seemed a foot. And her marvelous voice was speaking directly to me. I was stricken with awe.

Before long Gordon had spotted another one of my favorites, Anne Baxter. He grabbed my hand and pulled me across the room, "We have to see her. Sondra, come on."

Her back was turned but the throaty voice was unmistakable as she gestured dramatically holding a champagne glass. Gordon seized the moment to tap her gently on the shoulder, but there was no back to her gown. I watched as his index finger deliberated for a split second, until finally it tentatively settled on a shoulder strap, and tapped lightly.

"Miss Baxter?"

She whirled around dramatically, at the same time putting her weight on her back foot, her arched shoulders lurching backward as she seductively

tilted her chin. I had seen her use this movement both in *All About Eve*
and *The Ten Commandments*. It was *très dramatique*. "Yes?" she purred.
She was "on."

Gordon introduced us and told her how we'd won my role in *The Heart Is a Lonely Hunter* by dressing up "in character" and pretending, just as she had as Eve Harrington in the first moments of *All About Eve*.

"Divine! I love it! It's the quintessential Hollywood story, isn't it? You were sensational in the picture, darling," she replied. Later, Ms. Baxter would become one of my sponsors to become a member of the Academy of Motion Picture Arts and Sciences. Then we were quickly pulled away to meet Joanne Woodward and Paul Newman, as well as many others. Rosalind Russell was incredible. She *was* Auntie Mame. She and Gordon got along like old cronies once she learned that he knew all the dialogue from *Auntie Mame* and *The Women*. He even elicited that robust Russell laugh from her when he quoted a snatch of her two-hundred-miles-per-hour babble as Sylvia Fowler in the latter.

Toward the end of the party, I suddenly heard a voice behind me and turned to find myself looking up once again at Ingrid Bergman. "Forgive me," she said. "When we were introduced I did not recognize you, and I wanted to tell you how truly wonderful I thought you were in your film. I voted for you; in fact" — she paused with a smile — "you made me cry. Not many actresses have been able to do that."

I was astonished and so touched that *she* had come across that enormous room just to tell me this. I thanked her and told her that if I were lucky enough to continue on and have a career, no review would ever mean as much to me as those words from her. She smiled radiantly, putting her arm around my shoulder, giving me a hug. "I wouldn't worry. You are an actress!"

Filming soon began on *Run Shadow Run* and although it didn't turn out to be a successful film for me, it was a very fulfilling experience. It gave me a glimpse of what it was like to have been a part of the movies in the Golden Age of Hollywood, the Hollywood of my fantasy, the Hollywood Gordon and I had imagined in those many, many hours in the Princess Theatre and in the womb of his attic. It was filmed right on the studio back lot on the huge soundstages that had been inhabited by the greats of Old Hollywood. For me there was nothing like walking through the large three-story sliding doors of the cavernous soundstage into the mélange of all the actors, the technicians, the equipment, and high above on the catwalks, all the lights and the grips — the men who position the lights when the gaffer or the director of photography calls out, "Swing the brute to the left; close the right barn door," or "Throw me a number two warm gel on Miss Locke's key." And down below, in the middle of it all, there I was with the microphone "boom" right above me, just out of camera range, and the all-seeing eye—the camera—dollying in on me. The set I stood on was a manufactured world, a perfectly realized beach apartment with all the touches that made it seem unquestionably real, down to the smudges on the wall around the electric switch plates. Through the windows could be seen a perfect view of the Santa Monica pier—in reality a cyclorama executed by the talented studio scenic painters. I got to experience the elaborate studio costume and makeup tests, and I will never forget a rumor that came back to me through my agent, who asked, "Mr. Zanuck wants to know if there is something wrong with your arms because all your costumes have long sleeves?" I laughed. "You can tell him that he'll find out later, since I have a nude scene in this film!"

While filming *Run Shadow Run* I was also preparing for the actual Academy Award ceremonies. That meant I had to determine what to wear. I looked at numerous gowns by famous, and not so famous, designers, and found them either on the one hand too severe or on the other that in them I looked like a Christmas package. Money wasn't a concern, as the studio would buy it for me, but I wanted something special and personal, so I asked Gordon to design it. He agreed, and seamstresses in Warner Bros.' costume department were set to carry out his design. Those women in wardrobe were artists and some of the nicest people I would ever meet.

After they established all my measurements they constructed my form by altering one of their old ones. I enjoyed knowing that the one closest to my size was one that had been made for the enormous-eyed character actress Estelle Winwood (*The Producers, The Swan*, and Leslie Caron's elfin fairy godmother in *The Glass Slipper*).

Gordon designed my dress to be made of dull crepe-backed satin, cut on the bias. It was an amalgam of the thirties-style bias-cut gowns of Harlow and Lombard, only fuller, yet it was touched with the shimmering fantasy of *A Midsummer Night's Dream*, because all the edges of its slender straps, the bust area, and the open back and the small train were to be covered with tiny flowers, bits of antique embroidery, small handpainted tendrils and leaves, and then encrusted with jewels—tiny pearls, antique sequins, and minute glass stars in the palest shades of rose, amethyst, topaz, and aquamarine. And affixed to an invisible netting that was delicately stitched in the deep opening between my breasts, Gordon placed tiny stars, seed pearls, and antique sequins, which appeared to be floating mysteriously above my skin there. The wardrobe department had on hand an immense inventory of decorative trim from the turn of the century, from which Gordon was allowed to choose anything he liked.

It took the seamstresses two and a half weeks to complete the dress itself, then it was Gordon's turn. It was he who had to apply all the trim, a delicate surgery that was only finished the very day of the Academy Awards. As Gordon said, "Hand me one more of those teeny dull aqua sequins; it needs one more right here," I collapsed. At last the worst was over, I thought. Until, with the clock ticking away, we watched our designated Oscar-departure time come . . . and pass . . . with no sign whatsoever of the limousine that was to pick us up and take us to the biggest night of our lives. PANIC! I stared at the telegram that had arrived that very afternoon: "We lobbied for you; we voted for you; and now we pray for you! Love, Noel and Lester." I too was beginning to pray—that I would even get there for the awards.

Finally the chagrined driver who'd gotten lost showed up fifteen minutes late but miraculously somehow managed to get us there on time. Then we were in the middle of it all—the "red carpet," thousands of flashbulbs going off, security guards, police, and then a mélange of cleavages, whiter-than-white teeth set off against tanner-than-real tans, smiling ruby red lips, tuxedos for days. Glitter, flash, and glamour.

"It's just like the beginning of Judy Garland's A Star Is Born," Gordon whispered excitedly as our attendant propelled us forward, and toward Army Archerd, who announced, "Here comes Academy Award nominee Sondra Locke for The Heart Is a Lonely Hunter." More flashbulbs accompanied by screams. I remember the fans yelling out my name and one voice in particular calling out, "I love you, Mick, I hope you win!" And on down the red carpet, having to stop in front of other endless microphones to say what the world has always heard everyone else say, on Hollywood's most Holy Night.

Once inside, the nominees were seated in the first few rows in the beautiful pavilion of the Los Angeles County Music Center. It was the very first year the awards were held there. And what an incredible assembly of talent, I thought. With billions watching us around the world, it seemed strange how little tension there was as the show got under way. At each commercial break there was a complete dissipation of that breathless anticipation viewers on Oscar Night are so accustomed to seeing. It was as if the entire audience itself were an actor and the director had called "Cut."

Fortunately, my nervousness didn't last long, because my category was presented at the top of the show. Ruth Gordon, who'd been nominated for Rosemary's Baby, sat on Gordon's left, and he later said that he could feel her tense as the big screen dropped down for the photographs of the nominees. Most pundits had agreed that the winner would either be Ruth Gordon or me, but I never truly believed that I would be the one.

I watched with an almost detached fascination as Tony Curtis, the presenter, called out the nominees and suddenly a photograph of me from *Heart* filled the enormous screen. The moment froze until "the winner is . . ." and then a flurry of pink maribou and chiffon as Ruth Gordon hurried up to claim her well-earned Academy Award.

Part of me, of course, wanted to win but another part of me was happy for her. She had been in the business forever and had been nominated only once before. As a child, I had loved *The Actress*, the charming film version of her autobiography, *My Side*, on television back in Shelbyville, and had identified with the character and her impossible dream of becoming an actress.

Although it sounds trite, being nominated for my first picture *was* already like having won. Perhaps if I had been nominated several times and never won, I wouldn't have felt that way, but having been discovered, having received the reviews I had, two Golden Globe nominations, *Mademoiselle's* award, Find of the Year in the national critics poll, and others, plus an Academy Award nomination, were absolutely more than enough.

Out of the blue Mrs. Uhl, the owner of the apartment building we had loved, the Andalusia, contacted us, not only to congratulate me but to let us know that the tenant to whom she had rented the very apartment Gordon and I had looked at had moved out, and she wanted to know if we were interested in it. We were astounded since we knew there was a long waiting list; but given the way we'd stumbled upon it and the way we'd instantly connected with it, we decided we were just meant to live there. Happily we moved in as soon as possible.

Living at the Andalusia was a special adventure all its own. We learned that it was one of Hollywood's architectural landmarks. It was built around 1926 and Mr. Uhl's parents had acquired it not long afterward. He had met his wife, Marianne, when she, like so many others, had come to Hollywood to be discovered for the movies; but instead, she had been discovered by Mr. Uhl.

If it's possible to fall in love at first sight with a building, then we certainly had with the Andalusia. There was a timelessness about the building, a sense of enchantment. It was more than a building—it was an artwork. The beautiful front garages were built around a bricked motor court. Spanish turned posts and elaborate-shaped corbels ran across the front upstairs balcony, where huge hibiscus trees, like some giant vines, had been carefully trained over it. To arrive at our apartment we passed through a deep archway, and everything opened up into a beautiful garden that had at its center a spectacular Moorish tile fountain in the shape of a six-pointed star made of hundreds of tiles in at least ten different patterns; in fact, everywhere was truly breathtakingly beautiful custom tile work. Huge paned windows and French doors and authentic hand-forged iron lanterns and hinges adorned the building. It was stately and Old World elegant, and at the same time romantic, country, charming, and inviting. It was like walking into a fairy tale.

Just like her building, dear Mrs. Uhl was also one of a kind. Her flaming red-orange hair was always generously teased into an upswept "do" that defied gravity and reminded us of a cockatoo's. "It needs volume, dears," she would always say to us. Her lips, too, were always afire with bright red lipstick, a perfect complement to her vivid tropical, floral-printed muumuus. And then there were the many-colored bangles on her arms that would clack and clatter as she went about tending the building, and particularly when she fed her trained goldfish which swam in the garden fountain. There was a virtual percussion symphony of jangling bracelets as she clanked the metal lid against the glass jar that contained their food. The fish would, right on cue, swim eagerly over to Mrs. Uhl, practically leaping up to her, like something out of *Snow White*. It was hard to believe she was in her seventies.

We learned that, just like the Andalusia, she was famous throughout Los Angeles. Whenever we told anyone that we lived in her building, they'd remark in amazement, "You live there! How did you get in? That woman is amazing; she practically asked me to take a blood test." The potential tenants she turned away were legion. There was six six man who was a basketball player. "His scale is wrong for the Andalusia. He'll dwarf the architecture!" she told Gordon and me in all seriousness. Then there was the man who owned a liquor store to whom she wouldn't rent because his money came from the sale of liquor and was therefore in her mind, tainted. Gordon used to make the joke that, if she could have, she would have put a chastity belt on the entire building.

Even to Gordon and me she had said, "Now you don't like to do a lot of cooking, do you? Not Italian, I hope. The smells are not compatible with the garden—the garlic simply overwhelms the jasmine—you do understand, I'm sure." It was certainly an amazing comment, and we smiled and agreed. She was quite a character, but in spite of her many idiosyncrasies, she was a cultured woman with a great love and appreciation for art and literature. She projected such an air of gracious gentility, however, that sometimes it seemed just a tad bit studied. It was as if, Gordon would say, "She's seen one Greer Garson movie too many." Mrs. Uhl loved us and called us her elves, and over the years she became something of a surrogate mother to us. During the seven years that we lived there together, and the six more that Gordon would stay on alone, she never once raised the rent. "I don't care about making money," she'd say. "This is my home. I want people like you and Gordon here, sensitive people who appreciate 'Aunt Lucy's heart.' That's important to me." "Aunt Lucy" was her pet name for the Andalusia.

Gordon and I became almost as protective of the Andalusia as Mrs. Uhl. To this day whenever I see Bud Cort (Harold of *Harold and Maude*), he never fails to remind me of the day he pulled into the Andalusia courtyard on his noisy motorcycle. "You gave me such a look of disdain I felt like I had desecrated a shrine," he told me, laughing.

Finally, word came that *Run Shadow Run* was completed. The studio screened it for me and we both liked the dark and quirky film. I would only see it once, but that would be more than most people ever saw it. And when it was finally released, it bore little resemblance to what Noel Black had envisioned and filmed because the studio executives had tried to make it "more commercial." Also, with the studio tightening their belts to save money after the big-budget flops like *Star*, little was spent on the advertising and release of *Run Shadow Run* and so audiences never discovered it. Then, in a desperate attempt to sound "with it," the film was suddenly renamed *Cover Me, Babe!*

My next film would ironically go on to be something of a cult classic. I can't recall who my agent was at that time—there were so many—but he phoned and said that Danny Mann wanted to meet with me, that he would be directing a script entitled "Ratman's Notebooks" for Bing Crosby Productions. Mann had directed *The Rose Tattoo*, which starred Anna Magnani, and *Come Back, Little Sheba*, which starred Shirley Booth. Both actresses had won Oscars for their films. I had loved Susan Hayward and Jo Van Fleet in *I'll Cry Tomorrow*, so I knew he must be wonderful with actresses.

"What's the part?" I asked.

"It's the romantic female lead, that's all I know," my agent answered.

I was excited but when I read the script, I had to laugh. Joan was described as a pretty, sensitive girl—a secretary—who, along with all the other characters in the movie, would take a back seat to *rats*. The movie was *Willard* and it was a modern-day tale of a boy and his rats, an updated take on the Pied Piper of Hamelin, except, instead of banishing the rats, he let them loose on all his enemies. The character of Joan "was there to offer solace, sensitivity, and a hint of romance."

Bruce Davison was the male lead and a wonderful actor. At the time he was an up-and-coming "someone to watch" of the younger set, having just starred in *Strawberry Statement*, which has proven forgettable but was a big deal at the time. We became close friends and had a great time working together.

The real thrill for me was working alongside Elsa Lanchester and Ernest Borgnine. The first time I met Miss Lanchester was at "Willard's" house, a formidable Hancock Park edifice that had an innate eeriness about it. I walked in, and among the jumble of cables and lighting and equipment, sat the *Bride of Frankenstein*. Gordon and I had grown up watching her in *The Bishop's Wife* at Christmastime, *Witness for the Prosecution, The Glass Slipper,* and so many others. I had to pinch myself. She was smaller than I had expected, her bright red hair always threatening to spring out wildly like some jack-in-the-box. Her large eyes twinkled and she had no end of anecdotes, ditties, tall tales, and observations — both comical and lethal — which she would discharge at a moment's notice. She was working on her memoirs at the time, and one afternoon I had tea with her in her dressing room, where she told me many ribald anecdotes, including a few about her late husband, the amazing Charles Laughton. This was going to be fun, I thought.

I had admired Ernest Borgnine's performances in the classic films *Marty* and *The Catered Affair,* among others. What a marvelous actor he is. He was also a warm gentleman, who shook my hand and made me feel as if we were old friends. That big-toothed smile of his was like a sunny day and I don't think I ever saw him without it.

The rats were not as terrifying as they seemed on-screen; they were clean and tame and had been bred especially for the production. The trainer, Moe DiSesso, had worked with them for months, using food and a clicker, which the rats had been trained to respond to. It was amazing what the little creatures had been taught to do.

My only real problem during the filming occurred one night when Gordon and I decided we just had to have some Southern fried chicken like his mother always made, and while I was cooking it, a drop of scalding oil spattered and hit me square on the forehead. Within moments I had a huge blister that soon drained, leaving a dull white empty sack of skin in its place. It was hideous. Instantly I panicked; I didn't know what to do. "Try and calm down and let me 'piddle' with it," Gordon said. I vaguely recall that

he put either finely ground cornmeal or perhaps baking powder on it. Whatever it was, even he didn't know, because he made it up as he went along.
The next morning I was afraid to look in the mirror but miraculously the
burn had vanished. There was no remnant of the blister or peeling skin. I
could see only the faintest blush of pink. I couldn't believe it.

When the producers screened *Willard* for Gordon and me, I thought it
was a nice little thriller and might do okay but nothing more. We then took
a three-week trip up the coastline and into northern California just to explore, and when we returned, I was amazed. *Willard* was the talk of the
industry; I certainly was not prepared for what a huge hit it turned out to
be. It was my first experience with owning a deferred percentage of profits.
And to their credit, the producers promptly paid in full. I would later own
many percentages of profits, as well as deferments, but I never saw a penny.
Willard was only my third film, and I had yet to learn how incredibly rare
that promptness and honesty would be.

A marvelous postscript to *Willard* was that *Mad Magazine* picked it for
one of their famous movie satires. I delighted over one of the bubbles over
my head, as Joan, that read "After my brilliant debut in *Heart Is a Lonely
Hunter*, what am I doing in this film?" I could have answered, "Because
that's Hollywood."

As much as I loved making movies I actively disliked most everything
about the business itself. But I soon understood that working in Hollywood
was much more about whom you know, getting invited places, being seen,
and "kissing up" than anything else. When invited somewhere, I never
stopped to consider how that invitation might "benefit" me; instead, I considered whether or not it sounded like an experience I wanted to have. After
a while I had no interest in giving endless interviews talking about myself.
Soon, my only industry outings were to the screenings for members of the
Academy of Motion Picture Arts and Sciences which Gordon and I attended, usually every Sunday afternoon. This whole attitude was not only
naïve, it was deadly for a career. To really work, and to make it all work,
you had to get out there and "Sparkle, darling, sparkle." Gordon and I
preferred to spend our private time scouring antique shops, looking for old
children's books and fairy tales. Eventually we discovered the antiquarian
bookstores and began to build a wonderful and rare collection. Rackham,
Dulac, Parrish, Nielsen, and W. Heath Robinson were some of our favorite
illustrators and we could hardly wait to discover the next treasure we had
never before seen. The rest of the time we'd spend haunting theaters like
the Vagabond, the Encore, the Nuart that specialized in showing thirty-

five-millimeter prints of all the classic films of early Hollywood I'd only seen on late-night television.

During this period, I had my first encounter with the tabloids. "JOHN WAYNE SAVES THE LIFE OF SONDRA LOCKE!" the story screamed. "Sondra Locke and her husband bad-tempered Gordon Anderson were seen dining at Scandia. It seems that Miss Locke didn't want the rest of her meal but Mr. Anderson was forcing it down, demanding she eat it because it was so expensive! Just as she began to choke, John Wayne came over and rescued Miss Locke. It was a lucky break for Miss Locke that he happened to be dining there that same night!" That story brought the first letter I'd gotten from my estranged family. My brother, Donald, wrote, in care of Warner Bros., to say that he didn't know how I could stay married to someone who tried to force food down my throat! It was ridiculous. We had never eaten at Scandia or met Mr. Wayne.

Probably the crushing blow with me for press agents was when I was talked into posing for a publicity photo that was meant to *really* change my image. I was photographed lying almost nude in a bed of flower petals, all carefully and discreetly positioned. It was a lovely idea—for someone else. It was subsequently published in an issue of *Playboy* in "Sex Stars of 1969," an article written by the film critic Arthur Knight. I still receive that photograph in fan mail for my autograph, and I cringe. Looking at that image of me, like some poked and pulled Pekingese, with my long Lady Godiva–like locks and those flower petals, I can't help but see something about the expression on my face that seems to be saying "What on earth does this mean and why?" I've always looked at that photograph as representative of all the things that were not "me" but that I did because I deferred to other people's experience or better judgment. Soon after that I decided not to have a press agent.

As I became more and more frustrated with the "business" of movies, I began to pay less and less attention to the rules which, according to my different agents, forbade me ever to do television. When I would become impatient or antsy and a guest star role interested me, I accepted it. Among the programs I was on were *The F.B.I, Barnaby Jones, Cannon, Kung Fu,* and my personal favorites, *Night Gallery* (an anthology series similar to *Twilight Zone*) and PBS's *American Playhouse* in a play called *The Gondola*—an experience I absolutely loved. In both of these pieces I starred opposite an extraordinary actor whom I adored—Norman Lloyd. Norman had an incredible Hollywood history, having worked for years with Alfred Hitchcock, and he kept me fascinated with his enthralling stories.

Along with Norman Lloyd, in the *Night Gallery* episode I worked with Hermione Baddeley, the wonderful British actress who was nominated for an Oscar for her performance in the marvelous film *Room at the Top* and also was the unforgettable Mrs. Cratchit in *A Christmas Carol* with Alastair Sim, which Gordon and I watched faithfully every Christmas. She played my aunt. Norman played an older man who falls in love with me and is spurned, but doesn't walk away so meekly — he gets even. My character was supposed to be British, so I had the chance to use an accent. One day, Ms. Baddeley turned to me and, in her perfect English accent, asked, "How long have you be-e-e-n in this country, dear?" She didn't have a clue who I was and had embraced me as a fellow "Brit." I was thrilled.

Though I had, for different reasons, enjoyed my second and third films, there was none of the passion that I had felt for the extraordinary character I had been lucky enough to portray in my first film. I wondered if I would ever feel that way again, when in August 1970, my agent told me there was a great part coming up at Columbia Pictures. The many-time Oscar-nominated director of photography William Fraker, who had recently made his debut directing *Monte Walsh* (starring Lee Marvin and Jeanne Moreau), was set to be its director. The script, entitled *The Daughter,* was a thriller whose pivotal character was Marguerite, a shatterglass girl of sixteen, enigmatic and mysterious, secluded in an old Tudor mansion. Her mysterious injections and her strange collection of toys, including her life-size doll, Aaron, who may or may not be more than he appears, gave her a very provocative and otherworldly quality. When her long-lost father returns with a girlfriend, murders begin to occur. I definitely wanted this role.

Gordon and I talked about it a lot when one afternoon, out of nowhere, he said, "I think you're going to get it. There's been an omen. Do you know who I read was at the Directors Guild screening of *Monte Walsh?* It was Miss Betty Hutton! Holly of *The Greatest Show on Earth* herself. She was there. It was a powerful sign."

Still, Gordon didn't leave it all to chance. He went to work again, this time painting an exquisite watercolor, dark and atmospheric. It was a stylized chiaroscuro portrait of "Marguerite," a pale young girl with enormous eyes peering out of a bramble of tangled vines; she just happened to look an awful lot like me! Across the bottom of the drawing, in brown calligraphy, Gordon wrote a note from a mystery actress who informed Mr. Fraker that she was dying to play the leading character in his film. Having gotten Mr. Fraker's address from my agent (who represented him as well), Gordon and I drove there and left it on the windshield of his car. And waited.

"Billy is fantastically excited. He's going crazy, wondering who the 'mystery actress' is. He pumped me and pumped me but I swore I didn't know anything," my agent gleefully reported.

A meeting was set. At the corner of Havenhurst and Sunset at 7:00 P.M. on a specific date, Mr. Fraker waited for the "someone" who was to meet him and take him to meet this mysterious actress. That "someone" (Gordon) appeared, wearing a peasant shirt and lederhosen and with a flawless German accent, invited Mr. Fraker to "follow" him for a short walk down the block, proceeded to lead him to the door of our apartment, then disappeared. When Mr. Fraker entered the room, it was illuminated only by a few strategically placed candles and the light from a flickering fire, and the far-off tinkle of a music box was the only sound that interrupted the silence. His eyes slowly searched the room, anxious, until at last they found me. I was seated halfway up the stairs, wearing an antique nightgown, just like Marguerite might wear. Billy didn't speak, but took his seat in a large wing back chair, just as he had been instructed. Suddenly from the landing at the top of the stairs came another voice, the whispery voice of a young boy who began to goad me and lead me into the scene and thereafter continued to give me my cues. The "voice" came from Gordon's gray Voice of Music tape recorder and had been recorded in advance by Gordon; he was careful to leave just the right amount of silent space for each of my replies in our scene. I had rehearsed endlessly to get the timing right and had turned the recorder on just as Mr. Fraker arrived at the front door and then had run to take my position on the stairs.

When I completed the scene, Mr. Fraker stood up. "My God, you're fabulous! This whole thing, the painting on my car, this rendezvous, everything's incredible. You're Sondra, aren't you, Sondra Locke?" He was thrilled by the whole performance and decided then and there that I was the perfect actress for his film. Unfortunately there were others to please.

The producer, who didn't want to pay my price, began scheduling meetings with some lesser-known actresses, and insisted that Billy shoot film tests with two of them. I decided that I too would do a test, hoping it would convince the producer. The day afterward Gordon and I flew to Shelbyville for the Christmas holidays. We waited and hoped. I felt the old *Heart* excitement. Both characters' names were Margaret (Marguerite) and I hoped that was a sign. On January 19 the call came from Billy saying that it was all approved. I had the part. I was absolutely ecstatic.

As the rest of the cast filled out I became even more excited. Robert Shaw, the English actor who had played Henry VIII in *A Man for All Seasons*, had been cast in the role of my father (Shaw later became even more famous for *Jaws* and *The Sting*). In the role of my mother the studio agreed to cast Robert's wife, Mary Ure, a marvelous actress who had once been married to John Osborne, and had starred in both *Sons and Lovers* and *Look Back in Anger*. Sally Kellerman, who had just played "Hot Lips" in *M*A*S*H*, was set to play Shaw's girlfriend, and Signe Hasso, the marvelous Swedish-born actress who had starred as the evil spy in *The House on 92nd Street*, was set to play my grandmother.

I was thrilled, too, that Gordon designed all my costumes, and they were all perfect for Marguerite, who had been isolated and hidden away from the real world, protected like some rare hothouse flower, existing only with her mother and grandmother. One blouse that I've kept all these years was made from French curtains of the Belle Epoque period and was a cream netting woven into a delicate lace of scrolls and arabesques with minute strands of French ribbon gathered and worked into delicate rosettes all through it. My favorite costume was white point d'esprit with delicate sprigs of forget-me-nots, and a neckline that was encircled by a delicate pleated collar of lawn, and edged with handmade lace. Since Gordon wasn't a member of the costume guild, he could not receive a screen credit. I was sorry for that, because he did an extraordinary job, but he didn't care; he had done it for me.

Although the film never achieved any great success, it meant a lot to me. Not only did I love my character and working with such talented people, but it was altogether a very colorful experience. We filmed in a magnificent old mansion that even had its own ballroom. It sat abandoned in a squalid section of downtown Los Angeles, but once the studio's art department swept in, its timeworn interior was turned into a grand home once again. We all took various suites as our respective dressing rooms and before we'd finished we felt as if we actually lived there.

Robert was an immensely talented actor with a great appetite for both a fifth of scotch a day and never-ending mischief. He seemed to take delight in undermining his wife, Mary Ure, who was very insecure, especially in the small and undemanding role she was playing, because she had always played leads. His Peck's Bad Boy behavior wasn't aimed exclusively at Mary; Sally Kellerman was also a target. He continually tried to keep both of them off balance. Though he tried the same with me, he was unable to get anywhere because I found him more entertaining than irritating. He was fond of dropping by my dressing room to settle down for nice chats about films and theater and intrigues of every sort. He also made numerous romantic overtures, which I, with great delicacy, rebuffed, and which he good-naturedly took in stride.

Another interesting thing I loved about Marguerite was that she had a split personality. She projected her "other self" onto Aaron, which was personified by an almost life-size doll, the favorite one in her vast collection. This meant that in several scenes my co-star was her doll, and I had to imagine it speaking its lines back to me, when really only the script supervisor was reading them off-camera (they would be added later in postproduction). It was very tricky and very difficult to give the performance and to be aware of so many technical aspects. It was further complicated because the audience was not meant to know this about her and, in fact, was meant to believe that Aaron's voice was coming from a mysterious playmate who hid in the bowels or rafters of the vast old house. This meant that every time "Aaron" spoke, my mouth had to be obstructed from view by some prop or piece of furniture or a camera move. It was very difficult to act and constantly gauge the position of my mouth for the camera.

Once we began filming, there was much dissension about our film. Suddenly the studio became very nervous about the original ending. Billy and the cinematographer and I got together and secretly filmed the few shots that were necessary to realize our original ending, which occurred in the dusty attic of the old house, where the young boy Aaron is at last revealed and is running from Marguerite's father after Aaron has attempted to kill him. Finally trapped, Aaron begins to tear his clothes from his body, in a paroxysm of psychosis. The camera pans slowly up the naked body, finally revealing the undeveloped genitals of a prepubescent boy, then continuing upward the camera shockingly reveals the face of Marguerite. Suddenly the clues in the picture add up—Marguerite's "insulin" injections are really hormones, and Aaron is her alter ego. Marguerite was actually born a boy who, because of his mother's and grandmother's hatred of men, was reared as, and made to believe she was, a girl.

The film was special too because Gordon also was the voice of Aaron. Billy had been testing many actors and was not happy. It was a tricky and crucial voice, because not only did it have to create a malevolent character by only the sound of it, the voice also had to seem remindful of my voice as Marguerite. I suggested that Billy test Gordon, and remembering Gordon's perfect German accent when he had first met him, Billy jumped at the idea. As soon as Gordon read for Billy, he was cast.

I was thrilled that Gordon performed the voice of my alter ego for a few reasons. First, because that voice (as my character's other personality) would ultimately be viewed as part of my own performance, and so naturally I wanted someone who was a great actor. Mostly I was tickled because I couldn't help but remember how, four years earlier, Gordon had done a perfect imitation of my voice over the phone to Marion Dougherty for *Heart*; it was somehow a completion, a perfect circle.

Our film seemed destined for nothing but problems. I learned that the negative of an entire sequence was lost by the lab, and so, one year after completion of photography, we all had to return and reshoot it. Not only did everyone naturally look different from before, but in addition we had all forgotten our characters. Subsequent to that calamity, Billy informed me that we would also have to loop the soundtrack for the entire film; the extraordinary old mansion in which we had filmed might have looked great but the noise of downtown Los Angeles could not be erased from the track. I was really provoked at the producer for this; he had refused Billy the better sound crew he'd asked for because they were a little more expensive. Now the studio would have to dole out many, many thousands of dollars to bring Robert and Mary back from England, put them up at some luxury hotel, pay additional salary for them, as well as for the rest of the actors in the film.

I did get some revenge. I had absolutely fallen in love with one of the professional marionettes they had rented for Marguerite's collection in the film and the producer had promised me that *if* I could accomplish the complicated technical scenes with Aaron quickly enough so that we could get back on schedule, he would purchase it for me. I pulled it off and we got back on schedule, but he reneged. So later, when he needed me for the reshoot and all the looping, I refused to show up until he delivered my marionette! She arrived with hardly a beat.

When finally we had completed the film, we all celebrated by having dinner together at Matteo's, a trendy Italian restaurant in Brentwood. It proved to be a memorable evening. Gordon and I sat next to Robert and Mary, and my agent, who had lately become more and more obnoxious, sat at the other end of the table with Billy. It was a fabulous evening and Robert and Gordon, who'd become great friends, were at their best. Afterward, while we walked to our cars, I noticed Robert putting his arm around Gordon's shoulder and whispering in his ear as they walked together. Typical of Robert the incorrigible, I wondered whose button he was about to push. Earlier, I had noticed that my agent John (who was gay) had had his eyes glued to Robert and Gordon all evening. Obviously realizing the same thing, Robert suddenly pulled Gordon into his arms and began kissing him. John choked and nearly levitated. We all fell apart laughing. Gordon and I would miss Robert's unique madness.

When I saw Billy's cut of the picture, I loved it. But Columbia executives went berserk when they saw the ending we had shot. "We won't have Sondra Locke wearing a penis; it's obscene. Those shots are out." So the conclusion was reduced to several shots of me on the floor of the attic with snatches of my nude back only, while a corny, badly acted, telephone voice-over of a nurse droned on, "On that date your wife gave birth to a seven-pound . . . four-ounce . . . baby. . . . boy." At a time when audiences were enthralled with the young girl in *The Exorcist* spewing vomit, masturbating with crucifixes, and mouthing lines like "Thy cunting daughter," Columbia's prim stance was ridiculous and seemed completely out of step with the times, as well as hurting the film's potential audience.

Nevertheless, making that film would remain an exciting time for me and produced a few very long-term friends, primarily Bill Fraker and his future wife, Denise.

The other friendship was that with Sandra Hume, the wife of Ed Hume, the film's screenwriter. Right away, Sandra interested both Gordon and me. "She reminds me of a character right out of *The Group*," Gordon had said. And she did. The three of us became even closer friends when soon after the film's completion, she and Ed began an acrimonious divorce. It was obvious to both of us that during the legalities she was being manipulated and deceived. Gordon gradually became so incensed watching it all that he became Sandra's "star witness" at the trial in the custody battle over the children. Gordon on the witness stand was quite something to see.

Sandra was a colorful character; the niece of George and Ira Gershwin, she had lived quite a privileged and interesting life. We spent many entertaining evenings after her divorce, listening to her adventures with new potential boyfriends, one of whom for a fleeting moment was Gene Kelly — Gordon advising her all along the way. She eventually moved to Houston and over the years we sadly lost touch with her.

During the editing process of *The Daughter*, Michael Barry, the director of my next film, *The Second Coming of Suzanne*, had, quite by chance, seen my image through the glass window of the projection room at Columbia, where some edited sections were being screened. The script of his upcoming film had been inspired by Leonard Cohen's haunting song "Suzanne" and was the story of three men — an artist and a director and a newsman — who all love Suzanne and are all changed in some way by her innate goodness and purity. The screenplay was quirky and dreamlike and I thought it would be interesting to work outside the structures of the major studios, so I agreed to play Suzanne. The cast included Paul Sand (the artist), Jared Martin (the director), and Gene Barry (the newsman). Richard Dreyfuss was also in the cast as the "director's" business manager. The production designer was Elayne Ceder, who has remained a good friend of mine.

Metaphorically, Suzanne was a Christ figure. The film within the film (the one that the director's character is making) called for me to be nailed to a cross high on the edge of a mountain's rocky crag. I was nervous but understood the importance of the shot. I warily allowed myself to be hauled up on that twenty-five-foot cross that was itself perched at a dizzying height. I was extremely uneasy as the helicopter that carried our camera whirled around me for the shot. It began as a close-up of me and pulled back until I was just a tiny speck in the distance. The roar of the helicopter was deafening and its blades seemed only twelve feet or so from my head. The cross was vibrating and I was absolutely terrified. Fortunately the shot was achieved quickly and soon I was down. Actors are crazy, I thought, and swore that I would never put myself in such a dangerous position again.

The film received good reviews (Rex Reed, *Variety*, etc.) and developed a cult following, even winning best picture at a few film festivals. I always feel a fondness for her whenever Suzanne shows up on television.

Once Gordon had had his initial success as an actor in New York, he had really meant it when he had said to me, "I know I'm an actor now; I don't need to keep performing for it to be true." He expressed no interest in using my agent to represent him, nor in using any of the contacts I'd developed to try to get a job as an actor. In fact after observing what it was like for me in the "business," he looked on it altogether with a certain caution. "Anyway, movies aren't like the ones they made when I was grow-ing up," he'd say. Although acting no longer held any attraction for him, he remained constantly creative. When he wasn't helping me with my ca-reer, or designing costumes for me, he was painting or sculpting or working on his miniatures. He had become very much in demand by private col-lectors who had discovered that he could sculpt perfect versions of whatever they might want. One collector who loved historical figures commissioned him to sculpt a two-and-a-half-inch-tall Thomas Jefferson with tiny eye-glasses, standing at his desk with a minute inkwell on it, and for another he made an entire set of characters from *Alice in Wonderland*, a set we later learned was eventually acquired by Demi Moore. These creations weren't your average miniatures. They were exquisitely detailed, of museum quality, and really magical. My favorites, of course, were always the extraordinary dwarfs and elves. For my Christmas present one year he sculpted an entire set of two-inch-tall brownies, after the characters in the famous Palmer Cox illustrated books of the early 1900s. I could marvel at them for hours be-cause of their delicate detail and their extraordinary personalities, which he captured so perfectly.

Also, Gordon's social life had become very busy. Just as in Nashville and in New York he had no shortage of suitors. None of them were up to snuff, however. Artie and I would listen as he regaled us with his exploits. First there was Fred, who was "into real estate." He was handsome and attentive and the beginnings of that relationship seemed promising, but after a month or so Gordon announced that it was going nowhere. The problem was his behavior with other people. A friend of Fred's had come to visit from New York, and he was eager to show Gordon off. During dinner, Fred persisted in minimizing his friend and his accomplishments in front of Gordon, as if to accentuate Gordon's place of importance. On top of that he was curt and abrupt with the waiters, always snapping his fingers — behavior Gordon could not tolerate. On another occasion Fred informed another couple who had just bought a new home located south of Sunset that anything south of Sunset was "GU" (geographically undesirable). As far as Gordon was concerned, that was it. He told Fred that he did not like the way he treated other people and that his "geographical crap" was not only rude but pretentious and snobbish. Another man was eliminated when he informed Gordon that he detested women. "Sondra, how in the hell could I ever be in love, much less have a relationship with, someone who hates half of humankind?" Then there was a famous sex symbol from the early sixties who, when we had first arrived in Hollywood at one of those "glittering" functions, had aggressively pursued Gordon — at that time to no avail. After their brief encounter, Gordon complained to me, "There are moments when nothing needs to be said, but afterwards, one would hope that something would be. But there were only endless discussions about the actor's career and show business." There was an artist who seemed wonderful, but that relationship was doomed from the start. His increasing need for recreational drugs and the fact that Gordon had never used any at all destroyed that chance. Whatever the elusive quality Gordon was looking for, he didn't seem able to find it.

Artie, our Nashville friend who had moved to California after he had tired of teaching French at an exclusive boys school in the East, would peer over his ever-present cup of coffee at Gordon and say, "Now Scarlett had fun at the barbecue, too, and no one could keep up with her either. At the fade-out, even poor Rhett couldn't cut the mustard. No, *mon ange*," he'd say with a smug little smile, "I'm afraid you'll just have to resign yourself to a life alone."

"Gee, if it's not India Wilkes, the maiden lady; I thought you'd shriveled up years ago," Gordon said. "Thanks a lot, Artie — you shrike!"

Artie shook his head sadly, clucked his tongue, remembering both an Olympic medalist as well as the man who had the moon and had offered it to Gordon. "Think of the jewels, the houses, the cars — the pretties," Artie admonished.

Artie was always great with Eve Arden asides and comebacks. And Gordon loved carrying on with him, but the truth was no matter how well Gordon could create fake freckles and a sunburned nose, when it came to love and feelings, he was incapable of being emotionally dishonest.

Finally in 1974 he met John. John was tall, good-looking, mustached, and with beautiful blue eyes. There was an exuberance, a boyishness, and an *openness* about him that Gordon found irresistible. And, perhaps most important of all for Gordon, he was very smart — Oberlin, Stanford, and at the time they met, he was working on his doctorate in English literature and teaching at UCLA. "There's an innocent quality about him; he was even in the air force. John McKee, the perfect boy next door from Indiana," Gordon mused.

"Perfect? Is that ever a laugh! Once he's in your clutches he'll be putty in your hands and you'll be sculpting away, turning that poor man into his 'new little life.' Auntie Mame's got nothing on you," Artie teased.

When Gordon and John first started seeing each other — as long as they were together — things were great. But when Gordon would speak to John over the telephone, John would be distant, curt, and sometimes downright rude. The truth was Gordon always brought out the child in people around him, and that's what was happening with John when they were together. Afterward, John would return to his own world, and — zap — he'd resent having to claim his grown-up self again.

"I wonder, when he's not around me," Gordon said, "if he might not be kinda dead, a constipated academic. Maybe I'm a shock to his nervous system." John later laughingly confirmed Gordon's diagnosis. "It was like I was being pulled between two worlds. You know, Sondra, there's something unnerving about him. He's like Holden Caulfield, the innocent seeker, and Max the mysterious, 'knowing' boy in Hesse's *Demian*. He's bigger than life — like about fifteen other characters you find only in literature. I love them all — some of them are wonderful; however, the rest can make your hair stand on end," he said. Then seriously he added, "In short, he's more."

In time John would become my dear friend too and an important part of my life. He is loving, generous, and one of the most admirable people I've ever met. And, though later he would cheerfully admit it was the best thing that could have happened to him, he didn't complete the dissertation!

I also began casually exploring for a romantic relationship, dating a few men along the way, but I had not fallen in love. Certainly no one even gave me the slightest desire to change my living arrangements with Gordon.

We liked living together, and we were still closer to each other than to anyone else.

Our visits to Shelbyville became fewer and fewer. We had always gone at Christmastime. But nothing really changes, I suppose. Mr. Anderson certainly hadn't. And Bill and his wife, Pat, were like strangers. Neither of us had ever really liked or trusted her; she, Bill, and Mr. Anderson seemed cut from the same cloth. She was a distinct Southern type, the sort who thrives on forecasting doom. Gordon's mother said, "I don't know what I've done wrong, but I can tell she doesn't like me." And for once Gordon agreed with Mr. Anderson when he groused, "I don't know what's the matter with that girl. She's got a chip on her shoulder a mile wide," except Gordon corrected him: "She hasn't got a chip on her shoulder, Daddy, she's got the whole lumberyard." Although Gordon and I did enjoy the fact that their son, Bill III, seemed far more like Gordon than Bill.

Gordon's room was still the same and so were Mrs. Anderson and her cocker spaniel, Muffy, and, of course, Ma Belle, who still dressed to the nines and reclined on a chaise longue like a queen watching "her stories" on television. Every night we perched on her bed, just as we had in high school, and Gordon lavished her with her latest compliments. She would trill her demure flutter of laughter and say, "Sondra darlin', hand me my little glass of sherry there on the bedside table."

That's why we returned home every year, but with every Christmas, Gordon's father became more impossible. After he was in bed, he thumped on the wall, signaling that everyone else was to be in bed too. The nadir finally came one evening as Mrs. Anderson began cooking what Mr. Anderson called "a mess of croppie." Baby Bill wanted none of that and begged for a hamburger from Hardy's. Gordon and I took one look at the fish, and Gordon said, "Would you pick up two extra hamburgers for us, too?" "Well, give me the money then," his father said. I went to my purse in disbelief and got the few dollars. "And for this we spend hundreds of dollars to come home?" Gordon whispered. It was just too petty. We promised each other it would be the last time.

However, it was on one of those visits that Gordon did something I would never forget. We visited MacKenzie, a friend we had known in Nashville, and met her brother and his family for the first time. He seemed to be "Mac's" hero, a professional army man, a good ol' boy, never at a loss for something to say. That evening while I was in the kitchen recounting tales of Hollywood, Gordon went into another room to watch television with two of the daughters.

The next morning found us in Mac's private office at work, with Gordon on the phone to a county social worker, who showed up within minutes. She put Gordon on the phone with one of the small town's judges and Gordon proceeded to tell how, when pleasantly chatting with Mac's nieces, the youngest one had suddenly said, "Would you please help me?" She then told Gordon that they were being sexually abused by their father. As I sat there listening to Gordon tell their sad story, I found myself wondering why the girls had not chosen to discuss something so difficult with me, a woman, instead of Gordon, a man and a complete stranger. I, of course, knew the answer: She had sensed something about him.

It was the early seventies and there were none of today's resources available, no help lines children could safely call; there wasn't the awareness of how rampant and enormous the problem of sexual abuse of children was. Within hours the social worker spoke directly with the children and they were placed in foster homes.

Gordon felt badly. He said, "I didn't want to have to do this, but there was no choice. I had to. I promised her I would help her." Several months later, Mac passed on letters from two of the girls, thanking Gordon for what he had done and telling him that he had helped change their lives for the better, and that they would never forget him.

MY CURRENT AGENT, Larry, told me that he had read a script that called for a "bad girl." This sounded like a good idea; I didn't often get the chance to play that. I accepted the job. Although the script was called "Mr. Manning's Weekend," it should have been "The Nightmare Begins." Never, never was I to go through such an ordeal.

It was an independent film and I had top billing. Seymour Cassel (an Oscar nominee for *Faces*) was set to play Mr. Manning, and Colleen Camp, who had been one of the All-American Misses in Michael Richie's *Smile*, was cast as my sidekick.

The tale turns around two girls who show up at Mr. Manning's front door one night, like wet and lost kittens in a rainstorm, and as quick as you can say "potboiler" they have seduced Mr. Manning and taken over and destroyed his house; then they play cat-and-mouse games with the poor man, pushing him to the edge of his limits and his sanity.

The film was shot in a lovely home in Hancock Park, and from day one was like falling into some hallucination. The director didn't have any idea what he needed to be, was, or should be doing. He knew nothing. He was handsome, charming, and dressed in nifty clothes with the obligatory gold chain around his tanned neck; "Hey, moviemaking's a learning experience," he'd say, always spraying his spittle as he spoke. He would be perfect casting, I thought, for a con man with shady associations, which is exactly what he turned out to be.

Whenever the director didn't know exactly what to do, which was all the time, he would suggest that either Colleen or I break something, or eat something. "When you say that line, knock those marble eggs off the coffee table and, Colleen, hey, maybe you could pour a little Coke all over the Aubusson."

For the first couple of days this was a grotesque joke between Colleen and me, but then gradually I found myself directing, not only my own performance, but Colleen's as well. Poor Seymour was so disgusted that every day he threatened to walk off and never come back, and as soon as the film wrapped that's precisely what he did. He did not come back to loop, so, of all things, the cameraman David Worth looped Seymour's *entire* performance. It was hellish and unheard of, and every time I see Seymour it now provides us both with a great laugh.

The makeup man had been antagonizing me for weeks until one day I told him that I didn't want to hear any more of his snide comments. In turn, he told me to go fuck myself and I uncharacteristically hauled off and slapped him. Amazingly, he tried to hit me back but I dodged him, then began a screaming match with him that brought everyone on the run. He was fired at once. I was glad—and mollified for maybe ten seconds, before I was brought back to the reality of all the other problems.

There just seemed to be some bad aura around the whole production because in the middle of that nightmare another occurred. One night when I returned home to the Andalusia, I got out of the car and unlocked the large sliding garage door, then pulled my little MGBGT inside. As I was turning off the motor, I felt a subtle change in the light and casually glanced into my rearview mirror so see the garage door slowly sliding shut behind me. The light from the streetlights outside was slowly disappearing and someone was there. Time stopped. It was dreamlike, almost as if it weren't really happening. In some weird way I felt calm. Then adrenaline took over and I quickly opened the car door as aggressively and noisily as I could, and—without thinking or planning it—I dropped the register of my voice and yelled, "Get the hell out of here." Instantly, the door slid open and I saw the silhouette of a figure run out into the street. I quickly grabbed my purse and bolted for the door. If only I had continued running straight into the Andalusia's courtyard I could have made it. But, feeling proud of my victory, I stopped and tried to slide the heavy door shut and lock it. Suddenly, I felt an arm whip quickly under my chin and something else pressing against my back. "I have a knife," the voice said. "Give me your purse." Dropping my bag I grabbed at the arm that was pressing tightly against my neck. I pried it off, but then he reached for my purse on the ground. Again, I should have run, but didn't. Instantly I grabbed at my purse. He straddled me and began to slide the door back open, pulling me into the garage. Then with a superhuman strength that people in terrible crises often report, I clamped my arms onto the edge of the door and screamed. He was pulling my feet with all his might but I was too strong. As he stepped over me—I guess to attempt to *push* me back inside—I swung my leg up and kicked him hard in the crotch. He lurched toward me, grabbed my hair, and hit me with his clenched fist. It was then I saw him for a brief instant, a black man in his twenties. As I slumped back down to the pavement, for some reason he took off across the street through the bank's parking lot. Again, I amazingly felt totally calm; it was an odd feeling. I don't think I realized that I was numb, in shock. But, I guess, the experience revealed I was a fighter at heart.

After I told Gordon what had happened, he took me to Mrs. Uhl's apartment where we waited for the police to arrive. After taking down the report, they told me what I already knew: I should have let him have my purse in the beginning, and of course I should never have stopped to lock the garage door. My eye was already turning dark blue and I was thankful that in the final scenes of the film I was wearing fantastic and surreal makeup that looked like something out of Fellini. That makeup would definitely cover the bruise.

I hoped no one would ever see the horrible film, but it was released finally with the title *Death Game*, still turns up on TV, and is in all the video stores. Ironically, it's turned into a cult movie of sorts. I remember once seeing that the Z channel (in L.A.) even had what it billed as "a Sondra Locke Double Feature" and *Death Game* was one of them.

I was still recovering from my *Death Game* experience when Gordon and I were invited to a party being given by Jessica Walter at her house. She was one of our favorite actresses (from *The Group*) and had just given a brilliant performance opposite Clint Eastwood in *Play Misty for Me*. During the evening she spoke in measured tones about Clint, and I got the distinct impression that she did not view him as a very generous actor or human being for that matter. At some point she mentioned that his next film was something I would be perfect for. *Breezy* was a romance between a young woman and a much older man. It sounded like *Love in the Afternoon*, the Audrey Hepburn and Gary Cooper film. Clint would be directing the film and William Holden was set to play the older man. Coincidentally

I had met the screenwriter, a woman named Jo Heims, and so I called her on the phone. Jo said she'd heard that an actress named Jo Ann Harris was most likely getting the role in *Breezy*; "she's a 'shoe-in' many had said." Jo wasn't sure about the rumors but had heard that Clint and Jo Ann had had an affair of sorts during the filming of *The Beguiled*. Jo didn't think that Jo Ann was right for the part because she felt the girl should be more of a gamine (à la Audrey Hepburn) and feared that if she was too obviously sexy or buxom (as Jo Ann was) that the uniqueness and sweetness of the May/December romance would be lost. That uniqueness was the point of her entire story. Jo was so enthusiastic about me for the part that she phoned Clint immediately. A meeting was set up.

I was greeted by the receptionist and then sent straight into a private office to meet the tall, lanky Eastwood and his producer, Bob Daley. They were both pleasant enough, but the meeting never seemed to have focus. It was as if I had just been wandering by their office, and they didn't know exactly why I was there. Clint held a golf club the entire time and kept chipping balls across the room while I tried to present my passionate plea that I was the *only* actress to play Edith Alice Breezerman. The atmosphere was so casual, as if he weren't even making the film, that my passion lost some of its fizzle.

"How did it go?" Gordon wanted to know.

"I don't have a clue," I replied. "I'm not sure he ever actually paid any attention to me, whatsoever."

Gordon took new photos of me, looking just like the character Edith Alice ("Breezy") Breezerman, and wrote a letter directly from Edith herself, but it apparently made no impact on Clint. We had only recently seen *The Eiger Sanction* and neither of us had been very impressed by it. So, we both concluded that I shouldn't be very disappointed anyway. Of course, neither Jo Ann Harris nor I got the part; Kay Lenz did. Jo Heims seemed even more disappointed than I was that Clint didn't cast me. I think she was beginning to feel that Clint didn't "get" her script. And, sure enough, the final film was a predictable, run-of-the-mill story about a man in his late fifties who chases a young teenage chick with lots of T and A.

Chapter 6 ～

It was another warm California day in 1975. I have always been amazed that Californians seemed to feel there is actually a change of seasons in Los Angeles, some of them boasting wardrobes to support it. Even the rain seemed rarer and rarer. At least when Gordon and I first arrived in Los Angeles I could count on January for that. In January the rains would come, and it would rain all month long. I would sit and stare out at the puddles and then Gordon would drag me out into it; we'd walk and walk until we were nearly soaked.

In the autumn I would search out the rare streets that had deciduous trees because in Los Angeles even the trees seemed never to change. I did discover one, Beverly Glen, a hilly street that wound from Santa Monica Boulevard north to Sunset; there I found rows and rows of sycamore and maple trees that each year would turn to flame.

On this particular day in 1975, though the sky was again a perfect blue, the lovely Santa Ana winds were blowing—warm and light and full of expectation. These winds even seemed an omen when my agent called: "Clint Eastwood's office wants to know if you'll come in for a meeting on *The Outlaw Josey Wales*. It seems he remembers you from your meeting on *Breezy* and thinks you might be right for his current film."

It was a special script, I thought. Josey had lost his home and family in the Civil War and, with nothing left to show for his life, mounted his horse, left his regiment, and rode out to find the Confederate "red leg" soldier who was responsible. In spite of his intentions to remain the lone figure on this mission, he collects all sorts of unlikely characters who attach themselves to his coattails as he moves across country—an ancient Indian chief played by Chief Dan George, a young Indian squaw, a young boy who wants to be a soldier, and a grandmother and her granddaughter who are trying to make it safely to their ranch out west. My character was the granddaughter, Laura Lee, who rarely spoke but seemed to exude an underlying mystery.

Philip Kaufman would be directing, and though I had certainly heard of him, I wasn't familiar with his work, so I went to a screening of his film *The Great Northfield, Minnesota Raid* and was very impressed.

As I drove through the gates of the Warner Bros. studio, suddenly I was hit with a wave of nostalgia. I hadn't been there since the days in 1968 when Gordon and I had first come to California for *The Heart Is a Lonely Hunter.* The casting director, Jack Koslyn, courteously greeted me, and after a little small talk apologized that Phil Kaufman had been unexpectedly detained scouting locations for the film but that Clint Eastwood was waiting for me in his office. "I'm very sorry about that," he said.

"That's fine," I replied. "I understand."

The "Taco Bell" everyone called Clint's office, because it looked just like one—a one-story stucco bungalow with a tile roof. Inside it was simple and unpretentious. Soon the door to Clint's private office opened and he appeared. With arms folded in front of him, he began to stroll toward me in that famous "S"-like posture, his lope leading with the knees. He was wearing what must have been his standard dress—jeans, a white T-shirt, and tennis shoes. But this time he was sporting long chin-length hair and a scruffy beard. Still I didn't view him as imposing. On the contrary, he had a light and carefree air about him; so much so, that I experienced an odd sensation, as if the school bell had just rung and I could throw my books into the air and run off to some unexpected celebration. I rose from the sofa to say hello, he took my hand in his, and then, as if we were old friends, he pulled me to him and kissed me on the cheek. I felt comfortable right away. In his private office we were joined by Jack Koslyn and Bob Daley.

The meeting was brief and casual. Sitting on the leather sofa, I told him how much I liked the script and how nice it was to see him again.

"So, what've you been up to since I saw you last," Clint asked as if it were just last week.

I rambled for a while, and soon running out of conversation yet wanting to extend the meeting, I turned to small talk, even to the subject of his wallpaper, which *did* look very out of character for him. "This wallpaper looks Edwardian . . . it looks like it came right out of Henry Higgins's house in *My Fair Lady*," I found myself surprisingly saying.

"Yeah . . . it's wild."

"Wild" seemed like an unlikely adjective to describe any wallpaper, particularly that wallpaper, but I found his use of the word disarming. I forged ahead in my chitchat . . . about how much I loved *My Fair Lady*, how much

I loved period movies in general, how much I'd always wanted to be in one but how few of them Hollywood made any more . . . and—finally getting back to the point—how interesting the early West was and how much I liked the script of *Josey Wales*.

"Yeah, it's a good time in history, and a good story," Clint said. He was definitely a man of few words. Within thirty minutes the entire meeting seemed over and I stood up to leave. "Thanks for coming in," Clint said. We shook hands, then I turned and walked out the "Taco Bell" door, wondering if I would ever see him again, but mainly wondering if I had the job. I had no idea what impression I had made, except that Clint seemed quite happy with me.

A few days later my agent made several unsuccessful attempts to orchestrate a meeting with Phil Kaufman, who I assumed would be making the choice. Just when I figured that they had hired someone else, my agent phoned to say that I'd gotten the part. I was thrilled but amazed that I *still* hadn't met the director.

Finally, several days later, Phil Kaufman and I had an anticlimactic meeting for lunch. He was gentle and soft-spoken but very serious as we picked at our salads in the Blue Room, the executive dining room at Warner Bros. Among other things, we made plans for my character's look; he thought my hair was too blond and I agreed to rinse it a darker color. He told me how he was looking forward to working with Clint, how he had written the current draft of the script, and about the other actors in the cast. I liked Phil right away, could see how dedicated and meticulous he was about his work, and I became even more excited about being a part of the film.

Within days my deal was closed. My agent was not happy because it was far less than I had received or should receive for a studio film, but I wanted to make this film, so I told him to accept. After all, it was a well-known fact that Clint was cheap with his budgets. "Under schedule and under budget" was his motto and so I joined in with his creed.

That night Gordon and John and I drove up to the very top of Mulholland and, standing on a grassy precipice, stared down at all of Los Angeles sprawling far and wide beneath us. Still enveloped in the Santa Ana winds, the city looked crystal clear, all the smog had been driven away, and the lights sparkled against the black night sky like newly polished windows in the noonday sun. We popped the top on our bottle of champagne and made a grateful toast to the new film. It was an exciting moment, as the beginning of a film always is to an actor; embarking on a new film and the creation of a new character is like beginning an exciting journey, an adventure in which anything can happen.

I walked onto the set of *The Outlaw Josey Wales* wearing full Western attire. The location, Lake Powell, Arizona, was breathtakingly surreal. We were in the middle of the desert with nothing but tall sand dunes as far as the eye could see. Phil Kaufman was working with Bruce Surtees, the cameraman, to set up a shot, so I stood waiting. Then I noticed Clint. He no longer appeared the easygoing guy I had talked with in his Burbank office. He was Josey Wales. His long and lanky body stood tall, high above everyone else's. His handsome, chiseled face seemed different behind that now-full beard, and, in that flat wide-brimmed hat he looked like some kind of mythic hero. But he was more than handsome; he was compelling. In spite of all the usual bustle and chaos on a movie set, there was a hushed aura surrounding him, like the quiet at the center of a storm. His movements were fluid, in control, and everyone watched him, careful to keep in tune with his every need. He mounted his horse, adeptly turned it around, then rode back in, rehearsing his entrance for the camera. His horse stood prancing in place as Clint gazed confidently around the set. What was different about him, I wondered? His face seemed to have taken on a soulful, almost haunted look. I watched as he touched his beard with his long, slender, and strangely elegant hands, then looked down at the sand. Just as he was about to look away into the distant desert, he caught sight of me. I wasn't prepared for the way our eyes seemed instantly to fuse. Then, I felt a soft stab in the pit of my stomach as I watched him dismount and walk toward me. Paula Trueman, the wonderful actress who played my grandmother, was standing not far from me. "What a man!" I heard her quietly say. The jangle of the spurs on his boots seemed magnified as he neared me. Then he stopped.

"Hello, elf," he said.

I guessed he was commenting on the funny hat I was wearing or my waiflike appearance in my long prairie skirt, but his choice of words struck to the very heart of me.

"Hello," I replied, trying to sound nonchalant.

"I didn't know you were working this afternoon." His voice sounded soft, almost whispery.

"I'm not. Phil just wanted to approve my costume for tomorrow."

"Looks good to me," he said. His eyes held mine, and his lips curled into a boyish smile, revealing the slightest chip on one of his two front teeth. An imperfection, I thought.

"Thanks" was all I could think of to say. It was as if we'd never been introduced, as if we were meeting for the very first time. I guess he couldn't think of what to say either, because we both just stood there, first looking at each other, then glancing away until he noticed that I was holding a second hat in my hands.

"What's that for?" he asked, gesturing toward the other hat.

"I can't decide which one I prefer for the film. I thought I'd show them both to Phil."

"Let me see," he said, taking it from my hand. He brought his hand up to my face, tipped my chin upward, and studied the hat I was wearing, then replaced it with the other one. "I like this one," he said, holding out the first one to me, the one I had been wearing, the one I had liked the best. "It shows off your big eyes."

"Boss, do you want me to take your jacket? It's kinda hot out here today," Glenn Wright, Clint's costumer, said.

"Yeah, I guess; just stick it in the FMC till they're ready," he replied, never taking his eyes off me as he removed the big olive-green wool flannel Civil War coat.

"Hey, C.E., you want to come look at the shot?" It was Fritz Manes, one of the producers and Clint's boyhood friend.

Clint reluctantly turned to go, tipped the edge of his hat with his forefinger, and said, "See you later, Miss Laura Lee." The crinkles formed at the edges of his gray-green eyes as he gave me one last mischievous smile before turning to walk away, his long lazy legs carrying him across the sand and away from me. I wasn't sure what had happened but I knew I had been transported . . . if only for that moment.

That evening in my room at the Wahweap Lodge, I was getting dressed for dinner and thinking about Clint when the phone rang. "Hello," I answered.

"Hey," his already familiar voice said, "how ya feelin'?"

"Fine, thanks." I managed to get out. I never expected it to be him.

"Wondered if you'd like to go get a bite to eat?"

I couldn't believe the bad luck. "Oh, I can't. I'd love to, but Phil already asked me to have dinner with him, here in the dining room." Maybe, I reasoned, if Clint knew where we would be eating, he might join us.

"Well, maybe I'll saunter by a little later."

"Okay."

Then he hung up. He probably wasn't accustomed to hearing no. As I replaced the phone on its receiver, I wondered if he'd felt insulted. And I wondered if he would ask me again.

Dinner that night in the Wahweap Lodge dining room seemed endless. I tried to talk with Phil about my character and the next day's scene, but instead I found my mind drifting to Clint. I kept glancing at the entrance hoping to see him "saunter" in. Why did he make me feel like a sixteen-year-old girl again? As the sound of Phil's voice ebbbed and flowed in my ears, I distractedly watched Chief Dan George, the "real-life" Indian chief who played Clint's sidekick in the film, dance the two-step with some young girl on the wooden dance floor across the way. Chief Dan George was very dapper. He must have been well over eighty but still mischievous, charming, and very much alive.

". . . Rose . . . my wife . . . understands that these kinds of things happen." Phil's voice cut sharply into my thoughts.

"What?" I asked.

"My wife, Rose . . . she's not well . . . problems."

"I'm sorry." I was lost; how much of his conversation had I missed? I wondered. I was embarrassed; I hardly knew this man, and I couldn't imagine why we were discussing such an intimate topic.

He then looked down at the table, and I watched as his fingers reached across for mine. "It's difficult. She likes you, you know. Your work, I mean," he said, correcting himself.

"Oh, I'm glad." I recovered. "And I really admire your work. I'm so happy for the chance to be directed by you." He was holding my hand. Oh my God, what was going on? Had he misunderstood? Had I? Or was it just "Hollywood"?

"What I'm trying to say is that she *understands* that it's perfectly natural to develop close relationships when we're working like this." He looked at me meaningfully. He was certainly getting right to the point. But I pretended I hadn't a clue what he meant, and soon, feigning exhaustion, I escaped from the dining room, down the long corridor and back to my room. I had no less respect for Kaufman because of this incident. Perhaps it was because I had so very much respect for his talent, or maybe because most of Hollywood is crazy anyway, or maybe because most of Hollywood takes for granted that film location is synonymous with romance. Still I was relieved to be back in my room.

I noticed the message light on my phone was blinking. "You have two messages," the operator said. "One is from someone named . . . Mr. Hobbit?" I laughed. "The other one has no name on it. It just said, 'Well, what about tomorrow night then?' " Oh my God. He called. He didn't need to leave his name.

The next night Clint sat across from me at a table for two in a cozy restaurant only a short drive from the Wahweap Lodge. We both ordered steak and baked potatoes. It was that kind of place.

His gray-green eyes studied me again. "I find it hard to think of what to say when I'm with someone I really like," he confided.

My pulse quickened. "Me too." Then my eyes returned to my plate for another long silence. I wanted to fill the empty space with words. But what words? I told him how happy I was that Kaufman wanted me to be in this film, and how much I was looking forward to the experience, and how much I loved the location and how—and how—

"*I* was the one who wanted you in the film," he interrupted.

"Hmmm?"

"Not Kaufman. *I* did. Kaufman kept dragging his feet, so, while he was out of town scouting locations, I gave the orders to hire you."

"Really?"

"I never forgot meeting you for *Breezy*, Sondra."

"But you didn't hire me for that film, did you?" I teased.

"No. I didn't. Big mistake." He smiled. I hadn't noticed how long his eyelashes were, how straight his aquiline nose. "But I've hired you now."

"I'm glad." I genuinely blushed.

Even though our instant rapport was completely different from our office meetings, it was still just as real, just as natural. I could almost forget that he was Clint Eastwood, could almost believe he was some handsome stranger that I had happened to meet while on vacation in Arizona. But after dinner as we walked to the car, I was quickly reminded of exactly who he was when I glanced back toward the restaurant. There with their noses glued to the window was every waitress and customer, straining to get a last glimpse.

We were both completely silent as we began that twenty-minute drive back to the hotel, where this dream of an evening would end. Then suddenly, but easily, I felt his large hand touch mine. My fingers involuntarily responded, instantly wrapping themselves around his—a perfect fit. He turned and looked at me, and, squeezing my hand a little tighter, pressed down on the accelerator, making our car surge forward, faster and faster, back toward the Wahweap Lodge.

Once at my door all that was necessary was another look at each other. There was no conversation, no maneuvering, it was all as natural as if it were happening for the thousandth time, but as exciting as any first time could be. He pulled me into his arms and kissed me gently, delicately. Then lifting me up, like some knight bearing his maiden, he carried me across the room to the bed. Physically I thought he was the most gorgeous man I had ever seen—his heroic face, his tall, lithe, muscular body. And in spite of his size and power, he was a gentle, affectionate, thoughtful, and yet intensely ardent lover. I thought of nothing except the moment. There was nothing in his past I wanted to know about, and nothing I wanted to tell, and certainly nothing I wanted to address about any future reality. We made love that night, not once, but several times. It was truly magic. Together, it seemed that, though we were two bodies, two hearts . . . in perfect accord we were one.

The next morning I awoke and found myself alone. Perhaps it had been a dream. But there on my pillow was a little scrawled reminder: "Miss you, duck." And I smiled.

From that moment on, Clint and I were inseparable. Even on the set, working together, we couldn't take our eyes off each other. He wanted me constantly with him, to go every place with him, even just to watch him play tennis with a friend. "I've never known anyone that I wanted to be around me all the time," he said seriously. "I guess I'm usually trying to get away."

I knew immediately that this was it; I was in love. I had had few other relationships with which to compare my feelings; in my life with Gordon I had dated infrequently and by choice had led a relatively cloistered life. But dating for the sake of it had always been of little interest to me. It seemed too planned, too forced, and, in my mind, even too unlikely a path to love. Love didn't need rehearsal, was not something to search out actively; it finds you, I believed. I guess I'd always felt that about most important things in life—a curious surrender to, and faith in, soul and even destiny. Follow your heart and everything else will take care of itself.

"Tonight we're going out on Lake Powell," Clint told me. "Fritz and Kaufman and I have rented a houseboat. It should be nice." From the start, anything he suggested was fine with me—just so long as we were together.

"Spaghetti is ready," called Rose Kaufman, Phil's wife, from inside the houseboat. She had come to visit for a few days. Any awkwardness that might have arisen between Phil and me had vanished. He was the consummate gentleman, once the signals were clear. Although somewhere on the very edge of it all, I felt that Clint, with the instinct of an animal, sensed something he didn't like.

Our boat drifted over Lake Powell, which was dramatically set between two tall red and rugged canyons. Clint and I stood alone on the back deck. Evening was turning to night—that halting, delicate space in time when everything seems to stand still. The lake was a dark green pool stretching into the distance until it met the deep blue pool of the sky filled with millions of incredibly brilliant stars. On one edge of the horizon was balanced a huge, full moon, seeming to rise from the water all fresh and renewed and clean, and on the other edge was a soft orange sun slowly sinking into the gradually darkening lake. The hushed and intermittent drifts of conversation from inside the boat faded to nonexistence as Clint leaned to kiss me. His lips skipped gently all around my face and ended on the very tip of my nose. "Hi, nose," he said like a schoolboy. I grinned and looked up into his eyes. Then in a gesture that for some reason would always tug at my heart, he took his two fingers, gently plucked at my nose, then, exposing his thumb between those two fingers, he proudly displayed it for me — he had stolen the tip of my nose, he always said. But truly he had stolen much more than that; he had stolen my heart. And it was that shy schoolboy who had stolen it.

"Hey C.E.," Fritz called out. "Food's getting cold. You guys come and get it."

Within a week the tension that had been growing between Phil and Clint came to a head. We were filming the scene in which a band of roving comancheros have attacked and plundered Laura Lee and her grandmother's wagon, and are about to rape Laura Lee. Josey and Chief Dan George arrive just in time to rescue them. Kaufman has an *entirely* different approach than Clint to making a film. He is very meticulous and thoughtful and layered about each shot — an intellectual as well as a visual approach. Clint is all guts and instinct. He, a "big picture" person in life as well as in filmmaking, is not at all interested in details. "If they're looking at that, then the film's not working and the audience is bored," I heard him say many times. I certainly knew nothing about directing at that time, but as a person and as an audience member I had always loved detail and richness. Certainly the play is the "thing," not the details, but the details are the subtext and must be *felt*. It seemed the first and only thing Clint and I had disagreed on, but these decisions were not mine and I said nothing. To Clint the differences in these two approaches mean time and money. Kaufman's approach took more time and therefore more money, and with Clint *that* was an impenetrable impasse. Clint's legendary "shoot the rehearsal" approach did not work for Kaufman.

Kaufman was directing me in the scene. He wanted me to run away from one comanchero, and toward the camera, while suddenly from behind me the comanchero draws his gun and shoots off my hat. To explain this Phil allowed his hands to guide me by the waist. I certainly thought nothing of it, but Clint didn't look at all happy. That night at dinner Clint said, "I don't like the way he touches you."

Within a few days Clint was talking about firing Phil, naturally assuming that *he* would take over. However, the Directors Guild did not like that idea at all. Soon Robert Wise (president of the guild and a very famous director of such films as *The Sound of Music*) was trying to prevent Clint from making such a move. *If* Clint wanted to fire Kaufman, he had to replace him with a different director and *not* himself, the producer and star! That would be nepotism to the nth degree. Clint reacted to this like the king of a country who's just been told by his court jester that he can't play croquet that afternoon. Someone had to fly to L.A., someone had to "fix it," because Clint had to have his way. He intended to direct the film himself, and, of course, he did. After that incident, the DGA introduced a new written guild *rule*, commonly referred to as the "Eastwood amendment." Now whenever a director is fired, another director from outside the company must be hired to come in.

From Lake Powell the film company moved to Tucson and then to the small western town of Kanab, Utah, where I finished my work and was free to go home. I had sworn to myself that I would not say anything to Clint about our parting. I was keenly aware that our future together had always been questionable at best. I knew Clint was married. He had told me that there was no real relationship left between him and Maggie and that the marriage had become a friendship primarily for the sake of their two children, Kyle, who was seven, and Alison, who was three. He had told me that he loved me, and that he had never felt this way about anyone else before, but still I didn't let myself hope.

"Sh-h-h-h," I said, delicately placing my finger over his lips. "You don't have to say anything more." Then wiping away my tears I couldn't stop, I said, "I'm sorry. I didn't mean to cry, but I didn't mean to fall in love with you. I . . ." my voice trailed off as I looked down at my wrist and the scrimshaw bracelet Clint had recently bought for me from a local Indian artist.

"Come here, Snow White," he said. Snow White was one of the pet names he had given me, because, he said, my skin was as white as snow and I reminded him of the heroine in a fairy tale. "Don't you worry. Just let your ol' dad take care of things. Okay?" He spoke gently, soothing me. Early on, the dynamics of our relationship was established as parent-child. He was Daddy and I was his "perfect little girl." He loved for me to call him Daddy, and in turn it made me feel safe, protected.

"Okay," I said, my tears subsiding.

"Now put your arms around me."

And I did, and I clung tightly—so tightly that I could feel the smooth and regular rhythm of his warm sweet breath caressing the curve of my neck and shoulder.

Of course, I had shared with Gordon everything that was developing between Clint and me and my feelings for him. It was a poignant moment between us, because although we knew that neither of us would ever let anyone come between us, we also knew that life as we had known it together would be changing. As happy as I was for all I felt for Clint, I was also sad; it had always just been Gordon and me against the world. Somehow it would work out, I thought, as long as we just followed our hearts. Gordon was loving and genuinely happy for me.

"That's wonderful, Hobbit. You deserve it. I just don't want you to get hurt," he said to me gently.

"I know, but don't worry. I'll be okay. Whatever happens we'll always be the same to each other. You and me, Hobbit. You know that, don't you? Nothing can change our relationship, ever."

"I know that, Shana," he said. We hugged and pledged that it was true.

Clint called often from location where he was still filming *Josey* and every time we hung up it seemed as painful for him as it was for me. "We'll be together soon," he'd say. But I didn't press him for the exact time. I never was the kind of woman who pressed for premature answers and commitments and this was probably one of the things that drew Clint to me. Likewise, Clint was perfect for me in similar ways. He was strong but not pushy; he seemed shy and self-effacing in spite of his fame. I was always amazed and impressed at how modest he appeared to be. Clint the Superstar was known for showing his identification pass when attending Warner Bros. executive screenings—as if he couldn't gain access without it! I thought it was a sign of extraordinary modesty, but early on Gordon said he found it curious, even specious. I was further impressed that Clint didn't seem to know anything about who's who in Hollywood or sometimes even in the world. For instance, he once asked me, "Who is Barbara Walters?"

"You've been gone two weeks and I can't take it anymore, sweetie," Clint finally said one day. "Why don't you fly up here Thanksgiving and visit me. It's beautiful here in Oroville [California, where they were still filming]." I was thrilled. Thanksgiving finally came and I boarded the plane, but not without trepidation. Maybe the magic that had surrounded us would have vanished. When he picked me up at the airport, it was as if not a moment had lapsed since we had last been together. We had dinner and wine at a cozy little restaurant, then drove to location and Clint's hotel. That night in an unremarkable hotel room, we made love again and the connection between us seemed even more powerful.

"I never knew I could love somebody so much, and feel so peaceful about it at the same time," he said to me. Then suddenly and unexpectedly he leapt out of bed, threw open the hotel room door, and standing stark naked for all the world, shouted . . .

"Sveeeeeeeeeetieeeeee! I love you-u-u-u-u."

After that came our first really difficult period. The film was finally finished and Clint went back to Carmel to visit his children. I had such mixed feelings about Maggie and the children. I believed Clint's story about the situation. He had even confided in me that several years earlier (before Kyle had been born) he had asked Maggie for a divorce, but, within a matter of weeks afterward, she fell very ill with hepatitis and had to be hospitalized. In fact, she had nearly died and as a result Clint had stayed in the relationship. He even agreed to something that Maggie had desperately wanted for a long time, to have children. And soon she became pregnant with Kyle and later with Alison. Still, none of this erased my angst about the situation. But I believed in Clint, and his truthfulness and kindness. And I was totally in love.

Soon Clint was in L.A. and I was peeking out my upstairs window of the Andalusia as he walked into the courtyard. My heart beat loudly, because I had not seen him in several days. Something was particularly scary about that moment, because it was the first time we had seen each other outside our film. It was our first moment in the "real world." Initially I was thrown—Josey had always had a beard and now arriving at my door was a clean-shaven Clint. Not only did he look ten years younger, he looked different altogether—his jawline appeared delicate in comparison to the way it had with a beard. I had grown so accustomed to Josey, had actually fallen in love with Josey, and now Clint had stripped Josey away. For perhaps thirty seconds there was a slight awkwardness between us, as if we had not met. But then it passed and the perfect and easy fit between us was powerfully recaptured. After a quick tour of my apartment (Gordon was visiting our friend John) we settled in on the big down sofa and listened to Nat King Cole and Ray Charles records, an interest of mine which seem to surprise and please Clint.

"Let's go get some grub," he finally said to me. "There's a little place I want to take you." The Steak Pit was almost invisible from the street. Joe, the owner, did business with a very elite and private clientele. During the first few years of our relationship, before our affair became public, Clint and I dined there many times. It was always the same, always simple yet somehow special—"Steak or lamb chops, tonight, Mr. Eastwood?" Joe would ask. "New York strip, rare, Joe, and don't forget those big beefsteak tomatoes and sweet Maui onions," Clint would say.

"I'm gonna edit *Josey Wales* in Carmel. Will you come up and spend some time there with me?" Carmel would always be home to Clint. He and Maggie had moved there some time after his success with *Rawhide* and he loved it. Located on the Pacific coastline a few hours south of San Francisco, Carmel is a charming little village with a European feel to it, full of "fairy tale"–looking houses and shops. Naturally I loved it too. While Clint worked, I wandered around studying the houses, the beach, the flowers. On that first visit, Clint had made reservations for me at Hofsas House, a little German-style hotel just a few blocks from the town and from the restaurant, the Hog's Breath Inn, in which he was part owner.

This was New Year's Eve 1975, but I spent the stroke of midnight alone at the Hofsas House. Clint and I had been together earlier in the evening when we had talked and made love. "I don't like this. I don't like not being with you. I have to go to all these events that Maggie arranges, and I just want to be with you," he said.

"It's all right," I replied. "I'll be okay. Just seeing you for half an hour is worth everything to me. I love you so much, Daddy."

"I love you too, Snow White. More than ever. It won't always be this way, I promise."

I meant it, and I knew he meant it as well, so that New Year's Eve was one of great happiness and expectation, even though at the same time there was sadness. Some of it was over Gordon. He had gone to Shelbyville without me. We were as close emotionally as ever, so it seemed strange not to be with him, especially at the holiday season. Christmas would forever be associated with Gordon and the extraordinary child within him. I missed him, and we talked daily by phone.

It was during that first Carmel visit with Clint that I met Jane Brolin. Jane was a very old friend of Clint and Maggie's. She had met them soon after she had arrived in Los Angeles from Texas, during the days when Clint was starring in *Rawhide*. Apparently Jane was ever present in their lives during those early years and remained close even after she married James Brolin, the actor. At first I was uncomfortable at the thought of having dinner with Jane; after all, she was also a longtime friend of Maggie's, but Jane was immediately ingratiating to me and told me the same story about Clint and Maggie's relationship that Clint had told me. I was convinced.

Then, out of the blue, my agent received an offer for me to star in a film being made in Little Rock, Arkansas. My character was a spirit who guarded a sacred Indian homeland against intruders. It also starred Joe Don Baker and Ted Neeley and was entitled *Shadow of Chikara*. I didn't want to leave Clint but I also knew I had to think of my own career and my own support. Who knew where this relationship with Clint could or would take me?

My schedule was only six or eight weeks but Clint called me every day, telling me how much he missed me. About three weeks into my stay there, he said he couldn't stand it without me any longer; he was flying to Arkansas. I booked a hotel away from the cast and crew, at an authentic old "fishing hole" not far away, and Clint and I spent the next several days catching up. While I worked, he toured the countryside, wearing his fishing hat disguise, and then in the evenings we were together. Sometimes we'd drive to the next town to some charming and hidden restaurant he would have discovered, and on other evenings he would have shopped for food that day and have dinner cooking and a fire going in the little rock fireplace when I returned to our motel. "I don't ever want to be without you," he said to me. "I've hated this separation."

"I feel the same way," I told him, "but I have to work."

"Then work with me. I want us to be together all the time. There's a part for you in my next film, a great part and you'll be great in it."

Although Clint was clearly Daddy in the dynamics of our relationship, I seemed to bring out the little boy in him. And although he loved me for my childlike nature, he brought out the woman in me. Clint seemed astonished at his need for me, even admitting that he'd never been faithful to one woman—because he'd "never been in love before," he confided. He even made up a song about it: "She made me monogamous." That flattered and delighted me. I would never doubt his faithfulness and his love for me.

I told Clint everything about my childhood, my life, and most important about Gordon and our relationship. Just as I had hoped, Clint embraced it; he smiled and told me it only proved what a tender spirit I had and that he admired "his girl's" loyalty and depth. His reaction was crucial, because Gordon was an intrinsic part of me that I couldn't sever for anyone. The fact that Clint was open and understanding enough to accept Gordon as my only family made my wholehearted commitment to him at last become complete.

The film Clint had referred to in Arkansas was *The Gauntlet*, and although the story didn't exactly appeal to me, I was glad the character was different from how I was then "typed." Most important, Clint and I would be together again. Soon, however, I learned that Warner Bros. wanted Clint and Barbra Streisand to star together in it. I was concerned. But I underestimated the way Clint would always have the last word. It was interesting to watch him manipulate it—never really telling anyone what he was doing. He would take the meetings with Warners, in which he would listen to them and *seem* to agree, but he just never followed through on anything that could make the final deal happen. It became a passive-aggressive standoff until it was time to make the film and there was no deal with Streisand— somehow Clint had *willed* that whole situation away. Which meant I was in. But I was comfortable only after Clint, Fritz, and others assured me that his decisions were never based on personal feelings alone. "Clint wouldn't give his own mother a job if he didn't think she was right for it," Fritz hooted.

Finally we were off to Phoenix and Las Vegas to film *The Gauntlet* and I was in heaven. When actors are working, the film company takes care of everything: Their clothes are prepared, their food is prepared, their schedule is arranged, a car is delivered. It's a great cocoon. With Clint, it became a double cocoon. He wanted to take charge of everything, and I thrived on it. I didn't have to think of Hollywood politics (Clint was above them), or nagging my agent (Clint wanted me to sign with his own agent), or what my next job would be (Clint wanted me to work only with him).

Making the situation even more perfect, one day Clint asked, "So, when am I gonna *meet* Gordon?" I felt as if they knew each other already because I had talked endlessly about each to the other, but they hadn't actually met. I asked Gordon if he'd like to visit us on location in Phoenix. I'll always remember the day he and John arrived by car. We had just returned from the day's filming and were standing near the motel pool when Gordon and John approached. To my knowledge, Clint had never even seen a picture of Gordon, and so I asked him, "Okay, which is Gordon? You pick." Clint immediately put out his hand toward Gordon and said, "How ya doin', Gordon?" They both smiled, shook hands, and that was that.

The four of us had dinner that night at a nearby restaurant. "Did you know that Gary Cooper wore a lace toupee?" Gordon suddenly asked Clint. "No. How could that be? I could see where it was growing!" Clint replied, nonplussed. To which, Gordon, the authority on lace wigs, only laughed and explained how it was done, adding, "In fact, I know how to make them myself." Clint seemed amazed and the evening was off and running. Gordon regaled us with hilarious stories about *The Heart Is a Lonely Hunter*, Hollywood, Shelbyville, New York, and off-Broadway. He had Clint nearly in tears laughing over his Truman Capote encounter. "Well," Gordon said dramatically, "it began in New York when I was playing this character, a libertine with literary connections, outrageous and shrewd with a saber's wit that he used to shred anyone who got in his way. I had really used Oscar Wilde's *Dorian Gray* and Laurence Harvey's character from *Darling* as my models for him, but one New York review said my performance created the same sort of theatrical excitement that Truman Capote himself had, when he'd first exploded on the New York literary scene. And, in all modesty, ahem . . . another review said my performance was exquisite and poignant . . . soon a telegram arrived: 'All right to be poignant, even better to be exquisite. . . . Truman Capote.' At first I thought it was a prank but then a few nights later this complete stranger showed up at the theater with an invitation from Capote to drop by and visit him on Saturday."

Clint seemed intrigued and asked, "Did you go?"

"Oh yes. We had a 'right nice' little chat for an hour or two, told each other stories about Southern eccentrics and all the New York gossip—"

"But tell him my favorite part," I interjected. "When you told Capote about your . . ."

"I'll tell it, Shana; you *know* I tell things better than you do," Gordon said, teasing. "Well, when I was eight, I had a little toy homemade guillotine. And I used to sit on my back porch and *decapitate* my dolls. Capote just loved that, and said: 'What an image! A lonely child in Arkansas, on a hot summer's day, having his own little French Revolution. How delicious.' "

"That's wild!" Clint said with his oft-used phrase which would later become the one Gordon used for his good-natured Clint imitations—which Clint himself loved. It seemed "Mr. He-Man" was captivated and not at all homophobic; he even told Gordon and John how to find some local gay bar there in Phoenix—although Gordon had never had any interest in them. (It surprised me that Clint knew about this.) Clint talked openly about his own early years and how desperate he'd been to work and how he'd become very close, a protégé actually, with his first mentor, a director, a Mr. Lubin, who Clint said was gay. "We spent a lot of time together, traveled together. He liked me a lot; got me into the talent program at Universal, gave me a lot of breaks. Bought me some nice clothes, too. That's when people started wondering about us!" Clint laughed.

Gordon, who never let anyone off the hook, prodded, "So come on, Clint. You can tell us the truth."

Clint glanced up sheepishly and said, "I'll never tell."

We all laughed. The ice was broken, the two most important people in the world to me seemed to like each other.

One of the things that I was proud to have contributed to *Gauntlet* was my suggestion to get the well-known artist Frank Frazetta to paint the artwork for the film's ad. It remains my favorite artwork for any of the films Clint and I made together. It was particularly exciting for me because I got to meet with him and pose for him because we had to be on the East Coast at that time. Warner Bros. had scheduled a sneak preview for *Gauntlet* and Clint decided to locate it in Pennsylvania because he had to pick up his new Ferrari Boxer, which was arriving on some ship; it would also give us the opportunity to pick up the Frazetta painting, in person. The paint was still wet as we placed it in the Ferrari!

The flurry of interest in me after the release of *Gauntlet* was perhaps the greatest since *The Heart Is a Lonely Hunter*. My reviews outshone Clint's but he didn't seem to mind. In fact, he seemed to thrive on the attention I was getting. The press wanted to know more about me and Clint, wanted to interview me, photograph me. The famous photographer Rebecca Blake asked to shoot me; her photos are still some of my favorites, probably because they barely look like me. They're very sophisticated and heavily made-up, very high fashion. Clint hated the way I looked in Blake's photos because he hated for me to wear any makeup at all. In our films together he never allowed the makeup man to touch me. In our personal lives he always looked askance at me if I applied the slightest bit of makeup, even when we were going out to dinner or a special event. He liked me best the way I looked around the house—that meant with hair hardly brushed.

Life with Clint went along in some perfect bubble that is almost impossible to describe—it was like living in a monarchy. No one questioned or threatened our existence together; the outside world knew only what Clint wanted it to know. After *Gauntlet*, Clint made *The Enforcer*, and even when I wasn't in a particular film, I would be on location with him. That became a pattern for us. On *The Enforcer* he rented a large apartment in the hills above Union Street, as well as one in nearby Sausalito. We stayed in San Francisco during the workweek, then on Saturday drove out to Sausalito, where we lounged on our deck and watched the sailboats go by. In the evenings we strolled down to his friend Patterson's place, the No Name Bar, and listened to Fats Waller on the jukebox singing "Your Feet's Too Big." Clint loved that I responded to the blues music of his own childhood. Next to working, listening to blues and jazz was Clint's favorite thing to do. Often in Los Angeles we could be found sitting together in a dark corner in Dante's, listening to Bill Watruss's saxophone softly wailing "Here's That Rainy Day." With his arm around me, we listened to the soulful music, and he gently and quietly sang the lyrics of "For All We Know" in my ear.

I was deeply in love with what I saw as a gentle little boy hiding inside the strongest daddy I could ever imagine. Every time we had to be away from each other, even for a few days, I cried like a schoolgirl.

After *The Enforcer* Clint rented a small house for me in Carmel. It was easy to forget the reality of any outside world because we essentially created our own. Whatever we needed, Clint snapped his fingers and it was there. I admired his ability to make things happen. I had also come to have respect for Clint's potential as a film director, which I thought was greater than he had allowed himself to believe or explore. This was at a time in the mid-1970s when Clint was getting no respect at all from the critics, even though he was enormously popular and loved by his die-hard fans. He was persona non grata in the world of awards.

As Gordon and I had promised and hoped our close bond was not changed by our physical separations. When Clint and I were in Los Angeles, I spent a lot of time with Gordon, and whenever I traveled we spoke almost every day. And anyway, when we were apart, I felt I carried him with me even if we were on separate continents.

Gordon was still living at the Andalusia and he and John were very close and spent a great deal of time together. Ultimately, theirs was not turning out to be the perfect *romance* they'd hoped it would be, but in spite of that they were devoted to each other; it remained a very important relationship for them both.

In the beginning when we were in Los Angeles, Clint and I stayed in his private apartment adjacent to his office on the Warners lot. Soon we moved into his small house in Sherman Oaks, which he and Maggie had acquired during his *Rawhide* success. It was a late-fifties hillside bungalow, aesthetically and architecturally everything that I didn't like. The main living area opened onto a back porch and a small lawn with a very pretty little swimming pool—Clint loved to tell me how he and some friends had dug it themselves. Not a single piece of furniture had been moved in that house for a decade; even when it had been in style, it was hideous. It wasn't because the house was small or inexpensively furnished—I was certainly not a snob about that—but it seemed to be a mix of every terrible color, every terrible fabric, ugly shag carpets, hanging beads for doors, a fifties matching bedroom set that looked as if it were made of plastic. Stacks and stacks of old papers and magazines had just been left around as if the house were a warehouse. Clint saw it as just another hotel room; to me it was a nightmare. Worst of all there were photographs of Maggie and Clint, on tabletops and on walls, as well as some paintings Maggie had done and signed. And the third small bedroom was still filled with Kyle's and Alison's baby furniture. It was all incredibly weird and painful to me and yet Clint didn't even seem to notice. For me living in that house made it hard to maintain the safe picture I had constructed about our life together. After all, whatever the private truth, here was Clint's official public life staring me in the face. I was constantly reminded that, to the world, I would be labeled only as an affair. Fortunately we spent little time there; usually we were traveling.

Clint's world remained a tight one. For many years the only people allowed at all close to us were, for the most part, the people employed by Clint: the cast and crew of each film we made (carefully hand-picked for their discretion); his attorney, Bruce Ramer; his agent, Lennie Hirshan of the William Morris Agency; his business managers, Roy Kaufman and Howard Bernstein; Fritz Manes; Bob Daley; and the top executives at Warner Bros. over the years. There was Frank Wells, who had been Clint's attorney before he became president of Warner Bros. (Frank eventually moved over to help run Disney and was later tragically killed in a helicopter accident returning from a skiing trip.) Then came the other Bob Daly (the CEO of Warners) and his then-wife, Nancy, Terry Semel (executive VP and eventual co-CEO of Warners) and his wife, Jane. Of course, Clint had his drinking and golfing buddies in Carmel. From my side I brought only Gordon. Any other of my friends or acquaintances slowly dropped away. At Clint's insistence his agent became my agent, his business manager mine, his attorney (though I rarely needed one) mine—even Clint's dentist became my dentist. I became encompassed by him in every way. Since Clint didn't want me working apart from him, and since living with Clint meant being ready at a moment's notice to jump on a plane, I no longer thought about making even the most casual plans of my own. Clint was the pilot. Without my even realizing it or feeling it was a bad thing, except regarding Gordon, Clint became more and more exclusively my world.

This didn't bother me at first, because by nature, we both preferred a quiet, private life and it would remain so throughout our years together. We would show up for occasional Hollywood special events or awards, but those were superficial occasions—no one there really knew us and we didn't really know them. Hollywood was a peculiar place where I was never quite sure who actually knew whom anyway; more often than not, it seemed that only the press agents actually knew each other. When The Variety Club honored Clint (years later on) hardly anyone in the large audience *knew* him personally. Jimmy Stewart, whom we'd never met, gave a speech; Joan Collins, whom we'd never met, sat very near us. Yet everyone acted like good friends. Once Clint and I were at the popular restaurant Spago. We were leaving, and as it goes, we were greeted by people at other tables as we passed by. Suddenly someone grabbed my hand. "Sondra, call me. I'm staying at the Beverly Wilshire and I don't know a person in town! Promise now!" It was Liza Minnelli. Liza Minnelli didn't know a person in town? I really doubted that one; after all, she had *grown up* in Beverly Hills and on the MGM soundstages of her mother's movies.

Partly because of denial, partly because of my lack of need for convention, and partly because of the way Clint and I existed in our own protected world, it was easy to slide along, conveniently forgetting the situation with Maggie, because it didn't seem to affect our activities in any way. And because Maggie lived in quiet, out-of-the-way Carmel, she didn't bring anything to a head; according to Clint, she still knew nothing about me. Apparently because of the nature of their relationship Clint had rarely been home anyway, so perhaps nothing seemed different from her perspective. We could have been living in separate realities. As was my nature I waited patiently for Clint to handle things in the best way for everyone involved, especially the children. Then, before I knew it years had gone by. Finally, however, it came to a head, but not as I had expected. One evening in 1978, shortly after Clint and I appeared together on the cover of *People* magazine, we were at home in the Sherman Oaks house when I heard a loud rumbling from our bedroom. When I went in to check, I saw Clint dragging out a large suitcase from the closet. This was especially odd because he rarely packed any luggage except his carry-on. He was usually in jeans and a T-shirt, so I soon changed my own ways. As the years went on, we rarely traveled any place that didn't already have a wardrobe waiting for us—whether it was to another one of our houses or to the film location, where the costumer would worry about it all.

"What are you doing with that big case, Clint?" I asked.

Almost as if it were a nonevent, he answered, "Maggie wants to go to Hawaii." I stood there dumbstruck.

"What do you mean, a vacation? You didn't mention anything to me." With Clint everything usually came out in little tiny snippets, but this one really threw me.

"Maggie asked me about you, and I told her," said Clint.

"What do you mean? What did she say?"

I couldn't fathom what it could mean that, after such a revelation, he was now on his way to Hawaii with Maggie. Had she convinced him to give me up?

"She wants us to go there with the kids to see if we can 'work things out,' save our marriage, I guess," he replied.

I was getting more and more agitated. "Clint, would you please sit down and tell me what's going on. Tell me from the beginning. This is making me very upset." Tears began to well up in my eyes. He walked toward me and put his arms around me. "Sveetie," he said, "I'm trying to make it as easy for her as possible. You know I've told you that she's emotionally fragile, and although we both have known our relationship was over years ago, still when the reality hits, it's hard."

"I understand that," I said through my tears, "but what if she convinces you that you and I shouldn't be together? I couldn't take that."

"Don't worry, Best-est in the west-est, in the whole universe-est; you're the only girl for me. I just have to do this the way I have to do it."

By now we were on the bed and he was kissing away my tears. "What did she say to you? What did you say to her?" I asked.

"Some so-called friend of hers told her of the rumors about us, and so she asked me directly if it was true, and I told her it was. Then she asked me how I felt about you, if it was just an affair, and I told her that I'm in love with you."

Like a small child who'd received approval, I said, "You told her that? Oh, Daddy, you told her you love me?" My emotions were so mixed up. In spite of the tangled skein of the situation, all I wanted to feel was relief that it was out in the open, and pride that Clint had told her he was in love with me, that I was not like any of his affairs of their past.

"Yes, I told her. And now I feel like I should take this trip with her and the kids, because she needs it."

"Of course, you should," I responded. "You're so sweet, Daddy. I love you."

"I love you too, baby," he whispered.

"As much as ever?" I asked.

"More than ever."

After Clint returned from Hawaii, it wasn't long before he told me Maggie had hired an attorney to file for a legal separation, but she was not filing for divorce. This puzzled me because those were not actions of a woman who had given up a relationship entirely. I was disappointed that there was not to be an immediate filing of the divorce papers, but Clint felt it was important for Maggie to conclude everything "her way." In retrospect, it's interesting how the whole "marriage or not" issue evolved for me with Clint. In the beginning, I guess I wanted Clint to be divorced and marry me. I'll always remember how on one of our trips to northern California to visit a childhood friend of his, an older gentleman had introduced me as Clint's "bride." Clint grinned from ear to ear and later said to me, "That sounded good, didn't it?" And it did. Then, as years went by (Maggie didn't actually divorce Clint until around 1984) somehow it no longer seemed to matter. I truly believed that Clint and I did not need papers to validate the commitments we had made to each other. Also at that time, more and more people were beginning to live together and not marry—marriage was, it seemed, no longer favored by convention. And Clint knew the nature of Gordon's and my relationship, and was unconcerned that legally *we* were still married. In my conscious mind then, my marriage with Gordon was a financial protection for him. If something happened to me, he would be saved from unnecessary taxes on any assets I would leave behind. If in the future, Clint and I were married, I would have turned over all those assets to Gordon anyway, so then of course it wouldn't have been an issue. Also, my marriage to Gordon probably remained symbolic of my commitment to care for him and of the special place he would always hold in my heart. Unconsciously, however, I suspect there were other reasons that I didn't rush to change the paperwork of my life. Later I would analyze many things more closely, from my point of view as well as from Clint's. Lili Zanuck would eventually say to me, "Sondra, you have less of an *agenda* than anyone I've ever known."

Thinking everything would be perfect if Gordon could also find someone as I had found Clint, I wished for that. I wanted him to have everything I had. And around that time I was especially concerned for him, because he had fallen into one of his depressions. However, I reminded myself that historically those depressions were often a prelude to something extraordinary.

For instance, in August 1975, three months before I was cast in *The Outlaw Josey Wales*, he had become completely obsessed with the fact that, as he put it, "You're so wonderful. It's not right that you should vegetate and spend your whole life with me. I'm gay." John didn't know what to think. "Gordon's miserable," he told me, "he can't stand the fact that romantically you're alone."

So in 1978, after examining a series of his omens and connections, Gordon was led to a particular ad in the personals column. None of us, including Gordon himself, could figure out exactly why he had chosen to answer that one ad, nothing in it seemed to fit Gordon at all. But answer it he did, and it marked his beginning with Bo.

His name was Harper Bowman (he was called Bo by all those close to him) and from the beginning there seemed something destined and full of magic about it all. Some of the magic Gordon and Bo made themselves, and some was unexplainable. It was extremely romantic and full of intrigue.

Even though they both lived in Los Angeles, they wrote to each other for three months before meeting—"Sort of like something you'd see in an old romantic MGM movie," Gordon said. Neither knew where the other lived, and they exchanged presents, tokens, and symbols through a go-between. Two of the things Gordon sent were especially meaningful to Bo, who was a poet. One was a little Baggie full of the earth from next to Gordon's front door and the other was an antique Arthur Rackham bookplate of Philemon and Baucis, done for Hawthorne's *A Book of Wonder*. In it, two trees, a long-married couple honored by the gods for their devotion to each other, an oak and a linden, have grown together so they seem to be one tree. In return, Bo sent back to Gordon his high school football letter jacket, and most magical of all—a pair of little wooden shoes he had worn at the *same age* as Gordon had worn his. Bo's aunt had brought them to him from Holland, and when Gordon turned them over, he was transfixed because, like his own, they were scarred and pitted from wear.

There were also other uncanny connections between them. For instance, Gordon was living at the Andalusia on Havenhurst Drive and the next street over from it was *Harper*. Bo's family's home was in Glendora, California; the next street over from them was *Gordon*. "There are—no accidents," Bo wrote. A year or so before Bo placed his ad, he had visited the chapel at the Mission of San Juan Bautista a few miles from *Hollister*, California, and prayed to God that love would enter his life. At the time Gordon replied to Bo's ad, Bo had moved to *Hollister* Street in Santa Monica. It seemed some perfect "Gordon omen." Artie exclaimed, "It is an old MGM movie; it's preordained!"

I loved Bo from the start. He was clearly a special human being: intelligent, sensitive, evolved, and extraordinary. He had such a beautiful face, with striking eyes that seemed to see right into your soul, not unlike Gordon's. And he was incredibly bright and gentle. At that time he was extremely health-conscious, a vegetarian, and knowledgeable in Eastern philosophy and religion. He wrote the most remarkable poetry, which deserved to be published—something he dreamed of. Much of his poetry explored themes of the light and dark of life's journey, and he seemed to "get" who Gordon was from the very first. This was clear in the poetry and letters he wrote to Gordon, before they met and over the course of their years together; he comprehended Gordon in ways that neither John nor I had. What had always been so special about Gordon, and what I had accepted as just innately and uniquely Gordon, Bo understood and embraced—in very specific ways—from a far more mythic and even spiritual point of reference.

Their first meeting was at once both poetic and intensely romantic. Although they had exchanged numerous photographs and talked daily by phone for a couple of months, they had decided that they wouldn't actually meet until a certain symbolic date, May 26. As time went on they couldn't stand the wait. And since they'd sworn not to see each other until then, they decided their early meeting must take place in the dark. The plan was that Gordon would wait for Bo in John's pitch-black bedroom. For the occasion, Bo brought Gordon a loaf of bread and red wine—a gesture Gordon saw as simply romantic, like "a jug of wine, a loaf of bread, and thou," until years later when he recognized through Bo's poetry and letters that, for Bo, a symbolic *communion* had been enacted.

Gordon arrived with two things he felt were symbols of himself: "Chimney," a realistic-looking, large-as-Gordon, beautifully handmade stuffed bear (which Gordon felt symbolized his innate animal instincts), and a very detailed model he had made of Bavaria's Castle Neuschwanstein (which symbolized his love for fables and "happily ever afters"). After they made love and as Bo was leaving, he quickly scribbled four or five little notes on a scratch pad for Gordon to later find, one of which said, "I love Chimney" and another that said, "I love Gordie because he makes me *see* things I know are *true*." Bo would later tell me, "If I am the poet, then Gordon is poetry."

Because they hadn't managed to wait until their predetermined May 26 "official" meeting date, they decided to reenact their earlier meeting but this time Bo did not leave. They stayed together and as the sun rose on April 26, they gazed upon each other's face for the first time. And they were in love.

chapter 7 ~

Sometime in late 1977 Clint's secretary, Judi, had brought a new script into the office. It had been floating around for several years, and had fallen into the hands of her husband, Bob, who thought it might be right for Clint. Bob was a sound-mixing engineer with aspirations to produce. Clint liked the script, and in mid-1978 he produced and starred in it (allowing his first assistant director, James Fargo, to direct) but didn't offer to bring Judi's husband, Bob, into it at all. I was not privy to what went on between them, but I always sensed there were some bad feelings as a result of it all, which eventually resulted in Judi leaving Clint's full-time employment.

The script was entitled *Every Which Way but Loose* and in it Clint plays a bare-fisted fighter (Philo Beddoe) who gets in over his head when he falls in love with a neurotic country and western singer (Lynn Halsey-Taylor) and pursues her across the country accompanied by his two best friends, a guy and an orangutan. I was to be Lynn Halsey-Taylor.

It was during the filming of it that another one of those peculiar Gordon things happened. At lunch Gordon, Bo, and I were in the caterer's line when a very crude member of the crew broke line. With some smart-aleck remark, he shoved Gordon aside to get in front of him. I could almost feel the energy around Gordon explode; I half expected Gordon to whirl around and let the man have it, but he remained quiet. We prepared our trays and headed for my trailer. As we mounted the steps, I noticed Gordon still glaring at the man, who had now paused to speak with another crew member. With his eyes still on the man, Gordon said quietly but intensely, "I want you to get that creep fired. He's mean."

I replied, "Hobbit, just ignore him; he's ignorant. Come on inside and let's eat." But Gordon just continued to glare at him. The next thing we knew, the man's entire tray flew out of his hands and fell to the ground. It was so spooky. Bo and I just looked at each other. And even creepier, the man looked straight at Gordon, who just smiled and turned away. "You did that, Gordon, didn't you! Somehow you did that!" Bo and I accused Gordon once we were inside the trailer. But Gordon laughed. "That's ridiculous," he said. "God did it because that man was mean to me." It would be a moment Bo and I wouldn't soon forget.

It was also on the set of *Every Which Way but Loose* that I first heard a name that eventually became very meaningful — Roxanne Tunis. We were filming in L.A. in the country and western club the Palomino, and I sensed something about this one particular extra. I noticed Fritz Manes (the producer) and his wife, Audie, talking with her, which seemed odd because rarely does the producer know the extras. I casually asked Fritz, with whom I had become very close, who she was. Fritz's face changed ever so subtly and he suddenly shifted the subject.

Shortly afterward, Jane Brolin, who was also visiting on the set, came to my dressing room. I sat and chatted with her, which mostly meant I listened to Jane talk. I couldn't help but feel that she was always studying me like some laboratory experiment. Then she manipulated the subject around to Roxanne Tunis, and finally I got the story. Roxanne was a person upon whom "Cl-i-i-nt had ta-a-ken pity," Jane told me in her Texas drawl. Roxanne had apparently been an extra on *Rawhide*. Now whenever Clint made a film, he always gave her a few days' work.

"That's really nice of Clint," I said to Jane.

"Yeah, Clint's like that. He's a ve-r-ry lo-o-y-al person, you know." There was something unnerving about it all but I let it pass.

Every Which Way but Loose was one of the few scripts I personally liked. Unlike its sequel, I thought, it was novel and quirky, but still I balked when Clint wanted me to sing my own songs for Lynn Halsey-Taylor.

"I can't sing. I can't even stay on pitch. I think I'm tone-deaf or something. It's just not possible, Clint. I'll make a fool of myself."

"You'll be great, lovey. I'll get you some singing lessons" were his final words.

Clint had rarely taken a hands-on approach with actors. He suggested that I part my hair on the side for *The Gauntlet*, and later for *Bronco Billy* he would kick me under the table when I couldn't work up tears for my crying scene. But that was the extent of his direction. He used to say, "I'm like Hitchcock; I believe when you *choose* the actors, that's the direction. Then you let them go." I never had a problem with that approach, although sometimes I thought that I could have benefited from a more specific hand, a more careful director.

So, just as Clint insisted, it was arranged for me to have singing lessons from an extraordinary coach, George Griffin. He was nearly eighty and had coached many famous people from the early years of Hollywood. I loved him at once and began looking forward to my lessons with him in his house in the Hollywood Hills, which was always filled with gigantic, sweet-smelling roses from his garden. "Did you feel the way the note *fit*? Like a ball in a glove?" he'd say to me on those rare occasions I was on pitch.

On the evening of my first recording session, which had become something of an event, Gordon stopped by to watch. I was having a terrible time staying on pitch or key or whatever it's called, and Clint was slowly but surely getting quietly hysterical. I could see right away that one of the reasons he and I had always been so perfect together was that I was the straight A student and had never disappointed Daddy. Now I was not only disappointing Daddy, I was doing it in front of all these people. Snuff Garrett, the album's producer and Clint's partner in what would become his own record label, Viva, which made millions of dollars for them both, had suggested that the pianist play the exact melody into my headphones. I would sing along with each piano note, but only my voice would go on the track. I thought it was a great idea, yet Clint resisted. "No, she doesn't need that. It'll inhibit her style!" What style, I thought? He went on, "She'll get it. Just do it again, Sondra." And I did it again and again, until finally we followed Snuff's suggestion and it worked beautifully. Clint just pouted. I had been imperfect, and was therefore I suppose a loser. I'd get no gold star that night.

It was also the first occasion he attacked Gordon. That night Gordon had a flat tire. Of course Gordon being Gordon didn't know what to do, so he simply locked the car and left it! When he told me about it, I called AAA and they took care of it. But, that night when Clint and I returned home to Sherman Oaks the drama escalated. "If Gordon hadn't told you about that damn flat tire, you would have been able to sing on key," he said, his voice rising.

"What? Don't be silly, Clint. He had nothing to do with the whole situation. I told you I cannot sing."

"And I told you you could! It was *his* fault—him and his damn flat tire!"

Clint's obsession with my singing persisted. The country and western singing star Eddie Rabbitt had a major hit with "Every Which Way but Loose." After the film was released and was also a major hit, Eddie Rabbitt was appearing at the Palomino. Clint decided that it would be a dandy idea if I would appear with Eddie and sing something from our film. Before I could stop this little brushfire it had swept through Warner Bros. and everybody except me also thought it was a great idea. (Did I think anyone would disgree with Clint?) I was signed and delivered to the Palomino before I could think straight, and it was a night out of *Mad Magazine*.

I had a dressing trailer parked behind the Palomino and it was bombarded by fans. Jane Brolin showed up and nominated herself to be my "guard." I'd never particularly connected with Jane on any real friendship level, but on that night, I began to see her in an entirely different light. Her face appeared troweled on: the drawn-on lips, the heavy mascara, the full-face makeup. I'd noticed in the past that she was prone to drinking a little too much alcohol, but on that particular night I wanted to run for cover as she kept consuming it. Clint had derided her about whatever her choice of alcohol used to be, tequila I think, so she had switched to Kahlúa coffees. As far as I could tell, this only seemed to make her worse, because she seemed not only inebriated from way too much Kahlúa, but jangled from all the caffeine. She was yelling and pushing everyone away from me, "Leave her alone! *You* can come in; you can't come in." I felt like a part of some Barnum and Bailey sideshow. Clint finally showed up and only laughed when I pleaded with him to stop her "scene." Jane seemed to supply Clint's comic relief in life; all her extreme behavior was one big hilarious joke to him. I can tell you, that night I wasn't laughing at all. And neither were Gordon and Bo, who had just arrived and been promptly ushered by Jane into the inner sanctum. "G-o-o-r-don, come on in. I've heard so much about you! Give me a big kiss." Giving me a look that said "What is this horror?" he kindly brushed her face with his cheek and moved away.

From inside the Palomino I could hear Eddie Rabbitt beginning the show. My stomach was in knots and I seriously considered running away. Let Clint go up there and sing with Eddie, for all I cared; it was all his fault anyway. But being the good little girl that I was, I took my cod-liver oil without a frown. A large burly man soon fetched me and walked me through the crowded room. I just kept saying to myself, "How bad can it be? No one's going to boo me or throw things at me, I don't think. And if they do, who cares anyway?"

There was Clint sitting next to the stage grinning widely and applauding louder than anyone else. At the same table with him were Frank and Luanne Wells, John Calley, Fritz Manes, and Bo and Gordon along with Artie, all looking at each other as if they were cats that had swallowed the canaries. Everyone seemed to be enjoying this except me. From then on I remembered little except for one moment when Eddie and I sang "You Are My Sunshine." Encouraging the audience to sing along, I looked for Gordon's face. I'll get him up here with me, I thought, but the only face I spotted was that of Frank Wells. His eyes, looking like Rasputin's, locked onto mine. "Don't you dare come near me with that microphone, Sondra, or you will pay!" they said to me. I empathized.

That debacle still wasn't the end of Clint's obsession with my singing. I got booked on *This Is Tom Jones* a few years later to sing something from the "orangutan" sequel, *Any Which Way You Can*. I sang my solo from the film, then Tom and I sang a duet. Was that scary. But I survived and happily banged the last nail in the coffin of my singing.

In the fall of 1978 I enjoyed a little break while Clint filmed *Escape from Alcatraz* in San Francisco. It was something of a vacation for Clint too because he wasn't directing and producing the film as he usually did. Clint left early each morning and took a private boat to the island, and I spent my time reading and relaxing. As was usually the case on every film location, Gordon came to visit. Clint booked Gordon and Bo a suite adjoining ours; while Clint worked, the three of us explored the city, and at night all four of us would have dinner. I was especially excited during this time because the film Clint had next planned was my absolute favorite. *Bronco Billy* was the only film project with Clint that truly reflected my own sensibilities. The tone was so off-center—absurd in one moment, touching the next. Bronco Billy and his ragtag band of circus performers were such a colorful and lovable group. *Bronco Billy* was also the first time I read a script and could see it through a directorial vision instead of a narrow focus on my own character. I'd forever been in love with the circus and carnival settings and I thought Clint would be extraordinary as that character. It was Gordon's favorite too, and he—naturally being an authority on circus music!—contributed the ideas for the ones Clint ultimately used for all Bronco Billy's horse tricks. I begged him to make the film, and to me, it became his finest performance. Even today when I think of the Clint I thought I knew and loved most, I think of Bronco Billy.

Bronco Billy was definitely not the kind of story that Clint usually produced, but neither was *Every Which Way but Loose*. No one had been more surprised than Warner Bros. when *Loose* became Clint's *biggest* box office hit. Even though *Bronco Billy* was not as huge, it made money. If it had starred someone less famous than Clint, any studio would have been proud of its grosses. But when you have a superstar like Clint, the studio expects megabucks in box office receipts. Even so, the film had a major impact on the way he was perceived by the critics. In fact, the release of *Bronco Billy* was the moment when Clint's respectability began to turn.

The New York Times gave it a great review. And the Museum of Modern Art paid a special tribute to the film and to Clint. I was very proud as they all swarmed around Clint at the huge affair. "I'd like to see Pauline Kael's face now," Clint said to me later. He then proceeded to quote verbatim from her past reviews of his work. I was truly astounded that he had them memorized, despite the fact that I knew Clint often talked about Ms. Kael and clearly had a long-held obsession with her because she never liked his work. She drove Clint crazy. After her review of *The Enforcer*, Clint asked a psychiatrist to do an analysis of her from her reviews; it concluded that Kael was actually physically attracted to Clint and because she couldn't have him she hated him. Therefore, it was some sort of vengeance according to Clint. He told others that Kael had recently phoned him to apologize, saying, "Sorry about those reviews, Clint, but you know that's what's expected of me." But Clint later admitted to me that she had never called him; his story was a fabrication. To me, the whole ordeal seemed rather silly.

During preparation for *Any Which Way You Can* Clint began a new obsession, to consume vast amounts of vitamins and amino acids. We met with all kinds of authorities on the subject: Durk Pearson, co-author of *Life Extension*, and various other doctors including Dr. Harry Demopoulos, who would later sue the Doris Duke estate, claiming that Duke had intended a large portion of her estate to go to him and his "research." I was never convinced of Dr. Demopoulos's authenticity and felt there was something a little sleazy about him. He was always a little too eager to pursue "Hollywood" and "stars." Although most people kissed Clint's behind whenever they got close enough, Demopoulos appeared unseemly attached to it.

At first Clint explained that his new "megavitamin" kick was part of getting beefed up and buffed out to play his character in *Any Which Way*, a street boxer. He would keep large bowls of boiled potatoes in the frige and eat them like popcorn throughout the day. And he and I would mix the vitamins from a recipe that Durk Pearson helped him develop—a tablespoonful of this, a teaspoonful of that. It was a never-ending, frustrating experience that Clint insisted only he and I could do. He kept all the concoctions in enormous glass jars on the kitchen cabinet shelves, and after carefully blending all the powders for our latest batch, we would sit on the living room sofa scooping and stuffing the miracle powder into these enormous clear gelatin capsules. Sometimes the two ends of the capsules would bend or refuse to fit back together, and Clint would go ballistic.

"These fucking capsules are crap; they don't even fit together half the time! Why don't they make them better?" He yelled as he threw the miscreant capsules across the room.

"Well, maybe you've packed it too tightly, lovey," I'd say. "They fit before you took them apart."

"I know what I'm doing."

"Why don't you have somebody at the office do this, anyway? It's only upsetting you."

"I don't want anybody else's hands touching this stuff!"

He was actually a very funny sight battling his capsules, sometimes even jumping up and down on them.

Slowly I was getting more familiar with Clint's temper, which at first seemed harmless and funny because it was usually directed at *things*. He could not tolerate *things* that would not function perfectly, exactly when he wanted them to. The very first example I witnessed was in Las Vegas at the Jockey Club, where we stayed during the filming of *Gauntlet*. The doors to the closets in our room were typical louvered slide-and-fold doors, and Clint's closet door made the mistake of sticking and all hell broke loose. He let go with language I had never before heard and in the blink of an eye he had punched his entire fist right through the door, then looked sheepishly at me and began to snicker. Later at dinner someone who could read palms insisted on reading Clint's. The reader looked deeply into Clint's palm and said, "You are a very tranquil man." Clint and I glanced at each other; the back side of his hand was still bleeding.

It was almost as if Clint had an actual phobia of *things* malfunctioning. Once I had accidentally reconfigured the television remote controls just as Clint sat down to watch TV. When the buttons didn't respond to his touch, I could feel even the air around him change, almost as if it were invisibly whirling. He became frantic and was convinced that I had somehow "erased" all reception. "Clint, that's not possible. Programming is still out there. If you'll just calm down, we can fix it," I said. But in an ever-more panicked voice he replied, "Don't touch it; you'll make it worse!" Whenever I sensed an attack coming on, I'd usually just leave the room until it was all over. Too he would insist on *unplugging machines* when we'd leave town (especially later on at the ranch he bought in northern California). It was almost as if he wanted to make sure the machines didn't "do" anything while we were gone. Maybe they had a life of their own when we were absent. Who knew what they might be up to? Once Alison (who was still very young) accidentally flipped the switch on our tennis court lights. "Don't touch that!" Clint yelped, and rushed at her. "Those lights are sodium; they'll blow out if you turn them off and on!" Alison's eyes were as large as saucers; then terrified she ran toward the house. It was not uncommon in our (later acquired) Los Angeles house for him to take a hammer to the antique reproduction French door slide bolts, which I'd had custom hand-forged. "Can't you get anything that's modern?" he yelled. Just a harmless eccentricity, I told myself.

It actually seemed to me that the more vitamins Clint took, the worse his temper became. Some of the mixtures that he consumed in such abundance began to worry me, like selenium and Hydergene, L-Argenine, Tryptophan, DMSO for bruises, so much carotene that his hands turned orange, and on and on. "Just try this Hydergene under your tongue, lovey; your thinking will improve," he'd say. I finally became accustomed to swallowing a few of the "multivitamins" without gagging (because they were so large) and the subsequent nausea, but I drew the line at everything else. Sometimes I would take one from him, then later secretly return it to his pile.

And gone were the days of red meat and any fat. Even the avocados with the dollop of mayonnaise that we'd always had for lunch.

"Not the avocados?" I asked with horror.

"They're full of fat. And the mayonnaise! You might as well shoot up Crisco, right into your veins."

"But we've always eaten this."

"It doesn't make it right," he'd say.

"Well, at least I don't have to worry about stocking his refrigerator with mayonnaise," his secretary, Judi, said one day. She, Fritz, and I laughed because Clint and his mayonnaise was one of our favorite anecdotes. *No one* was allowed to touch the food in Clint's office refrigerator. He was obsessive about it, always checking the contents. One day he was about to prepare tuna fish salad for his lunch and his mayonnaise jar was bare. He had come storming out to Judi yelling, "Who's been in my mayonnaise? I know there was more than this in the jar! How many times do I have to tell you to leave my mayonnaise alone?" Clint hated detail in his films yet in his life often the "small stuff" seemed more important than anything else.

Those same years (1977 through the early 1980s) were full and eventful, not only because of the several films we made together, but in other more important and deeply affecting personal ways. Many decisions were made that would change the course of my life, and alter my emotional fabric. And yet those years also exemplified how basically simple our lives seemed to be. No doubt many people imagine that Clint and I lived a luxurious and glamorous Hollywood life. Not true. Most of Clint's financial power was used, not in surrounding us with lavish riches, but in facilitating ease and mobility. After our breakup the overwhelming daily details of everyday life would be the most surprising and staggering experience for me, because I had forgotten what it was like to make the day happen. With Clint and me, everything seemed to happen as if by itself. The Warner Bros. jets were always available, as were the transportation captains with our cars. Eventually we had homes almost everywhere we traveled, and if hotels were necessary, someone else arranged it all—down to the finest detail. Someone was always there with whatever we needed—then they disappeared, because Clint never had an entourage and never wanted anyone hanging around us.

We acquired most of our homes during these years. The first was in Sun Valley, Idaho. Clint bought it on impulse from a friend whose corporation had owned it. It was built on the hillside overlooking historic Sun Valley Lodge and was spread out over three stories—five bedrooms, a wine cellar, a TV room, sauna, and spa. It was quite impressive but was not my personal taste. The lines were straight and modern and cold. It was completely furnished and felt a lot more like a hotel than a home. I was always appalled that it came fully equipped with its own dishes, linen—everything—even a station wagon in the garage, but that's the kind of thing Clint loved. The most wonderful part of the house was its setting; it looked out on Mount Baldy and down on the village of Sun Valley, and when it snowed the whole scene was magical.

Initially we visited the Sun Valley house only in the wintertime for skiing. We developed a tradition of going there the day after Christmas and staying well into the New Year. After we made friends with others who also had homes there (the Richard Zanucks, and eventually the Bud Yorkins and Arnold Schwarzenegger and Maria Shriver), we began to visit in the summer and autumn as well.

At some point in those same years Clint also bought a house in Carmel, in the small residential village only a block from the ocean. I was a little concerned when he bought that house, because I knew that Clint viewed Carmel as "home," while I viewed Los Angeles as "home"—primarily because that's where Gordon was, and I feared that he would want to be in Carmel all the time once we had a real home there. Clint must have sensed my feelings, because he said, "It's just to stay in when we're here, lovey. And for Gordon to stay in too when he wants to come up." Many times we would watch the sun set into the ocean from our upstairs bedroom window. Then we'd walk downtown to the Hog's Breath Inn. After a few drinks there, we'd decide what we felt like for dinner and wander off for a quiet conclusion to the evening. Little was ever planned very far in advance and Clint liked it that way. Many evenings we'd walk down to the local movie theater to catch a film, buying our tickets just like everyone else.

Like the Sun Valley house, the Carmel house was like a vacation escape to me. Except for adding stone to the exterior, Clint left the house very much as it was when we had acquired it. Even the last owner's furniture remained in the guest rooms—and, incomprehensibly, even the books on the bookshelves. I never made many friends in Carmel; it seemed the only people I met were Clint's drinking-golfing buddies from the Hog's Breath Inn. Clint's mother and stepfather lived there and we would occasionally meet them for dinner and almost always spend Thanksgiving at their home. Merv Griffin also had a home there, and we'd occasionally meet him for tennis, or lunch or dinner.

It was generally during our visits there that we spent the most time with Kyle and Alison, who lived with their mother, Maggie, who in her settlement took the Pebble Beach house. However, Maggie placed severe rules on my relationship with the kids. Apparently, she never forgave me. And though I believe it was true for Clint that their relationship had long been over, I'm not so sure it was true for her. After she learned that Clint had taken me onto her property to show me a baby deer that had just been born there, she laid down a rule that I was never to be allowed there again. I was not even allowed to phone the Pebble Beach house. The whole situation was very sad because the kids were always torn over how they should feel about me. We would spend time together and develop good feelings, then they'd go away and the next time we'd be together there would be a renewed strain between us. One of the more touching things to me occurred when Alison wrote a very flattering essay about me for one of her school classes. It gave me hope that one day things would be normal. But Clint never challenged Maggie on her rules and never made any attempt to introduce us or dispel her resentment. I thought he was terribly wrong for many reasons, not the least of which was that it impaired our life with the kids. I was never actively able to pursue plans or arrangements for the four of us, which meant that Clint had sole responsibility for planning and organizing that part of our lives. And planning and organizing anything more than twenty-four hours in advance was not something that Clint was great at. Clint wanted everyone around him to be completely spontaneous. I adapted because Clint seemed to need it, but we couldn't expect others to be available whenever he wanted them—especially the children. Maggie wanted to know in advance *when* Clint wanted the children for summer vacation, *when* Clint wanted them for this or that, and Clint never wanted to commit. So naturally Maggie would make her own plans and then Clint would become annoyed after the fact and call her names. It was a constant pattern. For years I believed that this was why Clint didn't spend more time with his children. Later I was to believe differently.

The third property we acquired during those years was our most beloved retreat, Rising River Ranch. As a boy, Clint had lived in Redding, California, near the beautiful volcano Mount Shasta, and had again fallen in love with the area when he later made a charity appearance there. Around 1978 the Rising River Ranch fell into probate. It had belonged to Bing Crosby, who had used it as a fishing escape.

"It has its own lake and river," Clint told me excitedly. "And the water rises out of natural springs in the ground and is so pure and clear that you can see all the way to the bottom. I've got to get it for 'my girl' and me," he concluded. Clint sometimes talked about me in the third person that way: "I sure do love my girl . . . she's a good girl . . . she deserves the best of everything." Clint sent Bruce Ramer, his attorney, and Howard Bernstein, one of his business managers, to bid at the auction. They were armed with a ton of money and Clint's top figure, which they were to avoid if possible. "One point nine mil, sweetie," he told me proudly. "I didn't even have to go to my top bid." Clint got what he wanted.

I too fell in love with Rising River Ranch. It was so beautiful and peaceful—all the huge pine trees and sagebrushes were laden with snow when we very first arrived there. More than any place we traveled to, more than any glamorous event we ever attended, Rising River was the place that brought the most pleasure, the best times. At Rising River we escaped from everything and everyone and only the most special people were allowed to visit: Clint's mother stayed with us from time to time, and Gordon and Bo came to visit. I'll always remember the most wonderful Fourth of July party when we barbecued and drifted on the houseboat on the lake surrounded by pines. The sky itself was more amazing than any fireworks we could set off because at the ranch the night sky was always like a cosmic jewel box. I never knew there were so many stars in the heavens and Clint loved pointing them out and naming them for me.

Rising River was a special place that remains powerfully vivid to me, and it was also the one place where Clint was most open, where he usually revealed any of his secrets to me. And it was at the ranch in 1983 that I learned who Kimber Tunis was.

"I thought I should tell you before someone else did" was the way Clint began his explanation. "Years and years ago when I was on *Rawhide*, I had

an affair. It didn't mean anything; it was just an affair. I was young and . . .
anyway she was a stand-in and extra on the show, and she was really crazy
about me, and always hanging out in my dressing room . . ."

"Her name was Roxanne?" I asked.

"How did you know?" he replied.

"It doesn't matter. Go on."

"Well, anyway. It was, of course, long before I knew anybody like you
even existed, sweetie. And so we had this affair. Then I went to Spain to
make Sergio's film. Roxanne didn't tell me but she was pregnant. It was
only later when I returned that I found out. Anyway, that's Kimber. And
I've kept up with them and given them money over the years. . . ." He
trailed off.

"Does Kimber know that you are her father?" I asked.

"Yeah, Roxanne told her. So anyway now she's older and she wants to
get into the [film] business. I don't know . . . I guess I'll give her a job on
Tightrope . . . in the office . . . and you might see her . . . and there are a few
people who know who she is . . . and something might slip out . . . and I
wouldn't want you to hear it that way . . ."

"Who?" I couldn't imagine who knew more about Clint than I did.

"Oh well, Glenn Wright [Clint's costumer since *Rawhide*] knows because, you know, he was there during *Rawhide* and all . . ."

Clint looked so vulnerable about the whole thing, so worried about how
I would receive this information that, instead of my head taking serious
note, my heart went out to him. After all, we all make mistakes. I threw
my arms around him. "Oh, Daddy, it doesn't matter."

"It happened before I met you, baby. Before I ever really knew what love
was."

"I know. It's okay. I understand."

It was also at the ranch that Clint and I would make a major decision
that would forever change the course of things, especially for me. Though
there is much I have blocked about it all, there is much that feels like
yesterday. The Warner Bros. jet landed at the private airstrip in Redding,
California. It was dry and warm, and I could smell the dust in the air as
Clint and I stepped onto the tarmac. Bob Moore, our ranch caretaker, was
standing beside the van and waiting to drive us over the mountain to Rising
River Ranch.

"Hey, Bob, how is everything?" I asked as I approached him.

"Oh, everything's fine, Sondra," he replied. "Sure is good to see you
two."

As usual I could feel the tension from the real world and life in Los Angeles leave my body as we all settled into the car for the hour's winding drive—Clint in the front seat with Bob, and me in the back.

"Are the lilacs still blooming? Are the Canadian honkers there with new babies yet? How's the garden?" Clint and I bombarded Bob with many of the same questions each time we visited the ranch. We could hardly wait to get there so we could luxuriate in doing nothing.

"The lupin, too. They're bloomin'," Bob said as we made the turn and headed up into the mountains.

"How are Floy and Smokey?" I asked. Floy was Bob's wife, and Smokey was their big black and white Manx cat.

"Floy's fine. Been puttin' up vegetables from the garden. And Smokey's the same as ever—gettin' fatter by the day."

I closed my eyes, leaned my head against the backseat, and listened to Bob and Clint exchange all the recent ranch news, about the wildlife, or the headwaters Clint wanted to acquire. Suddenly I felt Clint's hand reach over his backrest toward me, something he always did as we made that drive. When I put out my hand for him to take, he turned and looked back at me with a boyish grin on his face. I loved him so much. The hum of the ranch van and the drone of Clint's and Bob's voices began to lull me, and I drifted off to a sweet place. It was amazing how my body had such a deep, almost instant, response to being at the ranch, every inch of it letting go.

Before I knew it, the hour had passed and I could hear Clint opening his car door. I opened my eyes, and saw Clint working the combination lock on the big gate. Then he swung it open for Bob and me to drive through, and stretching out in front of us was the long narrow road that led to the main house.

I watched Clint pluck a few leaves from the sagebrushes near him. When he returned to the car, he rubbed them between his fingers and held it under my nose for me to smell. It was a tradition. Smelling the sage marked the beginning of our stays at the ranch.

"Um-m-m," I said as I inhaled it. "It always smells so good."

"Look, sweetie, there's a doe with her fawn," Clint said, pointing.

"Where?" I asked. Clint could always spot them long before I could.

"Over there behind that pine tree," he said.

"Oh, I see them. The baby is adorable. Oh, look at them."

As our car approached, the mother stared at us with her big eyes and moved her huge ears in our direction; then in complete unison mother and baby quickly bounded off in slow-motion leaps across the field.

We rounded the curve of the circular driveway that cut across the big front yard full of pine trees. Thanks to Bob, the grass was all lush and green. When we had moved in, this same lawn had been covered by at least a foot of old pine needles. Clint and I spent days raking it ourselves, just to see what plants might be underneath. We enjoyed doing simple things like that at the ranch.

Part of the special experience of the ranch was the particular rituals involved. We always made a quick change into our ranch clothes and were out the back door in a hurry to begin our traditional three-mile walk along the dirt and gravel road that meandered through the property.

First, we'd pass the chickens and the roosters and the turkeys in their big pen under the trees. "Gobble-obble-obble," I yelled at the turkeys as we passed by.

"Gobble-obble-obble-obble," one of the male turkeys with a big red wattle under his chin called back at me. Clint laughed. He loved the way I could talk to them. It seemed I was the only one they'd answer.

On our right on a natural rise in the field just behind the big green lawn of the ranch house was the swimming pool that Crosby had filled with dirt and we had unearthed like some wonderful buried treasure. The wild geese loved it as much as we did, especially Flapper, the one we hatched in our living room.

Next was the big old-fashioned barn with the tall hayloft. I loved to walk inside it; it was so cool and dark and mysterious. Clint, however, couldn't go there because of his allergy to animal hair, which was so severe that, when he had to ride horses in films, he would first have to sniff medication into his nose and lungs. On *Bronco Billy* it was really a nightmare and left him constantly miserable.

The vegetable garden Bob always planted for us was one of our delights. Just before dark we'd go there and "shop" for dinner each night. "Doesn't taste like this in the markets," Clint always said.

We continued our three-mile walk down toward the river to the log cabin we had built. We never actually lived in our cabin, but we visited it daily when we were at the ranch. Sometimes we'd have lunch there or take a nap in the lazy afternoons after making love. We'd had such fun building the cabin, except for the problem with the man who originally sold Clint the logs. It was one of those companies that provides all the exact pieces for the construction, like a kit made to order from the plans. He absconded with twenty-five thousand dollars which Clint never recovered; Clint *did not forget* it and tried for years to track him down.

Clint took the key from underneath the bench on the front porch, where we always left it hidden, opened the door, and we walked inside. Everything was just as we had left it.

"It looks like the bats are still getting in here," I said.

"Yeah, that sound machine isn't working," Clint replied.

We climbed the stairs to the bedroom, which held my favorite of the four beds I had had made in L.A. My eyes moved to the large framed color photograph that hung over it. It was of me, taken on the set of *The Outlaw Josey Wales*. I smiled as I looked at myself, standing there, eating an apple, in my full Western costume — with that hat I had loved. Whatever happened to that hat, I wondered. I had meant to keep it.

I walked out onto the upstairs balcony to join Clint and looked out at the river that as usual was nearly still, with only the tiniest of ripples blown by the wind. I glanced away and into the distance where Mount Shasta stood impressively, snow draped around its top like marshmallow topping on a sundae. Even in the summertime, with everything else green around us, Mount Shasta always stood majestically white in the distance. "It's like a brain massage, isn't it, lovey?" Clint said. Then we stood silently. Our visit to the ranch on that particular day in 1979 was not an aimless one as it usually was. We had something very serious to discuss.

"What are we gonna do?" I asked, gently approaching the subject we'd been postponing.

"Well, baby, you know how I feel," Clint said.

I had learned that I was pregnant.

It was not my first pregnancy. The previous year in the summer of 1978, we had had to face the same dilemma, and I had reluctantly agreed to an abortion. It was a hard and painful decision, but Clint had convinced me that it was the only reasonable answer. It was difficult for me to argue the point, because Maggie had only just learned about us then, and Kyle and Alison had had no time to adjust. However, the concept of abortion was not something I had ever even turned over in my mind; I had never been pregnant, no close friend of mine had been pregnant. Even Gordon, with whom I naturally talked about everything, only said, "It's something only you and Clint should decide."

In truth, I had never contemplated having a family or not. But "abortion," despite my "pro-choice" politics, was a horrible word and, if I had allowed myself to think about it, a horrible deed. But denial can be a short-term savior, so I flipped a switch somewhere in my head and heart and had taken denial's hand. After all, Clint had been clear and unmovable on what *he* wanted me to do. I abstracted it all. Through a reliable reference, Clint had arranged for a doctor at UCLA to perform the abortion for me. A woman. I liked her immediately; she was sensitive and thoughtful, and before I knew it, it was all over. And I tried to forget.

But now in 1979 we had to face the same decision again. Before I had met Clint my gynecologist had suggested and fitted for me an IUD. Because my sex life was not very active, he did not think I should be constantly taking birth control pills. Clint complained of the IUD—it was uncomfortable for him, he said. And he too was not in favor of birth control pills, so he suggested a special clinic at Cedars Hospital where they taught a "natural" method of birth control. It was the same "rhythm" system that historically has been used to determine the fertile days for those who are attempting to achieve pregnancy. Of course, it could be used for the opposite results as well. Not only was I taught their method but I was constantly monitored with regular pregnancy checks. The whole process was awkward and entailed taking my temperature every morning and marking the calender, etc. It was demanding and ultimately it had failed twice.

"Well, you know I feel the same way I did before, sweetie. I don't really want any more children," Clint told me softly. "I'm concerned about you're having another abortion, though."

I waited for Clint's lead, as I usually did in our life together, and eventually it came down to his unmovable desire not to have more children. I couldn't help but think that that baby, with both Clint's and my best qualities, would be extraordinary. Suddenly I hungered for it. But I shook it from my head. I knew that I would not make that decision on my own; I would again listen to Clint. I would please him.

"If you have a child our whole life will change, you know that," he said to me.

It was certainly true that we lived a life that was never homebound; we worked when we wanted, played when we wanted, got on a plane when we wanted. Clint needed it that way and I knew that he would not change his nature. If nothing else, our nearly constant physical togetherness would be over. And though I did not consciously accept it, I already understood on some deep level that life is good with Clint only when things go his way. And having things "good" with Clint was still all that mattered.

"I'll call my doctor and schedule the abortion," I told him.

Not looking at me, he continued on. "We should really make some final decision about this. I don't think it's healthy for you to keep having abortions; and I don't want you to go on the pill. You know, Jane had a surgery to prevent pregnancy. What would you think of that?"

I could feel my heart in my throat. It was not that Clint was taking something away from me that I had absolutely counted on or had consciously planned on . . . it was just that any decision from which there is no going back is a scary one.

"What is it like?" I asked quietly.

"She said that it was a very simple out-patient procedure. Nothing to it."

"And you think I should do that?"

"Well, sweetheart, I don't think we should go on this way. Do you think you want to spend your life with me?"

"I never want to be with any other man except you. How could you even think such a thing?" Then I began to cry. "Don't you always want to be with me? Like you said? How can you even say such a thing to me?"

He turned and put his arms around me. "Sh-h-h-h, don't cry. I know I've found the person for me. But I'm a lot older than you. I've been around and I know you're it. You're my 'best-est.' If you're sure you feel the same way about me, then, I think it would be the best thing for our life together. Aren't I enough for you?" he whispered, gently smoothing the hair behind my ear. Funny how it never even crossed my mind to ask *him* to have surgery.

I was in my early thirties. And the die was cast.

That night we curled up together in the big four-poster bed.

"Goodnight, sweetie," he said. "I love you."

"As much as ever?" I asked.

"More than ever," he replied. "We're still on our honeymoon. We'll always be on our honeymoon."

"Goodnight, 'only one,'" I whispered; then, snuggling deeper under the covers and pressing tight against him, I sighed and thought that everything would be okay. We were meant to be together, and would always be together.

I flew back to Los Angeles alone, insisting that Clint remain behind. Frank Wells and his wife, Luanne, were coming to the ranch and their trip had been scheduled for some time. Anyway I knew that Clint could not be seen at the hospital because the whole thing could turn into a big tabloid story. And I guess a part of me wanted to pretend that it wasn't the monumental event I knew it was. Gordon and Bo took me and picked me up afterward. Back at Gordon's apartment they tucked me into bed and brought me cool things to drink. I slept and slept until I could almost forget about it. In a few days, Clint returned and we went back to life as usual, pretending it had not happened.

After that I couldn't bear Clint and Maggie's old house in Sherman Oaks. I was constantly redesigning it in my mind. I could replace the metal and glass sliding doors with French doors, or lay hardwood floors, or retile the bathrooms and the kitchen. But I knew it was, after all, Maggie's house and that's what it would always be. Finally I told Clint that I couldn't live there any longer.

"Lovey, I told you you could do anything you wanted to this house. It's your house now."

Then, in a completely uncharacteristic move he even pulled out his will and showed me that he had already assigned it to me. I was a little surprised that he would bring up such a thing, but it was as if he thought it constituted proof to me. I responded that I didn't want the house, and though I had thought about renovating it, no matter what, psychologically it would always be Maggie's house. Clint was very sweet and understanding. "Well, of course, sweetie. I don't want you to be unhappy. Go find yourself a house you love and I'll buy it for you."

It wasn't possible for me to be any more excited. I had never owned a real house. I don't think I consciously understood it at the time, but finding a house, and building a nest, was also a way of licking my wounds about the tubal ligation. This home would be my baby.

My real estate broker was Denise Fraker, the wife of my old friend and director William Fraker. I trusted her, which was absolutely necessary because with Clint, secrecy was a necessity of life. No *outsiders* could know where he and I were at any time, nor could anyone know where we were *living*. And *God forbid* if it got in the tabloids or on a map to the stars' homes, the sky would surely fall. When Denise and I met prospective sellers or their agents, she introduced me as Mrs. Anderson. And on the few occasions Clint came along, he introduced himself as *Mr.* Anderson! Denise and I had a good laugh about that, because Clint and his six-four frame were so recognizable as Clint Eastwood that the sales agents, trying hard to keep a straight face, had always looked at their feet when they addressed him as "Mr. Anderson." On one occasion "Mr. Anderson" showed up wearing a T-shirt with *Thunderbolt and Lightfoot* printed across the back!

Denise and I drove day after day to every house that remotely matched my descriptions. Finally one day in 1980, lightning struck at 846 Stradella Road. It was love at first sight — even the name of the street was beautiful.

The house was set on the peak of one of the many rolling hills of Bel Air. One could see very little of the property from the street, which is exactly what Clint and I wanted. The style was Monterey Revival, which is a form of quasi-Spanish, a simplified Spanish, used widely in the northern California area of Monterey. It seemed to stare out at me and cry for attention like some beautiful orphan child who wanted someone to love and heal its wounds. It had been owned for many years by one woman who lived there until she was quite elderly; she had left it to her nephew and now it was being held for sale by the bank.

"Oh, Denise, I love it. It's just perfect. It reminds me of the Andalusia. I could make it look just like that!"

Actually it had none of the Andalusia's detail, but I saw how I could turn it into a near twin. It had two stories with the long balcony across the upstairs front. Inside, it was built in a U shape around a garden with a central fountain, just like the Andalusia. The living room had a similar two-story ceiling with an imposing fireplace at one end and French doors opened on to the garden from all sides. The house was about five thousand square feet, including the maid's room, laundry room, and garages, and was more rustic in nature than formal.

The back looked out on all the lights of Los Angeles and away off to one side you could see the distant ocean. The garden was overgrown and the fountain was a bit tacky. Beyond the back patio and fountain area there was a low stone wall, then a small lawn, and then the property started down the hillside. This area was magical too; I could almost feel the heart of the elderly lady who had planted and enjoyed it all. She had terraced the property all down the hill with little bridges and every kind of tree and bush imaginable. Underneath a kumquat tree was a bench with beautiful sculpted tiles of various fairy tale characters. Not since I had first laid eyes on the Andalusia had I felt such a strong emotional reaction to a building. I knew I was *home*. I could hardly wait to tell Clint.

When Clint saw it, he too liked it, especially for its views and its privacy. "Are you sure now, lovey? It looks like it needs an awful lot of work."

"I know, but I'll enjoy that. I'll be able to make it just the way I like. I know this is the only house I want . . . ever. And you can probably get it for a good price since it does need so much work."

"All right. I'll call Roy and tell him to start negotiating for it," he said.

Ultimately Roy closed for $1.1 million, a very good price, considering the amount of land, which is at a premium in Los Angeles. Most similar properties in the area were valued anywhere from $3 million to $8 million—absurd, but Los Angeles westside property is *very* expensive.

"It's all yours, sweetie," Clint said one night. "Roy closed the deal."

I was so thrilled. Even though it was late, I had to go see it again. We explored every inch of it together, stumbling around in the dark because there was no power except the lights of the city beneath us. As we stood holding hands and looking out at them, I felt like the luckiest and happiest woman alive.

Clint later told me proudly about how he worked the purchase of the Stradella house. He had borrowed from his own retirement plan, thus creating some sort of good deal for himself. I had no idea what it all meant, but he seemed proud that he could be open enough to share it with me, as if it were a great and intimate revelation: "I've never told anyone *anything* before you, sweetie." How sad, I thought, but heartbreakingly sweet. I didn't look on it as a clue to problems inside Clint; I looked on it as a confirmation of the uniqueness and importance of his love for me.

Over the next three years I poured my every extra moment and my very soul into renovating Stradella. It was a complete labor of love for me. I didn't hire a contractor, or a designer or decorator, or even a secretary. I did it all, including all the phone calls and all the endless legwork. Clint was away on location a lot at that time, first on *Firefox* (in Vienna) and then on *Honkytonk Man* (in and around Nevada), and so I had a lot of time on my hands. He knew I was not a big spender (something else he liked about me) and knew that I would scrutinize every cost.

As my own contractor, I had to hire the plasterers, painters, tile installers, electricians, plumbers, carpenters, landscapers, and even the drapery makers. I walked from store to store to find just the right fabric for the chairs and sofas, the window seat, the bedspread, the draperies. I wanted everything to be special, not necessarily the most expensive, just the most "me."

Mrs. Uhl, who was thrilled I wanted to copy her building, was a big help to me. I took exact plans off all the turned posts from the balconies, the corbels, the stair railings. She even loaned me the original plan for the brass finial atop the courtyard fountain, and I found someone to make an exact copy for mine. Finding workmen for all the specialty work was a major accomplishment in itself. No detail was too small or too unimportant for my attention.

The tiles were one of the biggest challenges. The ones at the Andalusia had been made by the California Tile company in the 1920s. Their designs and method of hand painting were very authentic Spanish. I searched for months to find someone to copy the tiles exactly as I wanted, and at one point Gordon and Bo and I even took the Warner Bros. jet to a small village in Mexico famous for its tiles, but with no success. Finally back in L.A. I happened upon a freelance artist, Jim Sullivan, who experimented with me to make what I wanted.

While all the work was in progress, I threw myself into the study of landscaping, purchasing and planting almost every vine and flower myself—jasmine, honeysuckle, clematis, all my favorites.

Even Warner Bros. pitched in on the project. I was told that I had carte blanche to use the studio facilities for whatever I needed. I especially took them up on their offer when it came to the stonework. I had the columns (which I copied from a book) and the fireplace façade for the living room sculpted and cast in cement to look like rotten stone at the Warner Bros. plaster department.

Every piece of furniture was lovingly hand chosen, mostly antique and rustic. My favorite piece in the whole house was one hand-painted cupboard from the Pyrenees. The only problem was the beds. I loved the designs of the antique beds but they were all too small. Gordon, who had already done much of the renovation artwork for me, helped again and designed our beds, which I had made by a company in Texas. They were perfection; you couldn't tell they were not as old as all the antiques.

Gordon was altogether a tremendous help, not only with his artistic eye, but once even on his hands and knees. Clint and I were at the ranch, and I had just had the floors refinished to an antique look. I asked Gordon to check on them. He found the floor drying with thousands of tiny bubbles all over it. He, Bo, and Tomas, my caretaker, spent the entire weekend hand-rubbing all the wood floors to smooth the finish. By the time Clint and I returned they were perfect. Of course, Gordon never let me forget that one! His knees were raw from it all and I had to buy him presents for some time to come.

Fortunately, Clint's business manager, Roy Kaufman, had been wrong about his concern that the renovation might possibly lead to conflict between Clint and me. Clint was very busy with his films and whenever he had time off, I would travel to the ranch or to Carmel or wherever he wanted to be. Clint seemed quite happy to leave all decisions to me, particularly since he had little interest in details and less in decor. I always teased, "Give Clint beige walls and a brown sofa and he's happy." He seemed amazed and proud at all that I had accomplished. After we moved in and gave Warners CEO Terry Semel and his wife, Jane, a tour, Clint told Terry that now he knew I could handle the production of *any* film after what I had done on the production of the house.

Building my home was an extraordinarily intensive and sometimes seemingly endless job but it became the fullest and most personally fulfilling creative experience I'd had. It inspired and utilized all my visual talents and I understood, for the first time, what enormous gratification an artist who paints a canvas or sculpts some clay can feel as he or she watches it all take shape before his or her eyes. In all ways the property did become my "baby." The renovation went on for three years. Even after we moved in in 1983, I continued perfecting the house and its gardens. It would become my favorite hobby, finding the tiniest little things that were just "perfect" for it. It brought me much creative pleasure and finally a sense of a real home to share with Clint.

Perhaps the most wonderful thing—and ultimately the most spiritual—about finding Stradella was that it led us to find our precious cat, Chloe. To me, she was like a guardian angel. Just after we'd bought the property I was giving Gordon and Bo a tour when we saw a flash of red scurrying through the underbrush. "Looks like you've got a fox on the property," Gordon said. Bo went off exploring and soon returned carrying a huge cat that at first glance looked like a bobcat. She was the largest, most beautiful cat I'd ever seen, an enormous orange-striped tabby, with the most beautiful green eyes. When Bo put her in Gordon's arms, she was completely relaxed, not tense like many cats; she was floppy and snuggly soft—"Like butter," Gordon always said. There was a feral quality about her and gradually we surmised that she lived alone in the wilds of old Bel Air. "Maybe she had belonged to the elderly lady who had lived here until she died," I wondered aloud. When we put her down, she immediately began to pad along after us, making the most peculiar little trilling sound. Gordon sent Bo to the Bel Air market for a can of sardines and a half pint of cream, which she hungrily devoured. "She looks like the cat your character gave to Bruce Davison in the film *Willard*," Gordon said, "so I think I'll call her Chloe." As we sat in the overgrown back courtyard, Gordon called to her, "Here, Chloe," and she instantly came to him. Bo and I were amazed and soon discovered that she'd come to us as well. It was clear she understood she had been given a name, and that afternoon, when it was time to leave, we left her sitting like a little sentinel crying out loudly after us. Gordon said, "She doesn't want us to leave."

Gordon would often go up at night to draw blueprints and leave instructions for all the workmen. And when he did, the first thing he would always do was call out into the overgrown hillside, "Chloe, Chloe-e-e." And always in a matter of minutes, off in the distance, a trilling answer would come until she'd break through the brush running to spring up into his arms. "I swear, she seems more like a dog than a cat," Gordon marveled. I couldn't take her with me to Sherman Oaks because of Clint's allergies. And Mrs. Uhl allowed no animals at all at the Andalusia. Occasionally Gordon would take her for visits to his apartment; if Mrs. Uhl had only observed, it would have occurred to her that Gordon had begun doing an inordinate amount of grocery shopping, for he was always coming in with a big brown grocery bag! The first time Gordon put her into a grocery bag, she lay perfectly still, like a little secret agent, until they were safely inside. After that, she *knew* and would, on her own, crawl into the big brown bag and quietly wait. For the most part we decided to leave her where she was, but we worried about her and sometimes each of us would go up at night and call her for no other reason than to make sure she was all right. It was clear that Chloe could take care of herself; she had once happily come bringing Gordon an offering. He looked down to see her walking across the Spanish tiles of Stradella, positively strutting with power—a large mouse's body hanging out of her mouth. Another time, she answered his call but didn't come. He followed the sound of her "voice" until he found her lying regally in the underbrush with an enormous rabbit by her side; she had broken its neck and lay there looking up at Gordon, as proud as any lion on the African savanna purring over its kill. But after Gordon saw a coyote pursuing her, he decided to find out if she would live in his apartment at the Andalusia. It was to be her decision. She loved it, especially the bed. And during the year she lived there, never once did Mrs. Uhl have a clue that Chloe was there. Although cats are notoriously curious and Chloe love to prowl and snoop in every nook and cranny inside, she never once poked her head through the curtains. It was clear that somehow she "understood" she was in hiding and had completely given up one of most cats' favorite pastimes—spying out of windows.

Clint's attitude regarding Chloe was rather funny. He exhibited a proprietary air because she had been found crossing our property, and Clint, who had never had a cat because of his allergies, suddenly became an expert on feline behavior. One afternoon Clint and I stopped by Gordon's apartment for something. It was after Chloe had moved in, and Gordon was feeding her and petting her as she ate. "You don't want to touch her while she's eating, Gordon," Clint said, as if he really knew anything about her. "And you wanna make sure she doesn't get out the front door." I almost laughed; Clint could hardly keep his hands to his sides he was so anxious to direct everyone. Gordon, who always took Clint with "a grain of salt," replied in one of his "voices," not unlike our high school English teacher's, "Well, I'm just go-o-nna have to take that un-dah advisement, Mistah Eastwood." Clint laughed self-consciously as Gordon continued stroking Chloe's silky fur.

No one treated Clint as casually as Gordon did, and I think that amused and intrigued Clint—at least at first. He would often make me tell him and others the latest "Gordon" story, and his favorite remained the time Gordon walked out of a dentist's office right in the middle of treatment. Gordon had a sudden abscess and his regular dentist was on vacation, so he was forced to go to someone he'd never met. I had driven him there and was waiting in the outer room, when the door suddenly flew open and Gordon came tearing out, ripping off the heavy X-ray bib and throwing it on the reception counter dramatically. "I don't like it here and I'm going home," he said with the candor characteristic of a child. "The *assistant* kept trying to stick a pointy tool in my mouth with no concern to the hellacious pain it caused me. And she couldn't understand a word I said. She just kept saying 'Expectorate!' and, every time she said it, she spit all over me—plus she had 'big hair' and looked like a witch. I wanna go home," he said with no regard for what anyone might think or what he was going to do about his tooth. Then he exited, leaving me sitting on the sofa, magazine in hand, while the receptionist and the girls behind the counter stood there with their mouths hanging open.

Then there was the time during the filming of *Bronco Billy*, in Boise, Idaho, and Gordon and Bo were visiting. In Clint's and my bedroom was an elaborate sunken tub, which Gordon had spied and, as soon as Clint left, filled and jumped in like some child who's discovered his first swimming hole. In five minutes, Clint, who had forgotten something, returned to find Gordon splashing merrily around in our sunken tub. I wondered how he'd take it, but after a moment of astonishment, he suddenly began to laugh.

It was quite interesting that Clint seemed agreeable to almost anything Gordon asked him to do, such as amazingly staying up till 2:30 A.M. for a phone call. For Clint, who maintained a rigid health regime, this was unheard of.

Gordon and Bo were planning a trip to Europe and Gordon decided the time had come for him to *continue* his quest and unravel the mystery of France's most forbidden implement, La Guillotine, which he had tried to do once before in 1971. I was amused two weeks before that trip when he announced he was writing a letter to Alister Kershaw, the author of *A History of the Guillotine*, the book I felt he had almost willed into publication when we were in high school. He sent the letter to the publishers in London and I was amazed when a reply arrived from Mr. Kershaw himself, saying he would be delighted to meet Gordon and that he would also be bringing Jacques Delarue, a member of the Sûreté Nationale, who was also fascinated by the guillotine and its executioners and was planning to write his own book. (Delarue's book, *Le Métier de bourreau*, was published in 1979.)

Gordon, of course, was full of questions about the mechanics of the machine, but neither of them had ever been permitted to see it. "The only people who could have that privilege," Kershaw drolly commented, "are the executioner and his staff, the prison officials, the prison chaplain, the attorney for the condemned, and, unhappily, the condemned himself."

For Gordon's current foray to France, I had made as many calls as I could, using every imaginable connection from Merv Griffin to Christopher Lee, but Gordon had decided his best chance would be to pass himself off as a member of Warner Bros. research department ("it sounds much more official, Shana") and prepared a letter of introduction. He asked Clint to have it translated into French and German and typed on Warner Bros./Malpaso (his company) stationery. "No problem," Clint replied. "When you get all this research done, maybe you'll make me a model guillotine for my desk." Then it suddenly dawned on me that I knew the perfect person to help, a well-connected publicist in Paris who, if anyone could, would be able to accomplish the task. I told her that Gordon would be arriving to do research on the guillotine for one of our upcoming films. Unfortunately, poor Gordon had no idea that his arrival in France would coincide with a politically charged debate and then the vote on whether or not to *abolish the guillotine*! My publicist friend could get nowhere. It seemed that every French journalist was trying to obtain au courant pictures of "the machine," as it is referred to in judicial writs. It was, to put it mildly, the worst possible time for him to have tried to see it. He sent me numerous clippings about the upcoming vote on capital punishment, most of them showing prop guillotines from the movies, which Gordon noted with disdain. But shortly thereafter he called from Paris extremely excited. The publicist had arranged for him to speak with Pierre Salinger, who was the French correspondent for ABC television in America. Salinger knew France's Minister of Justice, Robert Badinter, socially and had made an official request to him to photograph the guillotine. Ironically, Badinter was himself a collector of guillotine memorabilia. Salinger assured Gordon that he felt quite certain that he would be allowed to film it for ABC News the next day, and that Gordon could accompany his film crew!

Gordon was tremendously excited and said they would be going to the prison at Fresnes the next day. I shook my head and conjured up the image of Gordon probably jabbering a mile a minute over the phone to John F. Kennedy's press secretary! "The only catch is Salinger wants to schmooze with Clint Eastwood. So put him on. I've got to beg him to stay up till 2:30 A.M. so Salinger can call him." Clint only laughed and did stay up for that call.

As it turned out, Badinter *denied* Salinger's and ABC's request. And that should have been the end of that. But, Gordon remained undaunted. Even when Bo had to return to California, he remained. A week or so later Bo and I were to meet Gordon at the airport. "Well, tell us, did you see it?" we asked. He then reached into his pocket and pulled out a small pocket tape recorder and clicked the button. Bo and I both listened, our eyes wide, to the sound of what must have been a ponderous mass falling downward and crashing loudly at the bottom. "There she is." Gordon smiled triumphantly. "No more secrets, the mystery solved."

The way it had all happened was totally improbable and filled with impossible details. It had involved adventures in three countries and, in spite of Clint (who was by that time in Europe filming *Firefox*) having furnished Gordon with a limo, a driver, a translator, and a still photographer, ultimately, it had been Gordon himself, with his what-if attitude and by paying close attention to his clues and omens, who had found the way to an official French guillotine. He returned with over three hundred pictures—detailed shots of everything down to the tiniest screw, as well as a sixteen-millimeter film made by a professional cameraman of Gordon himself working it! And an article from *Paris Match* containing an interview with a former executioner stating how in his twenty-nine-year career no photograph had *ever* been allowed.

The first time I worked apart from Clint since Arkansas in 1976 was in 1981 and it happened only because of unusual circumstances. We were at a celebrity tennis tournament hosted by Merv Griffin in Sedona, Arizona. I loved Sedona; it seemed tinged with a mystery and energy all its own. In front of Clint, Merv approached me: "Sondra, I promised my friend Rosemary Clooney that I would speak with you about the television movie they're going to make of her life. She's dying for you to portray her. She doesn't want anybody but you to do it. What do you think? You'll have a ball; Rosie is a great gal."

I remember looking at Clint, knowing his feelings about my working apart from him. And I had mixed feeling myself. I loved working with him too, and I wanted to make him happy, but I also knew that professionally I was clearly getting swallowed up in his shadow, and if I ever expected to do anything else on my own, now was the time. A flicker of anxiety passed across Clint's face before he glanced toward Merv, then said, "That'd be wild, sweetie. What do you think?" I guess I could tell he was pleased that Rosemary Clooney wanted me, but still I knew he was uncomfortable, or threatened, or something. Even though it was only a television movie with a short schedule, maybe he feared what it might lead to.

Everyone was staring at me, so I said, "Rosemary Clooney is wonderful. I'd love to do it, especially if *she* wants me."

"Well, she does; she loved you in *Bronco Billy*."

Merv's tennis tournament was a fabulous few days. On the last evening, during a beautiful dinner dance, Clint did something that I found baffling. After dinner, we got up to dance on the very crowded dance floor. It was a slow dance and I was enjoying just having his arms around me and moving to the strains of the orchestra, when suddenly he blurted out, "Would you let *me* do the leading!" It was a remark that seemed to come out of thin air; I had no idea what had led up to it. I certainly know how to dance, and I don't lead. In my many years with Clint, "leading" in anything was something that I had never been guilty of. I couldn't help but feel it had something to do with my decision on the Rosemary Clooney project.

⁓

AFTER THIRTEEN YEARS of accumulating things, Gordon finally decided that his apartment at the Andalusia felt too small and that sadly he would have to move. Also, now that I had Stradella, I wanted him to have his own home too. Denise helped me look for a house to buy for him, and it wasn't an easy task, for Gordon was unhappy with anything we showed him. He had very specific tastes. His childhood sketchbooks were filled with half-timbered medieval-looking cottages, like the charming dwarf's cottage in Disney's *Snow White and the Seven Dwarfs*. Where could one expect to find one of those in Los Angeles? There were many "fantasy" cottagelike houses around, but Gordon felt they were too exaggerated. In a way that only happens with Gordon, he found the perfect house. One afternoon he discovered the most magical house; it was a superbly realized Tudor cottage with irregular wooden shingles that gave the house the appearance of having a thatched roof. It seemed to be just waiting for the Seven Dwarfs to come home from the mines. There was only one problem: It wasn't for sale. Often he went out of his way just to drive past and admire it. And then one day, just as Denise and I were going out to look at a few more houses, he announced, "I just drove by that house I love, and guess what?" I answered, "There's a FOR SALE sign out front, naturally." And so there was.

When I told Clint the story and that it was more than I could afford, he asked how much it cost. Hesitantly I told him, but he merely shrugged his shoulders, and said, "I'll buy it for you." I was overjoyed, and although I knew it was expensive, it was certainly not very much money for Clint; also

he loved real estate. He had no interest in the stock market; he always said
he liked to own things that he could see and enjoy, and he appreciated it
when someone else felt that way. "Besides," he added, "you don't spend a
lot of money on jewelry and stupid stuff like some women. I'll get it for
Gordon. I'll call Roy and tell him to make it happen."

There was one strange glitch to the purchase of Gordon's house. After
Gordon had moved in, Roy presented me with a piece of paper that appeared to be a lease. He spoke in circuitous business language, saying that
it would be some sort of "write-off" to Clint's benefit if we did it that way.
The monthly "lease" amount was arbitrarily set at a thousand dollars and
he explained the arrangement: I would deposit that money with him, and
at the same time I would also forward all bills for any maintenance or other
costs (including phone, gas, etc.), which he would pay with the "lease"
money. I was a bit thrown by his suggestion, but after all, at Clint's insistence, Roy had also been advising me and invested all the fees I collected
from my film work. Still, this "lease" made me uncomfortable enough to
ask Clint about it. I even offered to take no fee for the next film in exchange
for Gordon's house. He seemed alarmed that I would suggest such a thing.
"Don't be silly. It's Gordon's house; it's just a business thing for me." I just
needed to hear it from Clint and I was fine about it.

Gordon was very excited, but leaving the Andalusia turned out to be
traumatic. And he began to photograph and document every artistic detail,
not only of his own apartment, but everyone else's as well, as if he were
about to construct the perfect replica. It was the closing of another chapter.
When everything was moved out, Bo had been waiting at the car for Gordon
for quite a while and decided to go retrieve him. As he entered the courtyard
garden, he saw Gordon through the large front window of his old apartment;
with raised arms he'd pressed himself against the wall of the empty apartment. "He was telling it goodbye, wasn't he?" I asked. Bo nodded with a
tender smile. "And I'll bet Gordon left lots of his little secret messages
hidden here and there." And, of course, I later found that he had.

Chapter 8 ～

In 1982, Clint and I made what would turn out to be our last film together. Only in hindsight can I wonder if it had anything to do with my decision to do the Rosemary Clooney film. Our film started out as a treatment sent to me by Earl Smith, who had written and directed the film I'd made in Arkansas. Earl's story was about a young woman and her sister who are raped as teenagers. The sister never recovers emotionally and becomes a hospitalized catatonic for the remainder of her life. The other girl, who carries a deep wound of another sort, decides to enact a revenge plot against the boys who raped them.

Things had seemed all right between Clint and me while I'd filmed the Rosemary Clooney movie, so I thought maybe I could stretch a little further. Earl's story was a good one and I believed it could be produced as a small and interesting film; I told Earl that I would develop it with him. Naturally, I talked about it with Clint, hoping that he would have no objections. But before I knew it, Clint had bought the treatment outright from Earl, had hired a writer of his own choice, and begun to turn my story into a Dirty Harry film, without even so much as a courteous "Do you mind, Sondra?"

It was doubly surprising because the process of developing stories was something Clint never bothered with. Although he had all the money and resources to develop any story or character for himself that he wanted, he never did. He'd always choose whatever appealed to him from those scripts offered him. It required less personal investment that way.

It was Fritz Manes who finally spoke with me about it. "I'm really surprised that Clint has taken over your story. I thought it was supposed to be something just for you. And, personally, I think you need to do something on your own."

In my heart I agreed but only answered, "I know what you're saying, Fritz, but I'm happy making it with Clint. I don't mind, really."

Fritz didn't leave it at that; he even mentioned it to Clint, who only said, "What are you talking about? It'll be even better for her if it's a Dirty Harry film." And I think Clint believed that at the time. It was so automatic for Clint to control things to his own advantage that, most of the time, I think he wasn't even aware that he *was* controlling. And right about then Clint needed a commercial story—preferably a Dirty Harry story. His recent film *Honkytonk Man*, in which he'd played a dying country and western singer alongside his son, Kyle, who played his nephew, had been a terrible flop. I was sorry about that because I had greatly admired the screenplay. "I guess they don't like your old dad anymore," Clint said to me when it had such a poor box office opening. His next film, *Firefox*, hadn't done very well either. Clint needed a sure thing; he needed a Dirty Harry, and I had a story that would work. At this point it was hardly any surprise to me that he was selfish, but then, I reasoned, so are many people who reach the tops of their professions. My project was scripted and filmed and was finally called *Sudden Impact*. It was the most commercially successful of any of the Dirty Harry films. Clint was happy. Therefore, I was happy.

Fritz, still disturbed by it all, made sure that I was given a substantial raise for that film. I had never really given much thought to the less-than-market-rate salaries I'd received for the films I did with Clint. I viewed those salaries as pocket money because Clint supported me and everything else. But I was stunned when Clint objected to Fritz's thoughtfulness. I had learned all too well that Clint was more than economical; he was downright cheap—but then that was something I'd known about him from the beginning. I just never thought it would apply to me. Fritz put through my raise nevertheless; more than likely Clint was too embarrassed to put his foot down. Clint never mentioned any of it to me, but in hindsight, it provides another possible reason *Sudden Impact* was the *last* time he ever hired me to work with him.

Another thing I noticed early on about Clint was a certain discomfort he had with other people's illnesses or physical imperfections. In Clint's opinion the physical well-being of a person was everything. If you were overweight, or out of shape, or had an illness, you aroused a certain amount of suspicion—there must be something lacking in you. He didn't want you around. I think he feared that it would somehow rub off on him. At times he even spoke about Alison with indignation because she had put on a few pounds—"She's getting a fat ass," he would say. "She'd better watch it; she's gonna have the 'Eastwood women's hips.'" It caused Clint no end of distress because he felt he too had wide hips. It was his only physical flaw—except the chipped front tooth that he eventually had fixed. I was disappointed about that, for I'd always loved that chipped tooth.

My first hint that Clint could not tolerate physical imperfection occurred as early on as *The Gauntlet*. Late one night when we were filming in downtown Phoenix, some locals were watching. Among them was a tiny man about three feet tall, who obviously had severe birth defects. I looked at him scrambling with difficulty trying to get a good view of us as we set up a shot. I felt an enormous compassion and said to Clint, "Did you see that little man over there? Do you think we could give him a job, make him an extra or something? I bet he'd be so excited." "Don't look at him" came Clint's reply, "don't make eye contact." This was the first time I'd heard him say that, but I would hear it again whenever he did not want to be "touched" by another person. It was as if Clint felt that he would be contaminated if he allowed the person to connect with him.

Rarely did Clint acknowledge any flaws of his own. I was really surprised when, sometime in the mid-eighties, he had hair transplants. He actually finally *admitted* that he was losing his hair, but like everything else he was unbelievably secretive about it. The surgery coincided with an unexpected visit from Kyle and Alison. The four of us sat around the dinner table, Clint with his head wrapped in white bandages (like *The Invisible Man*), acting as if the bandages weren't even there. Finally Alison asked, "What's wrong with your head, Dad?"

"Oh, I had a bicycle accident," Clint replied. Alison's and Kyle's eyes immediately cut across to me as if to say "Yeah, right. When does he ride a bicycle? What's really up?" Actually, the whole situation was so ridiculous that it was all I could do to keep from laughing.

I interpreted these quirks of Clint as either humorous eccentricity or simple human failing. I believed that they came out of ignorance or fear—but in any case they were forgivable—after all, we all have flaws. However, there were a few instances when Clint's aversion to illness or imperfection sent up a red flag I shouldn't have ignored. One of them involved something Gordon did, and it showed perfectly the vast difference between them when it came to human compassion.

It all began with a letter from Pat, Gordon's sister-in-law. Besides Pat never being very nice to us, she never failed to use my celebrity or Gordon's many talents to score points with whomever she was trying to impress. In this particular letter she was asking Gordon if we could help her find where to get information about getting a wig for a "little boy who has lost his hair due to leukemia." Annoyed, Gordon said, "Now why does she have to write us? Shelbyville's only fifty miles from one of the country's entertainment capitals; Nashville's got plenty of wigs and hair. She's not being altruistic about this. It's just about making herself the center of the melodrama."

Throwing the letter down in disgust, he went on, "Maybe she's trying to get in some new garden club."

Pat had enclosed a photograph of the young boy, whose name was Greg, and several hours later I found Gordon sitting on the sofa studying it. Clint was busy and asked me to fly to New York to publicize *Sudden Impact*. Out of the blue Gordon asked, "If you're taking the Warner Bros. jet when you go to New York, do you think Clint would let you fly straight into Shelbyville first?" I wondered about his change of heart, but Gordon explained that he had called his mother and asked her about Greg. She said Greg was a wonderful boy, fourteen, very sensitive, loved movies, and was currently wearing a knit toboggan cap to school to hide his bald head. He had refused to wear the wig his mother had bought him because it didn't look "real." Some of the country boys had bullied him and taken delight in yanking it from his head. Greg, Mrs. Anderson said, was in love with movies and everything to do with Hollywood. "Screw Pat and her agenda; I've gotten past that. This is *not* about her anyway." He paused thoughtfully, then continued, "Don't you agree it's *no coincidence* that I'm from Shelbyville; I live in Hollywood; he loves movies and you're a movie star; and most of all, when I was sixteen, I taught myself to *make* wigs?" He got up and picked up his car keys. "Okay, God wants me to do this," he said, and off he went.

Although at the time I knew that what he had decided to do was extraordinary and generous, I don't think I understood until many years later that what had happened in that moment—the change in his reaction to his sister-in-law's letter and his rising above his feelings about her—was that he had transcended his own ego. I would later come to believe that it is this gift of his that is the key to so many things about Gordon, and perhaps why so many unexplainable things seemed to happen, even arrange themselves, for him.

He returned with a wig he had purchased, which was the ugliest thing I'd ever seen. It was a hideous henna woman's wig, and the hair must have been twenty-two inches long. "Why on earth did you buy that thing?" I asked. "Well, he has cancer; he's sick; he needs a transformation and I want him to see this wig undergo one as well. I'm sure he feels horrible about himself and maybe even a little hopeless at times, and if I take something that looks like this mess and make it into something beautiful just for him, it then becomes a metaphor for him. Plus I intend to imbue it with a sense of magic for him by telling him that Arnold Schwarzenegger gave it to you just for Greg—one of the wigs from *Conan the Barbarian*, I'll say."

When we flew home, there was big excitement with the private Warner

Bros. jet arriving from Hollywood and landing on Shelbyville's tiny runway. Greg was brought on board and excitedly looked all over the plane. Thus began our friendship with Greg's parents. We were invited to their house the next day and Gordon began his alchemy. We fitted and pinned the wig's foundation, which I took back to Mrs. Anderson's and stitched up. The next day when we went back to check the fit, Gordon cut the hair of the wig, just the way Greg had worn his. We left with a sample of Greg's own hair his mother had saved, and that night Gordon spent hours matching the color perfectly and inserting a beautiful handmade part in the center. And the next day, in the blink of an eye, Greg found himself staring into the mirror looking exactly as he had before becoming ill. He was speechless, staring at his reflection transfixed. "I can't believe it. How . . . I mean, it looks so real. I look just like I used to." Then he threw his arms around Gordon and said, "Thank you, thank you, thank you." Greg's whole demeanor had changed. His father and mother instantly recognized the change and their eyes filled with tears. They too embraced Gordon, and said, "You've given us our son back. Isn't there anything we can do for you?" they asked, embracing Gordon.

"Absolutely not. I loved being able to do it for you, and who knows," he said, putting his arm around Greg's shoulder, "maybe this is the reason I had the knowledge of making wigs in the first place."

Gordon didn't stop there, however. The next day he called Greg, who wasn't feeling well enough to go to school, and invited him to come downtown with us for a walk. Greg was flushed and happy, wearing his new wig out for the first time. We rarely went downtown; word spread and many people peered out from the storefronts. We could tell Greg felt like a star, which is exactly what Gordon wanted. "Why don't you give Sondra and me a tour of the new high school?" Gordon asked, timing it perfectly because he knew we'd be arriving at the school just as it was letting out. As the three of us walked down the halls, students with shocked expressions began recognizing me. Becoming aware of footsteps behind us, we turned to find thirty or forty students walking in a hushed silence several paces behind us. The next time we turned around that number had multiplied to at least a few hundred. Kids suddenly eager to become part of our little parade began coming up to greet Greg and ask for my autograph. Then, as the three of us were getting into the car to leave, one boy yelled out at Gordon in a sullen and angry voice. "Hey man, who the fuck are you?" Gordon whispered, "I'll bet he's one of the ones who pulled your toboggan off, isn't he?" to Greg, who nodded shyly. "Well now, I must be a Somebody or you wouldn't be asking, would you?" Gordon said, embarrassing the boy.

"And if you want anyone ever to wonder who you are, you're going to have to change your lousy attitude." His line was a hit with the crowd, who let out war whoops of approval.

Gordon had not only made Greg a wig but had created the whole scenario just to bolster Greg's ego at a time when he needed it most. Perhaps it was all the pain Gordon had suffered in his childhood or maybe it was some innate gift that allowed him to put himself in another's place and seemingly be able to feel what that person was feeling that made Gordon the most empathetic person I have ever known.

Sadly, I began to suspect that Clint had no empathy for others. Though he had honored my request and ordered up the plane for me to fly to Shelbyville, at the same time he expressed disbelief and wonder that Gordon was going to so much trouble; after all, Clint pointed out, he didn't even know the boy and was getting nothing out of it. It was also clear that he viewed Greg's illness as something "not to be around." I told myself that somehow I hadn't explained it properly to him, but I knew I had.

I guess, even though I deeply loved Clint, I never viewed him as a highly evolved person. I accepted his limitations. He had always been incredibly tender with me and thoughtful. I always thought he would do anything for me, just to make me happy; he had never failed me. But I began to question my belief after the experience on *City Heat*. Blake Edwards called me about a script he owned and planned to direct, and asked me to read it with the thought of playing one of the two female leads, the society girlfriend. Blake had seen me in *Bronco Billy* and said he'd loved my performance. I liked Blake's script and thought it could do for me what I had initially wanted *Sudden Impact* to do, to take me out of Clint's shadow, so I told him I'd love to do it.

Out of the blue, he then asked me to pass the script to Clint, and before I knew it Blake and his wife, Julie Andrews, were having dinner with Clint and me. Then Burt Reynolds was suddenly brought in, and within a few weeks, I was simply out of the mix. And forgotten.

There was little question that Blake Edwards had used me just to get close to Clint. This is something not surprising in Hollywood, and I was hurt because Clint had been a party to it. He also didn't even notice, nor did he seem to care. We were at the ranch when I expressed my feelings.

"I can't make my career decisions on whether or not you get some job!" was Clint's response.

I was wounded and shocked that he only saw what had happened from a business point of view—he had a *job* and I didn't. Playing a role in *City Heat* wasn't what really mattered to me anyway. What mattered to me was that I had been used, deceived, and then dismissed, and I was hurt that Clint had not stood up for me. The least I needed was for him to acknowledge what had happened and to defend me in some way. I certainly hadn't suggested that he drop out of the film, although *I* would have done so if I had been in his place. And now I had apparently committed a mortal sin by even bringing this up. It was the first time he had made me feel this way and I was shocked. And, yes, I'd learned he was self-centered, but I chose to see it in stupid little ways that didn't really matter. And I knew he had personality problems when it came to connecting with most people. But he had connected with me and I loved him. In spite of his flaws, I had always thought that to him I was the most special thing on earth, but now I felt that he didn't even know who I was. So he wouldn't see the tears in my eyes, I turned, left the kitchen, and took a long walk down to Rising River.

My walk made me feel better, but after this experience, a little voice from time to time whispered in my ear, "Yes, but what *is* love to Clint? How much is he really *capable of?*" Because I was in love I was able to brush that voice aside. Clint and I had so much together, and circumstances also made it easy for me to brush it aside. Our life was so problem-free that only rarely were the boundaries of Clint's love for me tested. Ironically, our lack of problems was probably the glue that held us together for so long . . . with not even an argument.

On the surface Clint had what he wanted: unconditional love, admiration, and surrender. And I then thought I had what I wanted: a strong, uncomplicated, and gentle man who adored me, was the "Daddy" I had never really had, and took care of me. He freed me from grown-up responsibilities. This allowed me complete freedom to enjoy life and to be creative, and I guess, to remain the child I thought I wanted to be. It had all seemed so perfect.

IT DIDN'T BOTHER ME that right after *City Heat,* Clint went without me to New Orleans to film *Tightrope* (in 1984). I even recommended Genevieve Bujold for the role when Susan Sarandon had turned it down. I had always admired Genevieve's talent as an actress and had felt a little connection to her because her first Hollywood film, *Anne of a Thousand Days,* had been released around the same time as *Heart Is a Lonely Hunter.* At the time, I was still busy on Stradella. But then after *Tightrope* came *Pale Rider* and I found myself once again suggesting the actress Clint would work with, not playing the part myself. This time it was Carrie Snodgress, whom I had loved in *Diary of a Mad Housewife*. I was fine with it, but I was beginning to wonder why it was going that way. Then Steven Spielberg asked us, as a personal favor for him, if we would do an episode for his new television series, *Amazing Stories*. Clint directed and I starred in a piece called "Vanessa in the Garden." It was a period piece, which I'd always wanted to do. Steven and I had a bit of history of our own — actually more than I had realized at the time. One night at a dinner party, he was seated beside me and told me that he'd had a huge crush on me right after *Heart Is a Lonely Hunter*. He said that once he and I were in the same elevator together at Universal and all he could do was stare because he was so smitten. "Why on earth didn't you say something?" I asked him. "You could have introduced yourself at least." "Oh no," Steven replied, "I was a complete nobody then. You wouldn't even have spoken to me. I didn't know what to say." I assured him that I was never like that and I would have been very flattered. It became a little joke between us every time we met.

I also enjoyed the filming because it gave me the opportunity to work with Harvey Keitel, whose performances I had always admired. I had suggested him to Clint and was pleased when he had accepted. We shot it in a week's time, and during it Clint and I seemed as close as ever. My hurt from the Blake Edwards experience and any other lurking concerns were gone — I had successfully buried them. We were at home at Stradella, and I thought we were as happy and committed as ever. What I didn't know was that Clint had given a small part in *Vanessa* to a woman he'd met on *Tightrope* — someone he was *having an affair* with. As I look back on it, I'm repulsed how comfortable he was working with both of us side by side on the set. But that was a Clint I did not yet know.

Through chance or otherwise, I was no longer acting in Clint's films, my house on Stradella was finished, I was at a loss for what to do with my creativity. It was apparent that having acted so exclusively with Clint for such a long time had dramatically affected the way I was now perceived: It was Clint and Sondra, Sondra and Clint. In people's minds I seemed to be joined to him at the hip. However, one of the *advantages* of having worked with him so closely was that I had been around for the entire filmmaking process — reading the scripts, casting, filming, editing, and postproduction sound mix — and I loved all of it. So I began to explore the idea of turning to directing and mentioned it to Clint. "That'd be a great idea," he quickly responded. I was somewhat surprised because he had always been so weird when I'd talked about doing anything apart from him. When I had once talked about switching from the talent agent we both shared at Clint's insistence, he became very upset. But I thought okay, and started looking for a script that might give me a chance to express something different that would reflect my own individual sensibilities, something that would be "me." When I found it, I also found the beginning of the end of my relationship with Clint.

The script was *Ratboy* and it was a quirky adult fairy tale, a social satire of sorts, about a young woman named Nikki, who is so obsessed with fame and fortune that she is blinded to real values in life. She happens upon a creature, half boy, half rat, and decides he'll be her ticket to the "big time." Naturally, the little innocent Ratboy is almost killed in the process, but, in spite of that, à la Beauty and the Beast, he falls in love with her, and through his pure love for her, Nikki has an "awakening."

I shared the script with Clint and explained why I wanted to direct it. I wasn't sure what he'd say about it because it was very off-beat, atypical material for Clint. To my surprise, he said, "It's wild," which meant he approved. After one very brief meeting with Terry Semel (then president of Warner Bros. Pictures) I had a deal to direct, and star in, *Ratboy.* With Clint in your corner, it can be just that simple. Clint and Terry seemed to think that having me star in the film was an asset, and, as a first-time director, I could hardly imagine how difficult such a thing might be, so I agreed.

From the very beginning *Ratboy* seemed doomed. To begin with, it never seemed wise — or necessary to me — for Clint to be the producer. We had worked together with little dissension as director/actress, but director/producer has other dynamics altogether. As a director, I could not be Daddy's perfect little girl. If I had any talent at all, it would express itself in a passion for what I envisioned; after all, a director is the creative force behind the film. A producer is usually concerned mostly with the schedule and the budget, and more often than not, the director and producer are natural enemies.

I didn't want Clint to think that he wasn't welcome, or that I didn't want to share this experience with him, or that I wasn't grateful for the way he had helped facilitate the deal, but I also felt his involvement in it could be disastrous for me on several levels. For one, it might possibly threaten our personal relationship; for another, it would prevent me from reestablishing the professional respect I sought for myself within the business and from the critics — as separate from Clint. Others agreed with me and also felt he shouldn't be involved: "If you're the producer, Sondra's not going to get any real credit for making the film herself. Everybody's gonna think it's all yours, even if you do nothing. You can't put your name on it, Clint" seemed to be the overwhelming opinion.

"I'm not going to be the producer; Fritz is," Clint said. "And my name isn't going on the screen." Our initial understanding was that it would *not* be a Malpaso production and a new name would be invented for the producing company, but somewhere along the line Clint *conveniently* forgot all about that and ultimately *Ratboy* was a Malpaso film (in the business synonymous with Clint Eastwood) produced by Fritz Manes (again, synonymous with Clint).

"You should use my film crew, too," Clint said to me.

"I don't know," I replied tentatively. "I was thinking I'd like to work with some new people. If I'm going to direct I'll have to work with new people anyway . . ."

"That's stupid," Clint decreed, and turned away. That meant the subject was closed. Not only was I disappointed with the way I was being quashed from the outset, I couldn't understand how Clint could be so insensitive to my situation. But it was only to become more and more nightmarish.

Next, I had made it clear that I wanted to do some work on the script. Clint viewed this suspiciously, but I was dealing directly with Fritz as much as possible and hoped that Clint would keep his word that he was staying out of the decisions.

Knowing how creative and inventive Gordon was, I asked him to become involved and help me with the script, which I thought needed more quirk and life. At first he was reluctant, but finally he agreed to pitch in. Not surprisingly, his ideas were unique and hilarious. As Gordon began to reinvent the characters and dialogue, new life sprang out all over the script. I was elated.

I also asked Gordon to play one of the brothers in my film. I knew he wasn't that interested in acting anymore but I thought he was such a wonderful, rich character himself—not to mention a brilliant actor—that he would add much color to the film. He was just what a unique piece like *Ratboy* cried out for. I thought nothing of exercising my prerogative on that decision; I was, after all, the director and that was part of the director's job. I also knew the film didn't have the budget to pay for movie names. I could foresee no problem in my ideas. But soon, everything I did was a problem.

"Have you told Clint you're doing this?" Fritz asked, his tone foreboding.

"Well, why should he care?" I replied. "He's always talked about how talented Gordon is, and how funny he is. He even suggested that Gordon play the role Sam Bottoms played in *Bronco Billy*, but Gordon wasn't interested. Why would Clint care if I use him now? I know he'll be a great asset."

"I don't know . . ." Fritz just sat there. "Has Clint seen the changes you've been putting into the script?"

"Clint said he didn't want to be involved; that you are the producer. Is that not true?"

Fritz only continued to waffle, and I moved forward as a director is expected to do. I also made sure than any new drafts of the scenes stayed the same length and locations as in the original, so that I wouldn't create additional production needs. The changes were all about character and dialogue. Even so, when Clint heard what I was doing, the you know what hit the fan.

"You can't use Gordon in *Ratboy*—that's nepotism!" Clint said through clenched teeth. I couldn't believe he was getting into this conversation in a public restaurant; Clint hated any kind of display and there we were in the center of a room full of people.

"What are you talking about? He's a marvelous actor, and he's got very funny ideas for this. You've seen his reviews—right along with Dustin Hoffman and Gene Hackman, for goodness sakes. As far as nepotism is concerned, you've used Kyle and Alison in bigger roles than this, and they'd never even acted."

"That wasn't nepotism!" Clint's voice was rising. "I didn't use them in my *first* film."

"Clint, nepotism isn't defined by *when* it occurs," I defended myself.

"Well, I don't want him in it. He's not mainstream!"

"Mainstream? Do you think a story about a little boy who is half rat and falls in love with a woman is mainstream? There's nothing mainstream about this whole project. It's quirky, Clint."

"You don't think I know quirky? I'm quirky too!" he yelled. "I like PeeWee Herman and Benny Hill! Anyway I don't want Gordon helping you on the script; in fact, I don't want the script changed at all. Just shoot it the way it is."

"But, Clint, don't you love the new characters Gordon's invented: the brother who's a makeup artist for horror films, and the girlfriend from the Bronx who's a food stylist? He's written very funny dialogue for her and I found a great comedienne, Joy Behar. Won't you just look at a tape of her? She's hilarious. You can't want me to shoot the script as it is. Warner Bros. has shelved it for years that way!" I persisted in reasoning with him, reminding him that he had always said that Gordon should write a screenplay about my discovery on *The Heart Is a Lonely Hunter*. Clint had even wanted to produce and direct it, with Gordon and me playing ourselves. The only reason it never happened was because Gordon had refused: "Sondra, I know you love him, but trust me, Clint wouldn't know how to make that movie. He'd turn it into some cutesy caper movie. Everything special about it and our relationship would be missing; he wouldn't get it."

But that night in the restaurant Clint could not be budged. "And I know you've been taking the location stills out of the office! Probably to show to *Gordon!*" His voice was becoming more and more strident, and the vein on his temple was beginning to protrude. I felt like a small child being scolded for stealing a book from the library. I didn't even recognize the Clint before me.

"And I hope you know what you're doing casting a *girl* as Ratboy!" he then spat out.

I had cast Sharon Baird, a professional for many years who had been one of the original Mousketeers on the *Mickey Mouse Club*. Since then she had had a lot of experience on various children's shows working in hot costumes and heavy makeup similar to what would be required for *Ratboy*. Also, she was very small, the perfect size. But Clint, almost arbitrarily, didn't like her. I wondered if Clint had heard that Sharon was teaching Gordon the tap-dancing routines from the *Mickey Mouse Club*. Was he annoyed by that? Why?

"I think she'll be wonderful, Clint. Did you see the makeup tests Rick Baker did?" Rick Baker was one of the top makeup artists in Hollywood and I was thrilled he agreed to do my film.

"Yes, I saw the tests! And that's what I'm talking about. I could tell that that was the neck of a female!" His voice was now loud enough that people's heads were turning. "This is Rat*boy*, not Rat*girl!*"

It was getting ridiculous. Who knew what the neck of a Ratboy looked like, anyway? Maybe this wasn't about the neck or anything else but Clint was certainly undermining my confidence. Maybe that's what he really wanted to do. I should have realized it was hopeless and given up, but I didn't.

"Well I liked the tests, Clint. And so did everybody else," I said, flinging my arms outward for emphasis and knocking my water glass onto the tile floor, where it shattered on impact. A hush came over the room and Clint glared at me triumphantly, as if by knocking over the glass, I had made a mistake and that proved I was incompetent or something and so everything I said had to be *wrong*, which meant, therefore, that everything he'd said had to be *right*. He looked at me and the broken glass with a smug expression, and uncharacteristically I went on the attack. "Haven't *you* ever had an accident, Clint? Or are you perfect?" I couldn't believe I'd said it. It wasn't like me, but then it wasn't like him to treat me the way he was.

When I did that, he had the strangest reaction. He ducked his head and began to giggle. It was so inappropriate that it was eerie. Then:

"I'd use Rick Baker himself as Ratboy, if I were you," Clint declared. He had loved a moment in the test when Rick had jokingly put on the Ratboy mask and, with a fake cigar, had carried on like Groucho Marx. "Then you get your Beauty and the Beast," Clint concluded.

"Why? Because he's taller than me? It's Rat*boy*, not Rat*man*. And I don't think Rat*boy* should be six feet tall. Spielberg knew E.T. had to be small. Can't you see it makes him vulnerable and endearing?"

The evening ended but not Clint's ceaseless and even unexpected need to control me completely. He remained unmovable on Gordon's script changes. I even agreed to let his son, Kyle, read both versions—as long as he did not know which was which. When Kyle preferred Gordon's version, Clint was a poor loser and went into a pout.

"Kyle was only being nice to you. That's not what he really thought."

"Clint, you're not playing fair. You're cheating. How can you say Kyle was being nice when he didn't even know which script was which?"

And it continued throughout the making of my film: I wasn't allowed to hire David Alan Grier (Clint thought he wasn't funny-*looking*—although later David went ahead to much acclaim in comedy on *In Living Color*); I wasn't allowed to use the location I wanted for Nikki's house (Clint thought it was too weird); I wasn't allowed to have Ratboy watching old TV clips (Clint didn't think anybody wanted to see a clip from the *Mickey Mouse Club* or *Father Knows Best*. "It's nostalgia, Clint," I said. "Don't you see how poignant it could be if little Ratboy is looking at the *Mouse*keteers or the perfect family on *Father Knows Best* when he has no family?" Clint was unmoved); I wasn't even allowed to use the composer I wanted (interestingly, the score *his* chosen composer wrote would later have to be thrown out because it was so over-the-top that the screening audience laughed at it).

Even during the editing phase, he dominated my every move. Looking over my shoulder at the KEM machine, forcing me to edit out any "weirdness" that was completely appropriate to the story. There was originally a marvelous scene in the beginning of the film: My character has just been fired and she's sitting on an employees' bathroom floor, eating a candy bar and crying. "Get rid of that scene," Clint demanded. "Sondra Locke eating on the floor in a rest room! It's disgusting!" and on and on. I couldn't figure out his problem. Maybe he sensed that I was getting out from under his control with my move into directing. Daddy's little girl was running amok; she might sprout wings and fly away. He'd better pull those reins in tight.

That I had to abandon Gordon's funny, eccentric script and all the new and interesting characters and details he had created was not only disheartening for me but disappointing for others. Christopher Hewett (star of the TV series *Mr. Belvedere*), who was playing Ratboy's voice coach, said, "I love these lines; why aren't we filming this instead?" The Golds, who were in charge of making the film trailers, agreed: "The first script *is* a little flat-footed, but this one's great!"

I was forced to film the flat-footed script instead of Gordon's, but with one exception. At one point Nikki pulls out a gun and says, "Come on, Dirty Harry, make my day!" Clint loved that. From Gordon's entire script *that line* alone remained in the final edited film. And Gordon was also out of the cast; he wouldn't have stayed in at that point even if Clint and I had begged him.

But I did take great pleasure in two things. One was that the scene Clint loved best—the one he praised several times—was a scene that Gordon secretly wrote for me, by telephone, the night before I filmed it. It was one of my favorites too, where Nikki and Ratboy blow bubbles together. The second was concerning the choosing of Ratboy's "voice." I knew that Gordon could do the perfect voice as he had on *The Daughter* but I didn't dare mention his name. The casting director started lining up auditions, but none of them was endearing or subtle, and I knew the charm of the character would be ruined with some hokey cartoon voice. Finally Gordon took pity on me and agreed to do it. I was sure Clint would say no, just because it was Gordon. To prove that I was making an objective decision, I selected and recorded about forty top voice people, secretly including Gordon's voice among them. When I played the audition tape for Clint, the casting director, Fritz, and a few others, they all—including Clint—unknowingly picked Gordon's voice as the best. Clint became stone-faced when he learned it. But what could he do? It had been a unanimous choice. I had to trick him but at least I got a great performance that made the whole character work.

Whenever Clint wasn't directly attacking my every decision he was passively-aggressively upsetting me by disappearing from town, not calling, being distant without explanation. Everything that had *ever* made me suspect that Clint was a complete and total control freak came into clear, sharp focus.

The early screenings for *Ratboy* were incredibly painful for me as a director. If I had ever felt vulnerable as an actress, it was nothing compared to being responsible for the entire end result. It would be just as comfortable to parade around the theater in the nude as to sit through an audience's reaction to a film I've directed. Every single reaction from the audience seems surreal, magnified. Even their good reactions are mitigated by the anxiety that their next reaction might be bad. I'll never forget the Seattle sneak preview of *Ratboy*. Despite the fact that I have always, even as a teenager, had a flawless complexion, I exited the theater that night with a pimple the size of a small volcano on my chin. It was excruciating.

Although I will always be proud of *Ratboy*, its ultimate fate was mixed. It was invited to the Deauville Film Festival in France, where the critics absolutely fell in love with it and raved about it beyond my wildest fantasies. They seemed to "get" all the subtext I had tried so hard to achieve. To this day, I am astounded by their reviews. "Run to see her film," they said. "A film beyond reproach by a genuine and gutsy filmmaker" "a lucid and moving film" "Sondra Locke displays a strong personality as a director and a rare sensibility . . . an exquisite, inspired, masterful, poignant film" "The revelation of the 1986 Deauville Film Festival. This subtle and moving film is a bittersweet fairy tale with an edge" "a jewel of a film." It was just the kind of pick-me-up I needed. When I called Clint from France to tell him about the standing ovation my film received at the festival, he responded with silence, and finally a mumbled, "That's good. So when are you coming back?"

In New York *Ratboy* was greeted less enthusiastically. As I had expected, the fact that it was a Malpaso picture gave the critics the opportunity to attack me by saying it was a "vanity" film. However, Gene Shalit of NBC invited me on the *Today* show, where he told me how much he admired it, and the *Los Angeles Times* gave it a rave review.

But Warner Bros. didn't know what to do with *Ratboy*, or how to sell it. It was put into one theater in the Beverly Center in Los Angeles, and one theater in New York, and that was the end of that. Nevertheless, Terry Semel, Lucy Fisher, and Mark Canton (the top executives at Warner Bros. at the time) seemed impressed with my work and with my reviews. I was encouraged to bring more material to them, and to get moving on another directorial project. By the end of 1987 I had three different stories optioned for me to develop and direct. It seemed that professionally and creatively I had a new horizon. In spite of Clint's punishment, I learned that I loved directing, and that it was something I had a "feel" for. It was more challenging for me than acting; it was much harder work, but ultimately was also more rewarding.

Looking back, I wish I had done more to seize that moment to develop my possibilities outside the familiar cocoon of Clint and Warner Bros. I should have used my film to move myself into new professional circles that might have been more sympatico with my own sensibilities. Despite Clint's continual objections over it, I should have gotten a new agent, who could have parleyed my film into a directorial career for me. After all, I was one of the first few women directors in Hollywood. But I was a complete innocent politically and businesswise. And, in spite of my excitement about directing, my primary thoughts were more about repairing my personal life. Clint and I had never before had such a major disagreement. Just as he'd always said to me, we'd still been "on our honeymoon."

But I feared that the spell between Clint and me had been cracked. I had glimpsed a different man from the one I had fallen in love with—a cold one—and no doubt he thought he had glimpsed a different woman in me—for the first time a disagreeing one. But I vowed to mend things. I was still in love with him, in spite of how horridly he had behaved.

And I gave much thought to why he had suddenly turned on Gordon. After our ten years together, was he actually jealous of my relationship with Gordon? And why? Maybe he perceived that I had not shared *Ratboy* with him but had wanted to share it with Gordon. I thought he'd understood that I was trying to move out of his professional shadow and establish my own venue again, and that it had nothing to do with our personal relationship. Of course, that didn't stop me from feeling just a little bit of guilt if he were jealous. I would always feel guilt if I didn't always make those I loved happy. It would forever be a problem of mine.

Chapter 9 ∼

Not only was 1986 the year of early problems between Clint and me, it was a year altogether full of terrible tumult and heightened emotions. It had begun badly in January with Mr. Anderson's death. I was still in post-production on *Ratboy* when I received the phone call from Shelbyville. I left at once for Gordon's and found him asleep. As I looked at him lying there, knowing nothing of the bad news I carried, I felt such an ache inside. It emphasized to me how vulnerable we all are every minute of our lives, without even realizing it—and usually when we least expect it. I took a deep breath, shook him gently, put my arms around him, and said, "Baby, something bad has happened to your daddy. He passed away from a heart attack early this morning."

Gordon just stared at me as if he might be dreaming. As close as we are, I'll never know exactly how he dealt with it. He got up and left the room and went out the back door into the yard, which contained a multilevel garden. From the window I could see him sitting on the stone steps, his face buried in his arms which rested across his knees. When, some twenty minutes later, he came inside, I could tell he'd been crying. "My tears weren't because of my loss," he said, as if he were analyzing his complex feelings, "they're because of what never was."

He spoke almost daily with his mother, and finally they agreed that Gordon shouldn't come to the funeral, but that he would come later on, after the workmen were finished in his house, and spend time alone with her.

The construction in Gordon's house dragged on, and then, only two months, another call came. Completely unexpectedly, Mrs. Anderson was in critical condition, in a coma, in the Shelbyville hospital. She had had a stroke. I was stunned. At least she was still alive, I told myself, and prayed for a miracle. Again Gordon was asleep. This time, I had phoned Bo to meet me at Gordon's house; they had been together for eight years and I knew he would want to be there. As Bo hung reticently in the doorway, I approached Gordon. "Hobbit," I said gently, "wake up." Suddenly, he shot straight up in bed, a fearful look on his face. He knew it was bad news. I threw my arms around him and told him. He froze; it was clear to both Bo and me that he was in shock. Finally, an hour later he broke down and sobbed so hard that it seemed there could be nothing left inside. Neither of us would accept the possibility that Mrs. Anderson wouldn't recover. I immediately made reservations on the red-eye flight to Nashville.

I phoned Clint at the office to tell him my terrible news. He had heard many times that Mrs Anderson had been more like a real mother to me than my own. By the time I reached him, I was beside myself with worry and anxiety. "Why are you so upset? She's not your mother," Clint said when I finally got him on the phone. "You don't need to go flying back there. You have a job on *Ratboy* and I'm not changing the schedule." I was shocked by his heartless response. I had invented explanations to myself for Clint's recent behavior, but this time there wasn't one. I couldn't even reply. There was dead silence over the phone until he finally said, "Never mind, you can go." And then he abruptly hung up, punishing me. Whatever had just occurred was his problem and not mine. I intended to go to Shelbyville with Gordon, and I didn't need his permission. At midnight Gordon and I boarded the plane.

When we arrived in Shelbyville, Gordon, trying to be optimistic, told his brother and sister-in-law that just because their mother was in a coma didn't mean that she couldn't come out of it and recover; many people had. His brother nonchalantly replied, "As far as I'm concerned, she was dead when they put her in the ambulance." Gordon's expression turned to stone. I felt as stunned as if I'd been slapped. Then Gordon whispered to me, "I will not set foot in my mother's room with *those people*. I can't believe my own brother could have said such a thing." When we reached the hospital, Gordon told them to go on in before us, that he would prefer to see his mother alone. They turned and walked away. "And can you believe Pat?" Gordon went on. "I don't sense any grief at all; she seems to be in her element." Pat never treated Mrs. Anderson well; she'd always been jealous of how much her own children loved their grandmother. Gordon would always believe it was no coincidence that his mother had a stroke the same day Pat insisted that, since Mr. Anderson had passed away, she must come move in with Bill and her. Gordon knew she didn't want to leave her home; he had recently asked her to come live with him in California, but she had replied, "Honey, I don't want to live with anyone. Muffy and I are happy in our little home and that's where we're gonna stay."

When Pat and Bill came from Mrs. Anderson's room, Pat announced, "She's brain-dead. If we're lucky, she'll go quickly." Gordon stood up, took my hand, and in a calm, measured tone said, "You have no business making such a remark. I've asked the nurses, and my mother hasn't even had an EEG." We turned, quickly moving away from them, and entered Mrs. Anderson's room, shutting the door behind us.

She lay there, appearing to be in a deep sleep. Gordon climbed on the bed with her and hugged her. "Mama, it's Gordie. I love you so much and Sondra and I are both here." I sat on the opposite side of her bed holding her hand, and as Gordon said those words, her hand, which had been completely relaxed, instantly gripped mine like a vise. Then she gave a low, urgent moan. It was clearly a sign of recognition. "Gordon," I said in wonder, "she knows we're here." "Of course, she does," he answered. And throughout that first visit, at key and telling points in Gordon's words to her, his mother would respond in that same way. We both felt a sense of elation.

Later, at Mrs. Anderson's house, Gordon sat staring at the plate of food I had cooked for him, unable to eat, when suddenly Pat sailed in with a yellow legal pad. "I thought maybe you would want to go over which things in the house you would particularly like to have." An indescribable look passed over his face. He stood up and said, "My mother isn't dead yet. This is not the appropriate time and I don't intend to have this conversation." With that, he turned and walked out of the room. Completely aghast, I followed him. Within fifteen minutes the phone rang. It was his brother, Bill, in a tirade. Pat had returned home and told him an entirely different story; she claimed she had been attacked and "blessed out." I told Bill that it wasn't true, and I then found myself in the peculiar position of having to remind him that his own mother was *still alive.*

That afternoon we returned to the hospital and stayed with Mrs. Anderson for hours. Gordon took her favorite perfume, Anjou, and held a rose for her to smell. Each time she responded. He then reached into his pocket and brought something out, which he gently placed under her nose to smell, and said, "Here's Muffy, Mama," referring to her buff cocker spaniel, who was the love of her life, and since his father's passing, her only companion. Tears filled my eyes. He had clipped some of Muffy's fur for her to smell. To have thought of something as unexpected and special as that was pure Gordon, and his mother's reaction to it was as specific and intense as when we had first arrived.

Hours later, we were joined by Gordon's brother's son, "Little Bill." He watched as Gordon brushed his mother's hair and talked to her. He was puzzled and whispered to me that he'd been told by his parents and the Shelbyville doctor that she couldn't hear us, that she was like dead. "They don't know what they're talking about," Gordon replied. "Don't you ever watch TV? There's been case after case where people came out of comas and they remembered a lot about what happened. But don't take the word of other people. Why don't you find out for yourself?"

Little Bill tentatively took his grandmother's hand and began to talk to her. Just when he called her his special name for her, "Mu-ie," she squeezed his hand. "She knows I'm here!" Because Little Bill had personally experienced his grandmother's responses, he began talking about it to his friends in school. In a very bizarre way, that Little Bill sided with us about hope for his grandmother's life created a kind of war with Bill and Pat. Pat began to call all her son's friends and even Little Bill's school principal, spreading ugly stories that "his uncle from Hollywood had put 'silly notions in his head' and had him in a terrible state of confusion." It was actually her own behavior that upset Little Bill; he was furious, and even confronted his parents, saying he was ashamed of them. It was all grotesque. But there were several people we could turn to—Margaret Turner, Gordon's mother's best friend, and poignantly, Bob and Helen, Greg's mother and father.

It was bittersweet to see them again, because this time they were without their son Greg, for whom Gordon had made the wig. In spite of a bone marrow transplant, leukemia had taken him from them. We were heartbroken when that had happened, and had sent flowers, a letter, and—most important—the photographs of Greg that Gordon had taken of him when he had first tried on his new wig, photographs that years later would become an amazing miracle all their own. Even though they were good friends of Bill and Pat, they were there to help us.

One afternoon things became even more unbearable when the phone rang. It was Clint. I can remember little of the conversation except Clint saying to me that Gordon's mother "doesn't even know you're there" and informing me that he was "going to take over postproduction on *Ratboy*" himself if I didn't return.

Gordon hadn't heard the conversation but intuited what was going on. "I heard the phone ring. Was that Clint?" I nodded. "He's pressuring you, isn't he; he's going to take over *Ratboy*. Go back, Hobbit, and don't feel bad. You came home and Mama knows you were here. I'll be okay. You've got enough problems out there." Everything seemed unbelievably sad— Mrs. Anderson, Clint, Bill and Pat's behavior. I didn't know what to do. "It's impossible to know how long Mama could remain like this. Go back to L.A.," Gordon insisted. In a welter of mixed feelings and trepidation, I returned to California.

I kept in touch with Gordon daily, and learned that things had only gotten worse. Pat had forbidden Little Bill and his sister, Margaret, to see Gordon. And Bill persisted in doing anything he could to drive Gordon away. He stopped the mail, turned off the air-conditioning, even tried to legally *evict* Gordon from Mrs. Anderson's house, half of which belonged to him. And why? All because Gordon believed in his mother's recovery. Unfortunately, in the early-morning hours of April 23, not long after I'd returned to Los Angeles, Mrs. Anderson slipped away. In spite of Gordon's having urged me to return to California, I was left with feelings of shame and regret. I thought of Gordon all alone on Belmont Avenue in the stone house with the seven gables, the musical door, and his little wooden shoes on the hearth, waiting for the funeral that had been scheduled immediately.

"I should have known hours before Mama passed," he told me on the phone. "Remember how Muffy always slept on Mother's empty bed and would never come upstairs? Yesterday morning when I woke up, she was lying on my bed studying me. She seemed so sad and listless that I thought she might be sick. But, of course, she wasn't. She knew beforehand the way animals can that it was Mama's 'time.' But with everything that's gone on here, I didn't put it together. I'm such a mess that I looked for my shoes for two hours yesterday and finally found them in the icebox. I guess I set them inside when I went to get a Coke.

"And last night there was something," he faltered for the right word. "I don't know how to describe it; last night at the hospital something wonderful happened." It had been around two in the morning when his mother had passed, and he had waited with her until they had wheeled her away. Then numbly he had gone out into the tiny and completely deserted waiting room, where even the nurses' glassed-in station had its blinds drawn. Feeling totally alone and lost, he sank down into one of the chairs and began to sob. In a matter of minutes he heard feet coming down the corridor behind him. When he glanced up, he saw an old woman approaching, wearing a long tan work apron over her dress. He assumed she was headed for the nurses' station or would continue down the corridor. His head was bowed again, when suddenly he saw her worn old work shoes stop so close to his own they were almost touching. With no word, she instantly lifted him to his feet and into her arms.

"Shana, I don't understand it," he told me. "I was in the midst of the most intense pain I think I've ever felt, how could I possibly, in the next instant, feel such peace? There was this bliss and almost an ecstasy as she held me in her arms. 'Mama loves you,' I remember she said to me. It felt like she *was* my mama or at least was saying goodbye to me *for* Mama."

He described her as plain, her skin lined and etched like old leather, and he remembered her hair the most. It was cut absolutely blunt like a Dutch boy's and parted in the center with two bobby pins holding it on each side. It stood out because the color was so beautiful, a mixture of pure white hairs blended with golden ones. The next thing he remembered clearly was standing at the nurses' station trying to find out who the elderly woman in the apron was. They, of course, hadn't seen her because their blinds were drawn, and they didn't recognize the description of her at all. Finally, one of them suggested that maybe it was the mother of one of the nurses, who had recently gone off duty. Gordon sent her flowers to the nurses' station. Then days later, feeling terrible and very alone, he wanted to talk to her again and drove to her house in the country. When the nurse's mother opened the door, he realized at once that she was not the same woman at all. He knew then that what he'd experienced at the hospital had no earthly explanation.

Thursday, the day before the funeral, Gordon was leaving to go to the funeral home to make sure his mother's makeup was just the way she'd always liked it—that they had carried out his instructions. He didn't want to go but knew it was one of the last things he could ever do for her. For his mother's sake, he had hoped for rain because she had always loved a good storm. But when he went to the back door and looked out, he could see only a deep blue sky, breathtakingly beautiful and filled with great cumulus clouds. As he stood there holding the door open, he gazed up and talked to his mother. He had no idea how long he had stood there—perhaps fifteen or twenty minutes—it was timeless. The door was positioned at the back left corner of the house, and the steep second-story steps leading down from the small wooden-planked porch with its wrought-iron railing were not even visible unless you turned and looked down around the corner. Suddenly Muffy came running up the back steps and around the corner. Gordon was startled because he hadn't even realized she had wandered outside. As he looked down and saw her scampering into the house past his feet, he was left with a sight that literally made him feel he had been hit in the stomach. There lying across the wooden planks—perfectly aligned and spaced equidistant from each other—were five of his mother's hairpins. It was completely impossible, and Gordon knew it. He and Muffy had been in and out that back door dozens of times over the past weeks. It was the door he used daily, because the car was parked in the large driveway in back, just down those back steps. And, of course, none of her hairpins had been out of the large top drawer of the dresser in her bedroom—none of her personal effects had been moved at that point. Even if they had somehow been moved and dropped, there was simply no way they could have fallen into that perfect arrangement. And there was no mistaking anyone else's hairpins for them; they were made of metal that was three times as heavy and thick as the hairpins currently sold. They not only belonged to his mother but in so many ways they *were* his mother. Until the day she died, she used those hairpins in her long and beautiful chestnut brown hair. There was an entire ritual around them; when she shampooed, she would roll her hair into what she called "kitchen curls" holding each curl with one of those hairpins. Then when her hair dried, she would brush it out into full, soft waves, pulling it into a big luxurious French twist, which she would secure with the same hairpins. Not only did they symbolize Gordon's mother to him, they were also an ever-present part of his childhood; he was always going into her drawer after one, using them to invent all kinds of toys and to "fix things." Although he tried to come up with something that would explain their presence there, there simply was nothing. He knew at once that they were another message to him from his mother; they were a sign. He had, after all, just been *talking to her.*

As he was standing numbly staring at the hairpins, the phone rang. It was Bo calling from Los Angeles to check on him. He told Bo what had happened, then added, "I wanted to call Margaret, Mama's best friend, and tell her, but I'm afraid she'll think I sound just like so many Southerners around here who exaggerate all the time, saying things like 'The night Big Jim died, I swear to God, honey, the moon just literally vanished from the sky! One minute it was there and the next minute it was gone!'"

Bo was curiously silent, then asked, "Did you read the newspaper yesterday or watch the news last night?" knowing that Gordon never did those things. "Why? What's happened?" Gordon asked, suddenly anxious. "No, no," Bo said. "It's just your story about the moon disappearing, there *was* a lunar eclipse last night, the *same* night your mom went to heaven. The example you just made up, Gordie, is *true!*" To Gordon this was an instant confirmation about the hairpins—they were a gift, a response from his mama or maybe even from God.

I was thankful that Bo and Helen took Gordon to the funeral. At the very end of the service, Gordon approached his mother's casket and unobtrusively tucked a bit of Muffy's fur under the flowers.

The last thing Gordon did before leaving Shelbyville was to chip out something very special to him, the five-inch section of baseboard in his bedroom where he had written P.D.G. (Please Dear God) nineteen years before, during the talent search for *Heart.* He packed it, along with his mother's bath powder, her rose-scented hand cream, her Windsor rose nail polish, even the tiny bit of cheese we'd found on her bedside table when we'd first arrived, and of course, those five precious hairpins, and brought them all back to California with him.

With all the ugliness that had gone on in Shelbyville, Gordon had never really had time to grieve. Sadly, it continued in Los Angeles when a letter arrived from Helen telling Gordon that she hadn't been able to give his things away to the underprivileged people as he'd requested; Pat had created an ugly scene and demanded she hand over everything Gordon had left with her. Helen, who was still fragile from the loss of her only child, apologized for letting her take them back, but said that Pat had so upset her that she could not deal with it. Hearing how Mrs. Garner had been treated was the last straw for Gordon, so he phoned his best male friend from high school, Billy Palmer, a successful attorney and professor in Miami, and asked him to send his brother and sister-in-law a letter stating he never wanted to see or hear from them again. They never again spoke.

Then Bo's behavior became completely erratic. For the last two years he had suffered crises of his own. His mother had a stroke; then they found cancer and she had to be placed in a convalescent home. We both thought Bo was having some sort of a breakdown, a fragmentation because of it. We knew of his complex relationship with his parents. His father was a Free Methodist minister and both of Bo's parents had been missionaries; "thou shalt not" seemed to have been the main theme of Bo's childhood. Bo had once said that his father had never hugged him until he was around seventeen, and, even then, it was Bo who had embraced his father. Gordon felt that, similar to examples in the book *The Drama of the Gifted Child*, early on Bo had created a false self to please the stringent demands of his parents. And it had haunted him.

It was certainly clear from Bo's poetry to Gordon that he felt Gordon and life were synonymous. Over and over again he would say that Gordon *was* life, that he had finally been *born*, that he was *feeling* for the first time. Then eight years later, his mother's illness, too many wounds troubling him, both consciously and unconsciously, had made Bo withdraw deeper into some private hell that he wouldn't or couldn't share with us. The tenderness and quiet strength that were his hallmarks seemed to have vanished. He no longer was the same Bo; there was a coldness and hardness about him. At times he would look at Gordon with an extraordinary love in his eyes, then fifteen minutes later he would look at him as if he hated him *because* he loved him. Gordon began to wonder whether it was good for either of them to continue the relationship, but he didn't want to hurt him. "I won't leave him at a time like this. And maybe when that situation is resolved, the real Bo will be back," Gordon said.

But one day, only two months after Gordon's return from Shelbyville, Bo just disappeared. He didn't "end" their relationship; it was as if it had never existed. He never came over, never called, never explained. Gordon was still in a very bad state over his mother and now suddenly, unexpectedly, Bo was gone. After a week of absence, Bo phoned me and casually asked me to tell Gordon that he was gone from his life, just like that. I was dumbstruck. I told him that, if he intended to do such a thing to Gordon, particularly at this time, he would have to do it himself. He began screaming at me, completely shocking and out-of-character behavior for Bo. Then he hung up. Finally, he did phone Gordon, and in the detached, businesslike voice of a stranger, said to him, "Although I love you and always will, I have to go ahead alone. You are addictive and I have to go cold turkey."

"What about your baby pictures and your family photograph albums, all your personal things that you've left here?" Gordon asked, numb, unable to assimilate it all.

"You keep them," Bo replied.

Even in Gordon's state of shock, he still had enough clarity to see the truth.

"He wants everything to do with his life, his photo albums, etc.—read that LIFE—left here with me. He wants to get far away and feel nothing. He said I was an emotional fascist. At first I didn't even understand what he meant, but then I put it together. I'm an enormous threat to him because he loves me, and when he's with me, I make him *feel* and that's to be avoided at all costs now," Gordon said.

Any progress Gordon had made toward recovery from grief over his mother's death was destroyed. Then, soon after Bo was gone, we learned that the last year he had been with Gordon he had been secretly doing cocaine and within a few months after walking out of our lives, he had become a crack addict. "Now I know why he said that I was 'addictive' and, even though he still loved me, he had to go 'cold turkey'!" Gordon said. "He couldn't bear to face that he's become a drug addict, so he projected and turned *me* into cocaine, and then turned his back on *me*."

This news sent Gordon deeper into despair, heartsick with worry over Bo's welfare and his very life, which, possibly, because of the drugs, could end at any moment. It was all further exacerbated by the fact that there had been no real closure. Bo would allow no further communication. It was as if Bo had died, except we knew that somewhere in Los Angeles he was living with a deadly disease—drug addiction. And we were helpless.

One afternoon as I watched Gordon lying on the sofa racked with sobs, I screamed, "I hate Bo. I wish you'd never met him." Gordon shook his head and said, "Don't say that. The truth is, if it weren't for Bo, I might have been dead from AIDS a long time ago. But I was faithful to him, and do you know why? Because he's the only man I ever met in whom I felt an overwhelming sense of God. Funny, Bo had a drug problem two years before we met but had turned his life around when he had 'an experience with God—a Tao experience.' Because of that experience, he told me he stopped using at once, started yoga and meditation, and began praying to God that love would enter his life" Gordon's eyes began to fill with tears. "He always said I was the answer to his prayers. You know, Sondra, if you think about it, if a person has an experience with God and because of it turns his life around and is able to give up drugs instantly and find the love he's prayed for, what does it mean if eight and a half years later he goes back on drugs again? He not only turned his back on me; he turned his back on his own experience with God."

Unable to deal with the last seven months, Gordon sought help from a psychiatrist for the first time in his life. He had always said he would never, ever go to a psychiatrist. He didn't know what "one of those" would think of "a funny thing like me." Now there was no choice. He was in the worst crisis of his life. Emotionally he was far beyond fragile; he seemed to have dissolved completely. I checked with friends of mine and was given the name of a doctor who even counted a number of superstars among his patients. Gordon wasn't interested, but at least I saw a flicker of the old Gordon when he said, "I could care less about going to the doctor of the stars. If I'm going to a psychiatrist, I know who I want to see." He told me he had read a nonfiction book several years ago concerning a murder and in it the killer's psychiatrist seemed extraordinary. Even the head of the psychiatric hospital said she had been caring but tough, and that the work she had done with the troubled young man had been brilliant. "I feel she evaluated him accurately but always with empathy and concern for his well-being," Gordon told me. "There was no question to me she was a loving individual who extended herself far beyond what one could have expected. That's who I want." The book had used a pseudonym for her real name and when the book was written, she wasn't practicing in Los Angeles. I couldn't imagine how to find her. Then Gordon got up and moved slowly like a very old man across to the bookcase, pulled out the book and, as if it were something he'd already memorized, said, "What you do is this: Call your friend at the police. Have him check the author's driver's license and maybe get his phone number. I believe this is who I'm supposed to see, and, if God agrees, the author will give you her number."

I did as he said, and within an hour I was on the phone with Mary Brenneman, M.D., who now practiced in Los Angeles. She agreed to see Gordon the following day—she was only *twenty minutes from his front door.* I wasn't surprised.

Gordon was Dr. Brenneman's patient for the next fourteen months and it was a remarkable experience for them both. Dr. Brenneman would later say that having Gordon as a patient had been momentous for her. And why? What were the doctor's findings about the "funny thing" who at last had been forced to see a psychiatrist?

Her feelings and insights regarding Gordon were recorded on tape. She described him as extraordinary and loving with a phenomenal ability for abstract thinking. She also said he was clearly psychic, but there was an uncanny aspect about him and that his ability to live and experience the moment was amazing. The way he was able to meet and embrace his pain touched her, even though she knew how much it hurt. When Gordon asked her why she thought people had often compared him to an animal (in one of Bo's beautiful poems he had summed up Gordon as animal, sorcerer, priestess, and purest child), Dr. Brenneman replied that she felt those comparisons were made because he was authentic, there was this great naturalness about him, an honesty and a lack of pretense as well. "Gee," Gordon said, mulling it over and then sounding quite pleased, "I sound just like a dog!"

Gordon nonchalantly told John and me we could listen to the tapes of his sessions, and we were aghast to find that along with analyzing and tearing Bo and himself apart, he had been equally diligent in analyzing our faults. But of course they were things he'd already told us to our faces. Nor was dear Dr. Brenneman safe from his scrutiny. With our mouths hanging open, John and I listened to a tape in which Gordon analyzed Dr. Brenneman's own dreams for her, and drew deductions that she laughingly admitted were remarkably accurate.

From the beginning Dr. Brenneman was amazed as she watched the most extraordinary synchronicities she had ever heard of or read about in her twenty years of practice begin to unfold before her eyes, which is the primary reason nearly all of his sessions were taped. Gordon had never heard the word, but one afternoon as he discussed Bo he said, "I know one day he'll return and knock on my door." As he said the word "knock," there

was a simultaneous loud knocking on the door to Dr. Brenneman's office.
She jumped and gasped. "Oh my goodness, that's an amazing example of
synchronicity." "What's that mean?" Gordon wanted to know. She explained that the knocking on her door had begun at the same instant he
had said "knock." "Oh, that's what I've always called my omens or signs;
that means that what I just said will happen; he will come back and knock
on my door." Now Gordon had at last learned there was a word for so many
of the experiences he'd always had. There would be times in the years to
come when all of us would wish we had never heard it.

"Synchronicity" is a word that the Swiss psychiatrist Carl Jung coined,
and although Dr. Brenneman is not a Jungian psychiatrist per se, she admired him and had studied his theories extensively. Dr. Brenneman opened
one of Jung's works and turned to the definition of synchronicity, which
Gordon read: "Meaningful coincidences are thinkable as pure chance, but
the more they multiply and the greater and more exact the correspondence
is, the more the probability sinks and the unthinkable increases, until they
can no longer be regarded as pure chance but, for lack of a causal explanation, have to be thought of as meaningful arrangements . . . their 'inexplicability' is not due to the fact that the cause is unknown but to the fact
that a cause is not even thinkable in intellectual terms. Synchronicity is no
more baffling or mysterious than the discontinuities of physics. It's only the
ingrained belief in the sovereign power of causality that creates intellectual
difficulties and makes it appear unthinkable that causeless events exist or
could ever occur."

Gordon replied, "I think I get it, but the events he's talking about aren't
really causeless—at least mine aren't. They're God telling me things." Dr.
Brenneman, a very spiritual woman although not religious, laughed and
nodded in agreement. Gordon would later find a confirmation of his naïve
statement confirmed by a writer he greatly admired, Colin Wilson. Wilson
has written countless books on mysticism, poetry, religion, expanded states
of consciousness, etc., and in one, referring to Jung's theory of synchronicity,
he says, "What emerges very clearly from Jung's book is that in spite of all
his talk about the archetypes and acausal connecting principles his real
feeling about synchronicities is a certain excitement, as if they were 'messages from God.'"

At first all this was fascinating to me as well. And I thanked God and
was relieved to see that Gordon was getting help. Unfortunately it didn't
take the pressure off my life with Clint and dealing with his recent distant
and unpredictable behavior.

I was determined to get things back on track with Clint, and at first, I thought I was succeeding. But actually it was ever so gradually changing for the worse. It was so gradual that I didn't realize it. I would learn that that was Clint's way. More and more, he began to leave me behind when he traveled. It was no longer like the days when we moved virtually in tandem.

When Clint was elected mayor of Carmel, it put geographical distance between us that compounded the emotional distance. Too often, one thing or another kept us from being there together. Once he suggested that I stay in Los Angeles because he was having "threats on [his] life in Carmel. There's an investigation; I don't want you to go. It's not safe." Admittedly, I wondered if it were true; I'd heard him use that excuse to get out of obligations in the past. Then too my budding career as a director placed additional strain and bad timing on us. Unlike in the past, I too had business meetings and commitments that had to be kept. I couldn't understand why he began never telling me travel plans until the very last second, as he was sliding out the door. Sometimes I'd find out at dinner with friends the night before when someone would say, "So, what time are you leaving for Carmel in the morning?" And I'd be sitting there with not a clue that he'd planned to go. Not only did it hurt and confuse me, it made me feel foolish in front of everyone else; I had always been the one closest to him, the one to know everything. Suddenly he was treating me like an outsider. At the same time he seemed to try to leave me behind, he accused me of "never wanting to go to Carmel anymore."

I decided that I would bend over backward to "fix" it. I packed a small bag and kept it ready. The day before Halloween in 1986 he got out of bed, dressed, and started toward the door. "What are you doing, Clint?" I asked. "Oh, it's nothing, I have to run up to Carmel on a meeting. I'll be right back," he said. I'd learned the pattern enough to know that he'd be gone a week. "I want to go with you," I replied. "Oh sveetie, I don't have time to wait for you to pack," he said. "I'm already packed," I quickly replied. With that, I grabbed my bag, flew down the stairs, and hopped in the car beside him. We had a wonderful weekend, particularly for me, since Halloween has always been one of my favorite times of the year; in Carmel the air was chilled, and with the many carved and painted jack-o'-lanterns and the crackling fire that warmed us at the Hog's Breath Inn, all seemed magical again. Clint introduced me to some of his political constituents, calling me the "light of his life." I beamed and all seemed right, for a while.

His new guarded behavior about Carmel persisted, and his last-minute mayoral trips continued to grow suspiciously in number. I knew he wasn't the dedicated mayor he pretended to be. After all, I knew why he had campaigned to be mayor. The Carmel city council had refused Clint's architectural plans for a new downtown Carmel building he wanted to construct for the Hog's Breath Inn restaurant and other tenants. The building was too tall, not set back enough, and architecturally wrong, they informed him. Clint was livid.

"They don't know who they're fuckin' with," he raged. "I'll build that damn building the way I want it if I have to *run* the fucking city council to do it." Before I knew it he had engaged a political consulting firm in Costa Mesa and was elected mayor. He controlled the city council and put up his building, right where he wanted it. And no one in Carmel seemed to be the wiser. "Isn't he wonderful," they'd said. "A busy movie star like that interested in serving our little community!" The truth was he'd just wanted to have his way. Who he was serving was Clint.

When his constituents asked him to consider a second two-year term, he replied, "I would love to help you out, but I need to spend more time with my children in their formative years." I would hear Clint use that excuse more than once; obviously, they were no longer in their formative years. Still, he loved the *idea* of being the mayor. "Come here, sveetie," he said to me once as the Warner Bros. G-2 was descending and we could see the entire area beneath us. "Look out the window here. That's my kingdom down there." I would think of that moment again, when a few years later, Clint and I were in Washington, D.C., for lunch at the White House with President Ronald Reagan. Later that night a limo drove Clint and me around the city, and, as we passed the White House, Clint said, "Look, sveetie, all this could be ours." I was flabbergasted.

Everything took a turn for the worse, when Clint began to distance himself from his longtime friend Fritz. Tentatively, I tried to intercede, partly because at first I thought it might have to do with my own recent problems with Fritz on *Ratboy*. I almost hoped that Clint *was* acting in my defense. "Clint," I offered, "why don't the three of us talk this out. Surely, we can do that after all these years." I had known Fritz as long as I had known Clint, and Fritz and Clint had been close friends since junior high days; it seemed a shame for things to deteriorate that way. Clint only responded, "Stay out of this. This has nothing to do with you! I don't like the way he's running my company. *He's* not Malpaso. I am, nobody else."

Clint then began a campaign of collecting petty details to discredit Fritz. And in the politically aggressive world of Malpaso there were always people waiting in line to score points with Clint by telling him whatever he wanted to hear. He reeled when he learned that Fritz had let Judi, Clint's own secretary, occasionally use the company gas credit card, and had let the accountant, Mike Maurer, and his wife make occasional long-distance phone calls that got charged to the company. When I suggested that Fritz probably only perceived these gestures as simple perks for such longtime employees, Clint only became annoyed with me. And he was absolutely up in arms when he learned that Fritz had recently been checking into the net profit reports on films for which he was *supposed* to receive a percentage that had never come through.

Clint did not actually confront Fritz. He played cat and mouse. He would no longer call the office on his own private line because he feared Fritz might see it light up and then pick up. When he'd go to the office, he'd walk straight past Fritz and close the door on him. That meant, don't approach me. On one of our trips to Rising River, Clint called Harry Demopoulos (the vitamin guru, who also knew Fritz). "Harry, it would be great if you'd call him up and 'suggest' that he quit." What seemed especially odious about this was that Harry was to be a double agent of sorts. Harry was meant to "suggest" this to Fritz as if he were in "Fritz's corner." But Fritz was not cooperating; he took none of the hints. Clint realized that he had to fire Fritz if he wanted to be rid of him. Still he didn't confront Fritz. We left town and Clint's business manager, Roy Kaufman, phoned Fritz. "Clint is closing down the office for a while. So maybe you should just pack up."

Fritz, of course, discovered that no one else knew the office was "closing down." Apparently "the closing" applied only to Fritz. So Fritz finally accepted it, packed his things, and left quietly. He didn't fight back; no one fought back with Clint. Clint's parting words about Fritz were: "He'll never work again in this business." And Fritz hasn't made another film since then. And neither has Bob Daley, Clint's other old friend and producer.

I was blind to the pattern because I hadn't been closely involved when Clint had done a similar thing to Bob Daley. Even after he had gotten rid of Daley, his anger toward him did not subside and Clint could never really explain what Bob had done to deserve it all. Years later Terry Semel, president of Warner Bros., approached Clint and said, "Clint, Bob Daley wants to rent office space on the lot; I just wanted to make sure you're comfortable with that before we give it an okay."

"I don't care what he does as long as *I* don't ever have to see his face," Clint replied.

Terry "understood" what he had to do and Bob was denied an office. He wasn't even allowed to rent space on the lot. And Clint had done it in a way that no one could say that he had actually told Terry *not* to rent the office to Bob. Typically, he had said it by *not* saying it.

Looking bewildered at an early age

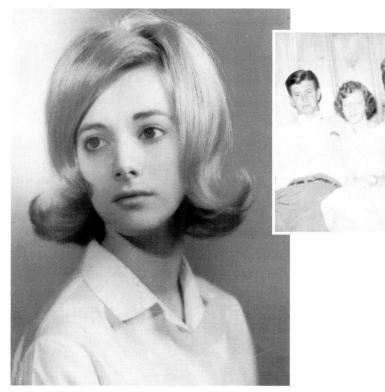

Above right: After my eighth grade valedictory address, my mother, step-father, and me sitting soulfully and silently on the sofa in the knotty pine living room on Horse Mountain Road *Above*: At eighteen, and with the perfect flip, I think I'm ready to meet the world but don't know where to find it.

Above left: Gordon's maternal grandmother, Ma Belle, would never be caught dead without her hat and furs. *Above right*: Gordon daydreaming in the grass just after high school graduation

Gordon in New York during
the run of his first play

Gordon and me in *Life with Mother* for Theater Nashville

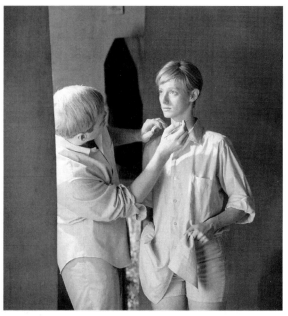

Here I go from ever-so-grown-up Nashville modeling to fourteen-year-old boyish waif. Gordon miraculously transformed me for my big Hollywood audition for *The Heart Is a Lonely Hunter*.

Discovered by Warner Bros. for *The Heart Is a Lonely Hunter*.
Filming began in Selma, Alabama. Gordon visited on the set. Famous
cameraman James Wong Howe checks my key light. (*Clockwise left to
right*) Alan Arkin, Thomas Ryan (writer-producer), Robert Ellis Miller
(director), and I pose on the steps of "Mick Kelly's" house.

ROMANTIC BLACK VELVET AND A NEW HEROINE— SONDRA LOCKE

Above right: This is my favorite photograph ever taken of me. Its haunting quality would resonate in the challenging years to come.

In the exciting times of promoting *The Heart Is a Lonely Hunter*, Gordon and I hit the fashion world.

Gordon and me arriving at the Academy Awards ceremonies in 1969, when I was nominated for Best Supporting Actress. I'm wearing the beautiful gown hand-sewn by Warner Bros. seamstresses from Gordon's design.

Gordon and me at the Hollywood Foreign Press Golden Globe Awards, when I was nominated as both Best Supporting Actress and Newcomer of the Year

Trying to show my acting versatility after "Mick Kelly," I accepted a range
of film roles: (*above right*) the beautiful girlfriend of Robert Forster in
Cover Me Babe, (*center*) the young troubled daughter of Robert Shaw
(with Sally Kellerman in the background) in A *Reflection of Fear*, (*bottom*)
the tough, seductive Southern girl in the PBS production of *Gondola* for
The American Playhouse, with Bo Hopkins and Norman Lloyd.

When Gordon wasn't helping
with my career, he was busy
sculpting extraordinary
miniatures for private collectors.

Top left: The Ancient, the oldest
and wisest of the elves, taking
away the new Baby Fairy King to
begin his instruction (11")

Top right: Thomas Jefferson
at his desk (2 1/2")

Middle: Kewpie in the chair
of kewpieology, inspired by
Rose O'Neill's creations,
with 2" Brownies, inspired by
Palmer Cox

Left: My favorite photograph
of Gordon

Love at first sight for Clint and me on *The Outlaw Josey Wales*

February 13, 1978. 60¢

People weekly

Clint Eastwood & Sondra Locke

He and his new star ride out a Gauntlet of gossip

PHOTO BY STEVE SHAPIRO. PEOPLE WEEKLY IS A REGISTERED TRADEMARK OF TIME, INC., USED WITH PERMISSION

Although Clint and I had been living together for a year, *The Gauntlet* began the public rumors.

Clint and I "play" during preproduction of *Every Which Way but Loose*.

I get to meet my "co-stars."

And I sing at the Palomino Club with Eddie Rabbitt, who recorded the hit single, "Every Which Way but Loose" for the film.

Top: Bronco Billy was my favorite film that Clint and I made together. "Antoinette Lily" was cool, classy, coldhearted, and fun to play. Gordon visited us on the set in Boise, Idaho. *Bottom:* Clint and me visiting Frank Frazetta to pick up the painting he did for the ad on *The Gauntlet.* The oil was still wet as we whisked it away in Clint's Ferrari.

Alison Eastwood and me sharing a birthday party
on the set of *Sudden Impact*

The Sun Valley Six at play on the lake:
(*clockwise from top right*) Bud Yorkin, Dick Zanuck, Clint,
Lili Zanuck, me, Cynthia Sikes Yorkin

My beloved home on Stradella Road which I spent years perfectly modeling after my longtime apartment at the Andalusia, a historic Hollywood building (the finished home, before renovations, and interior shots)

Immediately above and right: The Andalusia's back courtyard

Above: Gordon's mother with her dog, Muffy, on the back porch of her home in Shelbyville in the early 1980s. *Left*: Our much-beloved friend John McKee with Chloe Sr. curled around his neck

In 1990 during chemotherapy, I decorated the tree with Chloe Jr. perched on the ladder. This is one of countless photographs that contain unexplainable light phenomena, often in shapes of sacred symbols. Here a golden vesica piscis— a sacred Christian symbol—hovers, with no natural source, at the top of the ladder.

Left: Scott and me at the circus just as my hair
was growing back after chemotherapy
Above: Gordon at Magic Mountain in 1995

After the trial, the press ran photos like this one of me,
with copy that read "Life is a bed of roses—No wonder
Sondra Locke is so happy . . ."

Once Fritz was safely fired, Clint was on the warpath to recover every single, tiny, little thing that Fritz might have "stolen" from him. First he ordered Roy Kaufman to recover the GMC from Fritz, only to discover that it was last year's model and Fritz had actually *purchased* it. Undeterred, Clint then wanted Fritz's car phone returned; he didn't care that it was the old-fashioned kind that had been bolted down, he wanted it. The same thing happened with an old videotape machine—so old that it had piano key control—that Fritz had taken from the office. This was an amazing display that again supported my theory that some unknown stress was going on inside Clint and I knew that I had to get him to talk to me or there was no way I could help.

He had even concocted a scheme in which he wanted Gordon to break into Fritz's home and make a sample of the type on Fritz's typewriter so that he could see if it matched that on the anonymous hate-filled letters he'd been receiving for several years.

Gordon was horrified. "He can count me out of his suburban espionage, Sondra. I'm not playing cat burglar for him. He's such a coward. Why does he always have to hide while everybody else does all his dirty work? If I were you, I'd start worrying about him. Something's wrong, Sondra. He's warped."

Those letters seemed an obsession with Clint; he had even had a friend of ours from LAPD homicide investigating them. And no one was above becoming a suspect. (I would later learn that even I had been investigated!) Another of the suspects was his longtime friend Jane Brolin, who had mostly been absent from our lives. Around this time, however, she reappeared in a very dramatic way. She and her husband, Jim, were getting a divorce. Jane was living in Santa Barbara, but she had to be in Los Angeles regularly to visit with attorneys. She was having a lot of difficulty with the whole thing, and slowly I found myself being sucked into all her problems. Before I knew what had happened she was spending at least one night a week with Clint and me, and I was holding her hand on visits to her attorney.

Jane was having problems as well with her two sons, Jess and Josh, who also no longer wanted to see her. I understood that Jess was in a special school for emotionally troubled children; Jane had once admitted to me, "He's got a lot of problems, and I guess a lot of 'em have to do with me." Josh was doing well on his own as an actor but he refused to see her.

When Jane began to have health problems, first a wrist that required surgery, then a lumpectomy followed by radiation and chemotherapy for breast cancer, I felt sorry for her, especially since, unbelievably, Clint didn't even go to the hospital to visit her. Once she had become so seriously ill I went to Josh and managed to reunite them, until Jane once again alienated him. Josh was a proud new father, and Jane, a first-time grandmother, refused to touch the baby. Gradually I began trying to pull myself away from her, doubting her motives for friendship, but before I knew it, she was not only staying with us nearly every week, she was also inviting herself along almost everywhere we traveled. She had even begun calling Gordon and trying to work her way into his confidence. Gordon tolerated her for a while, for my sake, but ultimately told her to stop calling him. I never knew what he said to her, but whatever it was there was so much truth he had her dialing her psychiatrist.

I was beginning to feel suffocated by her, and my relationship with Clint was getting worse in her presence. Opening up to Jane, talking about my problems and confusion about Clint, was coming back to haunt me. Always under the guise of being my "friend" she plagued me. Her deep gravelly sandpaper voice had begun to affect me like nails pulled across a blackboard. "Well, I think Cl-i-i-int doesn't treat you right. I wouldn't take it if I were you" or "Do you think Clint has a girl on the s-i-i-i-de, Sondra?"

Clint had freaked out when the tabloids had printed an untrue story about a big engagement ring that he had supposedly given me. Then for Christmas in 1987 Jane gave me a diamond and sapphire ring, which, except for the time I opened it in front of her, I've never put on my finger. She gave it to me clearly to emphasize that Clint *hadn't*. Then I learned it was Jane herself who had sold the ring story to the tabloids, knowing full well how Clint hated being written about even when it was the most harmless mention. Jane seemed so preoccupied with creating problems in other people's lives that it was as if *doing* that were *her* only life. Once a problem was created, she could then become the center of the aftermath.

Also during this same time Clint's son, Kyle, moved in with us in L.A., mostly because he was flunking out of the University of Southern California. Kyle and I had never had the opportunity to develop a close relationship, but we liked each other. Almost as soon as Kyle moved in, Clint was off for one reason or another, and Kyle also proceeded to move in a few of his friends whom I'd never even met before, along with their musical instruments. When I told Clint about it, he said, "I don't know why you care anyway; you're never there" (I think he had it mixed up; it was *he* who was never there). "I enjoy having Kyle there; I don't want him to leave," Clint insisted. I wondered when Clint expected to *enjoy* Kyle's company, since he himself *wasn't* there. He was clearly only assuaging his own guilt for not having been there for Kyle in those "formative years." Now he was at least able to claim they were "living together."

On one of the rare weekends during this time when Clint did happen to be in L.A., we noticed Kyle getting into a strange car with his suitcase. When Clint called out to ask where he was going, Kyle replied that he was going to Carmel. Clint was stunned. "Well, that's weird; he didn't even tell us he was leaving! I never heard of somebody walking out and not saying goodbye." I just shook my head; he had absolutely no idea that Kyle's actions were typical of his own.

So this had become my life with him: Clint being distant, rarely at home, and Kyle and his friends playing their instruments into the wee hours, sneaking girls in and out for overnight stays. It was humiliating to feel that I had nothing to say about circumstances in my own home. The final straw for me was the night I woke up and saw someone staring down at me. It was a friend of Kyle's. I threw him out and locked my bedroom door from that day forward. I vowed not to tell Clint, because I didn't want to hear him twist it and somehow make it my fault.

Suddenly he was blaming everyone at one time or another. Because of that, I was able to believe him when he said whatever was wrong had "nothing to do with us." Off and on, he would even turn on Kyle and Alison. He was angry that Alison expressed interest in modeling instead of acting. He wanted Alison to follow in his footsteps; he wanted his own little dynasty like Henry Fonda had, which he often referred to. When Steven Spielberg was beginning work on his Peter Pan project, he wanted to meet with Alison as a possible but she wasn't interested. You would have thought she had slapped Clint in the face. He was that furious. He almost threw "her ass out of the will," as he phrased it.

Clint was often complaining that all anybody wanted was "to get in the will. Kyle and Alison don't care anything about me anyway. They're only around when they want something. Everybody just wants in the will."

He sulked for days when Kimber, his daughter by Roxanne Tunis, whom he still kept hidden from the world, dared to ask him to buy her a used car, and had even registered in an acting class under the name of Eastwood.

"I feel like I should just throw myself off the Golden Gate Bridge," he said one night over pasta at Stradella, as if he were truly being manipulated and used by everyone.

Maybe because I had never known my own father, I always felt sorry for Kimber and often told Clint that I would love to meet her and have her visit in our home, but that never happened. Years later, I did see a photo of the two of them together at the ranch. I looked at it and wondered where I had been on that occasion, and where he had told me he would be. I always thought it was cruel that he admitted he was her father but never treated her accordingly. He once told me, "Oh, I give them a few thousand here and there, but I always give it in cash so they can't prove anything. Besides, Kimber is listed as a dependent on her stepfather's tax returns; she's not a dependent of *mine*. Legally, I'm not responsible." How, I wondered, did he know about Kimber's stepfather's tax returns?

But I was learning that Clint had a habit of collecting information that he might later twist to his own advantage. He even had information about Maggie's second husband, Henry Weinberg. One night while he was having dinner with Sydney Beckerman, Clint told me, he "ran into" a woman named Joy Long, who apparently knew Weinberg and agreed to *spy* on him for Clint. I always thought Clint disliked Weinberg, just because Weinberg was benefiting from Maggie's settlement which Clint still called "his" money.

All of us began to feel distanced by Clint. If Kyle and Alison felt distant from him, it was because "distant" had been his own nature and habit with them. Alison once said to me, "He talks funny. It just drives me crazy. Like he walked into the bathroom while I was taking a shower and when I looked up to see what he wanted, he said, 'You up? You taking a shower?' What did he expect me to say, no? I was standing there *taking a shower!*"

I didn't feel right explaining Eastwood-ese to Alison, but I had spent more time with him and I knew what he had meant: "I didn't want you to be taking a shower right now, because I had something else in mind at this moment. Now that I've informed you, I think you should stop your shower immediately and ask me what it is that I need." That's what he was saying to her inside his head.

Then for a few weeks Clint would be "sweetie this and sweetie that," and everything would seem like the old days, and I would think our problems were behind us. But inevitably he would go back to being distant and weird again.

Fortunately during this time, some welcome and positive changes began to occur in our social life. I had grown tired of being only with people who were employed by Clint, and the occasional socializing we did with people like Merv Griffin was very unsatisfying. Though I had enjoyed dinner and tennis at his homes, and he always had interesting people around him like Cary Grant or Lucille Ball, I did not feel he was a close friend of ours. But soon we developed a circle of friends that included Bud Yorkin and his girlfriend, Cynthia Sikes, Arnold Schwarzenegger and Maria Shriver (who were not yet married), Al Ruddy (whom Clint had known for many years) and his wife, Wanda, and Dick and Lili Zanuck. Almost immediately we

became a tight little clique, especially because most of us had homes in
Sun Valley, Idaho.

Something about the dynamics of this group really worked. Al Ruddy was
a well-known colorful character and the producer of *The Godfather*. I occasionally enjoyed his wife, Wanda, but was never as close to her; she struck me
as being more interested in social climbing than anything else. Professionally
she had started out writing a social column for the *Herald Examiner* in Los
Angeles and eventually ended up with a job in publicity for Georgio Armani.
Cynthia was light and bubbly, and she and Bud were very funny together and
made for great company. I especially liked Lili very much. Though I recognized a certain shrewdness that I didn't underestimate, she was smart and
straightforward. Also, she and I had the most in common, our real interest in
filmmaking. She and Dick were also a great, and very entertaining, couple.
Arnold, too, though a little self-absorbed, was very charming and fun to be
with. But, in many ways Maria Shriver was my favorite. She was down-to-
earth, easy to spend time with, and very trustworthy.

Gordon's sessions with Dr. Brenneman were continuing. It was clear that
he was being extraordinarily open with her, telling her everything about
himself, good and bad. So, of course, she had heard about his Number
One and Number Two and the little words and initial codes he'd always
written in hidden places, and how he'd often even include little figures he'd
made. Of course the synchronicities were still whirling around Gordon, so
it was perfectly fitting that it was on Halloween in 1986 that Dr Brenneman
suddenly added everything up and saw Gordon with a clarity that at last
allowed her to "place" him.

She pointed out that Jung himself had what he called personality
number one and·number two, that he also hid little mannequins and secret inscriptions and, of course, Jung had invented the word "synchronicity." She said she thought that Gordon had what Jung himself had. On
the tape she said, "I've always felt an enormous respect for you, Gordon,
but today I've seen something that has given me chills. Jung thinks that
one of the problems with modern man is that he's lost touch with myth.
And it's true. But you haven't. Look at the way you met Bo and how you
saw each other for the first time. You were in the dark and waited for the
sun to come up. Have you read about Eros and Psyche?" Gordon said
he'd heard the names but didn't know the story. "Well, it doesn't matter,"
she continued. "You don't need to read it. It's intrinsically in you. What
you are, Gordon, is a *mystic*."

"Mystic" was a word that I had to learn about. So did Gordon; to him mystics were strange men with long beards who burned incense, read strange books, and wore flip-flops. He quibbled with Dr. Brenneman, "*If* I'm supposed to be such a mystic," he began, "then why in the hell—" but she interrupted with unusual vehemence, "There's no *if* about it. I don't *think* you're a mystic; I *know* you're a mystic."

She would later tell me that, although she had treated many members of the clergy, Gordon was the only true mystic she had ever encountered in her twenty-year practice. Then who, according to Dr, Brenneman, were mystics? Her definition did not include popular best-selling authors of books on religion, spirituality, or New Age philosophy. Boehme, Jung, Sweden-borg, and Blake were true mystics, she said. When I came to understand it all better, it was amazing what simple, perfect sense it made about who Gordon was and had always been.

I had sometimes wondered if I had done the right thing taking care of Gordon his entire adult life, and when I spoke with Dr. Brenneman about it she said, "You know, Sondra, in India people like Gordon are always taken care of." Almost to herself, she added, "He should be studied."

I looked at John, who was with me on that occasion. Only a few weeks earlier he had told me a story that one of his students from India had shared with him. In India the wise or holy men are taken care of by the villagers. They innately realize that the wise man cannot chop his own wood or gather his own food because he has a much greater responsibility—to experience and share wisdom. So others do those menial, worldly chores and in return the wise man imparts his secrets and his wisdom to them. Certainly, I thought, that was the relationship Gordon had with all who had come close to him. And I was at the very head of that line.

Throughout this time we all remained concerned for Bo but we also worried about Gordon's continued *feelings* and *connection* to him. Dr. Brenneman agreed that it would be best for Gordon to release him, but she also pointed out that Bo seemed *unwilling* to give Gordon a closure. She had read all Bo's letters and poems to Gordon and felt they were not only worthy of being published but were full of truth and insight. She felt that Bo didn't want a *release* or he could at least have written a letter allowing Gordon closure. "My feeling is he's unable to *write* a lie. He still loves Gordon," she said. Gordon explained to her: "I am Bo and Bo is me. The same goes for Sondra and John—at least most of the time," he teased. "That's rather profound," Dr. Brenneman said. "You can find that philosophy many places in the Bible. If it were better understood by all men the world would be a better place." It was further impossible for Gordon to forget Bo because so many of the *synchronicities* were continually connecting back to him. That was true not only symbolically but also physically. On key dates, at a precise moment to impart information or emphasize meaning, on a crowded street in a distant neighborhood, in a city of eight million people, Bo would be driving right next to Gordon. Usually Bo would not see Gordon, but he would see Bo. It was as if Bo *couldn't* see. Gordon even said that "metaphorically Bo was blind." During their eight and a half years together, they had *never once* accidentally spotted each other on the streets of L.A.

The synchronicities about Bo expanded to a preposterous degree. One of them began with a dream that, Dr. Brenneman pointed out, was filled with symbols of transformation. The dream took place in a shopping mall in Carmel. Several days later, Gordon and John went to Carmel for Thanksgiving; it was the first time in eight years without Bo. In an antique store Gordon found a hand-painted piece of stained glass that had been intended for the restoration of Chartres cathedral. He loved it but because it was cracked he didn't buy it. However, he couldn't stop thinking about it. Then, as they got in the car to return to L.A. Gordon suddenly said, "Go back to Anna Beck's in the Barnyard. Crack or no crack, I have to buy that stained-glass piece."

When John returned to school, he saw Bo. Despite eight years of friendship Bo rarely spoke to John. But this time Bo was waiting. "How is Gordon?" he asked, then quickly added, "I thought of him over the holiday. I went to France. While I was at Chartres cathedral, I lit a candle for him." John immediately thought of the stained glass from Carmel and literally felt the hair stand up on the back of his neck. He said Dr. Brenneman found it staggering too.

And that stunning instance of synchronicity did not end there. It opened up, expanded, and included other numinous stories that amplified its original meaning. The never-ending barrage of stunning synchronicities seemingly designed by unseen hands for Gordon alone was stupefying. It was about as improbable as winning the lottery every time one played.

One afternoon Gordon had a numinous dream that disturbed him. In it, Mrs. Bowman had been sitting in a chair. Behind her was a brilliant white light. Ten feet away sat Bo and behind him was a matching brilliant white light. Between them Gordon lay on the floor; something was wrong with his leg. "Get up. It's not broken. You can move forward," she said, pointing in the direction where Bo sat. The remainder of the dream was equally powerful and left him with an ominous feeling about Mrs. Bowman's health. Gordon felt so strange afterward that, for the first time in four years, he was compelled to call Greg's mother, Helen, in Shelbyville. He confided to her Bo's drug addiction, and his unsettling dream and his feelings of Bo's mother's imminent death, and what that might mean for Bo's recovery. While they were talking, John arrived at Gordon's and said, "I've just come from school. The principal told me that Bo's mother died today."

Both Gordon and Helen were shaken. It was the first phone call Gordon had made to Helen, who had lost her son, since he'd left Shelbyville after his own mother's passing. He'd made the call only because of his dream and premonition about Bo's mother. And he'd done it just before John arrived giving him the news he'd feared about her dying.

On the day a son lost his mother, Gordon had been impelled to call a mother who had lost her son.

At first the synchronicities and all their strangeness would first put Gordon in a state of almost rhapsodic euphoria, for he understood they were gifts, but later often left him drained, tense, and nervous, as if he had been singled out and was being watched somehow. When I spoke with Dr. Brenneman about it, she deliberated, choosing her words very carefully. "I truly believe that all these synchronicities are gifts and are occurring to Gordon because in some rare, unique way he is somehow in harmony with nature or the universe in a way that most of the rest of us aren't. And, although I can see how the synchronicity continually connects back to Bo, I think there is something far more profound going on here. Something extremely rare about Gordon is emerging. Observing and being a part of his transformation has been awe-inspiring for me."

Dr. Brenneman was particularly fascinated, as I had always been, by Gordon's telling her that as the two of them were talking to each other—although he was intently listening to every word she said—he seemed, at the same time, to be across the room observing both of them, from an entirely different angle, dispassionately evaluating two people sitting there conversing. Dr. Brenneman told me the term for that was "the witnessing ego." She went on to add that she felt a great deal of what was happening to Gordon was because he was able to transcend his own ego. In spite of Gordon's emotional devastation, his continued concern and love for Bo were evidence of that. She had learned early on that Gordon was no "victim."

On one taped session, which particularly moved me, Gordon was clearly overwrought and in an extreme state of agitation over the latest miracle, which had happened the night before, and began sobbing uncontrollably. "Why, why, why am I a freak like this? Why is all this happening to me? I wanna know what you think, I wanna know what you feel in your gut, not perhaps, not maybe, not there's a theory. I want to know if you think—this—is—God—or—not!"

The intensity of his question was matched by her answer, "I don't *think* it's God; I *know* it's God." Then, sounding like some weary child, he asked plaintively, "Well, why would God be involved if it weren't numinous?" "Gordon," she answered. "It is *all* absolutely numinous." And because of her firm convictions, seven months into his sessions with her she stopped charging him her hundred-dollar-an-hour fee.

On Good Friday, 1987, John and I were at Dr. Brenneman's with Gordon. She was deeply moved by something he said. "I don't want this to sound overblown or inflated," she said, "but when something so spiritual occurs like what you've just described happened to you, Gordon, I have an absolute sincere feeling that it can only be God." At that precise moment we all reacted to a deafening crash on the roof above us. It was a thunderous blow, as if something weighing tons had fallen on the roof of her small, one-story bungalow office. The four of us sat in stunned silence. When we went out and looked at her roof it looked completely normal. There were not even trees above it. John said, "We all live in L.A. and know what a sonic boom sounds like. And that sure as hell wasn't one. Nothing rattled or shook. The sound was distinctly only on the roof."

"Of course it wasn't a sonic boom," Gordon said. "It was God letting Dr. Brenneman know she was right when she'd just said 'it can only be God.' And it was! He was giving her roof a high-five."

Gordon's last session with Dr. Brenneman was Halloween, 1987. How appropriate, I thought, since it had been the previous Halloween when she had suddenly "seen" him so clearly. It was pouring rain, and, before he sloshed happily into it, he thanked her for all she had done for him, given him, and taught him. As they hugged, she reminded him he had also taught her a great deal.

Then synchronicities began happening in my life away from Gordon. First I noticed streetlights going off and on as I drove under them on my way to Stradella. I drove those streets at a slightly different hour every night and each time several streetlights would go out at the moment I drove under them. I started testing this by taking different routes home, and even with different lights and different streets it was always the same. It gave me a weird feeling, and deep down seemed like a message. "Don't you think that maybe you're driving toward the *darkness*?" Gordon said. It seemed that our lives were being inundated with light and dark symbolism, which, ironically, had been a primary theme in all of Bo's extraordinary poetry.

Then, more often than not, I'd return home to a ringing telephone. "Did you see that story in the *National Enquirer* on Clint and that older woman in Carmel?" It would be Jane, seemingly outraged for me. I had learned that, even if there was truth in what she was saying, her *help* would boomerang on me. After a while I decided to try to not respond at all. I'd change the subject and not let her know that she'd pressed my button.

What I regret most about the time I devoted to Jane was that I allowed her to pull me away for lunch on the last day my precious Chloe Sr. was alive. I'd always viewed Chloe as an angel visiting us; there was something about her that was mystical. For that last year of her life, she had been having kidney problems and I would regularly take her to the vet for IV treatments so that she would not dehydrate. Just after I picked her up from the last treatment, I dropped her off at Gordon's and drove away to lunch with Jane, whom I felt I was somehow bound or obligated to baby-sit because of her association with Clint.

Then, the next day I went to check on her. "Chloe? Where's my baby girl?" I called out as I climbed Gordon's stairs to the second floor, but before I reached the top I saw her there, lying on the floor, in one of her favorite poses underneath the *only* wall sconce that held a *candle* in the entire house. It was a red candle left there from Christmas. "Chloe, come to Mommy." I knew at once something was wrong. Slowly I crept toward her. My own breathing stopped as I realized her little body was all that was left of that beautiful spirit. My whole being screamed out with regret because even though Gordon was with her all night I should have been there. Then came the most amazing series of what I can only describe as miracles.

When Chloe "crossed over," Clint was out of town and I spent the next few nights with Gordon, who was destroyed. The next morning, as we lay across the bed silently grieving over her, we both, at exactly the same moment, heard the sound of little fur-padded feet hitting the floor. There was no mistaking it was the exact same sound we had heard for eight years, and then we heard that singular Maine coon chatter, as if she were down the hall in Gordon's bedroom.

Several nights that week I had the most vivid, numinous dreams about her. In them, she always comforted me and reassured me she wasn't gone and that she loved me. Suddenly I had to know everything about her; I went to all our neighbors in Bel Air and asked, but they could tell me very little. They said they had all tried to get friendly with her, but she wouldn't let them near, even if they offered food. They all assumed she was a wild cat. Then one neighbor said something odd, "You know the neighbors across the street from you lost a *white cat*. It disappeared shortly before I first began seeing your orange one." Gordon told me that he had read that in the Far East a white cat is sacred. And, of course, as it went in synchronicity the thread of the "white cat" story would connect to yet another one, and on it went.

As soon as Chloe passed, Gordon asked for a sign to tell him what we should do about her. He got an amazing one. "I'm having her freeze-dried," he told me. At first I must have looked surprised. "I really don't know why that seems to bother some people so much," Gordon said, "since it's perfectly okay for all of them to dress up Aunt Hattie in all her finery and pearls, have her hair done, and then put her in a box in the ground. Or keep Uncle Josh's ashes in a golden epergne on the mantel. What's the difference?" I had to laugh because he was right. Gordon had a way of cutting through pretensions.

We were told that, before sending her, we were to place her in a freezer for a week. Alongside her, Gordon put some of her favorite toys and some yellow roses our wonderful friend John brought. Chloe had adored John and seemed to feel he was *her* pet. Along with the roses John enclosed a card with the words "With Love for Your Apotheosis, Little Friend."

John had chosen that word "apotheosis" because mere hours before Chloe passed away, Gordon had had a numinous dream in which he was told to look up the word "apotheosis" in a big, jeweled medieval dictionary. In his dream the definition was "look in another book." At that point Gordon woke up, and looked in the only book of symbols he had at the time, but he could not find the word there. He went back to sleep and it was not long after that that Chloe "passed away."

That night we all knelt down in front of the floor-level freezer, talked to Chloe, petted and kissed her. Gordon stayed for hours.

"I don't know how long I must have sat on that kitchen floor, crying, with my head sticking in that freezer," he told me the next morning. "When I finally stood up, said goodnight to her, and swung the icebox door shut, I heard a sound; it seemed to be coming from the icebox. It was sort of a pneumatic sound, like the kind of sound fireplace bellows could make, almost like breathing. A sound of *life* was coming from a refrigerator where I'd just put my beloved baby to rest."

He immediately started opening and shutting that door to see if the rubber seal or gasket along its edge was suddenly loose, but it wasn't. Then he put his ear right next to the door and realized that the sound was coming from the inside. Testing it, he slammed it again and again. Finally the sound stopped. Just as he turned around to leave, a high-pitched vibrating trill sound suddenly started. "I swear, it sounded just like Chloe's trill, a mechanical version of it [Maine coons are famous for their trilling]. I mean I had to grab hold of the counter, I swear to God my legs were giving way."

He recorded the whole thing and played it for John and me the next day. It sounded exactly like Chloe. It would be months later before John and I would hear it firsthand. We were both in the kitchen making a salad and one of us spoke about Chloe. At that exact moment the incredible sound, the Chloe-like trill, came from the freezer and continued for almost a minute and a half. Several other people would eventually also get to hear the sound, but, intriguingly, the refrigerator wouldn't make the sound when they wanted it to. It was always just when they had given up and were walking away from it.

Chloe was finally sent away to be prepared like a little pharaoh and when she came home, Gordon placed her in a big trunk full of antique ribbons and lace fabric that she'd always loved to browse through and sleep in. And there she resides.

The amazing story continued when Gordon wanted another cat. No, what he really wanted was another Chloe. "I wonder what God wants me to do?" was Gordon's frequent question. "We found her as a stray, but she looks so much like the pictures of a Maine coon." After visiting several California catteries, we saw that the cats didn't have the same look as Chloe. Maybe she wasn't really a Maine coon. Maybe we should go to the pound, we thought. One breeder told us that that month's *Cat Fancy* centerfold was an orange Maine coon and that we should get it. I was standing beside Gordon when he opened it and yelled out, "Oh my God! I'm meant to get a Maine coon. Look at the first word my eye fell on! You won't believe it." I looked directly where he had pointed and saw the word "guillotine." In a way I was flabbergasted, but on the other hand, I thought—of course! The article indicated that Maine coons may have originally come from France aboard the ship that had been prepared for Marie Antoinette's escape. When she was captured and sent to the guillotine, the queen's own cats, that were already on board, sailed on without her. It was the most unlikely, ridiculous synchronicity yet. Gordon certainly had his sign. And the signs continued until they led us all the way to New York and Marge Beebe's cattery in Schenectady, which was called Heaven Gift. This was amazing, since we'd always called Chloe our "gift from heaven." And unlike the Maine coons we'd seen, her cats looked *exactly* like Chloe.

Although Marge had a policy of never sending photos of the newly born kittens, she did for Gordon because the most unusual coincidences which kept connecting her to him began happening. We were completely surprised when her photos of Chloe Jr. arrived exactly on my birthday inside a card to Gordon saying "Happy Un-birthday!" Marge had no idea that May 28 was my birthday. It was also the day that Bo's parents were married. And last, but not least, it was also the birthday of the man who invented the guillotine, Dr. Joseph Ignace Guillotin. The first photo showed Chloe with only one other kitten, a little *white cat*, and the next photo showed her playing with a peacock feather on the floor. Gordon, sensing that was meaningful, pulled out Cirlot's *Dictionary of Symbols* to look up the word "peacock" and read that a peacock (feather) stands for the *apotheosis* of a princess! It was too much. Gordon summed his feelings up, "We're not living *life* anymore, we're living *poetry*."

The amazing postscript to it all was that we learned why the California Maine coons we'd seen didn't look like our Chloe Sr. Marge, an accredited authority on the subject, informed us that Chloe was a Whittemore, which is the original gene pool of Maine coons before they became mixed. She then told us that her cats were Whittemores and from that *same* bloodline. "You're getting an actual relative of the mystery cat you found in Bel Air!"

And it was perfect that Chloe Jr. was born on the most magical date of the year, magical because it's the date that occurs only once every four years—February 29. When she finally arrived in Los Angeles, she was terrified from her ordeal. She was so tiny that she could crawl under furniture only a few inches off the floor and it was very hard to keep up with her, but after a few hours she calmed down and nestled on the sofa. When Gordon walked into his kitchen to get ice from the freezer, it began to trill. Gordon stood there staring as Chloe Jr. suddenly appeared and *sprang* into the freezer, lying down *in the exact spot* where Chloe Sr. had been.

The next morning while Gordon was describing this to me, Chloe did it all over again, almost as if she wanted me to see. Gordon happened to have a loaded camera on the kitchen counter and he snapped her picture, whereupon his camera, a Minolta SRT 101, broke. The *diaphragm* no longer worked. And thus began a new thread being woven into the tapestry—this one concerned other people's cameras breaking when they photographed things having to do with Gordon or his sacred stories. One of them happened to Marge. Christmas, 1988, Gordon sent Marge an ornament of a little orange tabby kitten sleeping inside a Santa's cap. Marge loved it and went to take a picture of it hanging on her tree. At least she tried to, but her camera broke!

Between the synchronicities and Clint's weirdness I was constantly off balance. Clint's actions were increasingly bizarre. Yet he continually insisted that there was nothing wrong between us. I wanted to believe that because, sadly, I still loved him.

One night Clint, Richard Fox (a Warners executive, president of foreign distribution), the ever-present Jane Brolin, and I were going out to dinner and everyone was first meeting at our house. I was upstairs in our bedroom and glancing out the window I happened to see Clint returning from the office. Before coming inside, he walked over to my car and placed his hand on its hood.

About an hour later, after Richard had arrived, I went to open a bottle of wine for us, but I couldn't find the key to the wine room. Tomas, the caretaker, who used it to get into the basement area, had apparently not returned it to its usual spot. "Why don't you know where it is?" Clint yelled at me. "I'll tell you why—you aren't here all day, that's why! I could feel how hot the engine of your car was." Then he blurted out the most amazing thing yet, "And you never come running to the door to greet me anymore when I come home!" It was all untrue, over-the-top, and a little scary. I hardly knew how to respond. In fact, it again confirmed to me that there was something *wrong* with Clint. He had some serious problem he was not yet able to talk about. And much the way you deal with someone who is not well, I tried to control my reactions toward him. I tried not to take him literally.

Yet another incident was even more peculiar: "Were you at Tower Records two weeks ago?" he said with brows furrowed one evening. I felt like a criminal caught in the helicopter searchlight. While I was still trying to make sense of the question, he rushed forward.

"I hope you're happy now; you've probably managed to get me sued!"

"What on earth are you talking about, Clint?"

"Don't act innocent. There were a lot of witnesses who saw you hit that motorcycle and keep going."

I finally remembered that I *had* been to Tower Records and for the sake of convenience I'd taken Clint's pickup which had been parked in front of our house, but I certainly didn't remember anything about a motorcycle. Perhaps it had been illegally parked behind me and I hadn't seen or felt it from inside that big truck. But, after all, the truck was insured. And the GMC cars were strickly loaners covered by the leasing company. Yet Clint was unrelenting.

"I think you'd just better drive your own car from now on. I don't want you driving mine. And I've told Keith [his transportation captain] not to give free gas to *anybody*. And I don't want Gordon in these cars either; don't think I've forgotten how you took my blue Mercedes without telling me!"

I was even more aghast at that one. He was referring to an unimportant

event that had occurred at least *nine years earlier*; furthermore, this was the
first time he'd ever said it had bothered him. During one of his trips to
Carmel I had driven his blue Mercedes on a day trip to nearby Solvang in
search of antiques and collectibles, and Gordon and Bo had accompanied me.

Finally I snapped, "Clint, stop it! You are ridiculous. And you're the one
who suggested Gordon use the pickup anytime he needs it, which he almost
never does."

Clint just walked away. The whole Gordon issue seemed to have died
away after *Ratboy* but recently he had been on Gordon again, and I genuinely couldn't understand why. Was it real or pretend? Hoping to get to
the bottom of it, I asked Gordon to stop calling me for a while; I would
call him, I said. He had not phoned our house for nearly a year when, in
the middle of some conversation, Clint blurted out, "I got rid of my friend
for you and you didn't get rid of yours for me!"

His friend, of course, was Fritz, and mine, without question, was Gordon.

"If you think I should turn my back on Gordon because you turned
yours on Fritz, that's insane. We have to talk honestly about this problem
you now have with Gordon, Clint. You never had problems before. What
is this *really* all about?"

"Well, I've divorced Maggie and you haven't divorced him."

That wasn't *exactly* the case. Maggie had divorced Clint, finally. I found
out about it on the *television news*.

"Do you want us to get married now, Clint?" I replied. "You know how
I've always felt. You know what you've always meant to me. Now that you're
divorced, go ahead and ask me."

"That's not the point!" he yelled back. "You should do it without my
asking you; you should make yourself available. I can't ask you if you're not
available!"

Sophomoric. Clint knew that the piece of paper between Gordon and
me was mostly business and could have been changed at any time over our
dozen years together. At this point, although I definitely still loved Clint, I
didn't much like him, nor did I much trust him anymore. So I said, "Clint,
if you'll go into therapy with me, I'll file the divorce papers as you suggest."

This sent him into a rage. "What!" he exploded. "Are you calling me
crazy? You think I need help!" He slammed the door of his dressing room
and soon I heard the water in the shower. Another dead end.

One day I later noticed that the gun he kept in the house for my protection was no longer there. When I asked him about it, he said that he'd
taken it to Carmel for something or other, brushing it all aside. Still, given

his current behavior, it struck me as strange because I couldn't help but remember that he'd done the same thing at the office and removed all the guns just before he fired Fritz.

Sometimes there was even a darkly comedic aspect to his behavior. Clint began referring to himself in the third person. "This house doesn't look like Clint EastWOOOOD!" he said one day about Stradella, where we'd been living for years. He was using his "movie voice" and sounded like an exaggerated impression of himself as Dirty Harry. I was reminded of the time he told me how he had developed this way of whispering in his performance during the Dollar films. He said he'd noticed Marilyn Monroe's breathy whisper and he thought it was very sexy and since it had worked so well for her, he decided he'd "do" a male version of it himself.

I was growing weary searching for the answer to Clint, who constantly flip-flopped on me. I even phoned his vitamin guru, Harry Demopoulous, about the megadoses of vitamins and amino acids Clint had taken for years. Just when I thought I could take no more, Al Ruddy came to me with a script, and an escape. It was a psychological suspense story, with a little action and a female lead. He thought it would be great for a woman director.

Al also hired a woman screenwriter, Leigh Chapman, and the three of us met regularly at Al's office in Beverly Hills. At Al's suggestion we took the current draft to Warner Bros., where Terry Semel and Lucy Fisher got the studio on board and we went forward, rewriting and casting. It was originally called *Sudden Impulse*, but I suggested we change it to *Impulse* because it sounded too much like *Sudden Impact*, in which I'd starred with Clint.

It would be the first feature film since the very beginning of my relationship with Clint that I would be making *completely* apart from him. It was time, and it was necessary for my own emotional well-being, but I didn't know what impact it would have on our already wounded relationship. It seemed *Ratboy* had been a disaster for us, but maybe my directing would be easier on us if we *weren't* working together as director/producer. Maybe.

From the start, however, Clint seemed intent on doing everything he could to make me feel insecure and uncomfortable. Suddenly, he'd want me to travel with him only when he *knew* I had an important meeting. When we were at the ranch, each time Al Ruddy would phone me, Clint would sit down at the piano and immediately start banging out Scott Joplin tunes as loudly as he could. Was he jealous? His actions also seemed another confirmation that he wasn't trying to end our relationship; otherwise, he'd be *glad* I had a film to direct, something that might keep me out of his hair, give me my own independence again. Clint was nothing those days if not a constantly confusing tangle of mixed signals.

But just when I was the most confused about us, Clint pulled the pettiest, most mean-spirited, and cruelest act of all.

Over the years we had established certain traditions for the Christmas season. We'd always spend Christmas Eve with just the two of us, or a friend might have a party, usually Arnold and Maria. Then on Christmas Day we'd always go to Gordon's, and the next day to Sun Valley with the kids. This plan allowed us both to accomplish everything that mattered to us.

Clint knew what a personal and complicated commitment Christmas was for me with Gordon. Every year since childhood it had been a major event for him. In recent years I always spent weeks helping him decorate his home for it, and the result was so elaborate and magical that even Clint called it "Christmas Cottage." It was the only time during the year that I placed any demand on our schedule. And Clint's ease about Gordon as my only *family*, and especially at Christmas, was one of the many reasons I loved and respected him.

That year, Christmas, 1988, Clint suddenly announced on the day before Christmas Eve, "I think I'll go on up to Carmel and play golf."

I was crushed but also angry. However, I was still determined to do everything possible to set things back on track with us, so I told him I would drop everything and go with him.

"Don't be dumb," he said. "It's no big deal. Christmas is nothing to me, you know that. I feel like hitting some golf balls, that's all. You stay here with Gordon, do your thing, then bring the plane and pick me up and we'll go to Sun Valley like always; maybe the kids will come along and we'll have a great time, just us." I had to admit that the thought of spending Christmas Day with Clint on the golf course was a dreary one, so a part of me was relieved when he'd insisted I not go. He made it *seem* harmless, but something told me it wasn't.

Christmas with Gordon and John was completely magical, as usual. Every year so much work goes into the endless details of the hundreds of decorations and ornaments. And after presents are opened and dinner is over, it's with a deep sigh of relief that we relax and glory in it all: the twelve-foot tree in the living room ablaze with its big old-fashioned multi-colored lights interspersed with tiny sparkling white ones that seem to dance in rhythm to the Christmas music from the CD player, the delicate white-flocked one in the Gothic room with all its carefully collected Gothic or-naments, the elegant noble one with its clear glass balls and silver snowflakes in the guest room, and the seven-foot old-fashioned fir loaded down with tiny toy ornaments and candy garlands in Gordon's bedroom, the antique toys everywhere, and real candles lighting all the rooms. Gordon was wearing his red-and-white-candy-striped stockings and his handmade leather curled-toed elf shoes that he brought out annually, and we forgot about everything that plagued us. But I was soon reminded.

When Gordon and John drove me home to Stradella so that I could pack for Sun Valley, there was a phone message waiting from Clint. "Will you bring my tuxedo to Sun Valley with you?" it said. I couldn't imagine why because there was no black-tie event I'd ever heard of in Sun Valley, nor did he suggest I bring an evening dress. In any case, I followed his request and packed it, but before I could get out of the house the phone rang. I rushed to it, hoping it was Clint again; we hadn't spoken all Christmas Eve or Christmas Day.

Instead of Clint's voice, I found Jane Brolin's. "So-o-o-o,o," she said like grating sandpaper. "Clint thinks I should come along to Sun Valley."

"What do you mean?" My pulse quickened.

"We-e-l-l-l, he called me from Carmel and told me that you should stop the plane here in Santa Barbara and pick me up first on your way to Carmel to get him," she gloated.

"And you said yes? After I specifically told you that Clint and I needed time alone?"

"Well, you won't be alone anyway. The kids will be there. And I guess Cl-i-i-i-nt doesn't think you need time alone," she oozed.

"Having Kyle and Alison along is hardly the same thing, and you know it," I threw back at her. "They're always out doing their own thing."

"Well, what could I sa-a-a-y to him, Sondra? If Clint wants you to do-o-o something, you just do-o-o it. You know that. Of co-o-o-urse, I wonder what he has up his sleeve. We all know he's not inviting me cause he really ca-a-a-res about me," she said with all the innuendo Jane was all too capable of.

I hung up the phone. One look at Gordon told me I didn't have to explain what had happened; he just shook his head. Then I noticed he was holding the curly stuffed lamb I'd bought for Clint's mother. "I'm taking this home with me," he said. "He's sad here; he wants to go." I smiled at Gordon's unique perception of things, crossed over to my tree and turned on the Christmas lights for a few brief minutes, then sadly switched them off. Gordon, the lamb, John, and I got into the car and headed back to Gordon's house.

That night I was hit by chills like I had never before, or since, experienced. It came out of nowhere, with no warning, no fever or flu aches. I just began to shake, and my teeth began to chatter so violently I thought they'd break. Gordon forced me to sit in a hot tub, with lighted candles everywhere, and played my favorite Christmas carols sung by the Little Irish Singers. I felt myself returning and within minutes the chills went away and never came back. It was strange, and I will always wonder if I was experiencing a premonition of what lay ahead.

The next morning I was aboard the G-2 to pick up Jane in Santa Barbara and then Clint in Carmel. I prayed for what seemed like a miracle—a romantic rejuvenation, and a sweeping away of the old, as Clint and I spent New Year's Eve, 1988, together. But a slight sense of dread and anxiety plagued me as I sat alone on the G-2 on my way into the future. I reached into my purse to bring out a Toni Morrison book I was reading and saw, stuck inside it, my Christmas card from Gordon. It was a foldout Victorian one with the image of a little girl standing in a winter garden beside a tree all laden with snow and decorated with candles. Near her was a little sled filled with presents, and on the back Gordon had written:

Darling Shana,
What can I say? Sometimes I see something about us and our unique life in a new and strange way. Sometimes just a quick odd glimpse and it is overwhelming and profound. Who can explain or know—minds, hearts, and spirit and you and me and God and the critters and where the road winds and the names lead. Don't be afraid. Just remember you are "protected."

Your Hob——

The warm shower felt healing as it pelted my aching muscles. I closed my eyes and let the water hit my face, my hair. In what had begun to seem like a constant hum in my brain I analyzed and reanalyzed my life. Was Jane herself creating this ever-widening gap between Clint and me, or was she just Clint's willing tool, doing his dirty work? Was there an honest explanation to be found or was it all petty manipulation? I stepped out of the shower and toweled off. The snow was beautiful and deeply piled against the big bathroom window, and I breathed a long sigh as I stared at it and began to comb my wet hair. Thank God, I had locked the bathroom door, I thought, or Jane probably would have followed me even there. It seemed my life had become her own private interactive soap opera.

I headed for my closet to get ready to face them. The sweater that frugal Clint had given me for Christmas lay on the shelf in my dressing room. My hand reached for it, then hesitated. Jane was probably wearing hers. He'd given us matching sweaters—*just* what I wanted. Suddenly I began to wonder where he was. Usually at that hour after skiing he was napping or lying on the bed watching the news. I looked around but didn't see him. Pulling on a warm towel robe, I left our bedroom and walked down the long carpeted hallway. I tiptoed past Jane's room, praying she wasn't there, and soon I realized that my quiet footsteps were the only sounds in the entire house. Kyle and Alison were probably out with friends, but where were Jane and Clint?

I walked into the living room and over to Putty and Roseanna, our birds. Their water bowl was empty, so I filled it. Putty wanted to walk around on my shoulder as usual but instead I gave him a eucalyptus twig and a few fresh peanuts to crack. I was becoming more and more unnerved by the deadly quiet and called out, "Clint! Jane!" No response. That was strange.

I remembered a passing conversation about a tea at Sam someone's house, but Clint had only smiled enigmatically at that. Typical Clint, never giving out information no matter how inconsequential. He would have been the perfect spy. Whenever we'd run into friends and they would say, "Hey, you two. We didn't know you were in town. Let's have dinner," Clint would respond, "Great, call us tomorrow."

As we'd walk away, I'd say, "Clint, we're leaving town early in the morning. Why didn't you tell them?"

"Why? I don't need to tell them anything" would be his response.

Earlier I had asked Clint if he wanted to go to the tea and he'd said, "Do I look like I want to go to a tea?" Surely he hadn't snuck out while I was in the shower.

Worried, I picked up the phone and dialed our next-door neighbor, Tom. Jane didn't ski, so she had spent the days at his house. She was probably well on her way to finding out the innermost secrets about him and his girlfriend, Anne, searching out their weak spots, chipping away at their relationship like a new toy for her to play with. Embarrassed to admit I didn't have a clue where Clint was, instead I asked, "Tom, hi, is Jane over there?"

He paused awkwardly, then finally said, "She was here, Sondra, but Clint picked her up about thirty minutes ago. They went to *Sam's tea*."

"Oh right." I feigned knowledge. "I . . . uh . . . fell asleep. I didn't know Jane was going too."

After a few more words of small talk, I hung up. It was unbelievable. Clint had actually gone while I was in the shower. I could feel myself getting very depressed. The phone rang sharply, interrupting the heavy silence. It was Lili Zanuck.

"Sondra, what's going on?"

"I wish I knew. Where are you, Lili?"

"We're at the tea. Why aren't you here?"

"You know about as much as I do, Lili. Have you seen Jane and Clint there?"

"Oh yeah, she's here with him. I asked her where you were and in that voice of hers, she said, 'I'll have to ask Cl-i-i-i-nt if I can tell you.' What does that mean? Could they be having an affair?"

I laughed. That concept was so ludicrous it was perhaps the *only* scenario I hadn't yet considered. "I can't imagine Clint could ever be that desperate, but it's all getting so weird, who knows?"

"That broad makes my skin crawl. Dick said, 'Doing this to Sondra is one of the cruelest things I've ever heard.' "

"Well, I'm glad to know *I'm* not crazy. I swear, I really do feel like Ingrid Bergman in *Gaslight* half the time now. I have to hang up, Lili. I just can't talk about Clint anymore; I think I'm gonna be sick. I'll call you later."

I hung up the phone and sat in the quiet with my thoughts. The night before, he had been cold and distant. Forget sex; it would have been nice to feel we were in the same room together. In bed there was a chasm miles wide between us. I laughed to myself; at least I hadn't had to hear him ask, "sveetie, did you floss?" He'd begun asking that before he wanted to make love. I started to wonder if there was something wrong with my teeth. Was spinach sticking out or something? Had he always been obsessed with hygiene? I tried to remember. He had recently even begun carrying a little kit of his very own professional dental tools.

Why did I love him anymore, anyway? He had become little more than a spoiled child. There was no longer any joy. If the least little thing didn't go his way, he pitched a fit.

The sun had set, and I realized that the house was dark. I wandered back to the bedroom to get dressed. Just as I turned on the light in my dressing room, I heard the downstairs door slam, and then Jane's ugly croak, "Well, is she just sitting in the da-a-r-k?"

I pulled on some jeans and a shirt, closed my eyes, and waited just inside my dressing room. I could hear Clint as he crept in on little cat's feet, down the hall and into our bedroom. He turned on more lights.

"Where have you been?" I asked.

He seemed startled. "What are you trying to do, scare the hell out of me?"

I ignored him, picked up my shoes and, sitting on the edge of the bed, began to put them on.

"Where have you been?" I simply repeated.

"I went to the tea."

"Why didn't you tell me you wanted to go? Why did you leave me behind?"

"I didn't think you wanted to go," he responded from inside his closet.

"Why on earth would you think *I* didn't want to go?" I said. "You're the one who said *you* didn't want to go. You've never done such a thing like that to me before."

"What's the big deal?"

"It's weird, that's what's the big deal. And you humiliated me," I said, trying my shoelace. "Everybody knows that you just left me here, in the shower." There was a sudden silence.

"What do you mean, everybody knows? Who knows what?" he pressed, suddenly paranoid.

"Lili, for one. She called wondering where I was."

"What business is it of hers?" Clint responded a little too quickly, then began stacking up the pillows at the head of the bed. I could tell he was about to do TM (transcendental meditation), which was becoming a joke to me, considering what I was learning about Clint's spiritual capabilities.

"She's a friend of mine. It was a normal reaction for her to be concerned, Clint."

He sat on the bed with his back against the pillows. "You *talked* about me to her? What did you say?"

It was so like him. He expected me to be loyal to the death. Even while he was mistreating me, betraying me, I was supposed to cover for *him*.

"No, Clint. We talked about *me*. This is my life too, you know."

"I need some TM," he said, ignoring me, closing his eyes, and slightly dropping his head.

I stared at him. I didn't want to set foot outside our room for fear the shark Jane would be waiting. Suddenly completely exhausted, I plumped up my own pillows and joined him. It was right out of some sitcom—or a tragedy. I drifted, refocused, and retreated into more positive thoughts about the days when things were good.

Clint's prescribed twenty minutes went quickly and he was up and dressing. He grabbed a down jacket from the chair in front of the fireplace and said, "I don't know about you, but I'm having dinner with Maria and Arnold. Are you coming or not?"

Dinner came and went that night and in true Dr. Jekyll and Mr. Hyde style, Clint held my hand and kissed my cheek between courses.

After tossing and turning most of the night I woke up early the next morning and found Clint still stretched out, relaxed and sleeping soundly. So I went to the kitchen and began making a pot of coffee, then stood staring out the window at the frozen vistas that looked as cold and lonely as I felt inside. Then, without the benefit of a warning sound, Jane slid in like a snake in search of its prey.

"We-e-l-l," she said, pouring herself a cup of coffee. "Clint's upset. You said you weren't going to make him do any socializing while he was here. He didn't want to go out to dinner last night. He only went because you arranged it."

"Jane, just leave me alone."

"You've treated me horribly this entire trip. All you care about are your fancy friends like Lili and Maria."

"I'm sure you remember that I asked you not to come," I responded without emotion.

"That's right. Like you can tell me what to do. And you know, Sondra, Clint is fed up with you telling him what to do, too."

Suddenly the draining manipulative tact she'd been using for months was turning aggressive. Demanding.

"That's a joke. And, you know, Jane, I just can't take this any longer. I have to tell you it's getting sick the way you're making us your constant business."

"I'm getting Clint in here," she suddenly threatened.

At that moment, as if he'd been listening at the door, Clint edged into the room swathed in one of the short white terry cloth robes that had come with the dishes and everything else in the house when he bought it. With his eyes looking downward he said, "Hey, how are you gals doin'?" and casually began making his morning oatbran.

Jane took that as her cue. "I'm really hurt, Clint. Sondra has done nothing but try to *leave me out* of *everything* this whole trip. You know how hard it is to be the fifth wheel, and she's just not helping at all." I sat staring as she then turned to me, "Clint *knows* you're just trying to get rid of me the way you got rid of Fritz, Maggie, Bob Daley, and all the other people in his life. You think you're the Queen Bee."

This was a brand-new thought; I almost laughed out loud. The idea that I could control anything about Clint was hilarious. As for me being the Queen Bee, I guess I hadn't noticed my maid, my chauffeur, my cook, my footman. I hadn't noticed them because all of them were *me*.

"Clint," I finally said. "Why don't you speak for yourself. Just *once*, I want to know what's really going on with you."

"I don't know what you're talking about. I'm not a part of this fight," he said casually, hiding behind the refrigerator door.

"And," Jane railed on. "You may as well know too that Clint is fed up with Gordon and the way he calls all the time."

"Are you crazy? Gordon hasn't called our house in ages." I turned to Clint. "Clint, what is this deal with Gordon? He's never around anymore. I don't get it." But Clint just stood, silently munching his oatbran. "And you know, Jane, you were the one who was *defending* Gordon! Actually crying at the ranch, because Clint was being so cruel about him. You were the one who said that Clint was '*obsessed* with Gordon' and acting like an 'asshole'—and that was your word, not mine."

"Well yeah, I did," she said, seeming to forget for the moment which side of the fence she was on, then glancing at Clint for his reaction. But he had no reaction—he could have been Mount Rushmore.

"Well, Gordon called *last night*, didn't he!" She suddenly remembered.

"Yes, he did," I yelled back. "Chloe swallowed a sewing needle and he wanted the phone number for the vet, for Christ's sakes." I couldn't believe I was *explaining*. And to her.

"He shouldn't have needles lying around," Clint clucked. "That's not very healthy."

"That's right," Jane eagerly pounced. "And you know, a few weeks ago Gordon said things to me then hung up the phone and hurt my feelings so bad that I cried for an hour. I even had to get my psychiatrist on the phone, Clint. All because of *them*. You know how fragile I am lately, but you don't care, Sondra."

"You? Fragile? And don't think that I don't know why he hung up on you. You and your games—you're a very disturbed person, Jane. If I'd only listened to Gordon, I wouldn't be standing here talking with you now."

By then Clint had neatly washed his cereal bowl and was just standing there, turning the kitchen faucet off and on for no reason. He looked like such a coward, standing there saying nothing. I was beginning to feel dirty, for being involved with this pathetic three-way argument. I stared at Jane coiled in front of me, all charged up, her eyes bulging like some jungle animal enjoying its kill. Then she finally blurted it out.

"Face it, Sondra. Clint doesn't want this relationship anymore!" she screamed, her veins popping.

Instant fury hit me that *she* was saying it, and I wheeled on Clint. "Then say it, Clint. If that's what you want, say it. You've done nothing but deny it, and make me worry about you and what the hell was wrong. I don't deserve this; if it's true, I want you to admit it. Say it out loud. You don't need to hide behind Jane and use *her* to carry your messages anymore, to break me down with all her negative—"

"You're the one who's negative," Clint, suddenly and completely unleashed now, bellowed at me. "You don't even like *Meryl Streep!*"

My mouth dropped. Meryl Streep? How did *she* get into this? We had never even talked about her, had never even met the woman. "Clint, *what* are you talking about?"

". . . and," he searched, "once Bruce Ramer was horrified when you made that snide remark about Sid Sheinberg. *That* was negative."

"This is insane! I have no idea what you're talking about. I don't *know* Sid Sheinberg, and even if I hated Sid Sheinberg's guts, what does that have to do with any of this?" It was amazing. Maybe Clint *was* having some sort of breakdown after all. When had he dreamed up those particular accusations? Clint had never been exactly quick-witted, and that meant he'd *prepared* those statements, just *waiting* for an opportunity to work them in. It was inconceivable.

"You committed the *cardinal sin*," he went on. "You went against *blood!*"

"Blood? I'm not *related* to Sid Sheinberg."

"With Kyle," he screamed. "The cardinal sin! You were *mean* to Kyle. You didn't want him living at Stradella."

"I was never mean to Kyle."

"Well, he's moving out and getting a house!"

"So what! He's almost twenty-one years old. He wants his own place," I said, insanely trying to be logical. "If you were *ever* home or if you ever *talked* to Kyle, you'd know that he and Mike have been looking for a house since the day Mike arrived. Kyle asked me to help them. It wasn't some big *scheme* of mine, for God's sake. Did you ever realize how all our problems seemed to start when Jane started hanging around? She's carrying twisted stories back and forth. This isn't like us! Can't you see it? She's continually goaded me about Kyle, and you . . ."

I waited for a response from him but there was none. "Well, you know what?" I said. "I give up. I'm tired . . . I'm sick of walking on eggshells, sick of trying to beg you to explain yourself, sick of trying to make excuses . . . all these games . . . this cowardly . . ."

"Don't you call me a coward," Jane leapt in. "I *told* Clint that Kyle should get a place of his own, and Clint said, 'It's none of your fucking business,' and it isn't. It's not my relationship. What *I* think doesn't matter."

"Then why are you in the middle of it? Get out of my life!"

"See! I told you she was trying to get rid of me, Clint!" she screamed.

"Both of you shut up," Clint suddenly spoke. "He's my son and I wanted him there."

In utter frustration I said, "You know I've never been anything except nice to Kyle. Let's just wake him and ask him." I started moving out of the room.

"Leave him out of this." Clint's voice was rising. "I already asked him, and he said you *weren't*, but *I* know you were."

That was pure Clint logic. He would always bend the facts to support his desired end. I watched him standing there, his eyebrows flying wildly, his forehead cruelly scrunched up, his mouth curled cruelly, his bare feet still planted firmly before the sink, and incredibly I suddenly felt sorry for him and sad for us. Almost unconsciously I moved toward him.

"Clint, please just look at me," I pleaded in one last effort. "Why are we talking to each other this way? Why is this happening? Can you possibly believe any of what you're saying?"

But Clint seemed determined and set on his path. "I'm tired of all this talking. I want you both to get out of here and leave me at peace with *my children*. The Warners plane is going to L.A. tonight, and I think both of you should get on it!"

Not believing him, I reached my hand out; he jerked away and turned his back on me. As if I'd been hit, tears instantly welled up in my eyes, but they cleared my vision. "Well, Jane, you wondered why he wanted you to come along on this trip? I think now we all know the answer to that."

Numbly, I moved into the living room, buried my head in the sofa pillows, and emptied my pain in tears. Clint was a stranger to me after all. I had trusted completely in our relationship, and let it consume my entire adult life. Now it seemed nothing but a joke. Back in Los Angeles, an entire film company was waiting for me to return and direct *Impulse*. Somehow I had to keep it together so that I could direct this film and go on.

At least now the *invisible war* between us was no longer invisible.

As I lay there sobbing, I felt a touch. For a brief second I thought it was Clint, sorry now, wanting to change our course. Pathetically, I lifted my head in hope, but saw only the long, manicured claws of Jane Brolin.

"It's for the be-e-e-st, Sondra. We'll both leave."

I pushed her away and screamed. "Don't touch me! Don't ever come near me again! I hate you!" I wanted to hit her, to pull every hair out of her head. But it seemed pointless, like everything else in that moment. She immediately turned and left.

I called Maria, then Cynthia, then Lili to tell them that I was going back to L.A. Maria was stunned and begged me to me to stay on with her and Arnold. "Don't you dare leave, Sondra," she said. "What's *wrong* with Clint?"

And Lili, who never edited her language, said, "The stupid fuck. Who does he think he is, treating you like this? What an asshole! I'd tell him to shove it." Then the Hollywood movie producer inside her took over. "On the other hand, if I were you, I'd go back to L.A. and see an attorney. The way he's acting I wouldn't trust him for one second."

Call an attorney? My God, I hadn't made *that* leap. I definitely couldn't think about that. I was still working on pretending that thirteen years of my life hadn't been a lie. But I knew one thing for sure, I wanted out of there.

As Lili and I made the twenty-minute drive to the private airport, the snow was beginning to fall. The flakes were large and plump and airy. I'd been hoping it would snow. But that day, looking at it only made me sadder, and I marveled how something that had always looked so beautiful could suddenly look so desolate and depressing. So many feelings were colliding: fear, regret, shame, hurt, anger, but none so powerful as disbelief.

We had arrived at the private airport, and as I opened the entrance door, Hank, one of the pilots, greeted me, "Hey, Sondra. What are you doing going back to L.A.?"

"Oh, this film I'm directing. Just a minor crisis." I tried to laugh.

"Too bad, right before New Year's. Well, I hope we can get out of here. We're just gonna have to sit around and wait for an opening in this cloud bank. You know these facilities don't have radar, so we have to take off by sight," he warned. "Hope you got some reading material."

Oh great, I thought. Just what I needed. It was like purgatory; I couldn't go backward, and I couldn't go forward. I'd hoped to be alone on the flight, but inside I discovered Joe and Dolores Hyams. Joe and I went all the way back to *The Heart Is a Lonely Hunter* when he was a vice president of publicity at Warner Bros. Now he worked mainly on Clint's films.

"You're going back too?" I asked, moving to hug them.

"Yeah, we have New Year's plans in L.A.," Joe said.

"Gotta get back to our cats and dogs," Dolores added. "But why are you leaving?"

I guess no one suspected that there could be a problem, a reason *not* to ask. I feigned my excuse about *Impulse*, and they let it drop. Wanting to get away from everyone, I turned and began to walk Lili back to her car.

"Sondra, I know you don't want to hear this," Lili said, "but I think you have to see an attorney as soon as you get back."

"Lili, please, I can't. I don't even know an attorney."

Before I realized what was happening, Lili had picked up the outside pay phone and was dialing. "I'm calling Norman, our attorney. He'll make sure you're all right. I just don't trust Clint."

The ironies of life. Norman Oberstein was Jane Brolin's attorney in her divorce action against Jim. Of course, I then remembered, it was the Zanucks who had referred her to Norman. Suddenly she was passing the phone to me and I stared at it as if it were poisonous, then began to sob. "It doesn't mean anything, Sondra," Lili said, putting her arms around me. "You may not need him. It's just a precaution."

I shivered and took the phone. "Hi, Norman," I said, my voice still quivering. "I never expected to be having this conversation."

We arranged to meet the following day at his house just to talk, because I continued to insist I didn't need an attorney. Then I watched Lili drive

away. Back to her life: her husband, her home, her guests. I knew tomorrow
night that she would be having her annual New Year's Eve party, a party
Clint and I always attended, a party where last year Lili and Cynthia and I
harmonized old songs with Richard Baskin. As her car disappeared from
sight, I could hear our voices ringing in my ears: "Go-o-oin' to the cha-pel
and we're go-o-o-na get ma-ah-ah-ah-ried . . ."

"Sondra, this storm doesn't look good." It was Hank, the pilot. "I don't think
we can get out tonight. Someone can drive you back home, or we can get
you a room here."

"Get me a room, please." I smiled.

The motel looked like the Bates Motel in *Psycho*. I splashed cold water
on my face, took a deep breath. Then Joe phoned, asking if I'd join them
for dinner.

The car that greeted me was an old dilapidated station wagon. "There
was nothing available, so I borrowed this one," the pilot said. "I'm just
gonna drop you off." I opened the back door to join Joe and saw that he
was sitting on the bare floor on a cardboard box. "Sorry, but this thing only
has one seat," said the pilot, continuing to apologize. I began to laugh and
pulled up another box for myself. It was somehow perfect.

Inside, the farmhouselike restaurant had real cloth tablecloths and wait-
resses with crisp white aprons and hats. It must have been "the" spot in
town because it was packed. Apologetically, the host said there was absolutely no way that they could accommodate us. I looked around at the other
people with their safe little reservations, and I wondered about their lives.
There are so many different lives we could live in so many different places.
How, I wondered, do we get the ones we get? Do we really choose them?

Outside, Hank, of course, was gone already, never dreaming that we
wouldn't get a table in downtown Haley. I pulled my collar up around my
face and dug my hands deep into my pockets as we headed down the main
street in search of dinner. The big flakes were coming even faster and soon
decorated our heads. I looked up into them and opened my mouth to catch
a few. They were cool against my tongue and, strangely, made me feel safe,
alive, pure.

"Should we try this pizza place?" Joe asked.

We left the cold and stepped inside.

Spaghetti sounded comforting to me, the kind I loved as a child, soft
and squashy like canned Chef Boyardee, with the label that had the picture
of the chef himself, grinning in his big chef's hat. And at our small table

in the corner with a checkered oilcloth, we spent the evening talking in enigmatic circles about destiny and other indecipherable issues. They knew something was wrong—and I knew that they knew—but we all knew we wouldn't talk about anything real that night.

By the next afternoon, the long and awkward journey home to L.A. was finally over. As we taxied in at Tiger Air, a private airstrip in Burbank, I could see my car like an old friend, still sitting there exactly where I had left it when I had boarded this very same plane for what I had hoped would be a trip that would somehow renew the bond between Clint and me. It waited for me, not knowing that I was a changed person, that what I had hoped for was not to be.

"Happy New Year's early," Joe and Dolores said as we all hugged goodbye.

We walked toward our separate cars and our separate lives and I could feel an irreversible page had been turned in mine. In spite of the warm California air, I shivered, started the engine, and turned on the radio to drown out the sound of my own thoughts.

AFTER RETURNING FROM Sun Valley, I spent the evening at the movies with John and Gordon. I had hoped it would take my mind off my own life. But unfortunately, the film seemed to be *about* my life. It was *The Magic Toyshop*, and the leading character was an evil puppeteer, eerily like Clint.

The next day was Sunday, New Year's Eve day, and I found myself sitting in Norman Oberstein's study and telling my whole story. He offered to represent me if things were really over between Clint and me. "I'm only here because Lili insisted," I kept saying. "I don't want to pursue anything. I know that somehow this will all work out."

"I hope you're right, Sondra. Just keep focusing on your film and we'll see what happens. Keep me informed. I'm here if you need me."

That night Lili called from her New Year's Eve party in Sun Valley. I could hear the celebration in the background. I knew Clint was there. One by one—Lili, Cynthia, and Maria—wished me a Happy New Year. Yes, Jane was still there, they confirmed. Of course, it had been the ruse I suspected when Clint had told her to leave too.

My room was dark except for the light from the television and I lay there trying to stop thinking. I pulled the covers around me and finally drifted off to the television's sound of Times Square and the countdown into the new year, 1989.

The next day I threw myself into the preproduction of *Impulse*. I was in casting sessions or production meetings all day, then at night I went home and collapsed. A few weeks went by but I never heard from Clint. In all our years, Clint and I had never let a day go by without at least speaking by phone.

I heard rumors from Maria or Wanda or Lili that Clint had been seen in L.A. here or there at someone's dinner party. It was usually some party that in the past Clint would never have attended. But he didn't come home.

"What is Clint's obsession with Gordon?" Lili asked me one day. "He called today and was saying something about how you had even given Gordon the VCR machine from your bedroom at Stradella?"

"Oh my God. I can't believe he's saying that to you! Our video machine has been broken and has been at Sony for a while. Now I know why Clint has been acting weird about it."

"*Did* you give Gordon the video machine?"

"For God's sake no! If Gordon needed another video machine I guess he could buy one. This is crazy. You see, Lili?"

"It's pretty pathetic. It fits though; I was gonna tell you that I talked to Clint in Sun Valley after you left," Lili went on. "He acted as if *he* were the victim here, and nobody loved *him*. I told him, 'Clint, you were the one who threw Sondra out of the house. Why did you do it?' But all he said was 'Well, she didn't *have* to go.' "

"Can you believe that?" I stammered.

"I know. And then he said something else interesting; he said, 'Maybe I'm just not the man Sondra thought I was.' "

It was only days before the beginning of filming, and my two leading actors, Jeff Fahey and George Dzundza, insisted on taking me to dinner. I was alone, getting ready for the evening, and the house was completely quiet and dark, except for the lamp on my bedside table and the light in my dressing area. I suddenly heard a strange sound. Then, glancing toward the upstairs balcony, I saw the shadow of someone creeping up the dark stairs toward me. My eyes trained on the security panic button. Slowly I moved toward it, just as a man stepped out of the darkness. It was Clint.

"You scared me," I said, letting out my breath.

"Uh," he mumbled.

"Why didn't you turn on the lights?" I asked but he didn't answer me. He hadn't been home in at least two weeks. "How is your mother?" I asked him. I had heard that Ruth had been in the hospital with pneumonia. I had called the hospital and been told that she was improving.

"She's okay now." A long pause. And then, "I thought for a minute there, it was gonna be the end of an era." He chuckled.

The end of an era? I thought. If his mother died, it would be the end of an *era*? A slogan. Clint lately had been describing any event concerning himself as if it might someday be a chapter title in his biography.

"Do you know if she received my flowers?" I asked him.

"Yeah, she got them." Long pause.

"Good. I'm glad she's okay."

"Where is the VCR machine?" Clint suddenly asked me with that certain accusatory tone.

"It's at Sony. I *told* you they haven't returned it yet." Then, ignoring that, I asked, "What are you doing? Where are you going?"

"The Golden Globes," he replied.

Just then the doorbell rang and I went to answer it. It was Lennie Hirshan, *our* agent. Obviously Clint and Lennie were going together. I had completely forgotten that *Bird* had been nominated. As I walked back upstairs, Clint was coming down in his tuxedo. "Goodnight, Sondra," said Lennie from the doorway. And they were gone.

~

"I HEARD CLINT'S in town; what's he saying?" It was Maria calling.

"He's not saying anything; I hadn't even heard he was in L.A. this time. He hasn't come home; I just wonder where he's staying."

"Can't you talk to him?" Maria pleaded as if it were all incomprehensible to her.

"You don't understand, Maria. Clint doesn't talk. And, I guess, a part of me doesn't want to talk to him now. He has acted awful. I guess I don't believe it's really over between us but this time he's gonna have to be the one to 'fix it.' And if there is anything left between us, he will. If he doesn't, maybe nothing's worth saving. I don't know. Maybe some time just needs to pass."

"I guess you're right . . . I have to tell you he showed up at our house the other day," she said after a pause.

"And?"

"It was very strange. He talked about losing the Golden Globe. He was real depressed over all that. And then he said something really weird. Like 'Maybe it's time for me to get rid of *everybody* in my life and start over.' I just didn't know what to say to him."

"That's a totally bizarre statement . . . 'get rid of everybody'?"

"Yeah. I know. He's weird," she said.

Impulse began filming, and that did a lot to occupy me. Theresa Russell, the female star, and I got along beautifully. She was a consummate professional, always ready and cooperative. We respected each other and she never balked at any direction I gave her. I thought she was perfect casting for Lottie—the police detective who works vice and, as a result, finds herself drifting toward the darker side of her own personality. Jeff Fahey needed a more diplomatic hand, but ultimately was always open and responsive. George Dzundza was my rock among all the actors. Not only is he enormously gifted, but his insight is keen and his heart big and encompassing.

I fully understood what Dickens meant when he said "It was the best of times; it was the worst of times," because that was certainly true of my life at that point. No matter how long the hours, or how intense my focus had to be, I hadn't been this happy in my work since *The Heart Is a Lonely Hunter.*

But at home the nightmarish standoff continued. I learned from my caretaker, Tomas, that Clint was creeping in and out of the house when I was not home, careful not to disturb anything. My mood ranged from missing him and wanting him back, to free-floating fears and loathing. I tried to sound brave to my friends, like a child whistling in the dark to keep away the monsters, but in my heart I was sad, frightened, and confused.

Of course Gordon's clarity was ever present. At the height of Clint's weirdness, Gordon had taken to calling him "Susi Pi"—short for Socio-Path—he said, *almost* making me laugh.

"Sondra, I think you're just going to have to face the facts that Clint is a sociopath; I don't think there is another explanation for the way he treats everyone. He cares for no one. I know it's a hard thing to accept but he's completely unevolved as a human being; he believes in nothing—he's a zero. I'm sorry to be so blunt, but that is it. He needs therapy."

I worried off and on about Clint's plans for me, because it had always seemed he got his way—no matter what.

"He doesn't always get his way," Gordon reminded me. "He just doesn't tell you about the times when he doesn't. Don't forget he didn't get his way with Kyle starring in the *Karate Kid*, did he?"

"Well, that's true," I answered. Clint had agreed to direct *Karate Kid* for Columbia *only* if Kyle played the lead, but they had refused. Clint forever more banned Coca-Cola from his sight (Coca-Cola and Columbia Pictures were connected).

"He doesn't have the power you think he does," Gordon went on. "Oh he has money and status but that's not real power. He has no *personal* power because there's no *person* there. Nobody's home. If he does, it's dark. And yours is light. You have God." And that's what Gordon believed.

Our first real confrontation since Sun Valley occurred when I was awakened by a call from my own production secretary telling me that Clint wanted me to call him. I had had approximately three hours of sleep because we had been filming nights. When he came on the phone, he acted as if nothing were wrong, "Hey, how's it goin'." From there the conversation continued in a perfectly Clint way: Nothing *real* was said. Finally he hung up, saying, "Well, maybe I'll be over a little later."

Within thirty minutes he was there, standing in the dining room with his arms crossed, gently swaying from side to side. "I washed the dish in the kitchen sink when I was here earlier," he confided. Was he trying to tell me how neat and thoughtful he was, or was he saying I was a slob for having left a dirty dish in the sink?

I sat down on one of the dining chairs, hoping the conversation would improve, hoping he'd finally decided to "fix" things between us.

"I hesitated to bring it up while you were shooting this film," he began, "but I was . . . uh . . . thinking, it's come to my attention that you . . . uh . . . and Gordon are sitting on my only *real estate* in Los Angeles."

Sitting on his real estate! Gordon and I? Incredible!

"*Your* real estate? Your real estate! That's outrageous, Clint." He actually looked caught.

"Well . . . uh . . . well . . . uh, I was thinking maybe you could go stay with Gordon for a while."

He said it as if it were a casual and normal request.

"What? Stay with Gordon?" I asked in shock. "Why on earth would you expect me to do that?"

"Well, you've stayed there before."

"Yes, overnight sometimes when you were out of town. Clint, look, what are we going to do here? Can we fix things with us or not?" He said nothing, just stared out the French door. I could feel the back of my neck growing hot. "I can tell you one thing, *I'm* not going anywhere. You don't even like Los Angeles. Go to one of your other houses in Carmel, in Sun Valley, or the ranch. Go there if you don't want to be around me. Rent some fancy condo whenever you have to be in L.A. Or stay wherever you're staying now! . . . Where *are* you staying, Clint?"

He looked away.

"I want you to tell me that you don't love me anymore, Clint. Can you say it?"

I waited. He couldn't. "Well," he mumbled. "Maybe you could just put it on the back burner until you finish your film." And with that he turned and left the house. That was April 4, 1989.

I dialed Gordon—and then hung up. I couldn't tell him; he had enough problems of his own then. I called Maria, Cynthia, John. What did they all think?

"It's just a knee-jerk reaction, Sondra," said Al Ruddy.

"Fucker . . . He's such a cheap screw," Lili said. "You need to tell Norman."

I called Norman Oberstein and told him about Clint's visit.

"Try to stay calm." Norman attempted to soothe me. "Clint *did* say to you, 'When your film is finished.' "

In my head I guess I knew it was over, but in my heart Clint and I were still not severed. I had, however, resigned myself to the idea that when my film was finished, I would go and visit Bruce Ramer, Clint's attorney. If Clint and I couldn't communicate, surely Bruce would help me sort out the separation. In a near-hypnotic manner I went back to work. Directing a film requires awesome stamina and with so much emotional drain in my life I could hardly stay afloat. A few days later on the set, my assistant handed me a phone message: Call your manicurist, Elaine, as soon as you can.

"Sondra, I'm a little concerned for you," she said. "Jane Brolin was here this morning and she said something really weird. She seemed to know that you had just been here on Sunday. Do you think Clint is having you followed?"

"What did Jane say?" I asked.

"Well, mainly that she knew you'd been here specifically on Sunday, and it was almost like she was threatening me because she said, 'Don't think I don't know you're telling Sondra things about me—about my face-lift.' And that was so spooky; how did she know?"

The only person I'd told that Jane's face-lift had gone wrong and that she was distorted and infected was Gordon. I remembered the phone conversation well from a few days earlier. I could never forget Gordon's response: "So now the outside matches the inside, huh?"

"Don't worry, Elaine," I said to her. "I appreciate your call."

As I put down the phone, I remembered Clint's words, about someone he was in conflict with, "He'd better never underestimate me." Apparently

I had done just that. That night when I told Gordon he said, "He probably has your phones tapped. I wouldn't put anything past that man. You know, Sondra, I've told you before and I'll tell you again, I really think you should start taking anything precious to you out of that house."

"How can I do that, Gordon, how can I just suddenly have things disappearing from the house? And what would I take; everything here is precious to me. That's no way to handle all this."

A week later, April 10, I was filming the most challenging scene in the script. I was very concerned about how to make it work. I had a crew of sixty standing by as I tried to focus every ounce of my attention and creativity on this key moment in my film, but I had just learned something disturbing.

Clint had hired Jeff Fahey and George Dzunzda to star in his next film, White Hunter, Black Heart. My words are inadequate to describe the way that news made me feel. More gaslighting? Not only had Clint never heard of them before I'd hired them, he'd even put them down when I showed him their pictures: "I don't know what you want with that pretty boy" (Jeff) he'd said, and, "Don't you think he's a little overweight?" (George) But he had hired them to go directly from my film into his. It felt creepy and incestuous. It was also "I'll take everyone away from you; I'll even win your actors over to my side." Then too, it was another way of putting his shadow over my project, if he did his usual rush release, his film with "his" actors would come out first and I'd be viewed as having copied him. It was perverse.

Before I could completely absorb that, I was handed a message to call Gordon as soon as possible. Gordon never called me on the set; I knew it was not good news.

"Listen to me carefully. Stay calm, do you understand?" Gordon said. With that my pulse quickened.

"What is it? Just tell me quick." I almost screamed.

"Clint has locked you out of your house. The sissy waited until you were safely at work, then he changed the locks."

I seemed to be somewhere far away. Fragmented responses were off in the distance . . . I could barely hear them . . . it was my voice . . . something about, God wouldn't let him do that . . . took my home . . . no one could be that despicable . . . I felt nonexistent . . .

Gordon began to read a letter that had been delivered to his house. It was from my friend Bruce Ramer. "Dear Mrs. Anderson. Please do not return to 846 Stradella Road where you have been allowed to stay rent free by Mr. Eastwood."

"Rent free! I hate Clint so much. I want to gouge out his eyes. I want to cut him up in little pieces. I wish he'd die of a heart attack right now!"

"Just listen," Gordon continued. "It says, 'The locks have been changed and your personal effects have all been sent to where you have *resided for nine years* with your *husband* Gordon Anderson' . . .'"

What! He stopped reading the letter and began describing what had happened next. "I heard the doorbell ring and I went to open the door; I thought it was probably UPS but for some reason I didn't open it. I decided to open the peephole instead. Then something stopped me from even that; I had the weirdest feeling. I walked to the dining room window to see if a car was in the driveway. I could only see the end of a truck, and a guy wearing a Warner Bros. T-shirt—and only one large box beside him. So I felt kinda silly and I went back to open the door, because I thought maybe they had gotten the addresses confused and were delivering something to do with *Impulse*. They were still knocking and ringing the doorbell as I walked back to open it. Just as soon as I was about to open it, it was as if *something* wouldn't let me. I stood there until I heard them walk away and the truck drive off."

As I listened to Gordon my mind couldn't leave that disgusting letter. "Dear Mrs. Anderson." I was no longer Sondra, lovey, sweetie, only-person-I've-ever-really-loved.

Gordon was still talking. "After they were gone, I opened the door and picked up the letter. Three minutes later the phone rang. Something told me not to use my own voice, so I answered in a 'dear old granny voice' and a man asked, 'Is Gertrude there?' I told him he had the wrong number. And as soon as I hung up, the phone rang again but this time I didn't answer it. You'd think he could have come up with a more subtle name."

"Where are my clothes?" I asked, panicking.

"They had to take them away. If I had opened the door or answered that phone, I know they would have dumped those boxes here. And, once they were here, Clint could claim that because I had accepted them, it proved this is where you live. He either took them back to Stradella or he's put them in storage."

"Oh God." I absolutely could not believe he had gone that far.

"You know how you're always saying, 'Gordon, tell me how something is gonna turn out' or wanting me to 'make this or that happen' . . . and I always tell you that I can't, that it's not me? Well, remember this, and don't forget it. This is not some prediction made in anger. This is a *fact* and, you can believe it, like it's written in stone somewhere. He will not get away with this, I swear to you, in the end he'll *pay*."

I hung up and walked outside where the key crew was staring, waiting for me to give them my clear thoughts, my "direction." I began to walk toward them. The last thing I remembered was a feeling of sinking in a soft mud. And then I passed out.

I called Norman Oberstein. He did not want me to stay at Gordon's house that night, because of the obvious game Clint was playing with the Gordon issue. Tom Stern, a friend and the gaffer on my film, took me to Lili's house. Lili, about to leave for location on *Driving Miss Daisy*, and Dick were living in a small rental in Beverly Hills because their new home was under construction. "I just talked with Cynthia in New York and she and Bud want you to stay at their house," Lili said to me. Cynthia was appearing on Broadway in the musical *Into the Woods*. Lili gave me a toothbrush and drove me to Bud and Cynthia's house.

Norman urged no delay in drafting the lawsuit against Clint. Norman also suggested something else. Because of Clint's obvious plan to wrongly represent my relationship with Gordon, Norman asked Gordon to sign a paper that surrendered any claim on any assets of mine as proof that our marriage was not a standard or "real" one. In an *extraordinary* gesture of love and faith in me, Gordon signed away *everything* without hesitation. Over that weekend I met Norman and his partner, Joe, in their completely empty offices. The legal papers were in front of me, laid out on the table, just waiting for my signature. I sat there, staring at them, sobbing uncontrollably.

"You have no choice, Sondra," Norman said as he handed me a pen. "He has cruelly thrown you out and unequivocally refused to do anything for you. You *have* to let us go after this man; what he has done to you is unconscionable."

I wiped my nose and, with my hand shaking, took the pen. The man I had once adored, the man with whom I had lived for so many years with never a fight before these recent months, was now to be my very ugly public enemy in a very ugly public fight. Reluctantly, I signed the papers, but still I begged Norman to try again to reason with Bruce Ramer. Norman reminded me that I stood to gain much more by taking Clint to court and demanding my fair share of what we'd built together. "I don't care about all the money, Norman. I just want my home and enough to support it."

Later, after meeting with Ramer, Norman reported, "I'm sorry, Sondra. The only thing Clint will agree to give you is Gordon's house. And that was with Ramer twisting his arm. I'm filing the lawsuit in downtown superior court today." I was standing at a pay phone in a café, where I was directing a scene in *Impulse*, and through my tears I told him to go ahead. I knew that the ceiling of my universe was now caving in completely.

The press went crazy. The story was in the *L.A. Times, Hard Copy, Inside Edition*, the tabloids, and on and on. All along Gordon encouraged a sense of humor about it; for instance, he laughed at the *National Enquirer*'s article that pictured both our houses and quoted "sources close to Clint" on how he had paid for Gordon's gardener and psychiatrist.

"Where did they [the *Enquirer*] get all these lies?" I asked.

"Don't you know?" Gordon answered. "Jane Brolin. I smell her all over it. But make no mistake, she's doing it for Clint. He knows *all* about it. It's his famous preemptive-strike syndrome."

The press was seeing to it that my life, such as it was, was an open book. And it was obvious to everyone around me that in my private life, I was a complete wreck, but professionally I was desperately trying to keep going. My split with Clint was personally devastating, but it was also about losing my ability to continue *working* in my profession. I had become completely enmeshed with and reliant on Clint. Hollywood is a very small town very concerned with who's "in" and who's "out." I *had* to complete *Impulse* and hope it would keep my career going. For the moment it was all I had.

On the set, I would direct a scene, discuss the next shot with the cameraman, then go to the bathroom and cry. When the lighting and camera were ready for the shot, my producer, Don Kolsrud, would come and get me. One day I woke up with my face so swollen that I hardly recognized myself. Hives, my doctor said, after I'd rushed to his office at 7:00 A.M. before going to the set.

My friends kept consoling me and reassuring me that Clint would settle with me respectably. They promised to do all they could to influence him.

"Clint just called Dick from his office," Lili said to me one afternoon, "and he said something strange. Remember how I once told you on the phone that Clint was so boring without you whenever we saw him in Sun Valley?"

"Yes, I remember that conversation well," I replied.

"Okay, good. Now listen." She paused. I waited. "What do you suppose he just said to Dick on the phone?" Again a dramatic pause. "Well, he said to Dick, 'I guess Lili thinks I'm kinda boring.'"

I felt queasy. Remembering Gordon's comment, and Elaine's (the manicurist) phone call, I said, "He must have had my phones tapped. My God, is there no end to what he'll do? I can't believe it! I'm telling you Lili, I remember *exactly* where I was when you and I had that phone conversation. I was lying on my bed at Stradella and you were speaking to me from Sun Valley."

"Are you sure you didn't tell someone else who might have told him?"

"Absolutely not. That is the one and only time that specific information was stated . . . by you on the telephone to me. He tapped it."

I phoned Norman. "Sondra, that is illegal," he said. "I doubt very seriously if Clint would have been so stupid as to do something like that. But I just received a call from Howard King demanding some gun Clint claims you've stolen from him."

What? I told Norman I had no idea what he was talking about. "There had been a gun Clint kept in a locked closet supposedly for my protection but he said he had taken it to Carmel; frankly, I thought it was strange. The only other gun I know anything about was one that he gave me to carry in my purse; *he* registered it in my name at Rising River."

"No," replied Norman. "He surely can't be talking about that . . . if it's yours that would be ridiculous. He can't be that stupid. What's he hoping to set up?"

"Who knows? Welcome to the world of Clint," I said sardonically.

I was still staying with Cynthia and Bud, whose house was also undergoing remodeling, and woke up every morning to the sound of hammering and sawing. At the end of each day's filming, I would return, step through the front door across the sawdust and debris and, feeling as if I were in some Fellini movie, lift the big sheet of plastic that partitioned off the entrance hall from the construction in the rest of the downstairs and drag myself up the long winding stairs that led to the second floor and the guest room, where I would crash.

I had finally been able to collect those fourteen Bekins boxes. The contents were a mess. Those fourteen boxes, according to Clint, contained all that I owned out of all our years together. He had dictated that it would only be the clothing from my closet—and even some of that had disappeared. Furthermore, he had conveniently withheld the personal things from my dresser drawers—every sweet note, every tender card he had given me over the years; all my snapshots of us together; the jewelry, especially the necklace handmade by his grandfather, that he had given me when he had told me we would always be together; even the sweet essay, which I had treasured, that Alison had written about me for her class at school— anything and everything that might have linked him and me in any *intimate* or *personal* way, anything that was evidence of the life we had shared together. All gone.

A few days prior to leaving for New York for a two-day shoot on *Impulse*, Cynthia phoned unexpectedly: "You'll have to be out of our house by Friday because Bud and I are coming back with our decorator and I've promised the guest room to him."

I was too stunned to speak, but that didn't stop Cynthia.

"Now don't try to make me feel guilty, Sondra. After all, when Laddie walked out on me, I simply picked up and went right on."

I stiffled a gasp and a laugh. Laddie was Alan Ladd, Jr., son of the famous movie star and himself a successful Hollywood producer. Cynthia had admittedly had only a brief affair with him and they never lived together. But according to Cynthia that compared to the thirteen years of my personal and professional life down the drain.

At first Maria wanted me to stay at her house, then finally she insisted it would be best that I stay with Nadine and her husband, Michael. Nadine was an old friend of Maria's and had worked with her in broadcasting. At one time she'd been a psychologist and Maria seemed to think that might be helpful to me. I agreed but when I returned from filming in New York I took a room at a beachside hotel in Santa Monica, just to clear my head and collect myself for a few days before moving in with them.

Upon my return I was informed that Clint's attorneys were ready to depose not only me, but Gordon as well. Then just before Gordon's deposition someone privy to the gossip in Clint's camp told me that he had heard from Fritz about Clint's game plan. Amazingly, the person had been sent by Clint to try and recruit *Fritz* for Clint's "team" against me! "I just want to warn you, Sondra, that Clint's gonna try and make you and Gordon out to be crazy," he told me. Things were getting weirder and weirder.

I waited by the phone while Gordon was being deposed by Clint's litigator, Howard King. I stared at the clock, whose hands didn't seem to move. I was concerned for Gordon, and yet I wasn't. He had always said that he was really two people. One, I knew, was childlike and vulnerable, but the other was fierce with insight as piercing as a laser beam, and the courage of a lion.

The phone call finally came. "Well, Sondra, I'll be happy if you do half as well as Gordon just did," Norman said. I breathed a sigh of relief.

That night Gordon regaled me with his deposition when we covertly met at the Tail o' the Pup because somehow it was "forbidden" that we talk — God forbid it should be construed as "consulting."

"You wouldn't have believed all the nonsense," Gordon said. "It seemed to me that King was shocked when he heard how you and Clint and Bo and I had traveled and socialized together. I'll bet Clint told him that he and I had barely ever met. I thought it was all just ridiculous. And really, I couldn't believe it when he started that whole inane line of questions about how often you and I spend time together. 'Do you celebrate birthdays together? How do you celebrate? Do you and Sondra celebrate Thanksgiving together? How many Thanksgivings have you *not* celebrated together?' When he asked me if there was 'some regular method by which you would celebrate Thanksgiving each year,' I answered, yes. He was positively panting, and then he pounced. 'Well, what was it?' he demanded. I smiled innocently and said, 'Just turkey.' " Gordon cackled. "You should have seen his face."

Then I began laughing so hard my eyes filled with tears. Thank God I could still laugh. But how could it be reduced to this?

Later when I read Gordon's transcript, I could appreciate what Norman had said. Gordon had full throttle let Clint have it. He said Clint had "no character," then went on to say: "He [Clint] is a person who, for whatever reason, has reached a point in his life where he is coming face-to-face with certain *truths* about himself that he does not want to face. And rather than try to deal with problems *he* might have, [he] would rather fire you, or blame you, or say it is the kids' fault, anybody's fault but *his own*. And I was the person that he picked to be the culprit. And I would also like to say that we have never had any unpleasant words ever between us. And, you know, I find it totally infantile and unreasonable to believe that because 'I fire Fritz, then you have to give up . . . your wife . . . or your best bowling buddy, etc. I gave up one; you give up one.' And that is what he said at one point to Sondra."

I returned that night to the small hotel at the beach, and at some point during the night a very curious thing occurred. The next morning when I went to get into the Jimmy, I discovered that the driver's window had been smashed. The timing—immediately after Gordon's deposition—was remarkable. Even more astounding was what was taken from it: my director's log for *Impulse*, where I kept all my notes, and some legal papers concerning my lawsuit against Clint. I had to wonder why the burglar hadn't taken more, or simply taken the car. Equally surprising, were the things *not* taken: the radio, the tapes, a jacket. And the whole thing had happened in a very nice neighborhood inside a security garage.

My deposition was nothing short of hell. In some ways it was the worst experience thus far. I was expected to prove my *existence*, and additionally the whole legal maze was so completely foreign and frightening. In fact, my body trembled as I raised my hand to be sworn to the truth. Almost from the start it was clear that my informant had been right about Clint's strategy. Howard King started in on the subject of fairy tales. "How long have you liked fairy tales?" "What is your favorite fairy tale, Miss Locke?"

Apparently, they hoped to convince a jury that because I liked fairy tales, I had *fantasized* my thirteen-year life with Clint. I was then taken through my entire life with Clint, and all those questions were slanted to make me feel sleazy that I'd had "stolen" a "married man." He even asked me about the last time Clint and I had made love. He made me defend my abortions. He asked endlessly about my relationship with Gordon: "Do you ever cook for him? Where do you take your clothes to the cleaners? Isn't that near *Gordon's* house? How many times in these years did you spend the night at *Gordon's* house?" The truth was *I didn't know* because I hadn't counted, *because it didn't matter*. But I was made to feel, even by my own attorney, that I *had* to give an answer. It was all simply a contrivance by Clint's attorney to upset me, and to distort the nature of *all* our relationships. I guess he thought if I spent several nights a year at Gordon's *that* would prove to a jury we had a true marriage regardless of the fact that Gordon was gay.

For the first time in my entire life I consulted a psychiatrist. I couldn't accept what was happening. The memory of the old Clint fought the present Clint. I couldn't reconcile the man I had loved with the ogre who was doing all these things to me. And *why* was he doing them? At times, I even blamed myself, and I didn't understand why.

"It's not unlike a rape victim, Sondra," my psychiatrist said to me.

"It just doesn't make any sense to me how I can still be so mixed up. I mean, I saw this film footage on A *Current Affair* and I actually felt pain for *Clint*. A *Current Affair's* cameras had caught, through the entry room window, a silhouette of a man peeking out, then quickly closing the wooden shutters. *I* knew it was Clint, and I knew the pain he was feeling because his privacy had been invaded. Worse than that, it was the pain he was feeling because strangers outside now knew something about him — they knew where he was, they knew things about his life that had been exposed in my legal papers, the pain he was feeling because, maybe for the first time, he wasn't in complete control. And I actually felt sorry for him. It's crazy!"

"Those are *your* feelings, Sondra, and that's fine. But Clint may feel something quite different, or he may *feel nothing*. You shouldn't try to imagine what he may feel or want at this time."

I laughed. "He *wants* me to disappear. He wants to *will* me away and he doesn't want it to cost him anything — not emotionally, not financially, not in any way whatsoever. That's what he wants. Poof. I never happened. Clint's magical thinking. He used to say that all the time, you know. 'I *will* things to be the way I want them.' "

"And what do *you* want?" the doctor asked.

"I want him not to be so cruel," I replied.

"You can't wish for him to change. You must ask yourself what *you* want for you."

"I want to be treated fairly, with the respect I deserve. I want my home. I want him to keep his promises. I want these thirteen years to have counted for something."

Often I felt my efforts were futile. How could I really win against Clint? No one else ever had; no one had even tried. What I didn't know was that I would wage my fight against him virtually alone. Slowly but surely all those friends who had urged me forward would disappear. All those dear, close friends who had said what a bad man Clint was, who had cheered me on, encouraged me to stand up to Clint and to fight him, all those concerned friends who had advised me and helped me get an attorney would conveniently bail out. As my attorney tried to prepare my case, they would barely return his calls. Lili spoke briefly with Norman, but Maria actually hung up on him. And she did it only because Norman called her hand, "What's to become of Sondra?" he said to her when she was reluctant to speak. "What's to become of her if her friends won't even speak up for her?" "How dare you call me disloyal!" Maria screeched. And then hung up.

When an early pretrial hearing was scheduled on the single issue of returning me to my home, none of those friends were available. Cynthia was in Hawaii. With accusation in her voice she said, "Well, I *did* sometimes phone you at Gordon's house, Sondra." I couldn't believe it. And yes, Cynthia, I *did* sometimes phone you at your mother's . . . even at your manicurist. Does that mean you lived there? I thought.

Maria was in New York and "couldn't possibly return in time," and Lili was still in Florida, quite unable to be away from the set for even one day to fly in on my behalf. She was apparently so important there that her husband, Richard Zanuck, the successful and powerful producer, couldn't run things in her absence. All afraid of the high-profile politics.

And while they were not at all part of my support system, they were also pretending to be totally "there" for me. *People* magazine, doing a story about the split-up, wanted friends of mine to say a word or two. I asked Maria, "Would you just call them and say a few nice words on my behalf? You don't have to repeat what you've said to me of your feelings about Clint, if that makes you uncomfortable. Just talk about me and what I'm like." I felt pathetic *asking* someone who purported to be my friend, and who claimed I was part of her "family," to validate me.

"Of course, Sondra," Maria had said. "I'll speak to them immediately. I'll call first thing in the morning." But she never did, which I found out from *People* magazine. I let her continue with her smiles and her pretensions, but I knew it was the beginning of the end of the real feelings I had had for her. But I had to remind myself, Maria had her own problems, being a Kennedy wasn't easy. And I knew she had always had a real fear of the press despite being one of them herself. She seemed terrified how she might be portrayed by them. When she and Arnold were dating, she used to scour the papers for any mention of them, just to make sure it was all "appropriately phrased." Many times she called on her powerful contacts to stop a story. The right image seemed imperative. And to that image, I felt, she sacrificed the truly real, potentially happy person underneath. Certainly living with Arnold was no picnic, and deep down a part of me empathized because I knew what she was living with; after all, I'd lived with one of them myself for thirteen years. I remembered a conversation she told me she'd had with Arnold after Clint had locked me out. She had asked him, "You would never do a cruel thing like that to me if we split up, would you, Arnold?" "Well," he had paused, thinking, "if the house was in my name, I suppose I could." As she recounted the story, I noticed how she sadly searched my eyes, waiting, hoping that I had some answer that would excuse his reply, and distinguish it from mine. I didn't.

Arnold had also told me *he* was disgusted with Clint's behavior, that before, he had always looked up to him. Clint's film *Pink Cadillac* was released when Maria and Arnold were on location for *Total Recall*. After they saw a preview of it, Maria proudly quoted Arnold: "*Pink Cadillac* is a mess. Clint has lost it. I think he's gone insane. I can't be friends with him anymore after what he's done to Sondra." Those words were easy, and time would prove otherwise. Arnold's loyalty to Clint seemed to be commensurate with the box office success of Clint's films.

Cynthia, whom I guess I'd always suspected was a little superficial, did the coldest thing of all, and when I needed it the least. Though opened, my boxes were still in her basement. I just couldn't take possession of them—my pulse would rise and my stomach twist any time the thought of them arose. But I was forced to deal with them when Cynthia called, wanting them removed.

"Bud really wants you to move your boxes out of the basement, darling," she said.

"Can't it please wait until I finish my film? I'm trying to edit it and find a place to live and deal with a lot emotionally, Cynthia. It's too painful even to look at those boxes right now," I begged her.

"I'm sorry, but I can't discuss it further. Please, don't make this difficult for me, Sondra. Try and understand."

I was beginning to understand a lot. I was beginning to understand that Cynthia was a vain, silly, shallow woman. If Bud had thrown her out, and she needed me to, I would have stacked her boxes in my small rented living room if that were the only space I had. But it didn't matter anymore to me who she really was.

But what could Clint Eastwood do to Mrs. Richard Zanuck? Nothing. So why had she run for cover? I had always sensed there was some key ingredient missing in her; she was able to flip a switch and forget the personal aspects of a situation. At the very least she could be dispassionate to a fault; in many ways she had the consummate personality for getting ahead in the movie business.

It was truly sad, yet illuminating, that the only person from my life with Clint who dared to come forward and tell the truth was the Guatemalan caretaker, Tomas. He agreed to be deposed and to answer all questions truthfully. It was very brave for Tomas to do such a thing because he stood to lose everything—his job, a good reference, his well-being. Yet he did it, in spite of others who tried to stop him. Mr. Fink, the contractor for our tennis court and pool, and the person who had also brought Tomas for employment, placed himself into the mix. To impress Clint, Fink tried to stop Tomas's deposition in my favor. Fink, who was also an attorney, phoned my attorney. He claimed to represent Tomas and said Tomas was ill and could not be deposed. He didn't know *when* he'd be well enough to speak with anyone. I phoned Tomas, who knew nothing of Fink's claim. Tomas presented himself to be deposed, and to testify at the subsequent hearing. While he sat in the waiting room, Jane Brolin bullied him, saying, "You're making a mistake . . . Cl-l-i-i-i-nt's going to win this." Immediately afterward Tomas fell off a ladder at Stradella and couldn't work for months. "It was no accident," Gordon said. "He wasn't meant to be up there without you."

While I waited for my hearing, I was still editing my film, and staying with Nadine and her husband, Michael, neither of whom knew Clint very well. I tried to remain calm but it was hard because so many unnerving things were going on. One day Nadine thought she was being followed, and felt she was probably being confused for me. We made some test drives to see what was going on, and there he was behind us. Later, we found him brazenly parked in front of her house and decided to confront him.

"Who are you? We know you're following us. Why?" we asked him.

He just sat silently in his car. We then pulled out a camera. He remained calm and silent as he opened his car door and walked straight toward his trunk and began to unlock it. I was suddenly terrified. What if he was some lunatic who was about to produce a shotgun from his trunk? My heart started pounding. We froze, just standing there watching him. He pulled out, not a shotgun, but a camera of his own and began taking pictures of us while we were taking pictures of him. It was theater of the absurd. Later, of course, we were able to confirm, again through my LAPD detective friend, that indeed he was a private eye . . . but, of course, he would never divulge the name of his client.

Chapter 11 ~

Clint's deposition was Thursday, May 25, 1989. Norman and I sat in his high-rise conference room, waiting for Clint to arrive with his henchmen. My emotions were mixed about being present for it, sitting face-to-face with him; still it could be like exorcising some evil demon. I hadn't laid eyes on him since that awful scene in our dining room on April 4.

The door opened and my pulse quickened, but it was only Norman's secretary. I breathed a sigh of relief, then looked away, out the window. Beyond the odd mixture of palm trees and skyscrapers, I could see the ocean miles away. I imagined the waves washing in and out, and my body relaxed. Just as I was settling into the view and wishing myself way out there, I heard the all-too-familiar voice. "Hey, how's it goin'?" said Clint as if nothing unusual were happening.

There he was, striding along, smiling at everyone, just a good ol' boy — as honest and endearing as the day is long. Clint was a far better actor off-screen than on, I thought. He and his attorneys made the perfunctory greeting, and, although I managed to keep my eyes on him, Clint never looked at me. He was very brave at destroying people behind their backs but not so courageous at looking them in the eye afterward. Everyone settled down around the long conference table. Norman and I were on one side; on the other were Clint and Dennis Wasser, the big-gun family law specialist Clint had brought in to try to destroy my case, and Howard King from the firm Gang, Tyre, Ramer & Brown which Clint kept on full-time retainer. Also present was Clint's business manager Roy Kaufman, who greeted me with a warm handshake and one of those looks that said, "Oh, Sondra, this is so horrible. And, by the way, I'm really on your side, but I can't say so. You do understand, don't you?"

We all sat down.

"Do you swear to tell the truth, the whole truth, and nothing but the truth, so help you God?" "I do," Clint replied. That traditional swearing-in seemed ironic to me; at that point the idea of Clint telling the truth about anything seemed unlikely.

As painful as this was, a part of me was curious to see what stories Clint was about to construct. As Lili had put it, "Clint's gonna have a big problem keeping his stories straight, Sondra. He is unable to cross-reference." And, because he couldn't keep the stories straight in his own mind, he didn't think anyone else could either, or didn't care.

The deposition began slowly with Clint "stonewalling," as Norman referred to it. Though it lasted only six hours, it seemed to go on and on for days. And, even at this point in my nightmare, Clint's extraordinarily brazen position with regard to our relationship stunned me. I had, of course, seen the letter he'd written to "Mrs. Gordon Anderson"; I knew in essence what he was going to claim, but hearing the cold hard lies actually come from his mouth caused more pain than I can say. "She never lived with me. She lived at Gordon's," he said in a hundred different ways.

When Norman asked Clint to describe his relationship with me "during the period you and Miss Locke were using the premises located at 846 Stradella Road," Clint said that "we were going together." When Norman asked him what that entailed, Clint said, "To go out on dates," then added, "going to the beach to going to the mountains to going to the desert." Suddenly I felt as if I were back in high school.

Finally Norman zeroed in on the key but simple question: "Did you *ever live together* with Miss Locke?" This began a series of exchanges between Norman, King, and Clint about the nature and definition of "living together," in which King and Clint did everything they could to avoid answering it. Finally, however, Clint begrudgingly responded, "We have spent nights together, yes." But just as quickly he retreated when Norman asked if he and I had ever "lived together under the same roof." "Not exclusively" was Clint's response. Norman asked again, "Have you ever on a *nonexclusive* basis lived together?" It was then that Clint dropped in his main angle: "It is hard to come up with a definition because Miss Locke is married." Clint then began to describe me as a "roommate," but then quickly redescribed me as a "part-time roommate," which he also admitted I'd been for "approximately ten years." From there my importance in his life diminished to that of his decorator: "Miss Locke helped with the *decorating* of the home," Clint said.

There was little that could be described as funny about what Clint was doing to me, but being able to see the dark comedic aspects of our whole breakup was one of the things that had kept me going. Clint was so over-the-top that I could almost laugh in his face.

Norman finally got to some grain of truth when Clint admitted that "the relationship had had its deteriorating moment approximately three and a half to four years ago." That was enlightening to know because he'd denied that to me at the time, which, interestingly, I noticed was around the same time I found the script for *Ratboy*. But even that turned into gobbledygook when Norman said, "The initial question is what was the *nature* of the relationship? Then we can talk about—" Clint interrupted and said, "Well, I have to go up to the four years ago because the two years ago was—if you want to change from the four year to the two year, then I would say it was *the same*." His mathematical calculation was not only a nonresponsive answer, it made no sense, but it had at least resulted in some definition—"the same." Now that Clint had described our relationship as "the same," Norman attempted to understand what he meant by "the same" and asked, "What *is* the relationship?" and this led to the most amazing exchange of dialogue yet. Clint answered, "Same relationship." Norman asked, "Same as what?" Clint said, "Same as it was." Norman: "And what was it?" "The same." "And what was it?" "The same." "The same as what, sir?" "Just the same." "You refuse to describe as to what it is the same as?" "Well, I don't know what you are referring to," Clint concluded.

It was amazing. The whole thing began to feel like the old Abbott and Costello routine "Who's on First, What's on Second, and I Don't Know's on Third." Then Clint topped himself by saying, "I can't answer the question because it requires me to 'speculate on my own mind.'" I certainly agreed that would be impossible, even for a panel of world renowned psychiatrists, to speculate on Clint's mind. In frustration Norman answered, "I am not asking you to speculate on your own mind. I am asking you whether or not at any time you had in your own mind any notion that you had ever made a commitment of any sort to Sondra Locke from the time that you first knew her." Without a pause Clint said, "What commitment are you referring to?"

I could take no more. I had to get out of there. I stood up and walked past Clint, pushed through the doors behind him, and moved into the hallway. I had to get some fresh air, any air that he wasn't currently breathing. But his lies and evasions kept assaulting me. "What commitment are you referring to?" Did he think we were all idiots? No, it didn't matter what "we" thought. He was Clint Eastwood. I stood in the hallway not knowing which way to turn, just wanting to bolt out of there. But as with everything in my life up to that moment, I knew I had to face it. I took a long drink of water, then reopened the door to the conference room and walked into another nightmare.

"And when did you place those recording devices on the telephone?" Norman asked Clint. "In March or April of eighty-nine," Clint answered.

I could see the shock on Norman's face as I took my seat; he hadn't believed me when I had told him that I suspected Clint had tapped my phones. Clint went on to claim that the phone taps were not there to record *my* conversation (of course mine were virtually the *only* conversations on those tapes), they were there because he'd been receiving "death threats" at home and at the office, off and on for three years. I recognized the "death threat" excuse as one he'd used in the past to get out of this or that. I *knew* there were no such threats at home; and if there were, why hadn't he told me about it? Clint then admitted that he had not put any taps on the office phone, which according to him received the *same* threats, *and* he admitted he had not even asked for assistance from his pals on the police force. It was all ridiculous and transparent; there was *no doubt* in my mind that the only reason he had placed the taps was to record me and my friends—*and* the conversations I had with my own attorney—so that he could calculate all his moves to get rid of me at no cost to him. It got worse. When Norman asked Clint, "What was the nature of the threats?" unfathomably, Clint responded, "Says, 'I am going to fuck you; I am going to fuck you. I am going to kill you.'"

I could not believe my ears. Just when I thought I might laugh, Norman asked the next question, "And who was the suspect?" and Clint answered, "I think it's Anderson." Disbelieving, Norman asked, "You are referring to who Anderson?" "Gordon Anderson" was Clint's extraordinary answer.

Like the pendulum on some clock, my emotions swung in the other direction. I almost came out of my chair. Now I was absolutely furious. What a completely evil, manipulating, lying excuse for a man he was. And what ultimate irony. Clint Eastwood, the man who symbolized to so many what a man should be, had turned out to have none of the acknowledged qualities of a real man—loyalty, honesty, bravery, and moral strength—and yet Gordon, a child-man, a gay man, had possessed them all.

Not only were Clint's claims of threatening phone calls a ridiculous, preposterous, and slanderous lie, it was a complete joke that the phantom caller had supposedly said, "I want to fuck you. I want to fuck you. I want to kill you." All this showed exactly how much his *money* meant to Clint; why else was he trying to deny our very history, destroy me, and even Gordon, unless it was to keep every penny of his money, and his "real estate." Of course, I knew this was just a game to "use" Gordon to escape his responsibility and promises to me, but I also figured that now he really did hate Gordon because Gordon had foiled his plan. First, Gordon hadn't accepted my Bekins boxes the way Clint had wanted him to. Norman had said, "Thank God you didn't take them, Gordon. If you had, Clint would have pointed to that and said, 'Her clothes are there; that alone proves that's where she lives.'" Idiotic but pure Clint. It would also have supported his other completely untrue and ridiculous claim that I "had a wardrobe at Gordon's house." Once my things were accepted into Gordon's house, who could ever prove what had actually been where? It was absurd but I learned that's the way Clint thought.

Another, and most important, way Gordon had foiled Clint was by coming forward and publicly admitting that he was gay—not only to Clint's attorneys but to everybody else involved. Gordon lived a very private life, and Clint assumed that he would never want to discuss his homosexuality in a deposition or in a trial. And if Gordon hadn't, it would support Clint's claim that Gordon and I were a happily married heterosexual couple. But he had underestimated Gordon's courage, and his genuine caring for me. And that caring was clearly something that, no doubt, did finally drive Clint crazy. I'd learned he was incapable of understanding genuine love between two people unless it was vested in "gain." I wasn't "getting" anything from Gordon that he could comprehend—not sex, not money, not servitude—and what else mattered? To cap it all off, I was certain that Clint had read every single word of Gordon's deposition that had exposed Clint's true nature like some virus under a microscope. Clint wasn't expecting *any* of these things to happen. And Clint didn't like not getting his way.

It boggled the mind that Clint was presenting Gordon as my heterosexual husband, on the one hand, and on the other he was claiming that Gordon was threatening to "fuck" him. One thing was clear to me, I no longer had to talk to my psychiatrist about my *empathy* for Clint. I cared nothing for his feelings. Clearly he'd stop at nothing. But then he'd always said to me, "Some people can get away with anything."

My spirits began to sink lower and lower. I had lost ten pounds, from an already slender figure, and I was constantly exhausted. Just getting dressed seemed like an awesome task. Those feelings were not just over the loss of the relationship; they were over the loss of faith in anything expected or counted on in life. If the man I had loved could cold-bloodedly lock me out of my home and deny me, then anything could happen. At times, I drove around in my car, just crying. My psychiatrist prescribed Prozac and Xanax which I took gratefully, as I continued editing my film.

I asked my attorney to plead with Clint at least to return my pet parrot, Putty, to me. I wanted him back, not just for my own comfort, but because I loved him and worried about him sitting there alone in the dining room.

Clint's response came through Howard King. "Notwithstanding any feelings

Clint's response came through Howard King. "Notwithstanding any feelings of affection that Sondra may have developed for it, the parrot named Putty was a gift to *Clint* from Jane Brolin. I am informed that Putty is one of the two parrots at the Stradella house [like one of two sofas?]. Clint thinks it would be inadvisable to separate them now. In all events, he does not wish to do so." It made no difference when I offered to take both birds.

Not only did he withhold my pet from me, he would also not return the Mercedes he had given me some years earlier. Finally, after much legal pressure, he agreed to return it, but only because it was one of the few things actually registered *in my name*. However, in retaliation, he demanded the Jimmy be returned to him immediately and subsequently took it without my knowledge while I was in the editing room working.

I learned that Clint had even tracked down poor Harper Bowman, whom he had never before phoned (not in all the years we'd known Bo). Clint hoped that Bo would assist him in some way, but Bo didn't. Incredibly, Clint also contacted my brother, Donald—with whom he had *never* before spoken—in an attempt to use my estranged family against me. He filled Donald's head full of lies that were subsequently printed in the Nashville newspaper. Clint claimed to have supported Gordon for years, and even to have paid for his psychiatrist—both complete lies. Although Clint did buy Gordon's house (which he then denied and was then trying to take back), Clint never spent one single penny on any support for Gordon. It was I who had always taken care of Gordon from my own earnings. Clint went on to tell Donald that it was I who had actually broken up with *him*, and that I was "obsessed" with doing research for Gordon on the guillotine (a truly bizarre claim—especially considering it was *he* who had assisted Gordon, and even asked for his own model guillotine!). It was all petty and ridiculous, and at the same time unbelievably evil.

⁓

MAY 31 CAME—the hearing on my request that the judge return me to my home. I would live to regret that I had agreed to a *private* judge and a *private* hearing. The hearing was held quietly in Norman's law offices instead of a public courthouse, with the press crawling all over. I naïvely had thought that if it were completely private, my high-profile friends might participate.

My witness list was a short one, consisting primarily of John, Tomas, and Gordon, whose presence was suddenly no longer demanded by Clint's attorneys. Apparently they hadn't liked his answers in deposition. But my attorney *had* liked them and was now calling Gordon as a witness for us. Norman had contacted Fritz Manes, but he had refused to testify. Fritz told Norman that he would not willingly testify, and if we supoenaed him, he would say things that would "hurt" me. To me, that meant he would be lying, since there was nothing in the truth that could possibly have hurt me. That Fritz did this was upsetting to me, but sadly understandable. Like so many people, he feared going against Clint; after all, he hadn't even done it for himself.

But Clint's witness list was not exactly stellar. It was no surprise that he brought in Jane Brolin, who finally confessed under oath that it was she who had sold those lies about the breakup to the *National Enquirer*. It was, however, a real shock that Clint brought in his son, Kyle, and had Kyle claim under oath that he was presently living in the Stradella house! I knew that Kyle was *not* living at Stradella; he and his friend Mike had rented a house in the Valley months earlier. But the evening before Kyle's testimony, Clint brought Kyle to spend the night at Stradella. Was that Clint's attempt to convince himself that he wasn't asking his son to lie? Clint wanted to cover every base. After all, he was preparing to leave for Africa to make *White Hunter, Black Heart*, which would mean that my house would be standing *empty*, and this might encourage the judge to allow me to return, but if Clint's own son were there . . . ? "That's the sickest thing Clint has done so far," Lili would later say.

Nothing could really have have shocked me at that point, especially not after what I had learned earlier that morning, when Gordon had arrived at Norman's offices. The moment I saw his face, I knew that something was terribly wrong. He pulled me into one of the conference rooms and handed me a piece of paper with a phone number. "You have to call this man right away; he's a journalist and he's been working on some big exposé on Clint."

"He probably just wants to get me to say something he can print. I don't want to call him."

"No, Hobbit, listen to me. Try to stay calm."

"Oh God, what now? What's happening?" My anxieties were rising.

"I have terrible news. Clint has two small children . . . right now, in Carmel."

I felt like I had been slapped in the face. The room I was standing in began to close in on me, like the scene from the old Olivia de Havilland movie *Snake Pit*. I couldn't get my breath — it was unexpected, unprepared-for pain. "I can't believe that's true," I said.

"I know it's unspeakable, but I believe this man's telling the truth. It was a complete miracle that I even got his message this morning. The only reason my phone was turned on was because John was supposed to wake me for this hearing."

I began to sob. "This is too much. Maybe he *never* loved me; I really believed he loved me."

"I know; I know how much it hurts, how much pain you're in, but if you weren't, I'd be worried. If you weren't in pain, you'd be just what he is—emotionless, dead. Whatever happens, you're lucky to be away from him. You have to remember that," he reassured me.

I couldn't answer, I numbly took the phone number and started to dial a man I didn't know, a man named David Shumacher, a man to whom I would remain indebted for being one of the few who told me the truth and wanted nothing in return.

"I've been working on an article about Clint for a while now," he said. "The title of it is 'The Man Behind the Mask.'"

Unexpectedly I began laughing. "Well, you've got the right title, anyway."

"Yes, I know. I have so much information on this man from so many different people, but none of them will speak officially on the record."

"I'm not surprised," I offered. "He seems to be able, in one way or another, to get control over everything and everybody. Either they're afraid of him or they're sticking around for some meager crumb he might someday toss them."

"Well, I know a lot of people who feel you're getting a bad deal."

"That's encouraging. I appreciate the support. How did you get Gordon's phone number?" I asked.

"It was someone in Roy Kaufman's office. She feels you're really getting screwed. She thought she'd be helping you by giving me the number," he explained.

"That's nice to hear. Well, go ahead . . . tell me all the bad news," I said to him.

"Do you know anyone by the name of Jacelyn Reeves? And a house Clint owns in Carmel at Carmelo and Eleventh?"

"No. Clint and I lived on San Antonio, not far from there," I explained.

"It's listed in Roy Kaufman's name—"

"Clint puts all property in Roy Kaufman's name," I interrupted. "He doesn't want anyone to be able to track anything about him. I could never even get mail at home."

He continued, "Well, I hate to tell you but during the four years since he moved Reeves into that house, they've had two children. Their names are Kathryn and Scott."

I had thought I was prepared to hear it. But now they had real names. Still I couldn't believe it. It was just so very weird I couldn't get my mind around it.

"I spoke with the nurse in the delivery room," he continued, "and she confirmed that they are Clint's children. I'll send copies of the birth certificates to you and a photo of Jacelyn, if you want them."

"When? When was this going on? When were they born?" I asked, still disbelieving.

"The girl, Kathryn, was born February 2, 1988."

"Oh my God! She's . . . she's just over a year old." I thought of last New Year's in Sun Valley and wondered if, only a short month later, after he'd created that awful scene with me, if he had shown up for Kathryn's birthday. And in between it all, he had been creeping in and out of my house on Stradella, collecting the secret tapes on *my* phone conversations.

"And the boy?" I asked like an automaton.

"Scott was born March 21, 1986," he replied.

The little boy had to have been conceived about four years ago. That was when the troubles began on *Ratboy*, but obviously whatever control issues he had over my directing were fueled by the hidden birth of a son. All Clint's gibberish in his deposition—"it was four years ago, two years ago"—had meaning after all. I could feel the heat of anger rising to the surface of my face as I thought of those times and all the games he had played on me, and how I had begged for the truth.

"Is Clint's name on the birth certificate?" I asked weakly.

"It says 'father declined,' but they're his, all right. A few other people there know about it too."

"Father declined." That sounded like Clint.

"I'm really sorry to upset you," the voice interrupted my silence. "But I felt, in view of what's happening to you, that you should have this information."

"Yes, I know, it's just that . . ." I trailed off.

My mind was still searching to get all his actions lined up. For at least the last four years, Clint had been living this double life, going between me and this other woman, and *having children with her.* Two babies had been born in the last three years of our relationship, and they weren't mine. More pain was heaped onto my pain about my own abortions and subsequent tubal ligation.

Then, the most unexpected and humorous thought flashed into my mind—the mincemeat pie I had sent him on the *Pink Cadillac* location that last Thanksgiving. Had he shared it with Jacelyn or with Frances Fisher (who worked with him on that film)? Or was it someone else I was yet to know about? What had he been doing while I had stood in my kitchen weaving the old-fashioned, open-lattice crust topping that he'd always loved so much?

I just wanted to get out of my attorney's offices, out of the building, go home. I just wanted to go somewhere and lie down for a very, very, long time. But I didn't. I assured Gordon that I was all right, left him sitting in the conference room, waiting to be called for his own later testimony, and walked straight into the hearing room. Clint was already inside, and as I brushed past him I could feel my anger pulsing, could almost feel my hands involuntarily reaching toward him, to grab him, shake him, scratch him, slap him, pull out his hair transplants. What therapy that would have been! Maybe I wouldn't ever have needed to see my psychiatrist again. Instead, I quietly walked past him, sat beside Norman, and began to write a note about what I had just learned. I slid it in front of Norman and saw a look of complete disbelief on his face.

"Today is Mr. Eastwood's birthday," Howard King announced proudly to Judge Hogoboom. Clint puffed up, and he and the judge smiled at each other. And so it began. As the hearing droned on, my anger subsided into a deadness, and I existed like a sleepwalker through most of it. And for that I was grateful.

Clint fought furiously when my attorneys demanded he submit his wills to the court but eventually he was ordered to turn them over. They were revealing in a few respects. They confirmed my testimony that he had bequeathed the Sherman Oaks house to me, and that fact lent credence to my testimony that he had bought Stradella as a replacement for me. But more stunning than that was *whom* Clint included in his wills: I was out, of course, but at the same time he removed me he had, coincidentally, added Jane Brolin. Jacelyn Reeves and her two children were in there too, completely confirming the story I'd been told. Most bizarre of all, he'd also included Jean Grace, the new mayor of Carmel whom Jane had called my attention to in the *National Enquirer*. There were no adjectives left to describe my feelings.

At the end of that first day, when no one was left in the offices except Gordon, John, me, and my attorneys, I noticed Gordon going through the hearing room wastebasket. "What are you doing?" I asked. But he only said, "Get me some Scotch tape." Norman and I watched over his shoulder as he placed torn scraps of yellow legal paper, which he'd pulled from the trash, onto the conference table. Then like pieces in a small puzzle he moved them around, taping them together until it read: "Susi Pi" . . . in Clint's own scrawled handwriting.

"How on earth did you know this was in the wastebasket, Gordon?" I asked. "I don't know," Gordon answered. "I just knew." Perhaps Gordon's nickname for Clint contained truth that even Clint could recognize, obviously it had struck a nerve that had remained tender. There was only one place Clint could *ever* have heard that word and that was on the phone tapes. However, when Norman gave me the awful task of listening to those tapes, *nowhere* did that word "Susi Pi" appear. To me this meant that Clint had never turned over all the tapes. Only those he'd hoped, in his twisted mind, to somehow use in his favor.

My motion to return me to my home had a fatal flaw in its framing: It requested that I be returned "to the exclusion of Clint." My psychiatrist had suggested that I not be in a house to which Clint also had access. Comparing my situation to a rape victim's, he felt that it would be too emotionally stressful for me, given the way Clint had acted. And ultimately Judge Hogoboom (whom Clint had paid to conduct the hearing) denied my motion on the basis that he could not "exclude Clint." Therefore, under the terms of my motion, I could not be returned.

The moment I met Judge Hogoboom, I hadn't liked him. And throughout the hearing he showed little interest in my obvious emotional distress, or in my psychiatrist's testimony. Hogoboom further astounded me when he stated in his ruling that he was "unconvinced I had sustained any emotional distress at all because, in the midst of all that had happened, I had managed to complete my film." I wondered how many men had had their emotional pain judged by whether or not they continued to show up for work during some crisis. I would lay odds that it was zero. But then, Hogoboom had also yelled out callously, "I don't want to hear about any parrot. Whoever gets the house gets both parrots!" I never did see Putty again. I learned that Clint changed Putty's name to Paco. After all, it would mean he hadn't really stolen Putty at all, wouldn't it? If Putty wasn't Putty any longer . . . With a wave of his wand, presto-chango, Putty was Paco . . . and not Sondra's bird at all.

And so for now, I had nothing. Except some cash in a separate bank account, fourteen Bekins boxes, and a deeply wounded spirit. My only real asset was an unfinished film owned by Warner Bros. — "Clint's studio."

It had been such a gloomy day. I had hoped for rain, but the sun merely hid behind layers of smog, which delivered nothing. The ever-increasing exhaustion sat like a heavy boulder on my neck and shoulders as I searched for an apartment. For some reason, it became overwhelmingly important to me that I connect emotionally with wherever I would be living. In my fragile state, I couldn't seem to view it as a temporary "hotel." At first I thought of returning to the Andalusia, but Mrs. Uhl had passed away a year earlier, and the building was no longer renting. Yet it was through Mrs. Uhl, after her death, that I was amazingly *led* to an apartment I rented on Fountain Avenue.

This particular story begins a year earlier when Gordon had ordered some Gothic corbels. They were months overdue, so I called the company. The clerk there told me they had been delivered to the Andalusia. The UPS paperwork showed that "the receipt was signed by a Mrs. Uhl, who claimed to be the manager." It seemed strange because Gordon hadn't lived at the Andalusia for six years and during that time UPS had regularly delivered to him at his current address. Gordon phoned Mrs. Uhl, and when she never answered her phone, he became concerned about her. He then called Louise, the Andalusia maid. Upon hearing the UPS story, Louise asked, "When did she sign for it?"

"On May thirteenth—that's what they said at UPS."

"Well, Gordon, that's just not possible. Mrs. Uhl passed on May ninth."

Mrs. Uhl had suddenly become ill and was taken to a hospital in Westwood, where she died shortly thereafter. We were shocked and deeply saddened to hear that news, and then a very strange thing happened. While still on the phone to Louise, Gordon heard someone say his name in an odd whispery tone.

"Louise. Did you just say my name?"

"No. I heard that too but I thought it was Sondra. I thought that she might have picked up the telephone."

"Sondra isn't even here, Louise. I'm completely alone."

After a palpable silence Louise said, "Well, since Mrs. Uhl passed, I can sure tell you there's been some strange things going on in her apartment. Several times when I've been in to clean, I've heard sounds coming from the upstairs, almost like she was walking around up there. It was spooky, if I may say." "If I may say" was one of Louise's favorite phrases.

When my requested copy of the UPS receipt arrived, it definitely showed Mrs. Uhl's familiar signature, and was clearly dated May 13. It made no sense. When I phoned UPS again, they reassured me that only the addressee or the manager could sign for UPS packages. At Gordon's request, Louise checked with all the current tenants to see if they knew anything about the delivery; no one did. "Nobody but me and the executor of her will was allowed in her apartment," Louise said, "and he didn't know about it either. It's spooky."

The whole thing became even more meaningful when Gordon noticed the name written on the UPS receipt immediately underneath Mrs. Uhl's signature. C. Shepherd, it read (as in Christ Shepherd), and underneath that signature, the next thing was D.E.U.S. (Latin for "God"). It was all further meaningful because Gordon had ordered the Gothic corbels for the Gothic room in his house he called "God's room." So, in a way, those corbels had been the "messenger" to let us know that someone dear to us had died. In the normal sense, it remained unexplainable and amazing, but the story didn't end there.

Because it was not possible to move back to the Andalusia, I thought of another building not far from it called the Villa d'Este. When I phoned there, the manager told me he had nothing at all available; and warned me that it was virtually impossible to find an availability in those older European buildings. Then, just as I was hanging up, he asked, "Excuse me, but your voice . . . you sound like the actress Sondra Locke. Are you? Oh, I'm so glad to hear from you. You know, Mrs. Uhl adored you so."

"You knew Mrs. Uhl?" I asked.

"Oh yes. We were friends for many years. I'm the executor of her will in fact."

I thought of Louise's comment that only she and the executor had access to Mrs. Uhl's apartment. Now, quite by accident, in a city of millions of people and telephones, I was on the phone with that *one person*. It seemed impossible. Before we hung up I asked him to please let me know if he heard of an apartment. "Wait. Why didn't I think of this?" he said. It turned out that a friend of his *did*, after all, have an available apartment in such a building—a *Gothic* building—on Fountain Avenue. And it just so happened that his friend was out of town for those two days and had given *him* the keys. He said, "I know that there is a long waiting list for it, but I'll ask him to let you have it as a personal favor to me because Mrs. Uhl was so fond of you." Because I'd phoned him on one of the two days he held the keys, he showed me the apartment.

When I saw the building I realized that it was one that I'd already been connected with. Rona Barrett had filmed a television interview with me there when I was nominated for *The Heart Is a Lonely Hunter*. A third connection was that the owner of this apartment building also owned a building on *Harper* (that recurring name). It seemed to me that I was meant to rent the apartment on Fountain Avenue.

I had affectionately begun calling some of our synchronicities "bread crumbs in the forest" — after the ones that led Hansel and Gretel along their path in the fairy tale. In this case the "bread crumbs" had clearly led me to Fountain Avenue, and I rented the apartment.

July 6, 1989, I moved in. The images and the feelings of my first nights there would be permanently burned into my memory; I will never forget sitting on that living room floor, staring at my only real remaining posses- sions — the haunting black-and-white portraits that the famous still photog- rapher Bob Willoughby had taken of me, all those years ago, after I had won the role of Mick in *The Heart Is a Lonely Hunter*. It seemed perfect somehow, in some strange, symbolic way, that I found myself left with little more than those photographs, as if I had come full circle. I stared and stared at the pictures, trying hard to understand the why and the meaning of all that had happened since they were taken in 1967. And the Mick Kelly eyes stared soulfully back at me, innocent and unknowing of what lay ahead. Somewhere behind Bob Willoughby's image of that gangly girl on the Staten Island Ferry was me. In so many ways, she hadn't changed at all; in so many ways, she no longer existed.

In those days I continued editing my film by day and welcomed with great relief the night. Night meant I could go to bed — to the Dial-A-Bed that I had ordered through the yellow pages when I hadn't the stamina to find one oth- erwise — and escape into sleep. But all too often anxiety attacks, like freight trains, awakened me — anxiety attacks that would leave me hyperventilating and shaking because of fears, both real and imagined, of what would become of me, fears of the future legal battle against Clint that loomed impossibly in front of me. When the anxiety attacks came, I often took refuge in painting my apartment, or listening to a tape I'd purchased, *Sounds of the Forest*. At times, only that tape seemed to soothe me. It would envelop my small apart- ment in the sounds of a jungle thunderstorm . . . the lightning cracked and the thunder rolled and the rain pelted on the giant forest leaves . . .

Clint's assaults to crush me seemed never ending: he raised the monthly "lease" payment on Gordon's house; he refused to return anything from my house to me — my fairy tale collection, or even Christmas gifts, and birthday gifts, some of which had even been given to me by other people.

First, he said the fairy tale collection, especially Red Riding Hood, was *his*. I couldn't imagine when he'd developed that interest! Then he said that the return of some of my requests would "cause some damage" to the wall — one of them barely weighed a pound. He even tried to negotiate one fairy tale piece for another, baiting me with the comparable costs of the items.

Somehow that made me hit the ceiling. I fired off a letter to my own attorney. "I want you to respond to Howard King's letter in the following words exactly:

"Sondra does not 'covet' the 'Tableaux' painting; like the other items on her list it is hers and she merely seeks its return. Sondra also wants you to convey to Clint that she does not now, nor has she ever, cherished anything for its monetary value. It means nothing to her that the 'Tableaux' painting cost $10,000 and the 'Baker Man' cost $1,000. Sondra also states that she personally hung every item on every wall in the house and does not recall that the hole for the 'Baker Man' was any larger than the hole for the painting. In any event, Clint certainly has the financial wherewithal to absorb the minimal cost of repairing any such holes or replacing any pieces with other items more to his own taste." I marveled how Clint had reduced everything to such a level of meanness. I felt better for having written the letter, but still Clint returned only a few items, holding on to "his" Red Riding Hood.

The year concluded for me in a card I received from Clint's mother, Ruth. It was actually in response to a Christmas card I had sent her. Hers, however, was not a Christmas card, but one with a tearful Winnie the Pooh drawing on the front, and printed inside, "I'm so sorry." But her own hand-written words inside made me feel even stranger: "Thank you for the Christmas card, it seemed odd not to send you one! We are both well and looking forward to 1990. Leaving for Indonesia March 10th. Best of luck on your picture. Ruth and Jack." Well, I suppose a "sympathy card" could be considered in order, but if it were so "odd" not to send me a Christmas card, why not just send one? Examining Ruth gave more insight into Clint. Ruth too had been able to flip a switch, I thought, on the relationship we had had, and just not call, not send a note, not send even a Christmas card. Although Ruth had always been accepting and cordial to me, she had never really opened up or gotten close. And there seemed something more than the obvious about her slight formality and distance. I had to wonder why, when she visited overnight, she often brought her own bedsheets. And even between Clint and her—I never observed the two of them really "talking." Most odd to me was the day Clint and I arrived at Rising River and on the kitchen counter lay a few dollars and change with a note from Ruth: "We made a long-distance phone call. Have fun. Mom." I was dumbstruck. Such a gesture seemed inconceivable to me. Yet Clint didn't seem to think so; he stuffed the money in his pocket and looked impressed that she'd paid— that she hadn't expected a "free ride."

Chapter 12 ∽

Christmas of 1989 enriched the ongoing tapestry of synchronicities in our lives to a new, completely unbelievable level. Like Gordon, I've always been a person open to possibilities; however, we are also both healthy skeptics. I guess that's why instinctively neither of us was ever really interested in most New Age or mystical accounts—they are usually too subjective, and if I don't know the individual who is claiming the experience or there is no tangible proof, how can I rely on it? Certainly Gordon was forever trying to tear it all apart, looking for some "normal" explanation; he had to find his own truth in the evidence. He said that he felt the way Alan Jones wrote in his book *Journey into Christ*: "In many cases we have to rely on second-hand information in order to function. I accept the word of a physician, a scientist, a farmer on trust. I do not like to do this. I have to because they possess vital knowledge of living of which I am ignorant. But when it comes to questions of meaning, purpose, and death, secondhand information will not do. I cannot survive on a secondhand faith in a secondhand God. There has to be a personal word, a unique confrontation if I am to come alive."

We still had no contact with Bo. Despite that, poor Gordon of course would learn that Bo was planning to move and exactly *where* he would move—a *month* before he left Santa Monica. On Gordon's *birthday*, a credit union called Gordon looking for Bo, but instead of getting information from Gordon, in a highly unlikely exchange, they gave out information: Bo's new address.

When John and I asked where it was, Gordon's expression told us we'd better get ready for another "story." "What's the name of the only street I knew in Hollywood when I was a little boy? Because it was the address of Paramount, which made *The Greatest Show on Earth*?—it's also a race of twenty-six miles, and the twenty-sixth of April being our anniversary. Of course."

"Marathon," John answered. (There used to be a Marathon Gate at Paramount.)

"Right. After Bo left us all and we looked back, we all figured out Bo's philosophy had always been? Eastern, right? So the opposite of Eastern is Western, or Occidental?"

"Occidental," John and I answered together. "He lives at . . ."

"Hold on, I'm not finished," Gordon baited us. "Now where are you from John — who before Bo walked out of my life, suddenly quit a better-paying job and began teaching at Bo's school, and ended up becoming a conduit that still connected Bo and me?"

"Lafayette," John said.

Gordon just shook his head. "Yep, that's right. They're all right there in Silverlake."

Bo's new apartment is at the end of a block bordered on its three sides by *Occidental* and *Marathon* and *Lafayette Park Place*. It was all just too pat.

And John continued to be that unwilling conduit: At a district school meeting that took place two years after John and Bo no longer worked together, John wished him a belated happy birthday two days late. Bo's fellow teachers said, "Bo, why didn't you tell us it was your birthday?" Bo told them it hadn't been, then looked straight at John and carefully enunciated, "It wasn't. My birthday is *April* 26." Of course, April 26 was Bo and Gordon's anniversary.

It was sad. It was as though Bo was trapped inside some prison and could only send out obtuse messages for help, then continually refuse the help. In a completely preposterous way one of Bo's poems had found its way into Gordon's hands — a poem that *answered* Gordon's continued question, "Did Bo ever really care about me at all? What was I to him? If he had really loved me, how could he have walked away at the worst time in my life?" In the poem Bo had written, three years after he'd left us, that Gordon was his Beloved, that he knew the relationship was "blessed by the cross," that he knew he had pledged himself years ago to Gordon but he was sick, addicted, and afraid. The last line was "In light and dark, my heart grows old."

Gordon was sick to death of all the synchronicities related to Bo. So that Christmas Eve he made a resolution that he would somehow try to stop them by removing any visible reminders of Bo from his house. He carefully boxed them all up and put them away. We'd planned to give Denise and her friend a quick tour of "Christmas Cottage" (Denise and Bill Fraker had remained friends of mine). Then for some reason, for the first time in my life I had wanted to go to Christmas Eve service. John had chosen a Gothic church because Gordon loved all things Gothic, and it was also legendary for its music and acoustics. We were concluding the tour in Gordon's bedroom, which was chock-full of antique toys, ornaments, dolls, and a myriad of other incredible details, when Denise exclaimed, "Gordon! This is an adorable picture of you posed in the little cowboy outfit on the little pony there." She was pointing to a framed mirror where Gordon had stuck Christmas cards all around the edges, among them was the photograph she described. But the photograph was *not* of Gordon. It was of Bo as a little boy. Denise had managed to point out the *one* reminder of Bo in the entire house that Gordon had overlooked. To Gordon it was a sign, and as we hurriedly threw on our coats to leave, he tucked it in his pocket and took it with him to church.

During the service I noticed Gordon occasionally taking the picture out and studying it. Then, after the lighting of candles and singing of carols, Gordon said, "Wait, I saw in the program there is communion afterward. I want to go." When he took communion that night, in a gesture meant to send Bo protection, he held his hand on that little picture.

Although we were all exhausted, and though Gordon knew Bo was in a hospital rehab program, he wanted to drive by Bo's apartment anyway, just to say another prayer. I reminded Gordon that, as usual, he would be up all night wrapping Christmas packages, but there was no stopping him. So John headed the car for Silverlake.

As we approached Bo's building, there were *only two cars* parked beside it. Without warning, John suddenly slammed on the brakes, jolting our car to a stop. "Jesus Christ! Look at that!"

"What? Where? What are you talking about?" Gordon and I both asked.

"That license plate, it's unbelievable," he replied. "It says 'CARITAS.' And right after church, too."

"Caritas?" Gordon questioned. "I know that word 'caritas' from somewhere. It was in something to do with Jung. I remember it was in a group of words like 'agape' and one or two others."

"It's Latin," John said. "Caritas is a word you often find in religious contexts. I believe it means 'a father's love for his children.'"

"Oh my God, think about what I just did back at the church!" Gordon, like a flash, had put it together and become excited. "I took communion touching Bo's picture with my hand, and then I came over here to say a prayer, and now there is a *message* waiting for us." We all sat there for a moment, staring at the incredible license plate.

"*Oh my God,*" Gordon suddenly gasped. "Look at the license plate on the car in front of this one! This isn't possible; it can't be real."

Our eyes all instantly fixed on the license plate of the only other car there. Bo's favorite nickname for Gordon was GoGo, and the license plate on the car in front of the one with "CARITAS" read "BOGO." I suddenly felt light-headed. "This is outrageous," I said. "It's a combination of both your names."

John shook his head. "Well, little boy," he said in amazement, "looks like God gave you your first Christmas present this year. You know it's after midnight; it's officially Christmas now."

I looked at Gordon's face. It was aglow, exactly like a child's on Christmas morning. He was oblivious to everything but the license plates; he was somewhere else. He just sat there staring.

Suddenly like a general, he commanded, "Okay, John, I have to go home and get the camera. We have to leave, right now. I have to take pictures of it or else nobody will ever believe me. Oh God! What if the cars are gone when we get back? John, get us home and step on it."

"Oh, Hobbit, what does it matter if anybody else believes it or not? It happened to us, not to them, and we know it's true." Gordon's constant documentation of everything often drove me crazier than the events themselves. Selfishly, I wanted to understand what it was that *I* was supposed to do or to learn from all this. I didn't care about convincing the rest of the world. After all, Gordon had never cared what "other people thought" either. Later I understood his reasons were less about convincing and much more about sharing, and that it was the skeptic in Gordon, studying in detail, preserving it. Which, in Gordon fashion, meant throwing everything in a disorganized mess into a box to add to a pile of rapidly multiplying boxes.

I would later be crushed that I stayed home and didn't go with Gordon and John when they went back to take the pictures. For when they returned, they found, sitting on the curb, almost as if waiting for them, an orange, mackerel-striped tabby that looked *exactly* like our beloved Chloe Sr. (who had at that point been gone for nearly two years). The cat stood up and walked about a foot onto the grass parallel to where they had parked and stood staring at Gordon, then slowly turned and padded back onto the sidewalk and up the steps, where it paused and looked back over its shoulder at Gordon. Gordon and John were mesmerized; they both felt they were watching our Chloe. Gordon, the artist, knew that little face intimately and staring at the cat that looked exactly like his old friend made him completely forget for an instant why they had come there and that they had a camera with them. Quickly, as the cat continued up the steps toward Bo's back door, he grabbed the camera and snapped a picture. Then they each sat staring in wonder as the cat disappeared from view, both feeling as if they were looking, once again, at the Chloe they had loved. That the cat was going straight to Bo's back door only amplified their awe, for Bo himself had been the one who had found her in a thicket at Stradella and placed her in Gordon's arms.

John began taking pictures of the two cars, both of which miraculously *were* still there. For a few of the shots Gordon stood by the license plates, holding the little church candle, the church bulletin, and the picture of little "cowboy Bo." It was a Christmas miracle — *It's a Wonderful Life*, *A Christmas Carol*, and *The Bishop's Wife* all rolled into one.

Two days later I picked up the photos from a custom lab. None of us were prepared for the numinous images that had been captured on film. The first photograph was a full-length shot of Gordon standing beside the car with the CARITAS license plate. There was nothing out of the ordinary about that picture, but there certainly was about the very next one. In that one, only Gordon's feet were visible. The rest of him was completely enveloped in a brilliant ball-like cloud of light.

In the next photograph, Gordon was kneeling by the CARITAS license plate, holding the church program, the candle, and Bo's picture. A brilliant red light shone down on Gordon and cut a wide swath through the center of the picture, forming the shape of a serifed "1."

The photograph of the orange cat came back with a mysterious light shining right down on the cat and its path — again a serifed "1." There was nothing supernatural or strange whatsoever about the cat, except the fact that she looked exactly like Chloe and that they had never seen it before and they would they never see it again. Several other photographs too had meaningful, spiritual, but completely unexplainable images floating on them. One had a perfect circle of white mist over the cars with little cometlike tails leading straight back to Bo's kitchen window.

The day after we'd studied them, John invited two friends of his to see Gordon's decorated house. Gordon had met them socially only once before, and they did not know anything personal about him and certainly nothing of his mystical journey. Because one of them, Nancy, was a professional photographer, he brought the pictures out to show her.

She was immediately intrigued and puzzled at the distinct shape of the unexplainable red swath. "This is totally bizarre. It doesn't look accidental like a light spill or leak and besides," she gasped as she noticed, "the light on the left edge of the '1' is married *precisely* to your profile, Gordon! That's impossible. If it were a light spill or a leak or any other natural thing, there is no way that the light could stop right at the edge of your face exactly — and not overlap it! My God! She went on, "Look at the light next to your nose — there the red light isn't even *touching* it. It's holding itself back from your nose, yet the edge of the light is re-creating the silhouette of your nose with the black night in between. That's impossible. This is the strangest thing I've ever seen. Where is the negative?"

Nancy studied the negative and the photograph intently for around ten minutes. On the negative the swath of cyan green—red's complementary color—touched Gordon only where the bottom edge of the serif at the top of the "1" cut across his blond hair, making it pink. Looking back to the photo she said, "It's so bizarre. Look, Gordon, it's like you're wearing a little pink hat. Gordon, you've been crowned by the red light!" She was clearly bewildered and kept repeating that what she was seeing wasn't explainable.

The following night after returning from showing the photos to some other friends, Gordon was saying to John that he *knew* that the amazing red light on the photograph was some sort of manifestation of God, but he also knew that because many people were prejudiced and homophobic that, even if they admitted the photos were "unexplainable," they might say that, because the light was a brilliant red, the image was really fire and brimstone. Minutes later when he again examined the photograph, he saw that the center of the red "1" now had a deep golden glow, a wide wash of beautiful light through the center of it, and three golden rays—a trinity of rays—shining right down on the word "CARITAS" in the license plate. This was more impossible than the photographs themselves. It had *changed.* We were all completely stunned. Gordon would later say that it was as if God had overheard his comments—about how ignorant hate-filled people would say that, because he was gay, the mystical red light was ominous. Therefore God had chosen to place the golden light and the three heavenly rays there as a sign that it was actually a gift from Him. This was confirmed for Gordon when he later looked up the word "caritas" in *Webster's Collegiate Thesaurus* and found that it was actually a synonym for "grace." We also learned the color that grace is most often associated with—*red.* And grace was precisely what the entire experience was all about that Christmas Eve.

His first thought was that he had to show the "changed" photo to Nancy. After all, she had only recently studied it carefully under an eye loop. He called and first he asked if she had a way to tape their conversation. She could. Then he asked her to describe the picture she had seen only two days before. She did—very accurately—the way it had been *before* but no longer was. He told her it had changed and about the rays and the pure golden light in the middle and she was aghast. They both decided Gordon should come over at once. Gordon also recorded her reactions to seeing the picture at her house. She was completely undone. All she could say was "God, oh God, my God . . . this was just not this way . . . this is impossible . . . I'm very visual. They've changed." Nancy's reaction was recorded a third time when she didn't even know it. It was the next morning when, in a panic, she phoned John to talk about what had happened. John picked up his phone just as his answering machine did and they both remained silent until they heard the voice-activated machine shut itself off. Unbeknownst to them, however, it continued to record, thus documenting their conversation. And what was really interesting is that hers was the reaction of someone completely outside of it all, experiencing it firsthand. "I'm telling you, John," Nancy said. "It just wasn't like that. God . . . oh God . . . I have a photographic memory and it just wasn't like that. It's impossible. No wonder it keeps Gordon whipped up, it would affect anybody that way! I mean . . . God" "Yep, Nancy," John said. "It's undermined all my traditional ways of knowing." To me, John's response to her would remain one of the most apt summaries about so many of our experiences: "Yes, Nancy, you have just entered a world where there are no longer distinctions between scientific reality and mythic reality."

Then on February 9, Bo's mother's birthday, the photograph of the mysterious orange tabby also changed. "I know the cat is a mystery, Hobbit, and it'll stay one," Gordon later said. "I keep turning it over and over in my mind to see if I've overlooked some clue. Was the cat I saw real or was it a vision? If it were a vision, how could John have seen exactly what I saw—and, can a vision be photographed? Or was it simply Chloe come again? I just wish I knew."

He was given his answer the following Christmas. Every Christmas on the tree in his bedroom he observes the tender ritual of tucking a *trinity* of pictures of both Chloes in among all the ornaments. I always love searching for them. That year one of Chloe Sr.'s pictures was one taken *nine* years before at the Andalusia. In it, she was perched on the sofa, her legs all tucked under her in what Gordon had called her "pagoda position," with her eyes half closed, looking like a little Buddha. It was one of my favorite pictures of her. Perhaps a week or so later, I noticed hanging on the tree, one of Gordon's mystical God photos from the previous Christmas, the one with the large red beam of light with the unexplainable gold center shining down on him—the one that had changed. When I went closer to look at it, I found it wasn't that picture at all. It was the little Buddha picture of Chloe at the Andalusia that had *now* also changed. It now had a radiant red beam with gold in the center shining down on her that matched the one in the picture of Gordon by the CARITAS license plate from the Christmas before.

It would be Easter naturally in Gordon's story when John would discover that Lafayette Park Place *begins* at the back of the Gothic church in the mid-Wilshire district, meanders for several miles, *and ends* in Silverlake on Bo's block, where the amazing "caritas" story all began. Gordon's experience that Christmas Eve began at the church and ended after midnight by Bo's apartment with the two mystical license plates and then the photographs. The street itself, Lafayette Park Place, John said, begins at the church and ends on Bo's block.

The word "caritas" would make its import felt so many times it's impossible to mention in this book. Two of them remain the most poignant and powerful to me. The first involved Gordon's mother. It was the anniversary of her death, April 23, and Gordon was climbing the stairs to his bedroom when suddenly he felt an unbearable pain in his right calf. Three days later, April 26, again the date of his and Bo's anniversary, a strange lesion appeared on that calf—a trinity of them, really. They were lined up in a perfect vertical display: a large downward-pointing triangle; centered under its point was a precisely shaped heart; and again centered under its point was an arrowhead pointing upward. Gordon immediately went to see his doctor to have it examined—and naturally recorded the examination. Dr. Mulry, who has a reputation as a doctor's doctor, said he'd never seen anything like it, that bruises do not form in perfect geometric shapes like that—it was not possible. "There are some things that are beyond even medical science," he said.

I was completely floored when Gordon later looked up "heart" in his most recent book of symbols. Beside the word "heart" there was only one illustration: numerous tiny *triangular* thorns surrounded a drawing of a *heart* with three upward-pointing *arrowheads* inside it and an inscription in the center. The inscription in the center read "caritas." It was too much! Then Gordon revealed what he'd been covering. The title of the illustration read "Saint Margaret's Heart"! Gordon's mother's name, of course, was Margaret.

The second "caritas" connection began *Christmas Day* of 1995. As we sat down to dinner, suddenly Gordon bolted from the table, instantly nauseated. This happened without warning several times over the next few weeks until finally I insisted he see Dr. Mulry. Dr. Mulry was concerned and arranged an appointment with a specialist for Gordon to undergo tests at another medical office building in Beverly Hills. I was extremely worried about him and drove him there myself. As we approached the corner of the street where the building was located—a building we'd never before heard of or seen—Gordon looked at the street sign and said, "God is doing It again." The street sign read *Bedford*; we were both from *Bedford* county. As we started through the door of the medical building, Gordon suddenly stopped dead and pointed to a word on the big bronze plaque near the entrance: "Caritas." We looked at each other and we both already knew he would be okay. The tests could show no reason for the mysterious nausea that had led us both to *Bedford* and the word *Caritas*.

These extraordinary events involve other people as well. In fact, it seems that the minute someone else becomes involved, unusual things also begin to happen to that person.

After Greg passed away, Gordon made an exquisite Christmas ornament using one of the original photos he had taken of Greg in his wig; it hangs every year on the Gothic room's Christmas tree.

It was, in fact, eight years after Greg's death and Gordon was looking at his scrapbook with all the photographs he had made of Greg when he noticed three rays and a halo of red light circling up over the wig; it had never been there before. There were three rays of red light surrounding the wig and arcing over it. Gordon, John, Bo, and I and numerous others had looked at the pictures of Greg many times over those years, and of course since that Christmas Eve of 1989, Gordon had examined *every photo* he had *ever* taken! There had never been anything out of the ordinary about any of the pictures Gordon had taken of Greg. Gordon no longer had the negatives to examine, since he had sent them along with a set of the prints to Greg's mother, immediately after she had lost Greg.

After stewing about it for several months, Gordon decided he had to call her in Shelbyville. Even though eight years had gone by, he knew she was still grieving over the loss of Greg. He did not mention the light but asked her to get her set of pictures, and by his describing them precisely, she was able to determine which photograph Gordon was referring to. "No, Gordon, there's no red light or anything like that on my print."

The following Christmas Gordon was going through his bedside drawer to find a box for a set of antique earrings he was giving me. He found an empty box from the Metropolitan Museum that was just the right size and removed a card that was inside it and tossed it onto the bed. Just as he was about to place cotton inside, he noticed touches of pale pink on the inside of the bottom of the box. When he examined it closely, he read the word "Kodak." He then realized that it was the back of a photograph turned facedown; it fit so flush to the inside edges of the bottom of the box that, except for the pink, he might never have known it was there. He took it out, turned it over, and saw it was the picture of Greg with what Gordon calls the *red God light* around his head. How could it have gotten from inside his scrapbook into the bottom of this little box, he wondered. Here we go again, he thought, and went to get his scrapbook, where the photo should have been. Shocked, he discovered his picture of Greg was still in the scrapbook. He then realized he had *two* copies of the same mystical photograph of Greg with his halo. Curious, he reached for the card he'd tossed on the bed to see what had originally been in the box and found that the museum card that accompanies all its reproduction gift items described an item too large to have ever come in that box. It was a card for a stained-glass rondelle for the Virgin of the Apocalypse, a reproduction detail from a window of a church in Cologne. He read that the original is "juxtaposed with the Trinity in a window whose subject stressed God's sacrifice for mankind." He looked at the photograph of Greg with its trinity of rays and thought, "that makes perfect sense."

Gordon stayed in bed two days after that one. He knew, of course, at once that the second copy was meant for Greg's mother, since her photo had not had the mystical light on it. It was several months before he sent it off to her. When she looked at it, she was shaken. She quickly went to get her own copy, and when she laid it down beside the one Gordon had sent her, she was stunned to find that her own photograph, which had been perfectly normal when Gordon had called her, now matched the duplicate that she had just received from Gordon. It had the same red halo and rays. Now there was *a trinity* of the photographs—the *same* word printed on the card for the rondelle, which Gordon had never owned or bought.

At some point in all these occurrences, even mechanical things began to "act up." Lamps in Gordon's house would sometimes turn off, and on, when some meaningful topic was being discussed—as if they were punctuating the conversation. His videotape machine acted in "impossible" ways, according to the experts at the Sony repair center. When it was preprogramed to record one thing, it would do something strange and record some other thing. That "other thing" would be about something very specific to Gordon and about what was going on in his mystical journey. It recorded a death scene played by an actor named Ron *Harper,* who was an actor I'd once worked with. When that happened, we were terrified for Bo. Completely spooked by it all, I took the machine back to Sony. They worked on it for five months but finally sent a letter saying that it was "the most puzzling experience they'd ever experienced with any Sony VCR. It's as if the machine has a mind of its own and is determined to do what it wants with or *without* an operator." In the same letter they stated they hoped to have it "ready on March 29," the anniversary of Mrs. Harper's death. It was all too much. That was a phrase I found myself constantly saying.

John and I and the others who knew had gradually become rather numb

to the onslaught of things mystical. And it would be completely inaccurate
to give the impression that Gordon was blissed out by the situation. He was
overwhelmed, particularly since the most minute seemed as important to
him as the seismic. When one member of the clergy I'd contacted stated,
"It is miraculous, but, if it were all from God, I think you would feel a
great *peace* and a gentle calm," Gordon looked at him as if he were nuts
and said, "You know, I've never really read the Bible. I didn't even know
what the Holy Ghost meant until all this started. But I did go to the movies,
and, correct me if I'm wrong, I don't think Job was too thrilled nor poor
Jonah and Jeremiah, who both tried to run away from Him, didn't they?
Do you suppose Abraham was in a state of bliss when He told him he was
gonna have to chop his son in two?" And then the light next to the minister's
chair began to flash.

Gordon would continue to document his experiences with photographs and
frequently the photographs themselves would again have unexplainable images on them, which sometimes later changed. Since I knew so many experts in the field of photography and cameras, I consulted them all.
Everyone said that there was *no plausible explanation* for what they were
examining. "Accidents and light spills don't make circles and crosses and
diaphanous triangles coming down on people's ears," they all said. Nor
could anyone explain what then happened to the *original print* of Gordon
standing beside the CARITAS license plate and disappearing into a ball of
light. Strange marks appeared on it that were not on the negative, and not
an any subsequent prints of it. Several scientists said it looked like a spec-
tograph reading. I looked that up in the dictionary: "a spectrum records the
distribution of energy from a radiant source, as by an incandescent body."
The only body within that ball of light was Gordon.

We were well beyond synchronicity. I began tentatively at first to seek
out the experts in the fields of the spirit, the miraculous, expanded states
of conciousness and the unknown, even some ministers and priests. They
all had something amazing to offer, and each in his own way, agreed.

Among them was Bella Karish. A man who had seen the photographs
told me, "Michael Crichton would love these," and suggested that I look
at some of the books written by Crichton's teacher, Dr. W. Brugh Joy, the
author of *Joy's Way* and *Avalanche*. In *Avalanche* (which had already syn-
chronistically made its way to Gordon), Dr. Joy said, "One person I often
recommend . . . is Bella Karish." He then went on to say that she dissected
him with "intuitive insight and compassion," and that if he had known she
was able to see so deeply, he might never have gone—at least until his

"more mature self" had developed to handle such candidness." This seemed hopeful; I also recalled her name from Michael York and his wife, Pat, who had spoken very highly of her, so I phoned. Bella spent time with Gordon, looked at the pictures, listened to the stories, and said, "You've been given such great gifts, Gordon, that I get chills. The stories and your photographs are magnificent. They need to be put down in a book. You have the proof the others don't. You're meant to do something with this; you've been chosen," she fussed. "Do you understand me? Chosen, chosen. Accept it and do what God means you to do!"

Stanislov Grof, M.D., formerly chief of the Maryland Psychiatric Research Center, a member of the teaching faculty at Johns Hopkins University's School of Medicine, founding president of the International Transperson Association, a protégé of Joseph Campbell, and author of more than ninety articles and six books, including *Adventures of Self-Discovery*, *The Holotropic Mind*, and *The Stormy Search for the Self*, invited us to lunch with him and his wife. The entire lunch was recorded. After hearing Gordon's experiences and examining the photographs, he said Gordon had made major contact with The Divine. He felt Gordon possessed "siddhis," the supernatural powers of yogis and avatars. (It was the second time I had heard that word. When Bella Karish had asked me to lunch alone, the week after she had met Gordon, she told me matter-of-factly that what Gordon is is an avatar.) Gordon disclaimed any such abilities to Dr. Grof and only said, "I don't think I'm causing this." Grof then recommended a book, *Future of the Body*, and said that it could also be something described there as *charisms*—or gifts of *Grace*.

Matthew Fox, then a Dominican priest and author of numerous books, among them *The Coming of the Cosmic Christ* and *A Spirituality Named Compassion*, termed Gordon a shaman and said he was being communicated with by "at the very least angels or at the most God." I even phoned Marianne Williamson. It was long before her first book was published and she became nationally well known. I didn't know anyone who had ever even met her, but because of a synchronicity that occurred about her, I phoned. What had happened was that Gordon had been staring at a photograph that had just changed at his house when suddenly the sound from Johnny Carson and *The Tonight Show* left the television and was replaced by a woman's voice that said, "They say that Jesus Christ is coming again. Maybe He's never left, but most of us just aren't able to see Him." Given the details of the photograph Gordon was looking at, hearing those words superimposed over the continuing visual of *The Tonight Show*, made Gordon feel as if this audio disruption had happened just for him. He checked the channels to try to find the voice and found it on public access. It was Marianne Williamson's. Because of this I phoned her. As she looked at numerous photographs and listened to me tell the stories that went with them, she said, "Gordon's a very old soul, I think. He's like a small water jar and They're pouring an ocean into him." She had no doubt that God was revealing Himself to Gordon.

The most wonderful encounter was with Colin Wilson, who has written over fifty books, including *The Outsider*, *Poetry and Mysticism*, *Religion and the Rebel*, a biography of Jung, and *Beyond the Occult*. He is keenly interested in the further expanses and potential of the human mind, considered a leading expert on the mysterious and the unexplainable, and has contributed to numerous encyclopedias on those subjects. Over a two-day period Colin shared a great deal of his valuable time in Los Angeles with Gordon.

From the beginning there were many synchronicities between them, including his accommodations which were — in the vast city of Los Angeles — only a minute or so from Gordon's. After our first afternoon with Colin, he invited us to dinner; since he wasn't certain where that would be, he told us to drop by the bookstore where he would later that night be lecturing and someone would tell us where to join him. We were given incorrect directions for the bookstore, and Gordon was on the verge of a panic attack, as I was stuck in a maze of Santa Monica's one-way streets. It seemed we were going to miss our opportunity to spend more time with the one person above all others Gordon had wanted to talk with. From reading Wilson, Gordon admired his intellect, his unpretentiousness, and above all, his natural skepticism.

Suddenly, Gordon threw open the car door and jumped out. "Gordon, get back in this car," I yelled. "I will not," he answered as he ran to the sidewalk. Tentatively then he walked about seventy-five feet, stopped, turned around, and came back to the car. "Hurry up and park; he's up that alley between those buildings having dinner." There's absolutely no way he could have known where Colin was, but I parked the car, and, sure enough, Gordon led us right to Colin.

When Colin asked if we'd stopped by the bookstore for directions, Gordon showed him the piece of paper with the wrong address and said, "There is *no* bookstore at this address. But it *is* an amazing synchronicity, don't you think," Gordon asked with a smile, "that you're here in Los Angeles lecturing at the Mandala Bookstore and that a mandala appeared mystically on my thigh a month or so before?" Gordon lifted the edge of his shorts, showing an instantly riveted Colin his "mandala" which had appeared on July 29 (the exact date Bo had left Gordon before). It was an incredible and complex story which Colin listened to with fascination. The "bruise" was a perfect circular ring, and within the ring was centered a perfect inverted heart. "That's a design by Jakob Boehm," Colin said, smiling up at him. "Do a little research, Gordon." Then still gazing at the amazing design on Gordon's thigh, he asked, "How *did* you find where I was?" "Oh, I smelled you," Gordon said, laughing. With that Colin instantly looked at his wife. "How interesting you used that phrase. It's one I use myself on occasion." He looked at me. "He's psychic, you know, Sondra."

Colin's explanation to me about Gordon was that he possessed something Colin had studied, written about, and defined as "Faculty X." As I best understood it, he had determined that most of us are living our lives as robots, virtually *asleep*. We do not see the obvious connectedness around us. He had even broken down these levels of consciousness and defined them from Level 1 through Level 8. Level 7 is the level connected with "Faculty X." Level 8, the highest level, is that of the mystic. It is the mystic who sees all the connectedness in life. "Of course, Gordon has Faculty X, and, above that, he's clearly a mystic," he said. Wilson's firm belief is that the future hope for mankind lies in that stage of consciousness—that of the mystic. "Gordon should be studied," he added.

I felt that Colin *saw* more and understood more from listening to Gordon's stories and looking at the pictures than anyone else did. When we asked if he had ever heard of so much all threaded together into *one long story*—he answered that he hadn't. "How could Gordon's VCR do something that even Sony maintained was mechanically impossible for it to do, something that had brought Gordon a message?" I asked. "Gordon's psychiatrist said all of this is *outside* of Gordon, but I want to know what you think. Do you think Gordon is somehow unconsciously causing all this?" Colin looked at me, paused, then spoke judiciously. "Let's just say that Gordon is being helped and watched over by *White Spirits*, shall we?" Instantly I felt goose bumps.

Gordon adored Colin, even wore his elf shoes to see him that night; and as he hugged Colin goodbye, he said, "I know you're a sly one. I can tell you have elf blood in you, too." Colin chuckled and wrote down his address for us. Gordon stared at it, then borrowing Colin's pen, quickly jotted something beneath it.

Underneath Colin's simple address, GORAN HAVEN, ENGLAND, Gordon had scribbled, GOR(don) AN(derson) HAVEN(hurst Dr.)

"You *are* quick, Gordon!" Colin said, amazed.

As Gordon and I walked to the end of the block and prepared to cross the street, I looked back and saw Colin standing alone, continuing to watch

Gordon. Before we lost sight of each other, we all again waved goodbye. "I love him," Gordon said, "He's wonderful."

It was all overwhelming. John (who had long been an atheist before all this) now called himself John the Witness because he'd witnessed so many "flat-out miracles," as he referred to them, and he even began reading religious books. In a book entitled *Report on the Shroud of Turin* he found a quotation that I particularly responded to: John H. Heller writes, "In the Marines, an odd event occurring once is random chance, twice is coincidence, three times is enemy action. Had the Marines been involved in the Shroud project, the prevalence of coincidence would have convinced them that our galaxy was being invaded." We laughed. We already *knew* our galaxy *had been!*

Although I had always know from childhood that Gordon was "other," I was completely unprepared for what came about over these years. None of us had known the definitions of any of the recurring words, symbols, and signs before this journey had begun, and what was most interesting to me was that they were familiar ones from all sorts of writings—Christian, Hindu, and Jewish. As Gordon had said, "God is a mystery; He is above knowing, above labels."

As time went on, I stopped looking for "experts," stopped trying to explain Gordon or his experiences and just let them happen. For myself, I continued to view my own occurrences as "messages." Sometimes the messages were extraordinarily dramatic; other times they were subtle and might have gone unnoticed if Gordon hadn't taught me to sharpen my awareness. Each one gave me courage and purpose and brought me a confirmation that life is "more" than the obvious, a confirmation that I was not alone. I came to believe there are unseen hands that will guide us and give us "clues" as we walk along. The more I recognized the clues, the more I felt comforted, and the more came to me. For me, the miraculous and synchronistic became a language, a communication, through which we can be guided. They became evidence of the existence of God in our everyday life.

Impulse was finally released (April 1990) and I was thrilled that it received wonderful reviews—especially for my direction. Siskel and Ebert gave it an enthusiastic "Two Thumbs-Up" and called it "the best directed film [they] had seen in a long time . . . watch out for Sondra Locke." I needed that pat on the back. I was so relieved—a new life, a new career . . . I thought.

Unfortunately, however, there was no escaping the shadow arm of Clint. In a story about Theresa Russell, the cinema magazine *Film Comment* said: "*Impulse,* Russell's current film, was *directed by Clint Eastwood* [italics mine] and his protégée Sondra Locke." Michael Wilmington, the *L.A. Times* film critic, wrote a positive review, but included the most inappropriate and unprofessional comments of all: "This movie's press book, unsurprisingly, makes no reference to Clint Eastwood, Locke's ex-lover and longtime director/co-star. Watching *Impulse*, you almost wonder whether this seemingly angry pair couldn't forget the tabloids and lawyers and call a truce. They might have a few more good movies together left in them." That didn't belong in a review! It was more like something from a fanzine magazine: "Dial 1-900 if you want to see Sondra and Clint together again." I was so angry when I read it that I almost picked up the phone and dialed Wilmington; I'd tell him exactly what I thought, I ranted. The moment passed, and I let it go.

Despite the excellent reviews, Warner Bros. barely released the film. And on opening weekend in the few theaters in Los Angeles, the ad in the newspaper didn't even use the Siskel and Ebert review. When I inquired and complained, they half-heartedly muttered *oops, we guess that was a mistake. Months later*, when the videotape came out, the "Two Thumbs-Up" review did not appear on the cover of its jacket either. Another mistake?

It was clear that not working with Clint, and even breaking up with him, hadn't severed my connection to him. And who knew when it would end. Actually, the worst thing of all had occurred even before the limited release of *Impulse*. Lucy Fisher, my day-to-day Warner Bros. executive, phoned me at my apartment. After expressing her sympathy on the sad news of my breakup with Clint, she informed me that they were "regrettably" dropping the projects I had in development at Warners. All three projects? One of which we hadn't even begun work on; it was in the exact same state as when they had loved it and contracted with me to develop it. I was devastated. I had thought I had hope of more work to get me through this transition, but now I didn't. Warners was, after all, virtually the only place I had worked since I'd been with Clint. What was I going to do now? When Clint "divorced" me, did Warners go along with the package? It was impossible not to draw that conclusion.

Then my Mercedes seemed to become a target. It was parked near my apartment in a security garage with an electric gate; nevertheless, someone removed the grille from the front of my car, touching nothing else, and leaving the screws lined up and neatly stacked on the garage floor beside it. It gave me a peculiar feeling, to say the least. With a Mercedes, the usual thief would have stripped off more parts, or just taken the car. And doing that would have been very easy, because once the thief was inside the security garage, the gate would open automatically for the car to drive out.

Not to mention, there were more desirable automobiles parked nearby, and none of them was touched.

Almost as soon as I had replaced the grille, something worse occurred. I parked and locked the car at an indoor shopping mall in Beverly Hills. I was gone for only twenty minutes, and when I returned, my car was gone. It was horrible; I thought I absolutely could not take one more thing. I kept walking around, not believing what had happened. Surely I just hadn't remembered correctly where I had parked it. The police told me my chances of getting it back were practically zero. Yet, a few weeks later, after another extraordinary series of synchronicities, a woman phoned Gordon and reported that a silver Mercedes was parked in front of her house. After noticing it abandoned there for several days, and becoming concerned, she looked inside and saw my address book. Miraculously she randomly chose Gordon's number from the many other names, most of whom no longer even knew where to contact me. Amazingly she had chosen the one person closest to me. The hardtop had been removed, but otherwise, the car was just as I had left it. Only a few incidental things had been taken from inside it, and they were strange choices—an envelope with notes about my lawsuit against Clint, and some photos of Gordon, Bo, John, and me from inside my address book. Music cassettes were still there, as was the radio, a bag of clothes, and even some unopened packages I had recently purchased. They hadn't even been curious to see what was inside. "You don't have anybody mad at you, do you?" asked one of the policemen when I reported the details of the recovery. Certainly the answer to that was an emphatic yes. When all these emotionally debilitating things happened to me, it was always the little miracles that followed (like the woman choosing Gordon's number from so many others) that gave me my hope and faith that, no matter what, God was there watching out for me.

Over a year had passed with no settlement offer from Clint. It was becoming clear that he was keeping his word on that incredible and shocking statement he'd made to Lili: "Does she want to be a director or become Michele Marvin? I'll drag her ass through court until there's nothing left. I'll never settle with her; I paid her for her jobs in movies; now she wants to be paid for love too?"

My attorneys were making slow progress with Howard King, and with all the other losses, the passage of time was wearing me down. It all had to stop. Maybe, I thought, if I spoke to Clint personally he would listen. With great trepidation, I dialed Stradella. In a conversation of few words we agreed to meet the next day at his office.

I showed up on time at the "Taco Bell," the same office I had entered almost exactly fifteen years earlier in 1975, when he was casting *The Outlaw Josey Wales.* This time he didn't greet me warmly, nor did he usher me into his private office. We walked into the conference room; I sat on the leather sofa and began by saying that I wanted to end all the ugliness, that, in spite of it all, there had to be a way to remember what we'd been to each other, how much we'd loved each other. He said nothing for a moment. Then he did something completely chilling. He came over, sat on the sofa beside me, took my hand in his, and to my complete amazement and horror, began flirting with me! He even kissed me on the cheek. It was the very last thing I expected. I didn't know what to do. As he looked into my eyes and held my hand, the hair on the back of my neck began to stand up. It dawned on me, all of a sudden, that he thought I was suggesting I *come back* to him! And he was telling me I could! In that moment I felt I could have apologized to Clint and he would have taken me back! He would have laid down new rules—no doubt the same that applied to Roxanne and Jacelyn and who knew who else—but I could come back. The last thing I wanted to do was upset him so, shifting away from him ever so slightly, I asked, "Clint, can't we put this behind us?"

"The ball is in your court," he replied, a little put off.

"No, it isn't, Clint. You have my home, you've kept everything. I have nothing—"

"The house is mine!" he yelled, jumping up from the sofa and beginning to pace.

"But, Clint, that's not what you told me, and you have so many others. You know you're not emotionally attached to Stradella and I am. It's all me!" I ventured. "I just don't understand why you want to do this. Why are you being so horrible to me?"

"Me? The *whole world* thinks what *you've* done to *me* is horrible! Don't think I don't know what's going on; I saw you on the *Joan Rivers Show!*"

I began to search my mind. What on earth had I said? The interview had been set up by Warner Bros. to promote *Impulse,* and a Warners representative had been sitting backstage listening to every word. I didn't remember saying much at all about Clint, but then even bringing up Clint's name constituted heresy. I'd learned that much.

Clint began quoting word for word everything he maintained I'd said. It was all so inconsequential that I can't even remember what it was, but clearly Clint did.

"You just *want* something like everybody else," he said. "I don't owe you anything. How much do you want for each time we did it? Huh?"

I tried to control my own anger and to remember that I wanted to walk out of that office with some positive result. So I ventured forth: "Look, Clint, do we *have* to be enemies? For your own good, if you don't stop distrusting everybody's every move, you're never going to be happy . . . ever. No matter who you put in your bed, you're going to be miserable."

"I *am* happy! I'm ecstatic!" he screamed. "I have lots of friends and lots of people I trust!"

Ignoring him, I went on. "Clint, I'm the one who's the victim here, the one who's been destroyed and dispossessed, yet I'm the one offering to be friendly. Go on with our lives. But you can't expect that I will just walk away with nothing. I can't even work now, after—"

"I can't help that!" he interrupted wildly. "It's an age-old lament; actors always say that. It's not my responsibility. Get a job as a waitress if you have to. It was you who decided to sue, to be Michelle Marvin instead of being a director!"

"I didn't want to sue, Clint. You gave me no choice."

"Yeah that's right. Blame me for it! Well, if you want to be friends. Prove it! Drop your lawsuit and come back to me *no strings attached*. And all that stuff you call syn-kro-ni-cit-y!" he spat out at me unexpectedly. At first I was confused because I had *never* discussed that with Clint. He could never have understood a word of it. But then I thought of the phone calls he had secretly taped and, no doubt, pored over—that's where he'd heard about it. Choking down my new outrage about his condescending tone about that subject, I let it lie—along with all the other things he'd done to me—all for the sake of some reasonable solution that wasn't happening. I barely controlled myself.

"You don't even believe in God, Clint. You think we're just buried and that's that. I wouldn't expect you to understand."

"What, I'm not smart enough? Oh yeah, well I know enough about that stuff to know it's weird. Jane told me about Gordon sending Bo some picture of a tree . . . oak tree . . . saying the tree was them or something. You tell me that's not weird?"

I would always regret that I hadn't taken the opportunity to tell him what I really thought of him that day. But I just wanted it over. In resignation I stood up to leave the room. He called after me, "Synchronicity!" I kept walking as he called out again, "I'll be your friend! No strings attached. Drop your suit, come back, and I'll see what I can do for you, but it has to be no strings attached."

"No strings attached" reverberated in my ears all the way to my car and back to my apartment and for days thereafter. It was such a telling phrase.

That was Clint entirely in a nutshell: "No strings attached," no responsibility, regret, remorse, or recollection of things past. An island. A stone wall. A cold, indifferent, narcissistic universe all his own.

Even so, I would try one more thing before giving up and proceeding to a painful and public trial. Incredibly I rationalized that maybe seeing me face-to-face had brought up too many emotions for Clint, perhaps even just a tinge of guilt; it was that, I told myself, that had made him hide behind his favorite tact: "The best defense is a great offense." I would deal with him from a distance, I thought. I would sit down and write Clint a letter. In my letter I tried to paint the picture of our past life together, recalling the love we'd had, the promises we'd shared. I also said that I could not accept his suggestion of "no strings attached."

My pleading letter was wasted time and emotion. Clint responded, weeks later, with a letter even colder than our meeting. In essence it stated: "I owe you nothing." There was no offering of a settlement, except that I walk away, take his word, and *hope* for some retroactive fairness from him. But I could not do that. I could not simply fall down on my knees in supplication with the same blind trust I had always given him.

Then some glimmer of future hope occurred. After the breakup with Clint I left Lennie Hirshan and the William Morris Agency and signed with a new agent, David Gersh of the Gersh Agency. Armed with my good reviews for *Impulse* he had a prospect for me. The script was entitled *Oh Baby* and it was to be produced and financed by Orion Pictures. It was a romantic comedy, the story of a scientist who makes himself the guinea pig for a drug he's testing. He implants an embryo in himself and becomes the first pregnant male in history. I met the producer, Beverly Camhe, then met the executives at Orion Pictures and they were all very eager for me to direct the film. I was ecstatic.

During the casting phase Beverly and I considered many different actors but Orion insisted we get a "star." We struck upon the idea of taking it to Arnold Schwarzenegger, who had often told me he'd like to work with me if the project was right. He seemed to view me as a director who understood actors and could him improve his acting range. I thought the idea of Arnold in this role could be very funny. So when he was filming *Kindergarten Cop* I visited him in his trailer. Arnold, who hates to read scripts, asked me to tell him the story, and I did. Right away he liked the idea but didn't know about his schedule. I sent the script to Maria, who loved it. We all waited.

Beverly and I took Arnold's then-agent, Lou Pitt, to lunch. "I don't know if Orion can afford Arnold," he said. Beverly and I pushed Orion to make any deal they could with him, but unbeknownst to any of us, Orion was about to go bankrupt and could never make such a deal. I was dejected, but before I could really focus on this, something else was going on that put things into a new perspective.

I discovered a lump in my right breast.

My gynecologist thought it was nothing, but after unsuccessfully attempting to aspirate it, she sent me for a mammogram. That mammogram wasn't conclusive, so I endured another, and yet another attempt at aspirating the lump. Finally I was sent to a surgeon for a "look-see" opinion.

The night before my appointment Nadine and her husband, Michael, took me for dinner in Beverly Hills, and we toasted to a good report the following day. But from the moment I disrobed for Dr. Marjorie Fine I had a deep gnawing in my chest and abdomen. Her face, though stonelike, somehow showed that she recognized something wrong in the shape of my lump.

"We need to do an immediate biopsy. Get dressed and my nurse will schedule you."

I wandered downstairs in the huge office building, walking in circles looking for a telephone to call Nadine. Finally, I found a row of pay phones. She answered and the floodgates holding back my tears cracked. "It's okay, sh-h-h," she said. "You don't know anything yet, not until after the biopsy." "But I . . . " I sobbed. "I . . . the look on her face. Oh, Nadine, I can't take any more; I really can't." "You're going to be okay, Sondra," she said in her voice of reason. I stood there, long after I had hung up the phone, unable to move, unable to think, unable to go on. Please God. Don't let it be true.

My biopsy was scheduled for the next day, and although I didn't feel much like eating, Gordon insisted that we go to Hamburger Hamlet. It would make me feel better, he promised, and added that I needed the nutrition.

"Now you're going to stay at my house tonight," he insisted. "I'll tuck you into the big Elizabethan tester bed and Chloe will curl up with you; you'll sleep much better there."

I agreed. I could feel safe there—a feeling I didn't often experience anymore.

When we arrived at Gordon's house, Chloe Jr. was there to greet us. Whenever Gordon returned home, he got on his knees and asked Chloe for a kiss. "Gimme a tiss," he'd say. She would then pad over to him and, kiss his face, first brushing him with the right side of her nose, then the left side. That night there were no kisses. Chloe just spun around and padded off toward the kitchen, trilling persistently as she went.

"I wonder what's going on with Miss Chloe," Gordon said. "I've never seen her carry on like this before."

A moment later she stuck her head around the kitchen door and trilled again, then, for good measure, added an urgent squawk and disappeared into the kitchen, still fussing nonstop.

"What is wrong with her?" Gordon said, puzzled. He crossed the dining room to follow her.

Exhausted, I had barely sat down when Gordon called out to me, "Sondra, come here. Hurry! I'm in the bathroom."

Oh God, what now? I thought. I couldn't take an emergency — not something broken, and certainly not anything mystical.

As I approached the bathroom, I could see Chloe standing on her hind legs with her front paws on the edge of the toilet seat. She was peering, transfixed, into the water. I followed her gaze and saw a strange, transparent substance slowing undulating in the perfectly still toilet water. I looked at Gordon, who was mesmerized.

"What on earth is that?" I asked him.

He didn't answer. He just kept staring at the frothy substance that suddenly began slowly to move and shift, leaving clear areas in the froth. Gradually, those clear areas themselves connected, making a distinct pattern.

"My God, that looks just like a cross," I said.

"It *is* a cross," Gordon replied, pushing past me and out of the room. "I'm gonna get the camera. Don't take your eyes off it," he called out to me as he ran upstairs.

I continued to stare at the water. "Gordon, hurry, it's changing!" I yelled.

"I can't find the camera," he called back. I could hear the racket of drawers opening, doors slamming, and hurried footsteps as he made his search for it. "What's it look like now?" he called again.

I could feel my pulse quickening at the impossibility of what I was staring at. "Now it's a circle! I can't believe it!"

Chloe and I both watched as it began to move again, silently drifting, closing in on itself, and shifting until it slowly became a triangle.

"Oh my God," I said to myself. "Gordon, you *have* to come down here. Now! Forget the camera. It's making more shapes. You have to see it."

Then I heard his feet flying down the stairs, charging through the Gothic room and into the bathroom behind me.

"What did it do?" he asked, nervously fumbling with the film box, his hands shaking.

"Well, it was a circle and then it was a triangle and now I don't know what it is," I answered helplessly.

"Which direction was the triangle pointing?" he asked quickly.

"I don't know. It was just a triangle."

"What do you mean you don't know?" He looked at me as if I were an idiot. "It could be very significant, Hobbit. Symbolically triangles have meanings depending on the direction they're pointing. Surely you remember—was the longest point toward you or toward the back of the bowl?"

"Pointing toward me, I think."

"Oh-h-h," Gordon said. "A downward triangle—that's a symbol of the Great Mother, just like the transparent ones that were flying down in a column toward my ear in the photo, the one I took on New Year's, a week after all the caritas pictures. Remember?"

I remembered it well; the resonance of that photograph was especially deep and rich. By what seemed awe-inspiring predestination, Gordon was *led* to a journal in which Bo had been writing his innermost thoughts about his drug problems (long after his breakup with Gordon). The first lines of that journal had read "Whose ears will hear this? God's ears move me most." It seemed that it was *Gordon* who God had wanted to hear them. Shortly after that, Gordon's camera, which was lying on the car seat beside him, went off, all by itself, and took a picture. When the photo came back from the lab, there was an unexplainable series of downward pointing triangles flying down onto Gordon's ear.

Gordon bent over and peered into the water, then began clicking the camera, photographing even Chloe, who would not budge from her spot overseeing it all. "Now it just sort of looks like random clouds floating in there," he said.

Then, putting his ear right above the water's surface, he said, "There's absolutely no sound at all coming from this water or the toilet, so nothing's running—and I'd love to know how Chloe knew that something was going on in here in the first place." Again, she stood up on her hind legs and peered in, her little face right next to his.

"Gordon, what on earth is it?" I asked hesitantly. "What does it mean?"

"There's no explanation. It's like the viscosity of the water has changed in certain places and is floating on top of other water. It's incredible. The images have to be a message."

Suddenly Gordon looked hypnotized. "Oh my God, look!" It was then that an image of what looked distinctly like a ram's horns began to form. This turned out to be a major religious symbol that, at the time, even Gordon hadn't learned the significance of.

"Hobbit, look!" I said. I could see a face was beginning to form. As it became clearer, we could see that the face was Eastern-looking—and a mark was slowly forming in the center of its forehead in the position of the classic third eye. And it absolutely looked as if I could detect a capital A coming out of its mouth.

"Please God, let this picture turn out," Gordon said, bringing up his camera, focusing it, and clicking. We watched the face dissolve, and the water, once again, become a sea of indistinct cloudlike drifts. Then suddenly it began to form what looked like the perfectly distinct shape of a ram's horns.

"Go in the kitchen and get me that empty jar sitting on the counter, the one with the screw-on lid. I'm going to preserve some of the liquid. Later we'll have it analyzed," Gordon, the "scientist," said.

Seconds later I returned with the jar and as I handed it to him, I bumped up against a bathroom cabinet drawer that was halfway opened. I knew that drawer had definitely been shut when I had left seconds ago because if the drawer had been open, I couldn't have moved past it without hitting it. When I leaned across to shut it, I froze. "Gordon, look."

Lined up in a neat row, resting on top of a box of Q-Tips, as if they had somehow been carefully arranged there, were the five hairpins that Gordon had been searching for since 1986. They were part of his mother's things he had brought back to California after her funeral. He knew the exact box in which he had packed the hairpins, but when he had unpacked and looked for them, they were *nowhere to be found.*

Now over *four years later,* here were these five unique hairpins lined up perfectly in a drawer that was opened and closed daily, on top of a box of Q-Tips that were used daily. As I stood there, staring at the hairpins, I recalled how hard we had searched everywhere in Gordon's house for them, and now here they were. The same hairpins that had mysteriously appeared on the back porch in Shelbyville right after Gordon's mother's death. We both stood there staring for a very long time, trying to assimilate what seemed impossible.

"What's going on in here is just not possible," Gordon said. "You know, you have to be able to have a certain amount of control over your life to be able to function, but the problem is that all this stuff makes me feel I *have* no control at all."

I understood but couldn't respond. There *was* no response. He knelt on the floor in front of the toilet and began carefully spooning the mysterious substance from the surface of the water. Looking at him there, I thought to myself, it's a shame that more adults aren't like him, so open and spontaneous, like a child. And I thought of the moving way Bo always described Gordon: "God's own powered orphan." Maybe all these things are happening to him because he *is* like a child.

"Tell us what it is, Chloe," Gordon said to Chloe, who still peered into the toilet. "How did you know it was in there?"

As if she understood, she turned and looked at him.

"Gimme a tiss," he whispered, and she bussed him on the mouth. "What are we gonna do, Chloe? God has turned our toilet into an Etch-A-Sketch."

He secured the lid tightly and, holding it up to examine it, said matter-of-factly, "It's holy water." Checking the label on the jar, he laughed. "Contained in a Del Monte pickled peach jar." He turned to me and said, "Hobbit, it's all a good sign. It's God. Don't worry about tomorrow. No matter what the outcome, you're going to be okay. You're protected."

I smiled. I didn't doubt that God or angels or Mrs. Anderson's spirit or Bo's mother's spirit—or all of them—were communicating with Gordon. After all, he was able to see beyond the barriers we're taught; he was able to see holy water in the toilet. And that seemed to be the point. We don't have to go to ashrams or Sedona or even to a church to get blessings. Maybe they are just as likely to be found in the commonplace if we have been given the *grace* to see them. I later teased Gordon, however, for referring to it as "holy water." And he replied, "Well, maybe God has a sense of humor." His comment reminded me of a *Life* magazine after-death article in which a Harvard professor spoke about such things: "Perhaps if God tried to communicate with us, he would have to speak to us poor mortals in language or symbols we would understand."

Gordon put the jar on a shelf for safekeeping. Weeks later, a doctor saw the substance and laughed at us. Almost immediately a perfect greenish downward-pointing triangle formed against the inside of the glass. The doctor said that he'd never seen anything like it, that scientifically it had to be mold, though he'd never heard of mold forming geometrically perfect shapes. When in another few weeks Gordon showed it to the doctor again by then a cross had formed in the middle of the triangle—both images the same as those that had previously formed in the toilet bowl. After that time, the water in the jar never again changed and the doctor stopped laughing.

Gordon went into the kitchen to feed Chloe when all of a sudden he was again calling out, "Sondra, come here."

Before I could even ask "What is it?" I saw, resting on top of Chloe's canned food, her favorite toy, a *circular* one that had been missing for almost two years.

Gordon spoke up. "And, of course, it was Chloe who led us in to look at the circular bowl of water (toilet) where you said you saw a circle forming. So, now, here is the circle (her toy) that's been returned to her. It's all connected, a perfect circle. That's the beauty of it all: Life has become like living poetry."

I felt exhilarated by the evening, and hopeful about the next day, but at the same time, drained. I knew Gordon would be up all night, thinking and searching his mind and his books for answers. I kissed him on the cheek and said goodnight.

The next morning Gordon brought me tea in bed and on my tray was a vase of beautiful pink flowers. I could tell they weren't from his yard. "Where did you get these?" I asked.

"Well, you won't believe it," he began. "I opened the living room curtain this morning and there it was: The tree in the front yard, the one that wouldn't bloom, has pink blossoms all over it."

It was a crepe myrtle tree and in the eight years that Gordon had lived there, I had tried everything to get it to bloom, but to no avail. Yet on that morning crucial to me it was blooming. Of course, it had to be an amazing sign. As I left Gordon's house, I glanced over at it, and, sure enough, it was in full bloom, just as he had said.

Denise Fraker was picking me up and driving me to Saint John's Hospital. I had told her that it was totally unnecessary for her to go with me, that it was a simple procedure that would be over in no time. I planned on going alone.

"Absolutely not. I'm going with you. We'll go to lunch afterward," she had said.

As Denise and I drove west toward the ocean and Santa Monica and the hospital, my head turned as I watched the Beverly Hills Hotel disappear behind us. Soon we would be approaching Bellagio Road, the West Gate entrance to Bel Air, and to my old home. I thought how often after the breakup I had automatically driven there, forgetting it was no longer "home."

"I wonder what he will feel if I do have breast cancer?" I said, not expecting an answer.

"Probably nothing," Denise said softly.

Before I knew it, Denise and I were in Santa Monica, then inside the hospital where someone handed me papers to fill out. Only as I followed the nurse to the room where I was to shed my clothes and put on a hospital gown did I realize that I was terrified. My hands trembled as I neatly put my dress on the hanger.

The next thing I knew I was lying on a surgical table, under a white sheet, looking up at all the doctors and nurses staring down at me—all of them faceless in their white garments and white masks.

Dr. Marjorie Fine didn't say a word as she went right to work. Suddenly, oddly, my mind drifted. I thought of the Christmas poem "A Visit from St. Nicholas": " 'Twas the night before Christmas" . . . when Santa "spoke not a word but went straight to his work . . ."

I had hoped that the doctor would put me to sleep so that I would be out until it was all over, but I wasn't to have that luxury. A nurse came toward me with a needle, which she injected into my breast. I couldn't feel it; I couldn't feel anything; I was already numb all over, yet I'd had no anesthesia. I was wide awake, but I had shut down.

My right breast was ready for Dr. Fine and as she began to move her scalpel, I could feel only a dull tugging sensation.

"It's all going to be fine." The voice inside my head was the only one talking to me. The fear was nauseating. Suddenly there was a strange odor in the room.

"What's that smell?" I asked.

"Nothing to be concerned about. I'm cauterizing the vessels," Dr. Fine's emotionless voice responded.

Burning flesh. My flesh. Dr. Fine turned away; everyone else seemed to walk away from me, too. Then a nurse left the room. She seemed to be carrying something in her hands. Was it the part of my breast they had removed? A part of me? Gone.

I couldn't move. I waited for someone to tell me what was happening. I didn't dare to ask anything else; I feared I wouldn't like the answers. So I just lay there under the sheet, with my life hanging by a single yes or no. I hadn't expected to lie there and wait for the results. Is that what was happening? I had expected them to remove the lump, and the next day I would hear that it was benign. In tiny baby steps, I could handle it all; inch by inch I could get through it, but not all at once.

Suddenly the phone rang.

"Yes . . . uh-huh . . . yes . . . okay, I see . . . uh-huh . . . thank you." I recognized Dr. Fine's voice, but who was she talking to? And as if she had read my mind, she turned and said, "Pathology." Then without a trace of emotion in her voice she said, "It's cancer."

It was as if a tourniquet tightened around my body and tears shot to my eyes, stinging like tiny pins, but I said nothing.

No one said a word. As they stitched me up, I tried to think only about my breathing . . . in . . . and . . . out. Before I knew it, someone was escorting me to a small, windowless room. "Shall I get your friend Mrs. Fraker?" I nodded a yes. Denise and I had planned to go to lunch, but Dr. Fine had said that word. Cancer. Or at least, I thought she had. Everything seemed unreal, as if I were underwater, yet, in spite of that, my body felt heavy. The nurse turned and walked out the door. It was quiet; the only sound was the pounding of my heart. Oh God.

The door opened and there was Denise. Everything that had seemed unreal became real when I saw the look on her face. She walked toward me with her arms outstretched and it wasn't a dream anymore. I knew it was actually happening. I collapsed in tears. She was followed closely behind by Dr. Fine, who immediately sat down.

"You'll have to have the breast removed," she announced with amazing certainty.

My mind began to race. How could she be so sure? Weren't there more tests? The whole breast? What about a lumpectomy? I had heard of that.

"The edge of your biopsy slide was not clean of cancer cells. I have to keep cutting until I have a clean edge," she said with no change of facial expression.

Keep cutting? I felt very hot. I wiped the beads of perspiration from my upper lip. The water that I had felt myself submerged in only moments ago had turned to heavy syrup. I couldn't move or breathe.

"We'll have to schedule more surgery," she said dispassionately, then stood up to leave. I wondered where she was going so abruptly. I couldn't remember having said a word to her. Had we talked about everything there was to talk about? Then, almost as if she had heard my thoughts, she looked straight into my eyes and said, "You'll never trust your body again." Then she walked out of my life forever.

I walked across the tiny room to the telephone and dialed Gordon, who was waiting to hear. His line was ringing. As I stood there, waiting for him to answer, I glanced down at my appointment book. It was the same appointment book of a week ago, a month ago, but now it was different. Its black leather surface, which I had touched every day, looked the same but it was changed because my life was irrevocably and completely and forever changed. I opened it at random and there, in a calendar entry from a week ago, I saw something I had written: "Nobody's child. Just like a flower, they're growing wild. No mama's kisses, no daddy's smile." And underneath: "crying." Suddenly Gordon answered his phone.

"It's malignant," I blurted out, wanting to get rid of it.

We both sat silently. Then he said, "I love you, and it will be all right. I promise. Are you coming here now?"

"Soon," I replied. Then I hung up.

"Do you want to go home? Or to Gordon's?" Denise asked.

"I want to go to lunch. Just like we planned." I wanted to pretend nothing had happened.

We ordered our usual salads, with raspberry vinaigrette on the side. Keep it normal. And for that moment I pretended that nothing existed except my lunch. I imagined Vivien Leigh in *Gone With the Wind*. I could hear Scarlett's words, "I'll think about that tomorrow." And I would. Many tomorrows.

When Gordon got off the phone he ran into the backyard, crying. John followed. After about forty minutes he sent John back into the house. Soon Gordon came striding back inside and said urgently, "I'm going to be given a sign. Put the television on channel eleven."

John did and in that very moment the television screen was filled with the name De Jesus. It was a close-up of the back of a football player's jersey, and the player's name was De Jesus. The *live simulcast* of the sportscaster's voice boomed out, "De Jesus will take care of it."

"Oh my God!" John exclaimed. At that moment, he felt something so powerful that, to this day, he says he has never been able to describe it.

Gordon only said, "Thank you."

DENISE AND I began searching for the right surgery, treatment, doctors, and hospital. I knew I never again wanted to see Dr. Fine. Everyone had a different opinion: Should I have radiation or chemotherapy—or both? Every door we entered seemed to lead to another, and though all the doctors seemed qualified, each had his or her own style. Maria sent me to an oncologist who was supposedly one of the best, but I couldn't wait to get out of his office. His manner was funereal, and his most famous patients had all died. Finally I chose an oncologist who was not only well recommended, but funny and lively, and played a musical instrument in his spare time. Right away, I knew Dr. Larry Heifetz was the doctor for me.

And to perform my surgery I chose Dr. Stephen Shapiro, one of the top surgeons at Cedars-Sinai Medical Center. I was to meet with him the following day.

"Do you want anything to drink? Can I get you something?" Gordon asked me as I sat down on his sofa.

"I guess. Maybe a diet soda."

"I'll put a big baked potato in the oven for you. Mama always said, 'They're the best thing in the world for you when you're feeling punk.' "

When I'd arrived at Gordon's he'd been watching the soap operas he'd previously recorded. They had ended, but the tape had continued running, and what began playing was the remainder of some previously taped program, an old episide of A Current Affair. I was just about to turn it off, when Gordon said, "Oh let's watch this. I just recently taped it, and I haven't had a chance to look at it yet, then I can erase it.' So we watched as the host began telling about the making of an old movie, The Conqueror, which had starred John Wayne and Susan Hayward.

"Oh, look! It's one of the best 'bad movies' ever made," Gordon said. "John Wayne as Genghis Khan; it's a hoot."

I watched casually as the program told about The Conqueror, which had been filmed in the same desert where the atomic bomb had been tested. Tragically many in the cast—including John Wayne, Susan Hayward, Agnes Moorehead, and the film's director, Dick Powell—had developed cancer and subsequently died. The host went on to say that, in fact, only one of actors from that film had survived. LEO GORDON was his name.

I began to watch more closely, nervous somehow. Was it a message about my own cancer? The program went on to explain how a study had concluded that the bomb was actually believed to be the cause of all the cancers. And the name given to that bomb was DIRTY HARRY. Gordon and I just stared dumbfounded. The coincidence that I too had just been diagnosed with *cancer* and was in the middle of a horrible battle with "*Dirty Harry*" was quite extraordinary. Even though there had been no history of breast cancer in my family, I certainly couldn't say that Clint had caused my cancer. But the connections and timing of the information on that program were stunning to me.

The next day, I made my way down the corridor toward the office of Dr. Shapiro, the surgeon who was scheduled to remove my cancer. I came to a dead stop when my eyes fell on the name plaque on his door. It read: Stephen Shapiro, M.D., and underneath, the name of his partner, the one who would assist him in my cancer surgery, was LEO GORDON.

I woke up early on the morning of my scheduled surgery. It was strange that I was on my way to Cedars-Sinai to have my breast removed, but I didn't feel panicky or upset. Glancing at my watch, I realized that I had only thirty minutes before I was meeting Denise at Gordon's house. I planned to leave my car at his house for safekeeping. For some strange reason, probably stress, I had convinced myself that I couldn't go to the hospital until I had a new toothbrush and bottle of mouthwash. So I decided first to drive to the small neighborhood market to pick it up. I arrived at Arrow market, where I had shopped for years, found a parking place right in front, got out of my car, and locked the door.

"Hey, Sondra, how's everything?" said Jim, one of the grocery clerks there. He was sitting on the nearby railing, drinking a soft drink, probably taking his morning break.

"Everything's fine, Jim," I replied. I walked inside, quickly grabbed the toothbrush and mouthwash, and walked straight to the cash register. As I paid, I could see my car parked just outside, through the glass entrance doors. The whole thing took no more than four minutes.

Jim was still sitting, drinking his soda, as I unlocked the door to my car and climbed in. "See you later, Sondra," he called out to me. "Bye, bye," I called back. Distractedly, I put the key into the ignition, then reached for the steering wheel. What on earth? I looked at it, and then I looked at it again, and then I just sat staring at it in disbelief! I even rubbed my eyes the way they do in cartoons, because I couldn't believe what I was seeing. My steering column was bent at an angle toward the dashboard, the edge of the steering wheel on one side was within a half an inch of touching the dashboard. I felt as if I had been swallowed by something unidentifiable, and pulled down into the center of some vortex. I knew no one had touched that car in the four minutes since I had left it locked, right in front of the glass doors to the market. And even if someone had gotten into my car, it would have been physically impossible to bend that steering wheel and certainly not in four minutes!

I got out and began walking around the car, helplessly searching for any logical explanation. Nothing had been touched. The passenger door was still locked, just as I had left it. I got back in my car and, slowly and carefully, headed back to Gordon's. By the time I arrived, I was ranting and raving, "I don't think I'm ever gonna be all right again. You won't believe what happened to my car. It's humanly impossible. I'm fed up. I'm fed up with synchronicity and Clint and lawyers and Bo and all of it—everything. Leave me alone! Everybody!"

Gordon just looked at me and said, "What's a steering wheel? A circle! I have to get the camera 'cause we have to photograph it, or who'll ever believe us?"

Later, when the car was delivered to Fred's Mercedes in Hollywood, the mechanic, with a disbelieving look on his face, shook his head and said, "How in the hell could this have happened? It would take a thousand-pound gorilla to do a thing like this to a Mercedes steering column." We made him sign a statement because we knew *no one* would ever believe us!

I checked into Cedars-Sinai under the name Chloe McCullers. The Chloe was for obvious reasons and McCullers, as in Carson, was for good luck. I was trying to keep the tabloids from knowing what was going on in my life. The last thing I needed was to have my cancer splashed all over the papers. I had been the subject of enough "feeding frenzies." In Hollywood it's unacceptable to appear weak, especially sick. No one wants to go near you; they might "catch" your bad luck. Since I had learned of my cancer, I had gone out of my way to be seen at screenings, just to show I was "happy" and "fine." Never let them know you're bleeding when you live in a shark tank.

After the first surgery Dr. Shapiro told me that the lumpectomy he had performed would not suffice. The slides were still not acceptably safe and he would have to remove the entire breast. He would also remove a section from my lymph nodes to determine if I needed additional chemo or radiation treatment. And that was not all; I had to make another major decision. Dr. Shapiro and Dr. Heifetz informed me that my particular cancer was the type that almost always occurred in both breasts. Would I consider having them both removed during the surgery, even though there was no evidence that my other breast was unhealthy? Did I, in order to keep that breast, want to live my life with a constant anxiety and watchfulness regarding it and most likely have surgery at a later date, or did I want to act aggressively then and there? It was not an easy decision, but after a sleepless night I said, "Remove them both."

That meant another member of my team was scheduled. Dr. Tearston would cosmetically reconstruct my breasts immediately after the mastectomy while I was still under anesthesia.

"But first, I want you to go home, Sondra," Dr. Shapiro told me. "It will be a few days before we can schedule the second surgery and the hospital is the 'dirtiest' place you can be." I had always thought of hospitals as being sterile, but of course they are full of very sick people. Denise packed me up and took me to Gordon's, where I stayed until my second surgery. When

Denise and I walked to her car that Saturday morning, a young intern named Dr. Scott Cunneen was carrying my bag. He had been another miracle in my life.

Scott had been the first image I had seen when I woke up from my surgery. He had been assigned as a member of my surgical team and had been performing the postsurgical checkup when I came out of the anesthesia. Where he stood beside my bed with my medical chart in his hands, the light from the window cast a brilliant backlit haze around him, and through my just-opened eyes and my still blurred vision, I saw his face. It was a face I instantly felt I knew but knew that I did not actually know — a face that was intelligent, gentle, and handsome in its strong bones and dark wavy hair. His brown eyes met mine directly from behind his gold-rimmed glasses, and something immediate happened.

Shortly afterward, Denise, who had been in the hallway, returned to my room. She has never let me forget my first drowsy words to her: "Who was that really cute doctor?" She looked at me as if I had lost my mind; how could I possibly have such a thought at such a moment in time? It had been an instantaneous connection for me and though he remained incredibly professional and discreet, it soon became obvious that it was the same for him. Like "gifts from God" the best things can happen at the worst times.

A few days later I returned for my second surgery. Afterward both my surgeon and oncologist greeted me with news, both bad and good. The testing on my second breast showed no evidence of abnormality, but most important, the tests on my nodes were *negative*. Thank God. I would need no follow-up treatments. I could go home and recover and adjust to the surgery.

No one could believe what a cheerful a patient I had been. Believing the typical "Hollywood image" that preceded me, they were apparently expecting a "witch who was suing that nice hero Clint Eastwood." I later learned that interns and nurses had cowered in the hallways, not wanting to enter my room. After all, the prototype of the Hollywood actress was a demanding, self-centered woman.

Even my friends were amazed at my positive attitude. "It's as if you aren't sick," they said with disbelief. All except Gordon, who understood completely the depth of all that had brought me to those feelings. One by one they visited, even my psychiatrist and my attorney, for which I was grateful. Cynthia and Lili put in an appearance, my newfound friend Joyce Rudolph (married to Alan Rudolph, the film director), Nadine, and Elaine Ceder (a very old friend with whom I had reunited since my breakup with Clint). Maria (who can barely walk into a hospital without literally fainting) brought balloons, her brother Bobby, and even Arnold. Of course there was no visit, no card, no phone message, and no word at all from Clint.

I faltered only once and that was when Dr. Tearston, my reconstruction surgeon, removed the bandages to examine my breast implants. I was seated on the side of the bed, and without warning, and without even seeing what he was seeing, I fainted.

Soon it was over. I was back in my apartment and released from any further treatment. Thank God, I didn't have to have chemotherapy. That alone merited a celebration. But I had barely unpacked my small bag when the phone rang.

"Sondra, It's Larry Heifetz." My oncologist. Oh God. "I need you to come over to my office right away." For the first time since Dr. Fine had said that terrifying word "cancer," I felt myself sinking into blackness, my heart pounding throughout my body. "What's wrong?" I hadn't expected to hear from him at all; I was "dismissed—no further treatment necessary."

"Just come on over here if you can."

He didn't want to tell me over the phone, which meant it had to be bad news. I called Denise, my constant support, but got no answer. So even though I was still in bandages and weak from surgery, I drove myself to Cedars and to Dr. Heifetz's office alone. I could feel the panic rising as I sat down in his small office and faced him.

"Sondra, what has occurred is so improbable that, at first, I didn't know how to interpret it. But Dr. Shapiro and I have talked it over and have decided that, if you were our sister or wife, both of us would recommend that you take no chances with it."

"What is it? What are you talking about? There was no cancer in my nodes. Was there?"

"Well," he began, "it seems that your slide was picked out randomly and anonymously—your name wasn't even on it—by the pathology department to test out this new cancer cell detecting dye. And one or two cells on your slide, which was made from the section taken from your lymph nodes, have apparently 'lit up' under it. That means those cells might possibly be abnormal cancer cells."

I thought that the earth had dropped out from under me. The cancer had entered the rest of my body. I was lost again, and I was angry. Why had I been allowed to believe I was fine for three days, then be jerked back and forth? First it's one breast, then two, then this.

"And so, I recommend we do some rounds of chemo," he said.

There was nothing to do but have faith and go forward. And so I did.

And I would later even view that random, "accidental" test as yet another gift.

After a few weeks of rest, I began the chemo. Denise again drove me and stayed with me through every single treatment, except one when Gordon took me. He had wanted to take me for all the treatments, but I said no. Having him watch would mean I would be suffering his anxiety on top of mine. "I'd rather you stay home, Hobbit," I had said.

No doctor could have made the whole experience any more comfortable and cheerful than Dr. Heifetz. Like many women, I have always been able to tolerate pain rather well, but for some reason I could never bear the thought of an intravenous needle and never ceased to dread that moment in chemotherapy and it was always that moment that was the most physically painful of the entire experience.

"Will I lose my hair?" I asked. "Maybe, maybe not" was the best answer I got. Denise made a special ice pack for my head, hoping that it would prevent my hair from falling out. I was certain it would work. But one day, standing in my shower, I ran my fingers through my hair as the water rushed over it, rinsing away the shampoo. When I removed my hands, there wrapped around all my fingers was a handful of hair. And it never stopped falling until there was almost none left. I couldn't bear to brush it. Finally I sat in Denise's little dressing room, looking at myself in her mirror, while she cut what was left to about an inch in length. Fluffing it around, she said, "See there, you look so cute."

"I look like Jean Seberg in *Breathless*, don't I?" I told myself and Denise. "I always wanted to have the nerve to cut my hair as short as hers."

I continued trying to keep my appearance together so that others didn't know what was really happening. There were leaks in the press but I always said I was fine and that no further treatment was necessary. I needed more than ever to find work, so I put on a smile and a strong front and continued meetings. The Orion film project *Oh Baby* (the one I had taken to Arnold on the set of his film *Kindergarten Cop*) was still alive and Beverly (my producer) and I were still in the process of trying to cast a leading man and keep our film on track against what seemed all odds.

My therapy became a problem for a planned meeting with Nicholas Cage and so I had to reschedule. Unexpected and mysterious lesions which I couldn't disguise had appeared on my face. My doctor was incredibly alarmed at first; he had never seen such a side effect. I was sent to numerous skin specialists until finally they agreed that the lesions were the result of a staph infection that my body had been unable to fight. These lesions were the least important part of my disease really, yet the most devastating to my inner strength. They etched giant holes in my courage. Still I never doubted that in the end I would heal.

Through it all I was helped, loved, and encouraged, mostly by Gordon, who put me in his guest room and waited on me constantly, by Denise, who took me everywhere with her, and also by Scott, who brushed my hair and told me that it would grow back "twice as beautiful" and even curly, the way I'd always wanted it to be. He held my head when I was so feverish and nauseated from the chemo that I felt I would turn inside out. The nausea left such a deep impression that for years I could not drive past the Cedars treatment center without being overcome by waves of it.

It was November and my lawsuit with Clint dragged on. Finally a trial date was scheduled for March. The thought of going to court still terrified me, and now after the cancer I was beginning to think I couldn't go on with such an impossible task. It no longer seemed to matter that I'd lost my home. I couldn't bear to think about the past anymore, about all the duplicity and mistreatment. If I could just get back to work, I thought, I could start over. Just as I'd begun to feel that way, the phone rang.

"Why don't you come on over to my office, Sondra. I've got something to talk to you about," Al Ruddy said to me.

I prayed it was a new film he wanted me to direct; it wasn't. It was a proposal he conveyed from Clint. "You don't want to keep going with this messy lawsuit, Sondra," Al said conspiratorially. "You've got so much talent; you don't need this. I saw Clint over the weekend and he said he was prepared to help you work; you're a good director; you should be directing movies. You know they all love you at Warner Bros. They've gotten caught in this mess too. Clint says that if you drop all your claims against him that he'll get you a contract at Warner Bros. and his power will assure you that you'll go back to work and direct movies there."

It sounded like a dream come true. I knew that Clint had the power, with the snap of his little finger, to produce such a thing for me. It seemed to make sense. After all, it was certainly a great deal for Clint: He wouldn't have any financial risk because Warner Bros. would, in effect, be assuming much of his debt to me. He'd also be rid of a potentially ugly public trial. And he'd be rid of me. By then I had resigned myself to the loss of my home and all the "things" in my life and only wanted to move on. The hard way I had learned that "things" don't really matter. Cancer had shown me that. So I agreed, and Al passed the word to Clint, who passed the word to his attorney. His attorney called my attorney. Clint met with Terry Semel, co-CEO of Warner Bros., and negotiations began. Within weeks, a contract was made and I could breathe again. Clint even returned a few more of my personal things, and I couldn't help but notice that among them was *every religious icon* I had ever collected, some of which I hadn't even asked for. Then, in a humorous postscript, he refused to return my skis. The skis were given to me by the manufacturer, but in "Clint logic" they were really *his* because they had only been given to me because I was with *him*. He was amazing.

During the final negotiations, it was agreed that I would receive $450,000 and Gordon's house. I'd asked for one other small consideration: that Clint buy back some bad investments that he'd requested his business manager, Roy Kaufman, put me in; Clint refused. I brushed it aside and focused on the future, and my Warner Bros. contract. With respect to that contract, my attorney asked for one special provision from Clint. "If Sondra gets sick again and can't direct some film, Warner Bros. could consider that a default and not pay. Then she'd be stuck, sick, and would have no salary." So Norman requested that Clint would agree to pay me those same funds under such an eventuality—only if I were ill and couldn't work and if Warner Bros. consequently would not pay me the dollar amount of my Warner Bros. contract: $1.5 million.

Clint outright refused. But after much pressure he finally agreed to pay some small percentage if I got sick and couldn't work, but *only* if I submitted to a checkup by his doctors. His position was incredible to me, but I told my attorney to close the deal; I would not get sick again, and I would not hear any further Clint Eastwood conversation.

So in December 1990, I moved into my offices on the Warner Bros. lot, hung up my posters from *Ratboy* and *Impulse*, hired an assistant, and rolled up my sleeves to work.

By this time *Oh Baby* had completely fallen apart because Orion was now officially in bankruptcy. Beverly suggested that I submit it to Warners, telling about the interest Arnold Schwarzenegger had had at one point. I was quite surprised when Terry Semel and Tom Lassally (another Warner executive) didn't go for it. Usually when a big star is even remotely interested in a story, the studios eagerly sit down with them. I knew that casting Arnold in this part was a bold move, and I also knew studios weren't often bold, so, very eager to get something going that Warner Bros. *did like*, I let it drop.

In a typical Hollywood move Arnold did something to me that was appalling. Whether he directly orchestrated it, or indirectly participated in it, or just allowed it to happen, he unnecessarily hurt me at a time I could ill afford another loss. *Oh Baby*, a very specific story which I had introduced Arnold to, was immediately taken—without me—to Arnold's friend and frequent director Ivan Reitman. The *Oh Baby* script was rewritten, with Arnold's involvement and participation, and produced by Universal Pictures with the new title *Junior*. I was never offered even a small "finder's fee" for having first brought him the project. He never offered me an explanation, or a phone call, and both he and Maria acted as if it had *never happened*.

For the next three years I talked day after day to various Warner executives, including my old friends Lucy Fisher, Terry Semel, Bob Daly—with whom I had worked and socialized for years. I met with agents and submitted project after project in good faith to Warner Bros. Before my breakup with Clint they had placed five projects in development for me and had had me direct two of them. Now that they were paying me $1.5 million in an Eastwood-orchestrated deal, not one executive would approve one single story for me to work on. Apparently they preferred to pay me just to sit there and do nothing, which would destroy me professionally as well as emotionally.

I even brought them a script I'd submitted to Madonna, who was interested. But the studio turned it down. I recast the film with Harvey Keitel, Jennifer Jason Leigh, and Glenne Headly, but again they said no. I got a foreign finance group interested in giving me the money to make the film if only Warner Bros. would give them *a letter of interest* saying they would release the film. Warners said no. I brought over thirty projects to them and they said an immediate no to them all.

I pleaded with Bob Daly and Terry Semel to give me some project off the shelves, something they had faith in that had no director assigned. I'd develop it, get actors interested in it, whatever it took to get it going. This wouldn't have cost them a penny over what they were already paying me, but they said no. Eventually agents stopped giving me scripts; they knew the score even if I hadn't figured it out. The thing that was most mystifying and made Warner Bros.' performance under my deal so obviously in bad faith, was *not* that they didn't let me direct a film, but that they did not let me even option a story so that I could *begin* the process. They had put me under contract, which normally meant they were interested in my creative ideas and judgment, but they never supported me, not even to first base.

In hindsight it's easy to look back and wonder why I wasn't suspicious of them sooner, but miraculously I was still unjaded. I stayed the "reasonable, good little girl" who knew how difficult it is to make films, and how expensive they are. I wanted to be cooperative, and I wanted to find just the *right* thing for Warner Bros. and me. And I was willing to take whatever time was necessary. Even if I directed only one film during my deal there, that would get me back on course and would say to the rest of the community that I was "in the club" even though I was no longer with Clint. That's exactly how they all think in Hollywood.

During the third year of my contract I grew depressed and desperate. I hired a new agent who got me a job directing a television movie for Robert Greenwald Productions and ABC. I knew that directing a television movie could very easily send a message that I was "coming down in class." This is an absurd prejudice, but a real one. I weighed it carefully and decided that I couldn't turn it down. I needed to get back on a film set for many reasons, and I believed that doing just one TV movie couldn't matter. After all, I would then follow it up with a big Warner Bros. feature.

Directing *Death in Small Doses*, which starred Richard Thomas and Tess Harper, was an arduous experience at best. As was the case with most television movies, I had only eighteen days to film it compared to the fifty-four days I'd had for *Impulse*. My longtime friend and brilliant cameraman, Bill Fraker, agreed, as a favor to me, to photograph it for me. I'll never forget Richard Thomas's first words to me when he arrived on location in North Carolina. "This is your first TV movie?" he said. "Well, buckle your seat belt; you're in for a wild ride!" He was right. The second challenge was that the story was based on a true event, so the script required massive annotating, 75 percent was done by me with a legal researcher, to avoid retaliatory lawsuits. But I was grateful to be working, and grateful for what I was learning.

After it was completed it was gratifying indeed when Richard Thomas phoned me to say, "I just saw our film and it's real 'filmmaking' and I'm proud to have worked with you on it." Then *TV Guide*, which rarely critiques the *director's* work in a TV movie, called my work "stylish." This was much needed encouragement when my own faith in my talent was faltering and my spirit was fading.

Back at Warners I was doing everything within my power to please them and make things work. I replaced my old assistant, hoping that a fresh voice would infuse new ideas and new contacts and help me bring in more material. I hired Mary Wellnitz who had had experience working with Lance Young when he had been a top executive at Paramount Studios. Lance was now one of the top executives at Warner Bros.; he and I had never worked together and I thought Mary would be very helpful with him.

I was supervising the editing and sound mix on *Death in Small Doses* when Mary handed me a surprising phone message. Clint had called. I couldn't imagine why he was phoning me after three years. I was of two minds about it; a part of me had still wished that for the sake of the past Clint and I could have ended on a more positive note in spite of who I'd learned he really was. The other part of me didn't ever want to hear his name, because even the sound of it brought along nothing but ominous and forboding feelings.

"Hey, how's it goin'," he said, once again as if nothing had ever happened.

"Fine," I replied. It suddenly occurred to me that he might be calling so that I would congratulate him for the Academy Award nominations he'd just gotten for *Unforgiven*. "Congratulations on your nominations," I offered.

"Oh thanks," he replied. "I'll just be glad when it's over one way or the other . . . there's just too much stress about it."

He proceeded to act as if he didn't care whether he won or not—he had forgotten how well I knew him. I knew he was desperate to win. Warner Bros. had spent a fortune on ads, and Clint had given numerous interviews, something he rarely did. He had always wanted to be legitimized by the critics. I'm sure he wanted to rub those nominations in Pauline Kael's face. Then Clint moved to another topic, which might also have been his reason for calling me.

"So, I hear you have a movie," he said.

I couldn't believe that he even knew about it. No one at Warner Bros. seemed even to know I existed. Was Clint still having me followed, or were my phones now tapped at the office? Why?

"I'd love to see it," he said. "Send me a tape of it when you have one." Within minutes he had hung up. I was completely mystified, and had no idea what that was about. A couple of weeks after that call I heard that Frances Fisher was pregnant. The news sent a shock through me. Although I was grateful that I hadn't had his child, this news reminded me of the permanent loss I suffered in my efforts to please him. Had Clint been "checking my temperature" about Frances's pregnancy? Was he worried I would go ballistic and mess up his Oscar campaign? (I was later told that Clint had made Frances keep her pregnancy a secret until after the Academy Awards. "I don't want that kinda thing taking attention away from my Oscar race!" he had said to her.)

When I'd heard the news, I called Lili, who hadn't yet completely disappeared from my life. This essentially meant that I was still getting invited to her annual "ladies birthday luncheon," an affair that was so "Hollywood" it should be a documentary. Most of the women there seemed invited strickly for political reasons because some said it was the only time during the year they ever *saw* Lili. We were all given instructions on what gift to purchase for her from the gift registry that Lili's secretary always put together. I generally refused to comply.

"I just heard Frances Fisher is pregnant!" I said to Lili. "Have you heard that? Is it true?"

"Yes, but I don't know much more about it than that. Dick and I had dinner with them one night not long ago and Frances announced, 'We're pregnant,' and Clint said, 'Who's this "we"? *You* are pregnant, not we!' "

Clint's remark was so disgusting that I began to defend Frances, whom I didn't even know. As I rambled on, Lili suddenly blurted out, "Sondra, do you have an agent representing you for 'voice-over' work?"

I paused, baffled. "What are you talking about?"

"Oh, I was just listening to your voice, and I never stopped to realize what a great voice you have. *You should do voice-over work.* You'd be great! I'm late for a meeting so I gotta rush off now, but I'll call you later." She was gone. Voice-over? I couldn't believe it. I marveled at her ability to disconnect. The idea that Lili and Clint had recently had dinner together was telling in itself, but then I recalled an earlier dinner they'd also had with Clint in London, shortly after our splitup, and after the *secret phone tapes* were revealed. At dinner, Lili had asked Clint, "Well, who was the worst person on the tapes?" "You were, Lili," Clint replied. "By far." They all laughed, as if it had meant nothing that Lili had "laid him open" and that Clint had secretly and illegally recorded (Lili's) private conversations. A great time was had by all—including Jane Brolin, the "trashy barfly" as Lili always called her.

While I was struggling to make my Warner Bros. deal work, I was forced to deal with something I'd never anticipated. "Hobbit, your mother has had a stroke and is in the hospital," Gordon haltingly said. "They don't know a lot yet, but Margaret Turner called, said it doesn't sound very good." It seemed ironic that I had given him the news about his mother's stroke, and now he was telling me about mine. I had not seen or talked with my mother since 1967, and now a deep, dull pain grabbed hold of me. I recoiled at the idea of opening up that old and still somewhat mystifying wound. Yet I was filled with a sudden and unexpected connection to her, a connection I had never felt during all my childhood.

"Are you okay?" Gordon asked. Then, "Do you think you'll go there?"

I don't remember anything clearly—not the packing, or the flight, or even my brother and his wife picking me up. Everything was a blur until I was walking down the corridor of the Shelbyville hospital with a nurse escorting me to my mother's room. As we drew closer I saw a man standing in the hallway; I recognized him right away. He looked the same, really—still thin and sinewy, just older, more stooped, and his close-cut, full dark hair was now flecked with gray. His eyes, made larger by the thick glasses he now wore, looked tired—one eyelid slightly closed by a small mole I hadn't remembered.

"Sondra," he said. "Lord, if it ain't you."

"Hi, Daddy," I responded. And after a hug, "Are you okay?"

"Better'n your mama, I reckon." he told me. "Come on in. She won't believe her eyes."

I approached her bed and looked at her lying there. Unexpectedly old. Her hair, cut short now, was solid gray. Her false teeth were on the bedside table, and her mouth looked so small and helpless without them. I had to stare deep into her eyes to find her, the person I had remembered, to recognize her. "Mother?" I said softly. "Can you hear me?"

She slowly opened her eyes and looked up at me. "Sondra honey," she said calmly, as if we'd only spoken yesterday. Then with mock impatience she said, "You two sit down." I sat down on the side of her bed and awkwardly took her hand; Daddy sat in the straight-backed chair. I was having trouble comprehending how I felt—time did not exist; reality did not exist. Oddly, we spoke of insignificant things . . . and nothing of the past.

"I had to clean her bed this mornin' myself," Daddy suddenly said. "Couldn't wait for those nurses. I came in here the other night, and they had even taken her oxygen tube right off her face and had it hangin' on the wall. I told 'em I don't want her passin' out on me again," Daddy said.

"Shut up now, Alfred," Mother teased. "He just worries, worries, worries. He's drivin' me crazy. Pokin' food in my mouth. Shinin' a flashlight in my eyes in the middle of the night."

"Polly," he said, "you pull off your tubes in your sleep. And you got to eat. You can't get well if you don't eat."

"I don't care. You scare me to death, shinin' that light at me."

He sat there, smiling, legs crossed, his face resting on one hand as she rambled on. She had always been stubborn. He had always worried. I remembered.

Silence. Only the gurgling of mother's oxygen tank filled the air.

"Don said you spent the night at his house last night," Mother said. "Did you like it?"

"It's very nice, Mother," I said. "And his wife and daughters too. I'm glad to see that Donald has become such a success with his air-conditioning business."

"Yeah, but he works all the time. I love those girls. They're all so sweet. My Amy is a character. I used to love to take her shopping. Me and her would have a ball," Mother went on.

"Where did you go shopping?" I wanted to make conversation, to make her feel better. After all, wasn't that why I had come? Like some absolution?

"Wal-Mart. They got everything you need at Wal-Mart."

"His oldest girl, Dawn, is a brain, just like you was, Sondra," Daddy added.

"Yeah, she is," Mother said. "I just got to get out of this bed for her wedding. I can't miss that."

"You'll be there, Mother," I told her. "I just know it. I hear you're getting better all the time."

"I sure hope so, honey. And I got to get home and run the dustmop." Images of the old house crowded my mind.

Soon the nurse brought in Mother's lunch. "I don't want any of this mess," she said.

"Polly, you got to eat," Daddy said, then turning to me, "We usually go out to eat once a week or so," he said. "We go over to the Ponderosa. They have a food bar. They said they would give us all a free meal when our daughter comes home. I reckon they thought that would never happen."

I didn't know what to say, so encouragingly I offered, "Well, we will just have to take the Ponderosa up on it."

And so we sat . . . and the rest of the day passed in long stretches of silence.

"Well, Mama," Daddy finally said, slowly rising from his chair. "Got to go feed my cats." He walked over to kiss her goodbye, and as he took her hands, he checked the nails to see if they were the proper shade of flesh tone, no more signs of the blue. Then turning to me, he said, "If you want to see the old house, you can follow me home."

"I'd like that, Daddy," I told him, making him smile. "I'll be back first thing tomorrow, Mother," I said to her, and kissed her cheek goodnight.

"That's good, hon. I'll just get a little sleep now."

It was about 5:00 P.M. and the light was soft and fading as I drove behind him, following his old yellow Chrysler across town toward Wartrace. My head turned to take in the high school, which still had the big stone-carved "Central" above the entrance doors. It was unchanged except for the modern black letters spelling "Harris Middle School," which scarred the side of its wall. Soon we were driving past nothing but green fields, where the fireflies were beginning to come out—magical candles, bordering the narrow black winding road as far as the eye could see—lighting up, then going out, all across the distance, until finally, up ahead, I could see the railroad tracks that marked the entrance to Wartrace. Soon I would see the old house. It was still hard to know what to feel. Curving alongside the railroad tracks, we rounded the corner past the old Walking Horse Hotel. And, there it was, the big corner lot, the huge trees, and the little white house with pink trim.

"Those shade trees in the front yard have certainly grown, Dad," I said after we had parked and were walking toward the house.

"Yeah, Mama won't let me cut those bottom limbs. They're practically layin' on the ground, but she says she don't want anybody lookin' at her. She can see out good enough, she says." Then he laughed.

As we climbed the four steps to the long front porch filled with rocking chairs he reminded me, "Polly likes to sit here when it rains." As I walked past them and into the house, I could almost smell the wet grass, could almost see my grandmother and me sitting on the Horse Mountain front porch swing, shelling peas.

"That's new," I said, pointing to a fireplace in the living room, its opening covered over by a vent for the black iron wood-burning stove that must heat the room.

"Yeah, but I'm gonna have to take it out 'fore winter 'cause Mama can't have wood heat 'cause of her breathin'. That's what the doctor says; she has emphysema." Emphysema, I hadn't known that. But she had smoked for years.

I glanced around me at the room full of photographs—of me, Donald, Donald's wife, and their daughters. Funny, I remembered no framed photographs when I was a child. But now, I noticed one in particular, sitting on the coffee table. I recognized it like yesterday—my short straight bangs. I could almost see the little bobby pins that had created the curls that fell around my face, the little sweater with pearls sewn across the front, like a necklace. Someone must have spent time buying that sweater and taking that picture. But now it was all gone. Was that my fifth grade photograph? Why couldn't I remember more? It was gone now.

Observing me looking at the photographs, Daddy said, "Mama likes to keep all these pictures of you and Donald and the grandkids. We got some more put away somewhere, if you wanna see 'em." "Of course," I said, and followed him through the back hall in search of others. As we walked past, I glimpsed my old room. Nothing there but the sliding closet doors would know me now; to the rest I'd be a stranger. Who was I when I had lived in that house? I tried hard to remember.

Their bedroom was way at the end of the back hall, just like always, but it was packed with furniture I didn't recognize. It was all very old and reminded me of Daddy's mother's old farmhouse where we used to visit. Images of churning butter and gathering up eggs in her big old apron came back to me.

"Here they are," he said as he pulled out a round, tin, lidded pan. A fruit-cake probably came in it, once upon some Christmastime. I followed him back into the living room, where we sat and opened the tin box. Just as he'd promised, inside were more old pictures. I was grateful to look at them, to re-construct, and I saved a few to take away with me. Then, running my fingers across a familiar nutcracker set still displayed on the coffee table I felt a rush of more memories. Memories that were now less painful, more poignant.

"You probably don't remember that coffee table, do you?" Daddy asked. "I made it at the shop."

"It's pretty. You should have made more furniture."

"I made this little round table here. You remember it, don't you?"

"Yes, I think so."

"I made it one Christmas for your mother. I didn't have money for a present and so I made that."

I looked at it, the round top, the cutting board style of the two woods blended together in the surface, the turned design on the one large center leg with three feet coming out from it. I could imagine him in the shop, working away on her Christmas present. It was sweet, I thought. I hadn't remembered.

"How's the world treatin' you, Sondra?" he said.

"Oh, I don't know. Fine, I guess. An awful lot of things have happened in the past few years." I didn't really know what to say next. I had brought along some of Gordon's "God" photographs to share with my mother, hop-ing they would lift her spirits as they had always done mine, so I pulled them out and shared them with him instead. He particularly liked the ones that showed unexplainable balls of light hovering over John's rose garden.

"That's a miracle," he said, surprising me. "I had a miracle once," he went on. "I had the biggest knot on my hand here, and it was startin' to hurt so bad I could hardly hammer; it was a-killin' me. At lunchtime I was sittin' underneath a tree, and I commenced to wonderin' which doctor I was gonna have to get to cut it out. I was feelin' real bad about it 'cause I'd had so much cuttin' done already on my ulcers. I finished my sandwich, folded up my sack, and my hand begun to feel a little funny, so I looked down at it and that blamed knot was *gone*. Nothin' left of it. And it never came back. But nobody believes in miracles anymore. The world is in a mess. I remember back years ago during the Depression, when there was soup lines down on the square in Shelbyville. People didn't have nothin'. I saw my dad lose everythin'. His bank account, his house, his land. I can remember my mama and daddy feedin' sometimes thirty people off our crops." After a long pause, he said, "There's always somethin' to be learned. I don't care how dumb a man is, there's always somethin' he can learn you. If you listen."

I found myself listening closely to this man who'd barely spoken to me while I was growing up.

Suddenly he stood up. "I gotta see if my cats are lookin' for food."

He walked past the old woodstove to the back door and peered out into the dusk. I followed him, anxious to share them with him. Then, shaking his head he said, "They ain't here. Well, I hope they're okay. They sometimes like to chase rabbits and mice, don't come back for dinner. They're awful pretty. Tails as big around as this." He made a big circle, connecting the thumbs and two fingers of his hands. "Long hair and just as silky."

He moved outside anyway and I followed.

"I see you still have a garden," I said, noticing the area carved out in the very back of the yard. He beamed, revealing for the first time his missing teeth. We wandered toward it—the okra, tomatoes, string beans, cabbage. All in neat rows.

"That over there is sweet corn. It ain't ready yet, but it's startin' to 'talk.' And it's time to tie up the tomatoes. I ain't had time, what with your mother sick."

"Do you have any scallions?" I asked him. I had always loved to pull them; there was something unexplainably satisfying about it.

"Oh yeah." He took me over to two rows of straight green stalks. "Pull yourself some. Take them from the back there, though. These in the front here are sweet onions."

As I pulled the scallions, I lifted them to my nose, inhaling the scent of the earth still on them. For a brief moment I was back at Rising River Ranch with Clint and pulling dinner from our garden there. But that was gone.

"The yard looks like a picture postcard," I said to him, noticing the ground was strewn with mimosa blossoms.

"Oh yeah, but these trees are awful messy," he replied. "I got some fence-row peaches. Probably the only ones left in the state. I dug them trees up out of the woods. Had three, but one died. Looks like I might lose another one."

I looked at them standing there and hoped they wouldn't die; it seemed important to me that he not lose them.

"This one over here is a peach tree; the squirrels are after 'em bad." He felt around for a peach soft enough to eat, pulled out his old pocketknife, and began to peel it. Cutting off a few slices, he handed them to me. Somehow, it was more delicious than any peach I ever recalled. In the distance a train sounded its whistle and roared past, leaving more memories in its wake. Night was falling. A breeze suddenly rustled the trees in the big front yard, and, as I stood there, I began to feel the first raindrops. Putting out my hand to them, I said, "It's starting to rain. That's a good sign."

He was already on the porch. "Is it sprinklin'?"

We stood there in silence until I said, "I guess I'll go on back now. Donald and Terri are expecting me for dinner." I walked over, hugged him goodbye, then turned and walked toward my car. "I'll see you tomorrow at the hospital. You get some rest now."

"You take care now, drive careful. It's slippery," he called after me.

As I closed the car door, I stared back at him, waving from the porch — this man I had never really known. I thought of the woman in the hospital bed, the mother I had never really known. The rain began to beat harder. As I drove slowly away, I turned on the windshield wipers, leaned back, and relaxed to the dull swish of their peaceful rhythm against the rain-covered windows. Over their sound, I heard the thunder begin to rumble. When I reached the corner, I looked back toward the old house, and, just at that moment, the lightning cut across the darkness, giving me one last glimpse of it all — the garden, the mimosa trees, the pink shutters, the empty porch with its empty rocking chairs looking out at the rain. In some weird way, I felt like Emily in *Our Town*. Suddenly I saw everything about my childhood and the people in it differently — as if I were looking through a veil and could more easily accept and claim a "good" I had never before understood that had come from it.

But, it was more than that. More surreal than real. Nothing made sense and yet everything made sense; nothing was possible and yet everything was. It was as if the separate sections of my life had been like separate stations on some radio dial — my childhood, Gordon, my old life with Clint, the cancer, the synchronicities, my current struggles many, many miles away . . . all the way to Warner Bros., where my Hollywood journey had first begun. They all were neatly separate, like different lives, even different me's. Then, one day, something unexpected causes all the radio stations to cross, giving me a glimpse of something I would never have seen. That glimpse changes nothing, but, at the same time, changes everything, because it changes the way I perceive and remember it all. I knew that when I was growing up I had not been a part of it, there, in that white house with pink shutters. I had had no "connection." Yet in a bigger sense, it was more likely that the words I spoke as an innocent seventeen-year-old valedictorian were wiser than I had understood at that time: "We are a part of all that we have met," I had said. We are connected even when we think we are not.

My mother recovered but remained an invalid. I phoned her often; we talked but still said nothing. I don't know if seeing me again gave her any peace or resolution; perhaps she had no need for it. Everything had changed but nothing had changed. In some ways I was glad that I had seen them all, and in other ways I was sorry because when I left, I took something with me that hadn't gone with me all those years ago. When I returned to Los Angeles and Warner Bros., I returned with a renewed sense of how brief life is, one that strangely even cancer had not given me.

MY NEW ASSISTANT, Mary, began to express her own concern to me about our seemingly hopeless situation at Warner Bros. One day, she pulled me aside. "Sondra, there's something Lance Young [her former boss at Paramount] said to me that I haven't told you. He said that personally he likes you and thinks you're talented but that he 'couldn't walk down that hall and tell Bob Daly to make a film with Sondra because Warners just isn't going to do it.'"

I was stunned, embarrassed, then furious. It was time for a last resort. I swallowed my anger and my pride, and I dialed Clint's office. "I don't know what's going on, Clint, but something's not right with Warners and my deal. Nothing at all has come together here. I mean, I hope that they aren't still uncomfortable about our splitup. I would hate to think that's what's been going on." Clint didn't say a word, and so I went on. "Look, I have a script now which has a lot of potential. I've submitted it to one executive who likes it, but he hasn't been able to get it past his boss, Bruce Berman. If you read it and like it, would you step in on my behalf? After all, the deal was I'd make some films here. And if you don't like it, I'd like to hear where you think I'm off-target."

"Sure. I'll take a look at it. Send it on over," he said in his friendliest tone. "Oh, and if they've made you a copy of your television movie yet, send it too."

I couldn't believe he was *still* thinking about that *television movie*, but since I'd just recently received my video copy of it I sent it over, along with the script *Paperback Hero*. Three weeks went by before we spoke. I had to phone him.

"I like this script," Clint said. "I mean it needs a little work; I don't like that scene where he parks the truck on top of that building in New York, but that could be fixed. It's just the kind of part I would have played ten years ago."

He was clearly inviting the compliment, so I complied, "Well, I'm sure you can play just about any part you want to, Clint." I wasn't suggesting that he play this one, but I *did* want him to get it approved by Warner Bros. for me to develop and direct. He promised that he would "get into it."

I waited but there was nothing. I called him, but he didn't return the call. Weeks went by, and finally I sent my assistant to pick up my videotape and wrote the whole thing off. There was hardly any question about his real intentions. He wasn't going to help me at all, but what, I wondered, did that mean about what had transpired all along?

I began asking some independent producers who had brought me projects and they all reluctantly confessed stories similar to Mary's conversation with Lance Young. When one producer, who had a deal with Warner Bros., had tried to hire me to direct a film, Bob Brassel, another high-up Warners executive, told him, "Joe, Warner Bros. isn't going to make a film with Sondra. Lay off that one. It's Clint's deal." Clint's deal? What did that mean?

By then, and at Mary's advice, I had changed agents to ICM, one of the most powerful talent agencies in the business. I immediately begged my agent to find me a job anywhere in town at that point. In a meeting, he said, "Well, it'll be difficult, Sondra. You haven't worked in a while now." Then he inadvertently said, "Don't bother looking at what's available at Warner Bros.; they're not gonna make a film with you." There was dead silence around the table. Mary and I looked at each other. "Exactly why do you say that, Tom?" I asked. Another dead silence. "Let's just move on" was his only response. Later, my former agent, the one who'd represented me at the time I had entered into the Warners deal, told me: "Sondra they used to give me the brush-off at Warners every time I called about finding a project for you. I've serviced a lot of deals and never been treated that way, but I can't get involved here. I do a lot of business with them." Apparently everybody in town knew this except me. I was livid.

I was anxious to get feedback from a "friend," someone who had been around at the time of the deal, and I called Maria. She and I rarely spoke anymore, but we still had some semblance of a relationship. "Maria, I have evidence that Warner Bros. has just been leading me on. They never intended to let me direct a film; I think they just said so to please Clint and get me to drop my lawsuit against him. It's outrageous! I'm not going to take it!"

There was a long pause before Maria said, "Well, Sondra, what do you expect from Warner Bros.; it *is* Clint's studio." And she said it as if it were perfectly normal and acceptable.

"What did I expect? I expected that we had a deal! I expected not to be tricked. If you thought that why didn't you say something, as a friend, when I made the deal?" Maria said nothing. I went on, "I gave up my claims fair and square. I kept my word and I kept my mouth shut. Also, the point is why wouldn't they just let me work, and then everybody would be happy!"

Unless of course Clint all along did not want me to work. Was that part of it for him? We were both quiet for a few seconds. "I'm going to talk with Norman about this, but if for any reason he can't help me, can you recommend an attorney, Maria? I'm going to sue them."

"I don't know what I think about this," she snapped back critically.

I don't know exactly what support I had expected to get when I had phoned Maria. None of them like conflict; public airing of the truth can be awkward.

Then Maria added portentiously, "They'll defame you, you know."

And that must have been unacceptable for her, because it would mark the beginning of the complete end of my relationship with both her and Arnold. Nadine did subsequently invite me to a surprise birthday party for Maria in Florida; Arnold was flying a small group of girl friends there and Nadine was organizing it. But, after that trip I saw each of them only one more time. I saw Arnold when I visited him on the Los Angeles film set of *True Lies*, when I directly asked him to throw something my way on *Junior* — associate producer perhaps, anything. I really needed it, I told him — both financially and professionally. "I'll do what I can, Sondra." But he never reported back to me one way or the other, and unlike on every one of his films in the past, I was *not* invited to his premiere of *True Lies*.

The final time I saw Maria was at a baby shower for Mimi Rogers. Mimi and I were only casual friends but I had always liked her and was happy that she was having a baby. I was standing on the patio chatting with Mimi when suddenly I heard Maria's voice. "Sondra, how are you, honey?" She reached out to give me a big hug. "I'm so glad to see you; it's been so long. You look great!" My body involuntarily recoiled from her. I just couldn't act as if it were okay any longer. But I smiled weakly and tried to drift toward the next group of people. Maria followed me, finally grabbing my hand and pulling me aside. "What's wrong?" she asked. "Why are you being so cold to me? I don't think I've ever received such a cold shoulder."

So I told her everything—how hurt I was about the way she had treated me—the invitations to her house that never came anymore, about the birthday gifts she used to give me that had deteriorated to flowers sent by her secretary, then to a card. I also told her how insulted I was not to be invited to *True Lies*. I asked her if it was because I had confronted Arnold about *Junior*.

"None of these *things* matter, Maria, except what they represent—a complete disregard," I said.

"There must be some mistake. You're on the family list. You *are* family," Maria blurted out.

"Then, Maria, please take me off the 'family list,' because apparently it doesn't mean much. After all this we can *at least* be honest. We are no longer friends and I can't act as if we are. I'm hurt and I can't act as if I'm not."

Everyone was congregating in the living room for Mimi to unwrap her presents, giving me the perfect excuse to break away.

"I'm so sorry, Sondra. I love you," I heard her say as I walked away. It was sad because I believe she thought she did. I had finally realized that Maria was friends with two kinds of people: those who were politically correct for her to pursue, a category I had once fallen into, and those who constantly pursued her, treating her as if she were the Queen Mother. And since I had refused to join that category, there was no place left for me.

I did speak with Norman Oberstein about my situation; he was empathetic and recommended another attorney. He said he couldn't handle the case himself, since he would be a precipient witness, having been a party to the negotiation of the contract in question. Through his and others' referrals I retained a prominent attorney from the Hollywood "boys club," thinking that, if one of their own went to Warner Bros., they'd extend my contract for a year and guarantee me one film just to close the books. But Terry Semel and Bob Daly only said, "We have no interest in making any *real* deal with Sondra. We can give her a twenty-five-thousand-dollar settlement for her trouble but that's it." Apparently they had *never* had any interest in any *real deal* with me. The twenty-five thousand dollars was some sort of "tip" for being a good girl and going away quietly, I guessed. I had done that before, and this time I wasn't interested. I moved out of my offices at Warner Bros. The attorney I was working with was extremely expensive and didn't take cases on contingency, so he referred me to a woman attorney in Santa Monica.

Peggy Garrity's offices were in a small Victorian house on a near-residential street in Santa Monica, where I poured my heart out to her. She advised me to file a lawsuit only against Warner Bros. because my contract was with them and Clint Eastwood might be a tough defendant to turn jurors against. Emotionally I no longer wanted to go back into things with Clint, which would only bring attention from the tabloids. I had been wronged in a "business" deal and I wanted to file a "business" lawsuit. I told her I would think about it.

"What do you think I should do, Hobbit?" I asked.

"I think you should sue them. You certainly shouldn't just let them get away with it," Gordon said.

Through this time two synchronicities had continued and often guided or supported my decisions. I was discussing Peggy with Gordon and he agreed that she sounded like a good choice. Just at that moment Chloe jumped on his coffee table and the flashlight that had been standing there toppled over. When Gordon reached over to pick it up, he just stared at it. Then pointing to something written on its side, he handed it to me saying, "Look at that." The name of the manufacturer of the flashlight was Garrity. "A flashlight lights the darkness," Gordon added. The next time I visited Peggy's office I saw a phone message from Mrs. *Harper*, her current plaintiff at trial. During Christmas of 1993 I hired Peggy, and on March 10, 1994, nearly three months after I had moved out of my offices, the lawsuit for fraud in *Locke* vs. *Warner Bros.* was filed. I knew I had to do it, but I was terrified just the same. On that very same day the brass lamp and the candlestick in Gordon's guest bedroom, the room where I slept whenever I visited him, bent unexplainably, and could be straightened only by taking them to a blacksmith. "Lamp and candlestick," Gordon said, "again, both have to do with light. God's saying don't worry. You'll be all right."

"Building a fraud case is like putting together a mosaic," Peggy said to me. "No individual pieces mean a lot on their own, but put them altogether and a picture emerges. Keep that in mind; we won't find any major piece of hard evidence that can stand alone. The very nature of fraud itself is something hidden."

As we also expected, almost no witnesses were coming forward for me, which meant that I was out on the ledge virtually alone. Everyone continued to tell me I shouldn't sue; Warner Bros. is too powerful, they said.

You'll be wiped out. You'll never work again. Everyone ran the other way. For me, the reality was that I wasn't working and hadn't worked since 1989 when Clint had locked me out of my house.

Warner Bros. predictably took the position that they had tried their best to work with me, but I hadn't been up to the challenge. But what had they done to show their good faith efforts to work with me? They hadn't even initiated one single phone call to me over the three years of my contract. They did, however, later remind me that they'd given me a parking space on the lot, as well as the lovely turkey every year at Thanksgiving. In September 1993, during the last year of my deal, I laughed out loud when I received a letter from Indian Hill Farms, the company that provided those turkeys, saying that "regrettably my turkey was being discontinued." That's odd, I thought. I'd been getting those turkeys since 1975. The very next month, after my first attorney had contacted Bob and Terry, I received another letter from Indian Hill Farms. This time the letter informed me with pleasure that I would indeed receive my turkey "as a gift from Bob Daly and Terry Semel." I guess I should have considered myself lucky to have the turkey and the parking space.

Around this time, someone removed the official Warner Bros. parking sticker from my car window while the car was parked on the lot. It was not something that could effectively be stolen for use again because the glue was so strong that the sticker would be destroyed upon removal. It was a petty and pointed gesture. I never knew for certain who did it, but I guessed that it was someone who was very practiced in petty gestures.

In July of that year I met someone I had long admired who offered to help me. I contacted Gloria Steinem when I learned she was going to be in Los Angeles, and she seemed pleased to hear from me; we agreed to meet for breakfast. She, Peggy, and I went to The Four Seasons, and Gloria listened intently to my story about Clint and corporate fraud. She told me about some ex-wives who were put on corporate boards as part of personal divorces and treated the same way I was. She said that if I'd been a man, they'd at least have given me the respect of treating me like a proper enemy. "I know Gerry Levin, the new president of Warner Bros. Inc. in New York," Gloria said. "I want a copy of all your legal paperwork. When I get back I'm going to give him a call; he should know this sort of thing has been done to you, and company money is being used this way. And I promise all the women will be on your side; I'm going to orchestrate a nationwide ban of Clint Eastwood films."

That evening at her sixtieth birthday celebration at the Beverly Wilshire, I had an amusing yet educational experience. I bumped into Gloria Allred and we exchanged words. At one point in my search for the right attorney I had met with Gloria, who was interested in my case but as gender discrimination. "Someone in the movie business needs to take that on. You have the profile to make one stick, Sondra," she said to me, but even though I knew there was gender bias at the core of what had happened to me that was not the primary issue in my case. I couldn't help but marvel that evening at the way Ms. Allred worked the room. She had brought her own personal still photographer to document the evening for her own press releases, and after she had gotten all the photos she wanted, she and her photographer quietly slipped out the kitchen door just as dinner was about to be served. It was such a crazy town, I thought.

I continued to stay in touch with Gloria Steinem, but she never followed through on anything she had so fervently discussed with me. There was no Levin conversation, no organization of women behind me, and no ban on Clint's movies. And no explanation of why not.

Throughout 1994, Peggy and I fought relentlessly against the giant Warner Bros. and their giant law firm O'Melveny & Myers. One Warner Bros. executive stated under oath in his deposition that he didn't even know I'd had a deal with Warner Bros., or that I'd had a relationship with Clint Eastwood, or that I'd ever acted in Clint's movies. This was the same executive who had told producer Joe Terry that "Warner Bros. would not make a film with Sondra . . . that's Clint's thing."

As we discovered how intertwined Clint and Warner Bros. were in this fraud, we realized that we could no longer avoid bringing Clint into the lawsuit. When Peggy filed a motion to add him on, Warner Bros. went ballistic, mounting a massive campaign to keep Clint out of the lawsuit.

"Plaintiff's motion denied on adding Eastwood," said Judge Thomas Murphy of the court in Burbank, also the home of Warner Bros. Judge Murphy ruled in favor of Warner Bros. on every single issue during the pretrial period. Murphy was about eighty years old and I had heard that he paid little attention to the law and instead saw himself as a kind of monarch in his courtroom. He was very right-wing, had been a fighter pilot in some war, and was said to have been a good friend of John Wayne. Throughout the proceedings he kept addressing my attorney as "Little Lady." One day during a preliminary motion, he asked, "How many men does it take to mop a kitchen floor? None, that's woman's work!" His dutiful audience laughed uproariously, and I felt we were in deep trouble.

Then a miracle occurred. I had suggested to Peggy that in our standard "document request" list we ask Warner Bros. for a copy of the final "cost run" for my studio deal—a printout of all the charges that had been placed

against my account over the three-year term. I'm not sure why it occurred
to me to ask for it. It was nothing more than the total amount of charges
Warner Bros. had paid me and my assistants over those years.

I hadn't even expected them to send it because they hadn't sent most of
the other documents we'd requested. We were stunned when it showed up,
stuck in between a bunch of other papers. It showed something I had never
suspected. At the end of February 1992, fourteen months into my three-
year deal, debits totaling $975,000 were transferred out of my account and
charged against Clint's film *Unforgiven*. I was in shock. Clint had been
secretly paying for my Warner Bros. deal. That left little doubt that the
whole thing had been a setup. Warner Bros. had just been a shill for Clint
to make a cheap settlement and get rid of my lawsuit. Warner Bros. never
had any intention of making films with me. They had only been laundering
Clint's money. Every month when they issued an official Warner Bros.
check to me, they knew they were secretly being reimbursed by Clint. They
had no investment in me whatsoever. And what irony that I was charged
off to *Unforgiven*. For me, the fact that I learned this critical information
will always seem a "gift from God."

Warner Bros. certainly didn't intend for us to have that document, and
as soon as we acknowledged receipt of it, they immediately filed a motion
with the judge to force us to return it. They declared it was sent by mistake
and that it was really their own attorney "work product." But it was too late
for that gobbledygook. We knew the truth. This secret arrangement between
Clint and Warner Bros. was devastating to me and my so-called deal, and
there were further ramifications for Warner Bros. in the way Clint had paid
for it. Charging unrelated costs against the budget of any film is like stealing
money from all other profit participants of that film. It raises the "cost" of
the film, thereby reducing the profits, and somebody loses his money. Their
cover story was that it hadn't affected any profit sharers because the money
all came from Clint's own fees and therefore did not affect anyone else
associated with the film. Of course they would never surrender any paperwork supporting this.

Clint also refused to make himself available for deposition. He was out
of town. He was unavailable. He was sick. His life was being threatened.
We asked his office to accept a subpoena, or for his attorney to accept it in
his absence, as is commonly done. He refused to authorize them to do so.
Clearly he was hiding.

One particular morning, the process server—an officer of the court—
waited on the street for Clint to leave the house. When Clint saw him, he
nearly ran the man down with his pickup truck. We would have to try to

catch him at his office. A pass was arranged for the process server, Mark Ryan, to get onto the lot and wait for Clint to arrive. "Mr. Eastwood, I have some papers for you," Ryan approached Clint as he parked in front of the "Taco Bell," and Clint said, "Got my hands full; come in the office." Once inside, Clint realized what the papers were and began screaming, "What the fuck!" "Close the door and call security," he ordered his assistant.

Within minutes of the "emperor's command" Warner Bros. security arrived in force, handcuffed Ryan, and forced him into a van, where they held and interrogated him for nearly two hours. They even tried to get the Burbank police to throw Ryan in jail, but the police refused to get involved. Mark Ryan, who is a very gentle man in his late twenties with a wife and a daughter, said that he'd never experienced such a thing in all his days doing the job. "I know enough about power, and I'd seen enough Clint Eastwood movies to make me worry," he said.

Ultimately, despite all our evidence, Judge Murphy ruled in favor of Warner Bros. Without blinking, he granted their motion against us that my claims contained absolutely no triable issue and should not be allowed to be heard by a jury. He bellowed at Peggy and me, "I made a decision. I invite appellate review. I am not thin-skinned. If I am wrong, I want to know it. I want the justices to educate me. So you've got the whole record before you. Now go on up and may God have mercy on your soul!"

Suddenly I lost hope. Maybe everyone had been right. How could I fight the biggest communications conglomerate in the entire world? I was no match. But Peggy said, "We have to appeal this. Come on over to my office and let's talk."

I got in my car and drove toward Santa Monica. And I cried. I was so tired. I felt so beaten. "Please Dear God, help me understand what to do. I can't be strong any longer."

I backed into a parking space on Peggy's street. Still crying, I turned off the ignition, dropped my head onto the steering wheel, and tried to calm myself. After a few minutes I raised my head and pulled the key out of the ignition, and as I turned to open the door, my eyes fell on the license plate of the car parked immediately in front of me. HV F8TH it read. A sign. And just when I'd asked for it. Just when I'd given up.

I closed my eyes, gave thanks for the "gift," took a deep breath, and walked into my attorney's office with a renewed sense of hope, and faith, and mission.

I agreed with Peggy to appeal the outrageous summary judgment decision in the Warner Bros. case and to file a separate action against Clint

Eastwood for fraud. I had tried to avoid it, but inevitably it all came back to Clint and me. Incredibly, I had set in to fight him again.

~

CHRISTMAS 1994 CAME and went and as usual, Gordon's Christmas trees remained for weeks. Their magic and beauty bolstered my spirits and gave me respite from all my legal battles. The unexplainable was continuing at his house, and, by then, his miraculous photographs had even been to Tibet, in hopes of seeing the Dalai Lama. Becky Johnston, who co-wrote the screenplay for *The Prince of Tides*, had taken them with her when she'd gone there to do research for her next screenplay. When she returned, she insisted that I show them to another screenwriter and friend of hers, Carol Caldwell. Carol had an interest in such things, and was writing a script about the famous English medium Dion Fortune. Her interpretation of Gordon was that he, too, was a medium. After all, he certainly seemed to be poised between two worlds, she said, after spending the evening with us and experiencing so many synchronicities that continually ricocheted between the two of them. We were all at the front door saying goodnight and Gordon was helping Carol on with her coat, when she said, "Could I take one more peek at the tree in the Gothic room? It's my favorite."

It was a noble fir and its boughs were heavily laden with "snow" and Gothic ornaments of clear spun glass and gold. Glittering stars on invisible wires seemed not to be touching the tree at all, but hovering inches away from it, each creating its own celestial halo, and its candle-shaped lights shimmered. Every year it looked like something that had just materialized, or like something stumbled upon while walking through the woods one night, as if it were Titania's winter hiding place in *A Midsummer Night's Dream*. "Magical" was the only word for it.

As we all followed Carol into the room, something unexplainable began to occur. It was both a presence and a sound; the whole room vibrated with it. We all stood completely still. What on earth? I thought. The sound was ethereal, an otherworldly tone. As we approached the tree, the sound grew louder. "It's coming from the tree," Carol said.

"From the heart of the tree," John added.

Gordon's face lit up. "Oh, it *has* a heart."

With those words he gently lifted a branch and revealed, hidden deep inside the tree, a heart of red brocade, encrusted with jewels and braided golden threads. The mysterious sound continued. "Oh, I know what that sound is like," Carol said excitedly, "it's exactly like a Tibetan prayer bell."

"Oh my God," I said. "Gordon's pictures just came back from Tibet. Did Becky tell you that?"

"No, I haven't spoken with her. That's amazing," Carol said.

"You see how it all fits together?" Gordon asked. "My pictures, which I call 'God' pictures, have been to *Tibet*. And we're standing in a room I call *God's* room, in front of a Christmas tree, a symbol of His son's birth. *From it is emanating an inexplicable sound that you have identified as a *Tibetan* prayer bell. So, that sound we all just heard has now become not just some random bit of unexplainable phenomena, however beautiful or mysterious. The sound now connects and completes a story. It's a perfect circle. Do you see?"

She saw. "Maybe Gordon is the 'Avatar of Synchronicity,'" she said, laughing. Later she sent him a copy of James Merrill's "The Changing Light at Sandover" because she said, "This is you." And so it seemed to be: "From time to time/God wants a child in his palm, a live one./ To feel the old clay, to hear that human electric beat . . . Yet not all can be trusted to withstand the moment and be/returned unchanged."

Not long after that I returned home one night and found a message from a voice I recognized but had not expected. It was Norman Oberstein. "Sondra, I just wanted to make sure you heard the news. A terrible shock. Jane Brolin is dead. An accident. Call me at home if you like." I felt stunned by such sudden news. "I don't have a lot of the details," Norman confided when I phoned him. "I was told that she had been drinking and had left her house, upset after some argument with her boyfriend. She was chasing him when her car just left the road and crashed head on into an *oak tree.*

"An *oak* tree!" Gordon exclaimed when I told him. We were both stunned. I instantly recalled the drawing of the oak tree that Gordon had framed and given to Bo as a symbol of the two of them. Jane had told that story to Clint, as Clint had so angrily reminded me on that day in his office when I'd gone in hopes of settling things between us. "An oak tree!" Clint had said to me. "That's weird!" Now Jane had crashed into an oak tree and killed herself. It was bizarre. A creepy feeling came over me, almost as if I could feel her energy around me, suddenly trying to reach out to attach itself. I shuttered and pulled myself tight against it. It was awful that she was dead, but that couldn't change who she had been.

Chapter 13 ~

Not unexpectedly, getting Clint into court had been an enormous feat. Clint's attorney, Ray Fisher, did everything he could to stop my case, including filing the same summary judgment motion that had worked for Warner Bros. The battle began when Peggy first filed the lawsuit against Clint in downtown Los Angeles. Without notifying Peggy, Clint's attorneys filed to have the case transferred to Burbank, and back to Judge Thomas Murphy—who had thrown out my case against Warner Bros. Peggy fought it, and though we were forced to remain in the Burbank court, we were assigned a different judge and that judge, one by one, denied Fisher's motions to stop me.

Judge D. M. Schacter's voice boomed out on the third day of trial as he humorously addressed the chosen jurors, "Everybody have their county-approved pencils? Has everybody's been prechewn? I just want you to know that the county is here to save money."

My pulse quickened as Peggy rose to deliver her opening remarks to the jury. "Your Honor, opposing counsel, Ladies and Gentlemen of the jury, Sondra Locke will prove in this case that she was defrauded into entering into a settlement agreement of an earlier lawsuit which was pending between Ms. Locke and Mr. Eastwood. The evidence will show that . . ."

I couldn't believe that I was actually sitting in a trial against Clint—something that I had always feared, something I had never wanted to happen, but something that obviously had to be.

". . . We believe that the evidence will show that this contract was entered into exclusively in order for Warner Bros. to accommodate Clint Eastwood." I listened as Peggy took a real, commonsense approach to explaining what had happened to me. And prayed.

Suddenly the room was quiet. Peggy had finished.

Fisher did not begin his opening address; instead he made the first of many motions during the trial; this time it was "nonsuit." Just because I had made it to a jury didn't seem to mean that I was staying there. With the jurors out of the room, Fisher tried to argue that Peggy's opening statement had not been enough to prove that we had a case against Clint. After Peggy rebutted his argument, Judge Schacter sat quietly for what seemed a solid five minutes, then said, "I'll take it under submission. Okay. Take a little break." He didn't rule on Fisher's motion at all. To me, a nonruling was the same as a victory. I felt like the little ant pushing the giant bread crumb uphill. They hadn't been able to stop me yet.

Fisher gave his opening statement, which was a very slick and carefully woven magic act that almost seemed convincing, except I knew the real truth behind his smoke. Peggy began calling our witnesses. The first was Terry Semel.

"Chairman and co-CEO of Warner Bros., Inc," Terry's voice rang out when asked about his job.

Terry looks like the typical slick Hollywood business shark. He's short, with a swarthy complexion and very thick dark, curly hair, which he always oils and smooths profusely to make it appear straighter. Someone once said, "I would never trust Terry Semel. How can you trust someone who works that hard to straighten his hair? He's not even honest with his hair!" I had laughed at the remark, but now looking at Terry, I was sadly reminded of my own naïveté. I had once thought he was my friend.

Peggy asked: "And would you say that you considered yourself to be social friends of Clint and Sondra as well as professional colleagues?"

"Yes. I would consider them to have been friends," Terry answered.

"And do you still socialize with Mr. Eastwood today?"

"From time to time."

"And do you still socialize with Sondra Locke today?"

"No."

"And in fact you have not socialized with Sondra Locke at all since her separation from Clint Eastwood, have you?"

"That might be the case."

Peggy handed Terry a card he had sent me right after the completion of *Impulse* and asked that he read it aloud.

Terry read: "Sondra, we're all pleased with the outcome of *Impulse*, a very well made commercial movie that looks like it could have cost $14 or $15 million. Congratulations to you . . . I'm sorry that you and Clint are over but do promise that the situation will not affect our business dealing in any way. Jane and I hope that 1990 is a great year for you. Terry."

"Mr. Semel," Peggy asked, "you have not done any business at all with Sondra Locke since that note was sent to her and since she entered into the deal that Clint Eastwood produced for her with Warner Bros., have you?"

"Of course I have."

"Have you had her direct a film?"

"No, but that's not the question you asked."

"Since you wrote that note to Sondra Locke in December of 1989 after the completion of the filming and the release of *Impulse*, Warner Bros. has not engaged Sondra Locke [as of] today?"

Terry skirted the obvious answer. Instead he tried to redefine my contract, saying it was for "developing," which he said I was "new" at and therefore it was my own fault that the deal had produced nothing. This was untrue, of course, because over my history with Warner Bros. I had developed five projects and directed two.

Peggy then asked him if he would ever enter into this kind of director's agreement with me today even though I had done nothing since *Impulse*. He answered, "If there were an appropriate project at Warner that Sondra would like to direct, and the people involved with the project would like to have Sondra as the director, I would be thrilled to be able to do that. Okay."

After this Peggy shifted her questions to the "secret indemnity." Terry kept using the expression "at the end of the day."

" . . . at the end of the day he [Clint] was very helpful," Terry said.

" . . . in fact he paid off the first $975,000 by the *beginning* of the second year of Sondra's three-year contract, didn't he?" Peggy asked.

"I don't know the specific amounts . . ."

"And in fact a full $1.5 million was paid for by Mr. Eastwood, was it not, on the Sondra Locke term deal."

"I don't know specifically, but I would assume that at the end of the day that his intentions were to underwrite the losses."

"And when is the *end of the day*?"

"Well . . . I guess the end of the day would have been when the term of this arrangement had ended."

That was what we were looking for. He admitted that it was an early payoff. That's all we needed from Terry.

EACH MORNING DURING the trial I woke up and walked to the shower. Then I'd walk to my closet and near robotlike, out the door of the cottage in the Hollywood Hills I shared with Scott. We'd been living together happily since 1991, the year after we'd met over my surgery at Cedars. His support throughout this awful business had been Herculean and I loved him even more for it. That morning, for no apparent reason, he had insisted that I drive his BMW instead of my Mercedes. As I entered Burbank and drove past the Warner Bros. studio, I recalled how many times I had made that drive. So much of my life had been tied up at that studio—from *Heart Is a Lonely Hunter*, to meeting Clint, to Clint's films, to our breakup and that awful scene in his office, to my great hopes for my Warners contract and the ultimate discovery that there really hadn't been a contract. But that day I wasn't making that turn into the lot. I drove past it and into downtown Burbank, to the courthouse where I was suing Warner Bros. and Clint. There seemed to be a strange poetry in it all.

I sat quietly at the red light just across from the courthouse, where I would make a right-hand turn to park in the allocated building. Then my eyes widened as the white car in front of me suddenly began to move rapidly backward. My hand flew up to hit the horn, but not before I felt the crunch of metal on metal. There seemed absolutely no explanation for this bizarre move.

The driver spoke hurriedly. He also needed to be in court that morning on a personal issue. He was uninsured, had no driver's license, and begged me to let him pay for the damage privately. I don't know what I said, but as he hurriedly drove away, I realized that I'd been so focused on getting to court myself that I hadn't even gotten his license plate number. I was especially nervous that day because I would be on the witness stand.

My heart was still racing when I heard Peggy say: "I call Sondra Locke as my next witness."

I stood up and walked to the front of the courtroom, swore to tell the truth, and sat down. Looking around the room at everyone, my eyes finally fell on Clint. He was unable to look at me and just stared down at the table. The room felt quiet and still as if someone had just pushed the pause button on the videotape of my life. The past seven years of it seemed somehow destined to arrive at this moment.

Peggy began asking questions about my professional history, how I had come to Warner Bros. and the film business in general, my years with Clint, my earlier relationship with Warner Bros. and the films that I had, in the past, developed and directed. She asked about the December 1990 Warner Bros. three-year contract over which I was suing. She asked about the nature of it, how it had produced nothing for me and how it differed from my past dealings with Warner Bros. My testimony continued throughout the day and all the next day. It was an intense experience, but at some point, my anxiety about it changed to a sense of satisfaction, even elation. I was telling my story; this was the moment I'd been fighting for for such a long time, maybe even since 1989 when I was locked from my home.

I had a big job: In order to prove that Clint had defrauded me, I had to convince the jury not only that Clint's "secret payment" had damaged me, but also that if I'd known about such an agreement, I would not have accepted the deal.

Peggy asked: "And did you at some point learn that Warner Bros. was *not* the source of the funds that you were paid?"

"Yes, I did."

"And who did you learn was the source of the funds behind your contract?"

"Clint."

"And if you had known that at the time you entered into the settlement agreements with Clint and with Warner Bros., would you have entered into both of those agreements?"

"Absolutely not. It would have made no sense whatsoever because it's like having an employer who's not really paying you. What—there's no logic in that."

"Now, at the time that you learned the source of the funds, how did you feel about that?"

"I felt amazed. I felt embarrassed. I felt humiliated. [I felt tricked.] I remembered all of the times over the course of the three years that I had gone in to Bob and Terry, and all the other executives there, and all the time I had spent, all the meetings that I had taken, all the work that I had tried to do, all the hope that I had had, all the expectations that I had had. I felt—I felt horrible. I felt completely defeated, really."

It was about 5:00 P.M. and court had been over for an hour when I took the elevator up to the top floor of the parking structure where I had left Scott's smashed BMW. Everyone had gone home and mine was the only car left on that level. After I got in, backed out, and began to drive forward, I saw a big dark four-wheel-drive vehicle slowly creeping toward me. Right away, it struck me as peculiar because the exit was in the *opposite* direction. Why would anyone be driving toward the top floor at that hour?

Before I advanced more than a few feet, the car pulled to a slow stop beside me, the driver's electric window rolled down revealing—Kevin Marks, Clint's full-time attorney from Gang, Tyre, Ramer & Brown, the man who sat in the front row in court, nodding yes or no to "Clint's litigating team." I had never met Mr. Marks before this trial, two days ago.

"Sondra," he said. "Too bad about your car. I saw the whole thing this morning. If you need a witness or if he tries to say it was your fault, I saw the whole thing. I'll testify for you." It took a moment to register but finally I smiled, thanked him, then drove away, feeling odd but at the same time thinking it had been a nice gesture on his part.

When I arrived at my house that night, I was still thinking about the strange encounter with Kevin Marks. I picked up the phone and called Peggy.

"Sondra, you amaze me," she said. "After all you've been through, you still aren't jaded. Believe me, all Marks wants to do is serve your head on a platter to Eastwood. If he had any honest intentions, he would have said something to you earlier in the day, or even to me. We were in court all day long with several rest breaks and a lunch break. Now, let me ask you why, you think, he waited until everyone had gone, and then crept up on you in such a peculiar way?"

I had no reply. The whole thing remained very puzzling. After the breakup with Clint, I had had so many assaults on the Mercedes he had given me, which by extraordinary coincidence only, I had not been driving on that particular morning. Such a small classic car would most likely have been destroyed by that accident.

"Get some sleep," Peggy said. "And I'll see you in the morning."

THE NEXT MORNING Ray Fisher rose from his seat next to Clint and moved toward me. Here it comes, I thought. He's going to try and confuse the jury, intimidate me to the point that I made no sense or portray me as the money-grasping scorned woman. Fisher was perfectly cast as Clint's attorney. Not only was he a police commissioner, it had dawned on me how much the sketches of Fisher on television looked like Clint. But in person, Fisher was much less attractive and reminded me of Lon Chaney in *The Phantom of the Opera*. As he stood before me I realized that he too represented so much of what I had come to despise and distrust.

"Good morning, Ms. Locke," he said. "I would like to ask you a few questions to clarify some of what you told us yesterday and today."

Fisher's questions attempted to portray Clint as this wonderful benefactor/mentor who had done so much for me, while I, the typical female, had only expected more. Then moving to our breakup, he phrased his questions to portray Clint as the victim of a scheming woman who had "behind Clint's back" done the unthinkable of retaining an attorney. It was all very predictable strategy, but his next move surprised me. I had never dreamed that in this lawsuit over my contract with Warner Bros., Clint would again dredge up *Gordon.*

Fisher asked: "Now under that settlement agreement, Mr. Eastwood . . . gifted or gave the Crescent Heights house to you; is that correct?"

"Yes," I said.

"And your *husband,* Mr. Anderson, lived in the Crescent Heights house; isn't that correct?"

"That's correct."

"He had lived there for quite a bit of time, had he not?"

"Since '82, when it was bought for him."

"And how big a house was that? Can you describe it for us?"

"1700 square feet or so."

"You, you had, with Mr. Anderson, spent some time decorating the house and furnishing it; is that correct?"

"I assisted him. It was something I enjoy doing."

"And you have told us about your affection for Mr. Anderson. It was important to you, was it not, that Mr. Anderson be able to continue to live in that house that you and he had helped furnish and decorate?"

"Yes, it was, of course, important to me."

"Because you have and still do have an opportunity, an understanding, that you want to support him?"

"I care about Mr. Anderson, yes, I do."

"I do understand that. So it was an important thing for you to get from Mr. Eastwood the Crescent Heights house out of the settlement?"

"Of course it was important, yes."

Then, as abruptly as he had brought this all up, Fisher dropped it. I wondered what that was all about, but I could see that all his questions were designed to make Clint look like the guy who had given and given and now was given out. I wish I'd thought to remind him of all that Clint had taken away from me, including *my* home, but then I hadn't come into this court to discuss any of that.

"So the purpose of Mr. Eastwood's call was to call and congratulate you about this movie [the ABC Movie of the Week *Death in Small Doses*]?" Fisher asked.

"I certainly could not tell you the purpose of anything that Mr. Eastwood has done . . . but after that phone call, I sent him the tape to get his reaction. He never returned my phone calls. After he had had the videotape for over a month and never called me back, I finally asked my assistant to go over to his office and pick it up."

Fisher then tried to destroy my earlier testimony that when I'd phoned

Clint for help in those last months of my deal, he had refused it. "And what did you—did you discuss [*Paperback Hero*] with Mr. Eastwood?"

"Yes, I did. I asked him if he would read it."

"And so you sent him a script?"

"Yes, I did."

"Did he read it?"

"Yes he did."

"Did he give you comments on it?"

"I recall that he said to me that he liked it a lot, that he thought it was a project that even he himself might have starred in maybe ten years ago, as a reference to his age being—that he was too old for the part. I do recall saying that 'I think that you could probably play whatever you wanted to play.' He did have some other comment to make. There was one scene where he was 'not sure the truck should be parked on top of a building.' And I said, oh, yeah, there are a few things. It needs a little improvement, it needs some work. And I—if Warners, if you could just ask them to let me do some work on this, I think I can even get the writer to do it free because I really believe in the project . . . Clint said he would follow up."

"Did Mr. Eastwood follow up on [*Paperback Hero*], to your knowledge?"

"No, I don't know if he did because he subsequently did not return my phone calls."

"So you don't know whether he did anything one way or the other with Warner Bros.?"

"I called him to get feedback and to get follow-up and he did not return my calls."

"This is a good time to break," said Fisher.

It was finally the end of my testimony and I was incredibly relieved. As tough and clever as Fisher was in his cross-examination, I felt he had not been able to twist my words. I knew I'd gotten in the truth and I felt it was obvious. And that meant everything to me.

Meanwhile, Fisher's latest trick was to exclude two of my witnesses. He convinced the judge to conduct 402 hearings, without the jurors present, to determine if Joe Terry and Mary Wellnitz—both of whom had had major conversations with Warner Bros. vice presidents who'd admitted that the company had no intention of working with me—would be allowed to testify in front of the jurors. Fisher claimed that their testimonies were "heresay" and "cumulative" to mine anyway. After one 402, the judge did dismiss Joe Terry, and I was really upset and nervous. After all, I had so few witnesses. Peggy and I were extremely worried that he would make the same ruling on Mary. There was only one hope in that instance and that was that Mary

had also been witness to my emotional state during the last year at Warner
Bros. Peggy pleaded with the judge.

Peggy and I breathed a sigh of relief when the judge allowed Mary to testify as an "emotional distress" witness. She spoke about the changes she'd seen in me over the course of that year, from my great enthusiasm in the beginning to general despair. She talked about the momentous meeting I had at ICM and how I'd felt afterward. Mary's testimony gave a very vivid portrait of me during that time. Listening to her recall that confusing and fearful time, I was carried back and couldn't stop the silent tears that rolled down my face.

The depression was still with me that night as I walked toward my car; when I got there I found a card had been left on the windshield. It read: "We're rooting for you, Sondra. A lot of us are on your side" and was signed by a complete stranger, a man. Little things like that continued to boost my morale throughout the trial.

A few days later, Clint and I arrived for court at the same time. It was relatively quiet at 8:00 A.M., hardly any cars were on the streets. I had parked behind the courthouse (something I'd begun doing after my strange encounter with Kevin Marks in the parking garage) and was entering the crosswalk when I noticed a big dark green GMC Yukon pull up to the traffic light. It was Clint, also alone. My light changed and the walk across that intersection, right in front of his vehicle, seemed to go on forever. Neither of us acknowledged the other's presence. I could only think how very sad and peculiar life can be. His light then changed and I watched as he turned the corner and drove through electric gates into a parking lot. In some perfect scenario I read the posted sign there. He had entered the private, gated lot for the Burbank Police Department.

One of the debates throughout my lawsuit had been over whether or not the actual records showing the inappropriate charging of my costs to the movie *Unforgiven* could be entered into court. Clint's attorneys—and Warner Bros.' before them—had fought hard to keep that out of the records. It was easy to understand why, and the judge himself put his finger on it when he said, "That's between them and their *investors*." Warners didn't want any *investors* asking questions, but Peggy argued on that it was "the very device of this fraud. It is the heart of the fraud. It was hidden, it was concealed, and it was concealed in the payment and the costs on *Unforgiven*."

It was a disappointment to both of us that the judge ultimately denied admittance of these documents. We were allowed to say that Eastwood paid but not *how* he paid. Peggy moved forward. "Plaintiff calls Clint Eastwood," she said.

Clint shot Fisher a look, then rose from his chair. I felt complete triumph as he walked behind me. His face looked hard and permanently etched by anger. I remembered the recent words of Gordon, "Clint doesn't look very good. It's sort of like what is on the inside of him has permeated to the outside." He took the witness chair and immediately stared straight at me. I stared back. Our eyes had finally connected. Incredibly, it was the first time it had happened in this court—maybe even in years. His look was one of intimidation; mine was of defiance. It was a stare that seemed to last forever and carried the intensity of the ultimate showdown. I was determined not to be the first to glance away. And finally, it was Clint who turned.

Through all our differences, Clint and I had never "had it out" privately. Our battle, whatever it was, had always been at arm's length. Even during the last bad months together, I had never told him what I thought of his behavior, never experienced the joy, the catharsis, of telling tell him off. At least, this fight I had waged showed him my determination, and my disregard for his power. I knew that he was infuriated that I had put him on the witness stand for all the world to judge. I wondered if any part of him was amazed, even impressed, at what I had managed—no matter how many times he and Warner Bros. had tried to stop and discourage me, I just kept coming back. As he turned to face Peggy I detected a look of hatred in his expression, which even the jury must have noticed.

"Mr. Eastwod, in approximately 1990, you entered into a settlement agreement with Sondra Locke, settling a lawsuit that was pending between the two of you at that time, didn't you?" Peggy asked.

"That's true."

"And at the same time, as part of that settlement, Sondra Locke entered into a contract with Warner Bros. To have—to develop and/or direct films with Warner Bros. over a three-year period; isn't that correct?"

"True."

"And at the time that those agreements were entered, you had also made an agreement with Terry Semel at Warner Bros. that you would indemnify Warner Bros. for expenses or losses under their deal with Sondra Locke, didn't you?"

"Yes."

"And with respect to that agreement, you did not tell Sondra Locke or have anyone on her behalf told that you had made this indemnity agreement with Terry Semel at Warner Bros., did you?"

"No."

"And you knew that she didn't know about that agreement; correct?"

"Yes."

"And in fact, you paid for that contract with respect to — let me withdraw that question. You paid for the indemnity agreement by the beginning of the second year of Sondra Locke's contract with Warner Bros., didn't you?"

"I paid part of it, yes."

"And in fact, you paid $975,000 in the beginning of the second year, did you not?"

"Yes."

"And at the same time, you also agreed to be bound to another $500,000; correct?"

"Yes."

"And you didn't, at that time, tell Sondra Locke that such payments had occurred, did you?"

"No."

"And at the time the Warner Bros. deal was entered into between Sondra Locke and Warner Bros., as part of the overall settlement, you did not offer to Sondra Locke any similar deal with Malpaso Productions, which is your company, did you?"

"No."

"No further questions."

As we left the courtroom after Clint's testimony, reporters were scurrying to get at the pay phones. "I'm telling you that's all he said: Yes, no, yes, yes, yes, no, no. And a 'that's true,' I think. That's it. That's all he said. I'm telling you that's all he said!"

The next day the *L.A. Times* carried an article on the front page calling Clint's responses the shortest in history.

Cameras and journalists were pressed against us as we made our way out of the courtroom and into the hallways. "Miss Locke, what do you think of Mr. Eastwood's admission?" they yelled at me. "What do you think the jury will make of it?" "Miss Locke, what do you hope to achieve by bringing all this out? You're pretty much on your own here, it seems." "Miss Locke, how do you feel?" Then it was my turn to speak out.

"Cleansed," I answered. "Whatever happens, I feel cleansed of the whole thing."

Leslie Sykes of ABC-TV approached me. "What do you say about Eastwood's admitting that he gave a million dollars to Warner Bros.? You said that you didn't know that. You had no knowledge of that."

"Absolutely not."

"What do you think that means?" she continued.

"It means I didn't have a real deal," I replied. "It means it was just . . . pushing his money around. I'm sorry I can't really say anything else right now."

As my attorney and I made our way down the hallway, another voice called, "Sondra, I wish you all the luck in the world. Honey, do *I* have *his* number!" I stared at her; something told me I should know her. I didn't recognize her face but then she said, "I'm Joy Long, honey."

The name rang a bell. "Oh I know who you are," I responded, "and thanks for the encouragement." Joy Long was the name Clint gave when he told me that he had "met a woman in Dan Tana's Restaurant, and she's gonna spy on Henry Weinberg for me." What an amazing turn of events, I thought.

Looking around her, she whispered, "Gotta go, I don't want him to see me talking to you." Then she turned and darted away.

We stepped into the elevator, and just as the door was moving, a security guard's hand stopped it from closing, letting someone else enter. It was Clint. He hadn't realized that I was in the elevator, and when he did, I noticed the slightest, almost slow-motion pause before he casually stepped inside accompanied by two security guards. "So where are *our* security guards?" Peggy said jokingly, referring to these employees of the court there to serve Clint. Clint never looked around; he stared straight toward the elevator door until it opened, then stepped out and quickly disappeared toward the courthouse back exit. Every day he arrived and exited (with security guards) through the back door. I always walked alone in and out of the front door. Of course, as soon as the press reported this routine, Clint began using the *front* door too — but still with security guards.

"Who was that woman?" Peggy asked. When I explained, she said, "Well, be careful. You never know what's going on."

That weekend I drove to the Century City shopping mall to pick up some new "court-appropriate clothing." I was inside the first store for no more than five minutes, and when I walked back out into the mall court-yard, I heard a voice calling my name. It was Joy Long. I had never met this woman in my life before the other day in the courthouse, now here she was again. The statistical improbability that she and I would just run into each other was staggering. In fact, it was pretty hard to believe that it wasn't calculated — that she wasn't following me.

"You know, Clint is so paranoid because I'm in the court watching," Joy said to me. "He had Jim McKeachan call me to ask me why I was there.

He was having McKeachan spy on *me*! McKeachan even asked me whose
side I'm on."

"Really," I said. I didn't want to engage with her and I was trying not to
be rude.

"Yeah. I said I'm not on anybody's side. But I do think he should take
care of you. You know what I wish he would do for you?"

"No, what?" I said, almost laughing.

"I wish he'd take out an ad in the trade papers asking people to hire
you."

My God, I thought. Something about that ridiculous proposal rang familiar. It was just the kind of settlement proposal Clint might suggest. I
laughed. "I'm afraid that's a little too late and a lot too little. Gotta go, Joy,
bye bye." And I walked away.

~

WHEN WE RETURNED to court after the weekend, Ray Fisher made yet another plea to have my case dismissed. This time he asked for a "nonsuit"
ruling based on the link he thought we were improperly making between
Warner Bros.'s performance during my deal and the suit against Clint. It
was all legalese. Frankly the two issues *seemed* inseparable. Again the judge
said he would "take it all under submission," which meant that he didn't
rule in either their favor or ours. Each time he did this I breathed a sigh
of relief because it meant I was still going forward, but, of course, I realized
that it also meant he was accumulating a stack of incomplete decisions,
and I had no idea what their impact could be in the end.

Fisher brought in Al Ruddy as his next witness. When Peggy first heard
Al speak, her mouth dropped. She leaned over and whispered to me, "Why
didn't you tell me that he *is* 'the Godfather'!" I was so accustomed to Al
that I didn't notice it anymore, but his voice is very deep and raspy (the
sound of a million cigarettes), he is tall and slender with a great crop of
gray hair. Al is very famous both as a colorful character and as the producer
of *The Godfather*. In Hollywood he is known as a "real schmoozer."

Al answered all his questions in such a way that he seemed to avoid
knowing much of anything. Then he came to the part of his story where
he became a go-between for Clint. Contradicting Clint's deposition, Al
said he'd *never even spoken to either Clint or me*, and in fact had only
acted as a *good influence* with both our attorneys. "To get them talking"
was how he described it. It was clear that Al was definitely there to say
how great Clint Eastwood was, but he was also being very careful to protect his own skin.

At one point he even said: "The whole settlement, I never had any idea—nor should I have been included, incidentally, in any discussion about any settlement of a lawsuit. I never had any idea when it was settled or what the terms of the settlement were." This was completely untrue. Al was the very one who approached me with Clint's proposal in 1990. Fisher then asked him: "Did Ms. Locke ever authorize you to come back to Mr. Eastwood and make some kind of settlement offer about the lawsuit?"

"Under no circumstances."

"And did Mr. Eastwood, in the same fashion, did he ever authorize you to make any settlement offers to Ms. Locke?"

"Under no circumstances."

"Did—do you recall Ms. Locke ever talking to you in the context of settling her lawsuit about a development deal with Warner Bros?"

"Never."

This was amazing. Not only had Al been Clint's "messenger," he knew all about the deal with Warner Bros. In fact, he had submitted a film script to me called *Alisha's Book*. After I submitted it to Warners and it was rejected, Al never again sent me another script. He got the picture real quick.

As Al left the stand, he did an amazing thing. He moved directly toward me and Peggy. Smiling his schmoozer's smile. I couldn't believe it. He was actually coming over as if this was some kind of cocktail party.

"Sondra, how are you, babe?" he said.

I looked at him with complete horror. Peggy instantly leaned toward me, shaking her head as if to ward me off him. It wasn't necessary.

"Oh, I'm not supposed to talk to you, I guess," he offered with mock innocence, then shrugged and walked away as if he just didn't understand why I would be so mean to him. Hollywood.

Al Ruddy was followed by Bill Gerber, a Warner Bros. executive who was supposed to testify about how much Clint supported me and wanted me to work, but it didn't come off as very effective testimony. When asked how many times during those three years that Clint had phoned him about me, he answered, "Probably two." Then, amazingly, he said that he didn't even know that I had a formal deal with Warner Bros.; he instead thought we were just "having conversations." Billy Gerber was known for his great political ambitions; he'd seemed ecstatic when Daly and Semel assigned him to be Clint's "day-to-day" executive. Of course, I knew Clint didn't even seem to know his correct name. He'd called him Phil Gerber on more than one occasion. Fisher was only lining things up so he could bring Clint to the stand, which he then did.

Already I could tell that Clint's demeanor and facial expressions were

entirely different than they had been when Peggy put him on the stand.
Now he was warm and friendly, almost chirpy, and he directed all his
answers to the jurors—romancing them in a nearly embarrassing way.

Clint proceeded to describe his poor childhood during the Great
Depression. Actually they were never poor, they lived in a very wealthy
part of town, had a swimming pool, belonged to the country club, and
each drove his own car. "My father was typical of the Depression era of
people," Clint said. "He always preached a hard work ethic: the world
doesn't owe you a living, nobody is going to give you anything, that sort
of mentality. And consequently, I started working when I was nine years
old ... and I have continued working ever since ... all my life ... and
then I was inducted into the army in 1951 into the military during the
Korean War."

Here it comes, I thought. I could hardly keep from shaking my head. So
much of it was familiar rhetoric; he always dropped the Korean War reference, hoping everyone would conclude that he was in combat and might
be some sort of hero. Actually, he'd been a lifeguard at Fort Ord in northern
California for his entire stint in the military.

As Clint began to describe his long Hollywood career, Fisher brought
out a large cardboard poster with a drawing at the top of a little director's
chair with Clint's name emblazoned on it and underneath it listed all of
Clint's many films. The jury was meant to be impressed with the number
of them.

After Fisher displayed the list, he then began discussing the many awards
Clint had recently been given, among them "the Image Award for [his] use
of women and minorities in films."

I couldn't help but recall the evening Clint, dressed in his tux, was ready
to walk out the door to go and accept that NAACP award for contributing
to the employment of black actors because of his film *Bird*, which was about
Charlie Parker, the black jazz musician. "I'm so excited, Clint," I said as I
came home from the studio, "I've found a great black actress to play the
police psychiatrist in *Impulse*." He looked at me as if I'd lost my mind and
replied, "Well, I hope you know what you're doing. Casting a black actress
to play a police psychiatrist!" Why not, I wondered, as he walked out the
door to pick up his NAACP award!

And the idea that Clint was considered a feminist director made my hair
stand on end. I had learned all too well about Clint's treatment of women,
both professional and otherwise.

Fisher asked him, "And with respect to women, what films have you
given women prominent roles in?"

"Play Misty for Me, Beguiled, Two Mules for Sister Sara, The Gauntlet, Tightrope," Clint replied.

I couldn't help but reflect: The woman in *Misty* was a psychotic killer; in *Beguiled* all the females cut off Clint's leg, then murdered him with poisonous mushrooms; in *Two Mules* the woman was a foul-mouthed person posing as a nun; in *The Gauntlet* I played a hooker who'd been raped in an unthinkable fashion; and in *Tightrope* almost every woman in it was a sadistic or masochistic hooker. That's a pretty good record for a feminist filmmaker.

Finally Fisher began asking Clint about our breakup. "What were your feelings toward Ms. Locke in 1989 once the lawsuit was filed?"

"My feelings were the normal feelings you have when somebody has been planning for many months to assault your children's inheritance! . . . Well, you know, I didn't feel very good about it, I must say. It was not the happiest moment in my life. Ms. Locke and I had never had a conversation regarding any requests or anything she wanted. She had never made a request to me personally. It all just came through this lawyer, this legal action that was sprung on me very suddenly."

I guess his mind had been someplace else all those many times I pleaded for answers. But, as usual, he was casting himself as the victim. To weaken the impact of my testimony about it, Fisher asked Clint about the time I visited him in his office, a year after the lawsuit had been filed, begging him to settle with me.

Clint answered, "I said I couldn't really have this discussion . . . as long as there was a lawsuit pending—this was sort of like holding a gun to your head. I felt it was like social extortion of a kind, blackmail or whatever you want to call it."

I was shocked. He had come up with a line that surprised even me. His face looked dark and angry, and his voice carried a bizarre sense of self-righteousness. By then I knew that Clint was capable of saying anything but I could not believe that he had *said* something like that in front of the jurors and the press.

Fisher then asked: ". . . had there been press coverage of your dispute with Ms. Locke?"

"Yes, there had. Ms. Locke—"

At that, Peggy objected.

"I'll interrupt him . . . we're not going to get into this," said the judge.

"Were you unhappy with the nature of the press coverage?" Fisher persisted.

"To say the least. That was one of the problems with this proposal she was making . . . that she had made these outrageous stories."

Peggy again objected, "Your Honor—"

Clint kept going, determined to get it in, "Outrageous stories, including the *National Enquirer*, interviews with anybody who would listen, including *National Enquirer*, and the stories were outright lies . . . this press coverage . . . and because of the lawsuit filed. Even though I had prevailed in the initial lawsuit."

"No, no, we can strike that . . . the jury is to disregard," the judge broke in.

It was all propaganda, of course. He had not "prevailed in the initial lawsuit"; it was settled. Unless, of course, he considered the fraud "prevailing." And he *knew* Jane Brolin had admitted under oath that she had sold all those stories. I couldn't believe that this was his defense. What did any of it have to do with this lawsuit about his having tricked me into my contract with Warners? The court called for a break, and as soon as Clint was off the stand and the jury was out of the room Fisher began complaining to the judge. "I will ask that people at plaintiff's counsel table stop engaging in a tremendous amount of body language during the testimony . . ."

He wanted the judge to make us stop having any reactions to Clint's testimony. That almost made me laugh. No doubt my face *had* conveyed horror but it was certainly not calculated for any reason; it was spontaneous. More appropriately, Fisher should have *controlled* the absurdity of his own client.

The judge brushed it aside and said, "Don't worry. We have a funny story to tell everybody here."

Then the bailiff told us that he'd learned a reporter had brought a baby into the courtroom and used it as a prop so he could hide his camera in its blankets! It was just one more example of the circuslike atmosphere.

Finally the jury was brought back in and Fisher began again with Clint. "Mr. Eastwood, I just have a couple more short questions. Can you tell this jury whether you intended to defraud Ms. Locke when entering into the indemnity agreement with Warner Bros.?"

"Absolutely not. I never intended to defraud anyone. I can't think of an instant in my lifetime where I ever tried to put somebody out of work. It just doesn't make sense. And why recommend somebody and then turn around—and recommend them for projects on a *constant* basis and then turn around and ask the studio to not make those projects, it just does not make sense. It monetarily did not make sense because I would—an indemnification means I would have to pay for it. I don't understand that philosophy. It sounds like a dime novel or something."

"Thank you. Your Honor, no further questions," said Fisher.

It was Peggy's turn.

"Now looking at the filmography that you have on the board," she began, "how many of those films did you do with Sondra? Just run through the list."

"There was *The Outlaw Josey Wales, Gauntlet, Every Which Way but Loose, Bronco Billy, Any Which Way You Can, Sudden Impact.*"

"And with respect to the following films, *City Heat, Tightrope, Pale Rider, Heartbreak Ridge, Bird,* and *The Dead Pool,* Ms. Locke assisted you in ways, such as editing or reviewing scripts or casting on an informal basis, didn't she?"

"Not particularly."

"Did she help you at all?"

"Not that I recall."

"Did you have an editing room at the ranch?"

"Yes."

"And isn't it true that Ms. Locke would assist you in the editing room at the ranch and that was one of the things that you did when you were up there?"

"She did at *Bronco Billy.*"

"After 1975, you only did two films that were not with Warner Bros.; isn't that correct?"

"Yes. *In the Line of Fire* was one . . . and the current one that I'm doing right now will be released through Sony [*Absolute Power*]."

"Now with respect to the lawsuit that was pending between you and Sondra in 1990, you were concerned about the fact that she was claiming an entitlement to half of everything that the two of you had acquired while you had been together for the preceeding thirteen years, weren't you?"

"You're telling me."

"Were you concerned about that?"

"Yes."

"And in settling that lawsuit with Sondra, you got out from under those claims, didn't you?"

"Well, she dropped the lawsuit, yes."

"And in fact, when she first came to talk with you, I think you said, on May 30 of 1990, you told her, I think you testified, that you would talk to her, but you did not want to talk to her with a lawsuit pending; isn't that true?"

"Yes."

"So you made her dropping that lawsuit a condition of talking to you about work, didn't you?"

"Yes. I felt that due to all the circumstances, being that this was the first conversation we had ever had face to face, I felt that there was no reason two people should have to finance the legal community."

"And when she filed the lawsuit against you in April of 1989 and while it was pending, you were pretty angry at her, weren't you?"

"Disappointed would be the word."

"Were you sad?"

"Yes."

"Did you tell her you were sad?"

"We didn't have any conversations."

This line of questioning was interrupted by some misunderstandings over language but then Peggy asked him about the 1989 settlement.

"She got the $450,000, and that was the settlement," Clint replied.

"Right. And as part of your settlement with Sondra, she was getting the Warner Bros. deal; correct?"

"Yes, I would go to bat for her."

"And if—in fact, the settlement agreement, which is in evidence between you and Sondra, references the Warner Bros. Agreement [meaning it was *part* of what I had agreed to settle for]?"

"Yes, I assume it does."

"And so worst case scenario, you settled the original case for a $1,500,000 indemnity agreement, the Crescent Heights house which Gordon lived in, and $450,000 to Sondra; correct?"

"Yes."

"And that was millions and millions of dollars less than what she was claiming in that lawsuit, isn't it?"

To this Fisher objected, and the judge sustained.

Peggy tried again, "That is a very small fraction of your earnings and accumulations during the thirteen years you were together, isn't it?"

Another objection that the judge sustained.

"You also indicated that you were aware that she had counsel for some months before that?" Peggy asked.

"Yes."

"And you were aware of that because you *tapped her phones*; isn't that true?"

Fisher shot from his chair. This began a round of objections and counters between Peggy and Fisher, until finally the judge just asked for the next question.

"Let me back up here. You met with Sondra on May 30th of 1990, isn't that right?"

"That seems to be the date that everyone agrees upon, yes."

"And then [months later] you met and spoke with Al Ruddy; correct?"

"Yes."

"And then there's a third conversation that's been referenced here, among many others, in which you spoke with Sondra by phone in which she told you about the cancer; correct?"

"Yes."

"In those conversations you tried to get her to drop the lawsuit, didn't you?"

"No, I had a discussion about the lawsuit."

"And when you learned—well, you were concerned about her, I take it, at this point in time; is that right?"

"Yes. I was very, very sad that she had been ill, and I told her that. I told her I was very sorry about it. [I, of course, didn't recall any such sympathy.] And we did discuss, like she mentioned, a mutual friend of mine who would—who had suffered from cancer."

"And in fact, she was upset when you referenced the fact that that friend had just died of cancer in this phone conversation, wasn't she?"

"I think she was sympathetic towards that, yes."

"Well, she was also scared herself, wasn't she?"

"I can't speak for her state of mind, but I assume so, yes."

I wondered if everyone else had the same question I did: *Why* did he bring up such a story to me when I'd been fighting for my own life?

"Now, she—well, you were asked at some point in the negotiations relative to the Warner Bros. deal with Sondra to indemnify *Sondra*, to pay *her*, if she became ill with cancer again and could not work under that deal, didn't you?"

"Yes."

"And you initially refused to do that [indemnify Sondra against a return of her illness]?"

"Yes."

"And subsequently, you agreed to guarantee her only a *part* of that [the Warner Bros. fee of $1.5 million] up to $450,000 if she was not able to work under the Warner Bros. contract and consequently couldn't collect the $1.5 million or any other proceeds she might get from directing a film?"

"I don't know the exact figures that you're dazzling around at the moment. I did say I would indemnify the Warner Bros. thing, yeah."

"Well, I'm talking about Sondra now; all right? . . . You have indicated
that Sondra had requested through her attorney that you agreed to guarantee
payments to her under the Warner Bros. deal *if* she became ill and couldn't
claim even the minimum payment under that contract. Do you recall that?"

"Yes. That's what her attorney was proposing."

"And you have indicated that you refused to do that, initially."

"Yes."

"So ultimately, you did agree to guarantee approximately one third of
the minimum payments she was entitled to under the Warner Bros. contract—if she became ill and couldn't work and couldn't collect anything
under that contract? Isn't that true?"

"My arrangement with Warner Bros. was indemnifying Warner Bros.,
not Sondra Locke or Oberstein."

"Exactly. That's my question. You refused to indemnify Sondra Locke,
but you agreed to indemnify Warner, correct?"

"Yes."

". . . at the time that you signed this agreement with Sondra and included
in there the amount of indemnification you were willing to give *her*
[$450,000], if she could NOT work [from illness] under the WB agreement
. . . you knew . . . and did not disclose [to her] your other agreement with
WB to pay them everything that they were obligated to pay [to Sondra]—
up to $1,500,000."

"Yes."

Peggy was finished. The judge sent the jury from the room. Fisher made
another motion.

"Your Honor. At this point, I move for *mistrial*."

Fisher claimed that Peggy had no right to bring up the phone tapping.
Peggy argued that Fisher had brought up the subject when he asked Clint
questions about the attorney I'd hired, and Clint's answers had clearly been
learned from those phone tapes. "He opened the door," Peggy said.

The judge denied Fisher's motion. I had never experienced such a roller
coaster ride.

At lunch Peggy and I debated further questioning of Clint—we knew
that Fisher would be coaching him during the break. We decided against
it, and Fisher was given his opportunity to rehabilitate Clint, though it
didn't appear that he was very successful. We had been led to believe
that Clint was their last witness, but they had a surprise waiting in the
lobby.

Fisher's associate announced, "Your Honor, I would like to call Mr. Steven Beale. He is out in the hall."

Steven Beale had been my assistant before Mary Wellnitz. He had been pretty ineffectual in the job, and eventually I had had to terminate him. Now they were dredging him up to discredit me, but I knew something about him that I hadn't even told Peggy. While Beale tattled his ugly and untrue tales about how I never worked, never even came into the office, I pulled the yellow pad toward me and scribbled a note to Peggy for her cross-examination.

Peggy stood up. "When Sondra Locke terminated your employment, she did so after finding you . . . going through her purse in the office, didn't she, Mr. Beale?" She asked.

"Absolutely not," he replied, coming ever so slightly out of his chair and looking at Clint's defense table for help.

Out of the corner of my eye I could see Clint's entire legal team looking at each other like, Oh shit! Peggy went on to inquire about the office files he had stolen and how Virginia Tweety of Warner Bros. payroll had held his check until he'd returned them. Clint's big secret witness, the only thing he could find to attempt to discredit me had not just fizzled, it had blown up in his face.

Clint's team followed Steven Beale with another Warner Bros. executive, Tom Lassally. Tom was to be their "authority" on all the projects I submitted during those three years of my deal, but actually I had submitted only about three projects to Tom. Fisher's assistant, Ms. Cohen, pulled out the big book of "Sondra Locke coverage" and began to ask Lassally to testify about all the ways in which Warners attempted to work with me. At some point the judge became so impatient with this process of going through all the "coverage records" that he took charge of the witness himself. Then began a long back and forth between Tom and the judge; the judge gave the titles of my many projects, one by one, and Tom answered what he knew about each of them. Finally when this so-called custodian of records had shown that he barely remembered anything I had submitted at Warners, Ms. Cohen took over again. She asked Lassally: "Did Mr. Eastwood ever talk to you about any of Ms. Locke's projects?" "Did he ever call you on the phone to talk about Ms. Locke or one of Ms. Locke's projects?" "Did he ever meet with you in person to discuss any of those projects?"

And to all of these questions Lassally answered no. You would have thought he was a witness for my side.

Lassally knew almost nothing about any of my thirty-plus projects, and Billy Gerber didn't even know I had a formal deal with Warner Bros. Terry

Semel, the co-CEO of the entire motion picture division, was apparently impotent in his own company, because all he could do was call the lower executives on the phone and ask them to do something that they never quite did. And Clint himself, who had tried and tried to "help" me, just didn't seem to have his old influence anymore. One of my favorite Eastwood witnesses was their fancy "expert," who couldn't actually *be called* an expert because we didn't use an expert (some legal quid pro quo). He outright stated under oath that what someone like Eastwood said, goes. "If you have a sponsor like Eastwood; it's a very different deal." Boy, he could say that again—especially if you're Sondra Locke.

It was clear that the case was nearing completion, but Fisher wasn't quite finished. "Defense recalls Sondra Locke to the stand," he said, also calling for my deposition (from the original Warner Bros. case) be given to me.

"Ms. Locke," Fisher began, "yesterday your former assistant, Mr. Steven Beale, testified . . . do you remember being asked at your deposition in front of you about the circumstances of your termination of Mr. Beale?"

"Yes."

"And were the answers that you gave at that time, you understood they were under oath? . . . under penalty of perjury?"

"Yes."

Fisher then read from my deposition, emphasizing that in it I had *not* said that Steven Beale had gone through my purse. Clearly Fisher intended to turn that into perjury, and then into "Sondra Locke cannot be believed." When he finished, he dramatically closed the folder, like Joan Crawford would have in some melodrama, and said, "I do not have any further questions, Your Honor."

Peggy stood up. "Ms. Locke, why didn't you include in this explanation, of why you let Steven Beale go and hired Mary Wellnitz, any reference to his dishonesty?"

Fisher objected that she was leading, the judge overruled him, and I was allowed to answer.

"I felt very badly for Steven. I didn't feel that he was really doing a very good job, but I didn't want to harm his ability to get another job. His brother was dying of AIDS, and I sought not to give out that information until he came in here and lied on the stand about me, and I then felt no more responsibility to him."

Peggy sat down and Fisher was up.

"He lied about you—is that right—is that what you're saying in this courtroom today, Ms. Locke?"

"Yes, I am."

"There's a security division over at Warner Brothers., isn't there?"

"Yes."

"So are you aware of Mr. Jack Egger, the director of studio protection, former captain of the Beverly Hills Police Department, who's in charge of security there? Or Mr. Scott Nelson, ex-member of the FBI, who is also head of security at Warner Brothers?"

"No, I'm not."

"So your testimony is that you saw Mr. Beale riffling through your purse. Is that what you're trying to say today?"

"Yes, I am."

"Did you call the security people at Warner Bros. about that?"

"No I didn't."

"Of course you didn't." He whirled, and, just on the word "course," he melodramatically slapped his hand against the papers he was holding. "Ms. Locke, did you file a report or a complaint with Warner Bros. about what you're now alleging against Mr. Beale?"

"I just stated that I chose to let it go."

"You were under oath [in the Warner Bros. deposition], and you were asked a question by counsel in a case that you were adverse to Warner Bros. about . . . you were fighting about the legitimacy of your deal . . . and you were trying to recover *money* [he spat out the word as if it were dirty] from Warner Bros., isn't that correct?"

Peggy objected and the judge sustained it.

"There were several reasons I let Mr. Beale go," I said, "many of which are stated here [in the deposition]. I chose not to state that particular reason because I didn't feel it [the case] related to Mr. Beale and that he had anything to do with the situation. I chose to protect him since he had nothing to do with the situation, and since the event itself didn't relate to the situation *at all.*"

"And your testimony is that when you found Mr. Beale committing this breach of trust, you didn't bother to call the security people at Warner Bros.?"

"It was not necessary."

Fisher threw up his hands in disgust and wheeled away from me. "No further questions," he *spat* out as if trying to convince the jury that he had "won." I couldn't help noticing, when he had begun his petty attack on me, that the mouths of several jurors dropped open in disbelief and shock.

•　•　•

That evening on the TV news Clint was still spinning his story, repeating his most recent sound bite from that day in court, "Sounds like a dime novel." This was followed by a clip of me in which a journalist asked me what I thought of all the things Clint had said about me on the witness stand. "Honestly, I thought it was ridiculous," I answered. "I thought it was sad and ridiculous."

THURSDAY, SEPTEMBER 19, was the first day of final arguments. I truly believed that no matter how this turned out I had already accomplished something amazing by being before a jury and telling my story. I also continued to be astounded that the press was reporting the story seriously, and even in my favor. From my experiences, I knew what the odds on that had been. I also had to admit the personal satisfaction I'd had in seeing Clint Eastwood, who had robbed me of so much, and who had hurt and cheated me in so many ways, sitting up there for all the world to see and answer for his actions. On top of it all, it was gratifying to have people approach me on the street and thank me for giving them the inspiration not to be afraid to do something similar in their own lives. It was already more than I had prayed for. Even so, I also knew that there would be a big downside to losing, not only financially, but in the eyes of the community and much of the public. All that I had fought for would be tainted if that one single jury didn't believe me.

When Peggy stood up to address the jurors I was one solid wall of tightly coiled nerves. I looked straight ahead with the jurors to my right, and Clint and his attorneys to my left. Suddenly I detected a movement from the left. When I glanced in that direction, I could not believe what I saw. Clint was picking up his chair and moving it to the head of his table, as if he were the host at some dinner party, so that he was staring head-on into the eyes of the jurors. My God. Did he think he could stare them down and seduce them just before deliberation? I only hoped it was as obvious to the jurors as it was to me.

"Your Honor, Ladies and Gentlemen of the jury, opposing counsel, Ms. Locke and Mr. Eastwood," Peggy began. "Ms. Locke has brought this case to trial before you because she was defrauded out of her professional reputation, her professional existence, her self-esteem, and her professional identity because she dared to challenge Clint Eastwood. And she was easy to trick, I guess, because she wanted desperately to work. She didn't want to be dependent upon Mr. Eastwood. She was willing to move on. He was through with her. That was okay, but she shouldn't have to give up her professional life because of it. Mr. Eastwood told you in his own testimony that he was angry at that lawsuit. He didn't like that, and he set down as a condition to any settlement discussions that her [1989] lawsuit get dropped *first*. He said [to Ms. Locke in the May 1990 meeting in his office], 'If you want to have a lawsuit I'll keep you in court for the rest of your life. You want to be Michelle Marvin or do you want to direct movies?' Ms. Locke wanted to direct movies. If this whole contract was really about the million and a half dollars she got, which is going to be waved in front of you as a diversion, as a smoke screen—if that's really what it was about [for Ms. Locke], and that's all she was after, he [Clint] would have gone to her and asked to settle that case for the million and a half dollars. You do not have to work for three years, but settle the case, take this money. And he didn't do it because he knew she would *not* go for that deal. So he tricked her into dropping that lawsuit by offering a contract for work that never came. She does not want to be here, but she has no choice." The tension in the room was palpable as she spoke on . . . Finally Peggy finished and sat down.

Then Ray Fisher stood up and spoke for hours. He had posters and charts, and endless words meant to confuse. He again painted Clint as the giving lover/mentor who had done everything possible for the woman. "[Eastwood] consistently acted to advance Ms. Locke's career," he said, "but Sondra Locke wants to blame everybody else for what went wrong in her life." He tried to convince the jurors that I was "shady" and that I was a liar. "Do you believe that young man [Steven Beale] really went through her purse?" he said to the jurors. "And if she lied about that she might be lying about everything." He flashed his smoke and mirrors to disguise Clint's early "secret payment" to Warner Bros.—in spite of the fact that the calendar proved, and Terry Semel admitted, Clint had paid two years early. According to Fisher, Clint tried his best to help me at Warner Bros., but I just couldn't hack it. "You saw him [Eastwood] on the witness stand. You have to make your judgment if you think he lied to you," he said. Then ultimately he argued that Clint had no *duty* to disclose to me the fact that he had a "side agreement" with Warner Bros.

This seemed to be the most important issue of the fraud. Did Clint have a legal duty to disclose to me his secret payment agreement with Warner Bros.? We believed that I had a definite right to *all* information so that I could evaluate the sincerity of the contract being offered. But Fisher had several explanations as to why Clint had no obligation to tell me about his secret payment. First, he said that I hadn't *asked* Clint to tell me, and therefore that showed that it didn't matter to me. This made no sense; how could I ask someone *not* to do something that I had no idea he was even thinking of doing? Second, he said that Clint's arrangement with Warner Bros. had nothing to do with me, and wasn't my business. (Even though it was *about* me.) Finally, he said Clint hadn't told me because he "didn't want to grandstand" in front of me that he was actually paying. Fisher also took great care to deny "my actual damages." Some interpret that the law states a *formula* exists for actual damages—how much money were you promised, minus how much you received. Fisher wanted to extrapolate that into: My contract stated a certain dollar amount; I received that dollar amount; therefore, I had no damages. What I hadn't received, of course, was the *work*, the opportunity. But, according to Fisher, that part of the promise or intent of the contract didn't count, because *no actual dollar figure* could be placed on it without speculation, which wasn't allowed.

As I sat listening to Fisher's tricky logic, I could feel myself turning inside out. I thought of all I had been put through since 1988: first the "gaslighting" by Clint, then the "lockout," then the cancer, then the three-year Warner Bros. fraud, then the two additional years I had fought my way to trial. I suddenly felt very tired and old. I began to cry. Quietly with my head in my hands, I sat there and let the tears roll down my face. Why? How could my life, which had always seemed so free of conflict, have become nothing but conflict? I had put my faith in a monster who thought nothing of destroying anything inconvenient to him. And yet, even through my tears, I knew in my heart I was better off than I'd ever been.

I opened my purse to get a tissue and found something unexpected. Gordon had tucked something in there. He often did things like that. It was a clear red plastic box that held a pebble with a piece of paper wrapped around it. The small piece of paper was as soft and worn as an old piece of Kleenex. The inscription on it was the address of the Roosevelt Hotel in New Orleans where we were to meet Joseph Strick for *The Heart Is a Lonely Hunter*: the stone was the one we'd picked up from his driveway in Shelbyville thirty years ago before we'd started that journey. It was a talisman. It had been all over the world with me. A little gray rock from a driveway, where it had been picked up so long ago and imbued with meaning and an incipient sense of magic. It was just an ordinary little pebble then, from faraway Shelbyville, Tennessee, but now, in a Burbank court, in the middle of Ray Fisher's damning words and my own anxieties, it reached out and reminded me of all the good and important things that had happened.

"Let me say this in closing . . ." Fisher's voice concluded his argument. "I said it before. You're being asked to say that Clint Eastwood committed fraud . . . fraud is a very serious accusation . . . that's a very weighty responsibility you have."

I felt flattened. Somehow he had confused even me with all his words, and if I felt confused, wouldn't the jurors be hopelessly confused?

After the lunch break, Peggy gave her rebuttal, our final word.

"Thank you, You Honor . . . Ladies and Gentlemen of the jury," Peggy began. "Mr. Fisher, I submit, went to great lengths and took a lot of time to try and confuse you because that is the best way he has to go with the evidence in this case. I submit that the attempt to trick you is not dissimilar from the fraud that was perpetrated on Sondra Locke. It's sleight of hand. It's shuffle the papers. It's look at the numbers. Let's look at this contract. Divert your attention from what you saw and what you know. And yes, fraud is serious, and it is particularly serious for Sondra Locke, who is defrauded out of her career. While it is serious, extremely serious and the damages are substantial, and substantial to her reputation, it is not complicated. And under this circumstance, it's not complicated. You're supposed to believe that it is."

Peggy's rebuttal was short and moving and soon it was over. The judge instructed the jury. The bailiff was sworn to take charge of them. The jurors left for the jury room to commence deliberations. Ray Fisher turned to Clint and said, "This'll be the shortest deliberation in history."

It was mid-afternoon on Thursday, September 18.

Peggy, her associate Christiann, Melanie, and I all went out and ordered martinis. It was a celebration, an anxious one but a definite celebration. The case was in the hands of the jurors and we were all still standing.

There was no word on Thursday, and on Friday I went in to my editing room to work and every time the phone rang I jumped off my chair. Each caller could be Peggy. Finally, she did call. "Don't get excited. There's no verdict, but I'm on my way over to the court because the jury has a question."

My heart pounded. I'd been told that the jurors' questions sometimes indicate what they might be thinking. On their special verdict form, there were five main questions that had to be answered before fraud could be established and they could rule in my favor. Each question had to be answered in order, and each one required at least nine jurors to vote yes or else they were *not* allowed to go to the next question. In that event, the deliberation would be over and I would have lost. It was terrifying. Under the rules of this special verdict form the jurors couldn't simply vote whether or not they felt I was defrauded; each question had to be deliberated separately. The five questions were: one, Clint's agreement to reimburse Warner Bros. was a *material fact*. Two, Clint was under a *legal duty to disclose* that fact to me. Three, Clint *intentionally concealed* the existence of the reimbursement agreement with the intent to defraud me. Four, I *would not* have entered into the settlement agreement with Clint and taken the Warner Bros. contract if I'd known about the reimbursement agreement. Five, the concealment of the existence of the reimbursement agreement caused me *damage*.

The jurors were now asking, "What is the definition of the word 'legal,' in question number two?" Peggy argued to the judge that if the jury had already answered yes to question number one, then under the law, Eastwood was *legally* bound to disclose it to me. She asked the judge to give those instructions to the jury, and he agreed. This told us that the jurors were in my favor and had moved to question number three. I was on pins for the rest of the day. When Saturday came and the jury was not in session, I could finally breathe. But that didn't last long. "I just got a message from Fisher," Peggy said when she called, "he wants to talk about settling this."

I didn't want to settle. I wanted the verdict and I told Peggy to say no. But Fisher was persistent. "Let's settle this before the jury comes back with a verdict and one of our careers is ruined," he said to Peggy. What he meant was before his own career was damaged. No matter what, Peggy was already victorious for having held her own against the power structure of Fisher and his law firm. We said no, and they began raising the offer. The next day, Sunday, it went up again. It had more than doubled. Monday was a holiday, and I continued to say no. The whole thing had never been about the money to me and I didn't want to settle. I kept telling Peggy to say no, but she was beginning to disagree with me. "Think about it carefully. If you hold out for the verdict, you could lose. I know the jury seems on our side, but you never know. We have very tricky jury instructions. Their hands are somewhat tied. I'd be remiss if I didn't remind you of that; you've been through so much I'd hate to see that happen to you. And let's say you do win the verdict, Eastwood will most assuredly appeal. Fisher has even promised it; he's said, 'If you force us through a verdict, I'll have to appeal this all the way to the Supreme Court.' "

"That sounds vaguely like Clint's old threats of 'I'll keep you in court for the rest of your life.' That only makes me angry," I said.

"I understand that but look at it this way. You've won. Look at what you've accomplished. It's amazing. Eastwood said he'd never settle; he even said it to the press. Now he's come to you begging to settle; and, believe me, at this late stage of the game, he wouldn't do such a thing unless they felt he had lost, that the jury is on your side. You should feel that is a major win. And it's over. You can walk away." I sat silently. "You sleep on it," Peggy said. "I'll talk to you in the morning."

I phoned Gordon. "Please, Hobbit, tell me what to do," I begged him. "If I wait for the jury, what's going to happen? What's the right thing here?"

"I can't tell you, Sondra," he replied. "You're always asking me to tell you what's going to happen about this or that and you know that I can't."

"Well, ask for a sign," I said.

"You know that they don't come on command whenever you ask for them."

"Well, I remember you've only asked maybe three or four times and each time you got an answer," I insisted.

"All right. I'll ask about it. I'll call you back," he said, and we hung up.

He phoned me back later and sure enough he had gotten a most extraordinary sign. "Stopping now is the right thing to do. I think you should settle it," he concluded.

The next morning I told Peggy what I'd decided, and I also told her, "I don't want any caveats that I can't talk about it because one of the main issues for me has been this controlling and secretive atmosphere. I won't agree to that no matter how much he ups the ante."

"They said nothing about that. The only thing they ask is that you don't reveal the amount of the settlement," Peggy said.

I laughed. "Who cares about that."

After I sent Peggy away with the authority to settle, I sat down and unexpectedly burst into tears. I didn't doubt my decision, but I was emotionally exhausted, and I felt unfinished. I longed to know what the jurors thought.

Three exhausted people, Peggy, Christiann, and I celebrated with lunch at the Bel Air Hotel, a beautiful garden hotel known for its ponds with elegant white swans. It was like the dead silence at the end of a raging storm. I didn't know what to feel, or what to do. It was hard to believe it was over. We clinked our champagne glasses and breathed sighs of relief.

I agreed to follow Peggy back to her office, where a few members of the press had asked me for a statement, because I had not been in court when the jurors were dismissed. As I got out of my car and walked toward her office, I was greeted by the most amazing sight. The little Victorian house that was Peggy's office was crawling with press. There must have been at least fifty or sixty press, crew, and photographers. There was even a live remote broadcast truck. They all began yelling out: "Miss Locke, could you please tell us how you feel? Are you happy with the settlement? Sondra, over here. Sondra, over here. Can you give us a few words? Congratulations! Can I get a photo of you this way? Sondra! Sondra! Hold this rose and pose with it, would you? After all, life is a bed of roses, huh?" I could feel their exhilaration that justice had been served against the odds. And, I couldn't believe they had come out in droves—from NBC, ABC, CBS, CNN, the L.A. *Times*, the British press, the Australian press. "I can't believe you're here with the live remote truck!" I said. "Oh, we were a few miles away with the O.J. trial, so when the office got wind that you were going to be here, we were ordered to come up and grab you." How perfect, I thought. It had started with an O.J. connection and ended with one. That must be another sign. I smiled at the circle.

That night as I looked at the television coverage of my "press conference" I received the one gift that made it a truly perfect ending. I found out what the jurors had concluded.

"After little more than one day of deliberation," one reporter said, "it was clear that the jurors were in Locke's favor . . . [they had] already concluded that Clint Eastwood had defrauded his former lover Sondra Locke, and were leaning toward awarding Ms. Locke a substantial amount of money. Some of the jurors expressed disappointment that they were not able to complete their deliberations and send a strong message to the movie industry regarding secret deals that movie studios negotiate. It did open their eyes as to how the industry is run."

Jury foreperson Brenda Williams was filmed saying, "We knew it was not real. It was fraudulent. It was done so . . . Clint Eastwood . . . [could] . . . get out of his palimony. The industry is run by a bunch of powerful men who'll do anything to protect their major stars who bring in millions of dollars for that industry. When the CEO of Warner Bros. comes in and says that he'll do whatever it takes to make Clint Eastwood happy that tells me a lot right there. So anyone who crosses him will pay for it. And Sondra Locke paid for it. Her career has been ruined; she's been put through a lot of emotional trauma and stress and she deserved compensation for that. We all understood and agreed that a fraud had been committed. I believe Eastwood never truly did anything to help her career. I don't feel bad that they settled because I'm not sure we could have given her enough money to compensate her for what she's been through."

Another juror, Robert Campbell, said, "It was already decided that she had won. It was only a matter of damages. Multimillions. That's personally what I would have voted for in the end. Her whole career was ruined and she needs to be compensated for that. As soon as [their relationship] ended she was left out in the cold. [I was convinced because of] everything from the Warner Bros. executives' testimonies. And especially Clint Eastwood's outburst on the stand, the second time he took the stand where he said she [Locke] was trying to 'defraud my children of their inheritance.' "

Another juror, Channel 4 news producer Yvonne Beltzer, said, "Eastwood's silent-partner involvement in the Warner Bros. deal should have been disclosed to Locke. My belief was that this was kept a secret and certainly was kept a secret from her. She had a right to know that. It was simply a sticky case that was hot in the media, that was getting bad publicity for Warner Bros. and Clint Eastwood and they didn't want any more exposure, so they decided that they had to get it settled. I think the whole thing was a way of protecting Clint Eastwood from a very, very damaging palimony suit."

Across town Clint also had a press conference, but he wasn't there. It was attended by Ray Fisher and there was only one microphone and one camera. "Clint, as far as I know, is at work editing his film *Absolute Power* and I think he's quite content with the settlement because it allows him to go on with his life, and to put an end to this war between Ms. Locke and him."

I couldn't help but wonder why he waited so long to "go on with his life." And I also loved the irony in the title of his new film.

"Sondra, we have a little problem," Peggy said to me two days later. Ray Fisher was expected to show up at the Burbank courthouse in two days with a check in the full amount of the settlement but he had fired off a letter to Peggy saying that Clint wasn't going to pay. This seemed too much, even for Clint. "Can he do this, Peggy?"

"Well, no, but it means we'll have to go after him for it; they can make it hard."

"I swear, if he does this I will file another fraud suit against him. Can you imagine making a fraudulent settlement on a fraud lawsuit? It's a comedy."

"Well, I'm glad you can laugh. Fisher claims that we broke the agreement because you told the amount of the settlement. Fisher says that in response to some journalist who threw a number at you that you 'nodded' to confirm."

"That is truly pitiful. And so truly Clint. I was surrounded by the press, all of whom were talking at once. I don't remember nodding at anyone, but if I did, I certainly didn't nod at something as pathetic as that. This is outrageous!"

"Just sit tight," Peggy said. And we hung up.

Peggy fired back a written response to Fisher and demanded payment by end of day Friday. Soon a phone call came. "Well, where do you want to meet to exchange?" Fisher asked.

"Exchange what?" Peggy said.

"Well, we have some papers we want you to sign."

"Oh no, we're not signing anything. We agreed on the court record on the day we settled and that's all that's necessary. We're not wading through a bunch of paperwork with all sorts of conditions. The deal is done and recorded by the court. That's it," Peggy responded.

Finally Fisher agreed. "I felt like he was going to ask me to meet at some phone booth halfway between our offices and pass me a bag of cash," Peggy said to me jokingly.

"Well, that's Clint. Everything is like an act of espionage. Paranoia central."

Peggy insisted they meet at the Burbank court. Fisher handed over the check, but not before saying, "Clint knows that Sondra is working on a book. She'd better watch out. It's libelous."

How, I wondered, could he know that when the book had not even been written.

"We hope this puts an end to the litigation between Ms. Locke and Mr. Eastwood," Peggy said to the press.

Epilogue ～

I truly felt like the heroine in some fairy tale who'd been swept up in a great but impossible adventure, and managed to survive it all. Fairy tales and myths are often full of ordinary people who in the beginning meet improbable, magical creatures—an old crone on the road, a talking bear, or perhaps an elf with wondrous shoes. Inevitably, the dark night arrives when she is challenged to do battle, whether it's against ogres, trolls, witches, or the Forces of Darkness. When she succeeds, she returns with a boon for others and many amazing riches—a golden harp, a treasure chest of jewels, the pot of gold buried beneath the slain dragon. Overall, my life has seemed like those stories.

But my reward was even greater than the "pot of gold" I received for winning. I was also freed from my metaphorical prison. The bogeyman had been forced out of the darkness and into the light and all that had been frightening about him no longer was. He was nothing. The air smelled good again. My shoulders felt light again. The albatross was gone. Christmas 1996 was approaching and I knew it would be the best yet. And it was.

A few weeks before Christmas, Gordon and I were frustrated and lost; we had been driving around for two hours in search of a particular furniture store that carried a certain display cabinet. Finally, we found the store in an ugly, barren, industrial part of Glendale. As we entered it, I heard an unexpected sound, like the wail of a cat, and turned to see a store employee hurrying past with a cardboard box. Concerned, I followed him outside and watched as he dumped out a little gray and white cat, so skinny that I could practically count its ribs. It scampered frightened underneath the garbage by the side of the store. For several minutes I stood alone staring at its little face peeking out, then turned and went back inside. But I couldn't stop thinking about it, so I walked outside again and called to it, "Kitty, kitty, kitty." Suddenly it appeared from behind some wild brush and came toward me, but ran away when a woman and her daughter approached. "Don't you need a little cat to take home?" I asked the woman, but she replied a chilly no.

Later, as we were leaving, I glanced around for one last image that might convince me the little cat was going to be fine when Gordon said, "I think you're meant to take that little baby home with you."

"With three dogs? You know I can't."

Because of my soft spot for animals I had already "inherited" three poodles a few years earlier when I had "baby sat" for the mother, Ginger. Then came her son, Spot, and then tiny, abandoned Hannah. And like *The Man Who Came to Dinner* none of them ever went home.

Gordon persisted, "Well, I had Chloe Jr. when my 'Christmas' was sent to me, and they get along fine."

"Yes, but you can't compare 'Christmas.' Everything about him and how he came to you is mythical. He doesn't even act like a dog," I replied. Just then I heard a tiny cry and looked up to see the little cat running across the field and straight to me. What could I do. Giving in, I scooped it up. "Okay, baby, you can stay with me, but only until I can find you a proper home."

"I think you should name her *Angel* since it's almost Christmas," Gordon said, getting into the car. "Or maybe Clarence for the angel in *It's a Wonderful Life*, or if it's a girl, Clara, of course."

"I'm *not* keeping her," I insisted.

The next morning I pulled out the furniture salesman's card to phone and confirm my order and, for the first time, stared at his name. It was Herman *Bustamante! Bustamante?* I'd seen that name only *once* before, and it was on Ginger's and Spot's registry papers—they're Bustamantes. I was astonished. Then, when I spoke with Mr. Bustamante and told him what I'd decided on, he replied, "Fine, but I won't be here if you come on Friday, so please ask for the other manager, *Angel*."

Angel! I couldn't believe it. It was the very name Gordon said I should give the cat. What were the odds!

"It's beyond odds, Sondra," Gordon said when I phoned him. "It's a confirmation, a sign that you were meant to keep her."

And so it seemed to be. The little lost cat became Angel Clara and that Christmas she had a whole new beginning, just as I have. I regard Clara's story with wonder for I believe that the fascinating and mysterious mosaic of life that had brought me to this enchanting synchronicity with her had also brought me from Shelbyville, Tennessee, all the way to the heights of Hollywood and into the Burbank court against Clint and Warner Bros.

After the trial my phone began ringing. One day my answering machine recorded fifty-seven phone calls. I received notes and cards, and, amazingly, even flowers. Suddenly I was the winner, and everyone wanted to be my friend. None of that truly mattered. The important thing was I felt vindicated and cleansed. I had won what everyone thought was a completely impossible battle. I couldn't help but remember what one very powerful acquaintance, an entertainment attorney, had said to me: "Sondra, you don't understand. *You can't win.* Think of Eastwood and Warner Bros. as a big powerful empire with high-tech weapons; whatever you fire at them can't touch them; they'll deflect it like popcorn and only laugh at you."

But I knew that Clint wasn't laughing. I'd been told that he was on a rampage. An insider from his camp reported to Peggy and me, "Clint's on a tirade; he's screaming at everybody and driving his attorneys up the wall. Kevin Marks even said that he wished they were back at their old law offices because, at least there, his office was on the ground floor and he wouldn't be tempted to jump out the window." It couldn't happen to a nicer group of guys, I thought.

And as for Clint, he seemed completely unchanged by his journey. After begging me to settle, and hearing what the journalists and the jurors had said, weeks later he was still attacking me in the press. "She plays the victim very well," he said to *Playboy* magazine, and heartlessly added, "Unfortunately she had cancer and so she plays that card." This statement brought a blistering response from Diane Blum, executive director of the National Cancer Care Foundation, who said, "Breast cancer is a devastating disease—forty-five thousand American women die from it every year. These women do not think of themselves as victims. The last thing they need is to have their disease trivialized." In addition, I received more than three hundred letters of outrage and sympathy over Clint's statement. In that same interview in which Clint talked in this *very ugly* way about me, he also congratulated himself for *not* doing exactly that: "I always think it's best to take the high road and *not* get involved with [talking about] that," he said.

The truth was I had waged a horrible, frightening battle *not* to be Clint's victim. Since childhood I had never wanted to fight; I had always tried to do what was expected of me, never making waves. Like so many women, I thought by *not* fighting everything would work out, everything would be okay, "Daddy" would take care of it all. But I learned "Daddy" would only take care of "Daddy." And so, in 1989 "Daddy's perfect little straight A girl" *had* to change or else.

It's ironic that it was Clint's own ugliness, his enormous betrayal and lies, that forced me to become a better, stronger person. If he had treated me fairly, our breakup would never have made headlines and his true character and all of his secrets would have remained hidden—even from me. Ultimately I'm grateful it didn't happen that way because I needed to grow up and to learn not to fear fighting, or becoming unpopular, or even losing. After all, I'd learned the hard way that what we lose by telling the truth was either never really ours, or never worth having to begin with.

I've been incredibly lucky in life, and I look forward to all that's waiting in the wings. I've signed a contract to direct my next film and that's exciting. I'm surrounded by a handful of friends whose love continues to sustain and nourish me.

And always, forever, there is Gordon. Being alongside him for much of his miraculous and continuing journey has inspired and taught me more than I can say. I continue to listen and look carefully for those "bread crumbs" of life.

I am grateful for all the miracles, especially the one that brought Scott and me together at the lowest moment in my life, and for the fact that six years later we are still living happily together in a real, supportive, and equal relationship—one in which there is honest communication. And most important of all, my health has never been better, and for that I constantly thank God. I've learned that "happily ever after" doesn't necessarily mean there won't be more difficulties ahead. But I'm confident because I've learned to stick with the choices that are true, and keep my faith that there can be *good* hidden in even the *bad* things that happen.

With a deep sigh of relief and gratitude I've nearly reached the end of this manuscript. I walk out onto my deck, and watch the sun setting over Los Angeles and the first lights of the city begin to twinkle far below me. The scents of night-blooming jasmine and the mock orange tree I just planted waft suddenly my way and I breathe in deeply. I hear Ginger, Spot, and Hannah squeal excitedly, and the little bell on Angel Clara's neck begins to jingle, and I know that Scott is home for the evening. I search the heavens for the sweet rain that I wish would come, and suddenly I feel an enormous sense of peace wash over and envelope me. Peace, how extraordinary. It's been a long time coming.

Postscript ~

On August 26, 1997, as this book was being put to bed, I received a phone call from my attorney, Peggy Garrity, giving me the extraordinary news that the Court of Appeal of the State of California, Second Appellate District, had unanimously ruled that my lawsuit against Warner Bros. does indeed contain proper and sufficient evidence to warrant a trial for fraud and breach of contract, and that Judge Thomas Murphy of the Burbank court, who in early 1995 had cavalierly dismissed my case, acted incorrectly in doing so. Furthermore, the three-judge panel certified their opinion for publication, and that means that my lawsuit against Warner Bros. has made law and will set a precedent in the future for the way major film studios can treat other artists in these kinds of contracts—although the film studios may have the contractural right to "creative discretion," they must act "honestly" and "in good faith." My case brings emphasis and clarity to that distinction.

Fleetingly, the words of Judge Murphy replayed themselves in my head: "Take it up on appeal, and may God have mercy on your souls!" I had done just that, and I felt a rush of gratefulness, satisfaction, and pride for this vindication by the higher court. Now Warner Bros. will have to deal with me in a public trial, just as Clint had. For, as the appellate judges stated in their ruling: "Such conduct [by Warner Bros.] is not beyond the reach of the law."

Acknowledgments ～

To those few closest to me who supported and encouraged me throughout these experiences and during the writing of this book, I would like to say a deeply felt thank you: Scott Cunneen, John McKee, Denise and William Fraker, and Gordon, whose contribution was enormous. A special thank you to my attorney, Peggy Garrity, who took on a very great challenge; to my excellent copyeditor, Kathy Antrim; and to my editor, Henry Ferris, who always supported the book that I wanted to write.